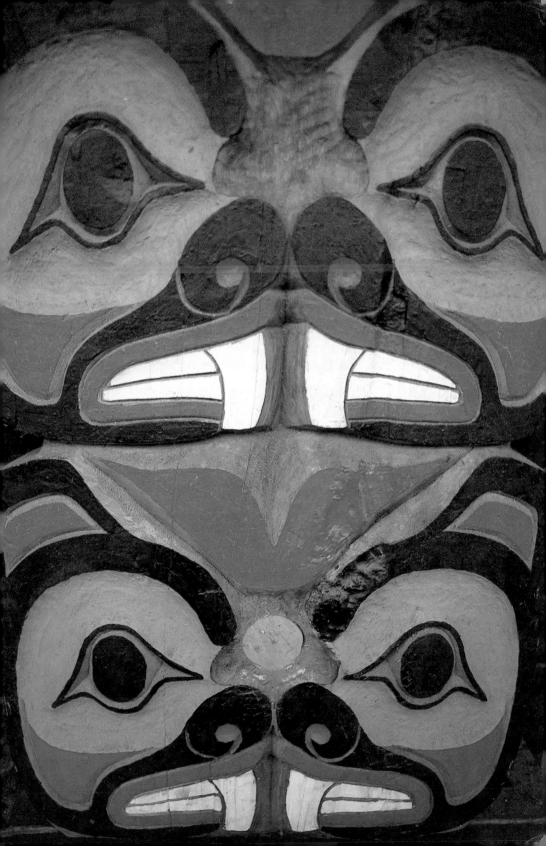

Directed and Designed by Hans Höfer

INSIGHT
GUIDES
alaska

Project Editors: Janie Freeburg and Diana Ackland
Field Editor: Roy Bailet
Updated by Gloria J. Maschmeyer

HOUGHTON MIFFLIN COMPANY

APA PUBLICATIONS

NO part of this book may be reproduced, stored in or introduced into a retrieval system, or transmitted in any form or by any means (electronic, mechanical, photocopying, recording or otherwise), without the prior written permission of the copyright owner of this book. Apa Publications (H.K.) Ltd. Brief text quotations with use of photographs are exempted for book review purposes only.

As every effort is made to provide accurate information in this publication, we would appreciate it if readers would call our attention to any errors that may occur by communicating with Höfer Media (Pte) Ltd., Orchard Point Post Office Box 219, Singapore 9123. Information has been obtained from sources believed to be reliable, but its accuracy and completeness, and the opinions based thereon, are not guaranteed.

alaska

Third Edition (5th Reprint)
© **1994 APA PUBLICATIONS (HK) LTD**
All Rights Reserved
Printed in Singapore by Höfer Press Pte. Ltd

Distributed in the United States by:
Houghton Mifflin Company
222 Berkeley Street
Boston, Massachusetts 02116-3764
ISBN: 0-395-66173-0

Distributed in Canada by:
Thomas Allen & Son
390 Steelcase Road East
Markham, Ontario L3R 1G2
ISBN: 0-395-66173-0

Distributed in the UK & Ireland by:
GeoCenter International UK Ltd
The Viables Center, Harrow Way
Basingstoke, Hampshire RG22 4BJ
ISBN: 9-62421-023-3

Worldwide distribution enquiries:
Höfer Communications Pte Ltd
38 Joo Koon Road
Singapore 2262
ISBN: 9-62421-023-3

ABOUT THIS BOOK

Insight Guide: *Alaska* was one of Apa Publications' most challenging projects. Although it is thought of as one of the newest of the United States–number 49 out of 50–it is really a country of its own. The state covers 586,412 square miles over four time zones. On the west Alaska is closer to the Soviet Union in miles that to the "lower 48" of the US to the southeast.

Nearly three times as large in area as Thailand or France, Alaska includes immense unexplored and uninhabited areas as well as huge reserves of oil and other minerals. The state displays Mt. McKinley, the highest peak in North America, and other treasures for the adventurous traveler. It was a natural but still bold subject for the series of unique travel guides published by Apa founder **Hans Höfer** from his headquarters in Singapore.

A native of West Germany who was trained in the Bauhaus traditions of book design, printing and photography, Höfer published his first Insight Guide in 1970. His book about Bali won several international awards for its blend of outstanding writing, fine photography and fresh journalistic information. These books are aimed at serious travelers who want a complete emotional and intellectual experience from tourism. As with all other Apa books, this edition was written and photographed by the best available local experts under the guidance of a project editor. **Janie Freeburg** carried the main responsibility with the assistance of **Diana Ackland**.

Freeburg has planned, edited and designed a number of publications in her eight years as a public relations specialist. Freeburg graduated from the University of California, Irving, with a degree in Comparative Cultures, followed by studies in commercial art and graphic design.

Diana Ackland was an editor in the Features and Articles department of *Good Housekeeping* magazines and now serves as Vice-President of Sequoia Communications, the Santa Barbara company Ackland and her husband Donald run. Ackland was educated at Pine Manor and Dickinson College on the U.S. East Coast.

Field Editor **Roy Bailet** wrote several of the chapters himself and compiled the mass of information on all parts of Alaska for the Guide in Brief. Bailet hails from Craig, Alaska, brought first-hand experience to his piece on the Alaska Bush Pilots.

Writer and photographer **Gloria J. Maschmeyer** co-authored the chapter on Anchorage and is also responsible for the 1989 update of the guide, which includes an extensive revision on the Guide in Brief section. Her written works and photos have appeared in a variety of publications in Asia and the United States. Maschmeyer holds a degree in print journalism and works as a free-lance writer in Anchorage.

Carol Phillips, who wrote "Life in the Land of Superlatives", moved to Alaska 22 years ago after growing up on the east coast. A favorite project was the editing and design of a book on Aleut Art.

Contributing the chapter on Alaska's Native Peoples, and the section on Katmai National Park, is **Kathy Hunter** of Palmer, Alaska. Hunter has worked as a free-lance writer and photographer, and is a graduate of University of Alaska, Fairbanks School of Journalism.

Freelance writer and editor **Kyle Lochalsh** contributed the long chapters on the geography and history of Alaska, as well as the informative piece on remote Cape Krusenstern National Monument.

Mike Miller, contributor of the pieces on Juneau, the Inland Passage communities, and

Freeburg

Ackland

Bill Bjork

Maschmeyer

Debby Bjork

Misty Fjords National Monument, is a member of the State House of Representatives, co-publisher and partner in the firm Alaska Books.

Jeff Brady, editor/publisher of the *Skagway News*, wrote the chapter on "Skagway, the Fun City". Brady moved to Skagway and started the paper immediately after college (at the University of North Carolina at Chapel Hill).

Writer **Mark Skok** was born in Anchorage, grew up in Washington state, and returned to continue his interest in Alaska's back country. His article on beautiful Prince William Sound, as well as an interview with noted bush pilot Lowell Thomas Jr., are in this book.

Chris Blackburn, writer of the Kodiak Island chapter, has contributed to a number of publications as diverse as the Kodiak Daily Mirror, Fish Boat Magazine and Redbook Magazine.

Chris Carson, who wrote the chapter on the Kenai Peninsula has worked on newspapers from Lewiston, Idaho, to Kenai, Alaska.

Katy Korbel, author of the Anchorage chapter, has lived in the Great Land since childhood. Born in Panama, she moved to Alaska as a young girl.

The substantial chapter on Fairbanks and the Interior of Alaska was penned by **Bill Bjork** and **Debby Drong-Bjork**, both native Minnesotans and teachers. A 1977 canoe trip in the far north led to teaching positions in a remote Athabascan village.

Park ranger/naturalist **Rick McIntyre** contributed the chapter on Denali National Park as well as the feature on Alaska's wild flowers and wildlife. For the past decade he has worked at Denali in the summers. Several of his photographs appear in this book.

Leslie Barber, author of the piece on Gates of the Arctic National Park, is a member of the Citizen's Advisory Commission on Public Lands.

Diane Brady contributed the piece on Glacier Bay National Park, and area she has toured many times as a commercial pilot for an air taxi service out of Skagway.

One of the most unusual pieces of writing in the *Insight Guide: Alaska* is the work of **Julie** and **Miki Collins**. Twin sisters who make their living hunting and trapping in the remote Alaska bush, the Collins have built their own cabins, grown and preserved their own food, and raised sled dogs.

Another look into the different styles of life in Alaska is the work of Fairbanks writer **Carol Kaynor**. Her article on "The Musher and the Entrepreneur". A Massachusetts native, Kaynor settled in Fairbanks in 1977.

Others whose images grace the pages of this book include **Mireille Vautier** and her **Photothéque Vautier-de Nanxe** in Paris, and **Jeff Shultz**, **Harry Walker**, **Allan Seiden** and **James McCann**, **Tonystone Worldwide**, **Mark Skok**, **Lee Foster**, **Maxine Cass**, **Kim Heacox**, **Angela White**, **Julie** & **Miki Collins** and **Carol Kaynor**. All historic pictorials are from the collections of **Bruce Bernstein**, by courtesy of the Princeton University Library. Maps were drawn under the direction of **Gunter Nelles** of Munich, West Germany. Indexing was done by **Karen Cheng**.

Judy Palmer, Marketing Vice-President of Princess Tours, deserves special credit for helping to get the project off the ground.

Thanks especially go to **Thomas F Honan**, Director of Marketing, Holland America Westours and in his capacity of Chairman of the Alaska Visitors Association Marketing Council (AVAMCO) and to **Dave Giersdorf**, Owner/Director of Exploration Holidays and Cruises for his support.

–Apa Publications

Jeff Brady

Diane Brady

Hunter

Miller

Barber

CONTENTS

Beginnings

Places

Features

Maps

TRAVEL TIPS

**For detailed Information
See Page 273**

WELCOME TO ALASKA

Alaska: The Great Land, The Last Frontier–more than 580,000 sq miles (1.5 million sq km) that taunted early explorers and still defies modern-day researchers. The hint of urban sophistication in Anchorage rapidly gives way to the frontier, where whale-hunting expertise may be far more useful than a college education.

Alaska has both lush rain-drenched forests and barren windswept tundras. It boasts lofty mountains and endless swamps–along with a handful of high-rise buildings and uncountable numbers of one-room log cabins. Within hours of dining sumptuously in a first-class restaurant it is possible to tread on ground that has never known a human footprint: ground belonging to the grizzly bear and wolf and only shared reluctantly.

This varied land is best viewed from a light plane or surveyed from a canoe; it cannot be seen from a car, and would take forever to cover on foot. Alaska is an outdoor world, a wilderness, a land of many faces, few of which can be explored by moving from hotel to hotel.

The Alaskan experience includes the sheer wonder of finding what hides beyond the horizon or over the next ridge. No one person has ever seen it all; no one person ever will. Therein lies the essence of Alaska. Something new, something different and something unique always waits around the next bend in the river or twist in the trail. Only those who have looked upon Alaska, however briefly, can appreciate its fierce and unforgiving majesty.

LIFE IN THE LAND OF SUPERLATIVES

"When we were young, my brother and I shared many enjoyable reading adventures. We were fascinated by everything related to the North, and our favorite book was the journal of a renowned arctic explorer. One line in particular stood out: 'Today it warmed up to 50 below.' The first time we read this, we broke up with hilarity; after that, whenever anyone complained about chilly weather, we would toss off that phrase. After I moved to the interior of Alaska as an adult, I could hardly wait until extreme winter conditions granted me my golden opportunity. At last, on one grand, shimmering, ice-rimmed morning, I was able to write the legendary line to my brother: 'Today it warmed up to 50 below.'"

Fifty below! A phrase to instill terror in warm hearts. Two stark words which challenge any positive appeal. But forget for a moment the obvious hazards of cold weather, the problems inherent in such a temperature and overcome by determination, ingenuity, the survival instinct and, often, sheer good luck. Think instead of the images which lead many Alaskans to declare unequivocally that winter is the state's best season.

Looking out at a frosty world from behind a ski mask or a furry hood, with layers of cozy clothing providing adequate protection, one views astounding beauty — skies of piercing clarity, hoar-frosted tree glittering with diamonds, mountainous horizons sharply distinct against the sky. A blood-red sunset paints the heavens, although midwinter's fleeting light leads to debate about whether it's sunrise or sunset!

Only the sibilance of sled runners against dry snow and the panting of the huskies intrude upon the perfect peace of a trail where snowshoes and skis and the tracks of myriad wildlife have traced patterns in the wilderness. In the silence an occasional note rings out, sharp as a rifle shot, as trees and house logs protest the cold's stress.

And then there are the northern lights. Have you ever been in wonderland, surrounded by a light show of gigantic proportions, with strobes pulsating, sweeping the sky as though commanded by a supernatural hand? Scientists claim the northern lights make no sound; perhaps the experts have never been alone on a tundra trail and experienced this phenomenon as Alaska artist/dog driver Jon Van Zyle did one winter night; he recorded in his journal how the dogs looked up and all around "when the

lights crackled and made whooshing sounds."

Cynics will be quick to note that winter is also Alaska's longest season. True enough; it lasts perhaps two months too long in most parts of the state, and, indeed, the Great Land is a poor place for those who don't enjoy cold weather and winter activities. But try telling that to the skiers and snowmobilers and outdoor enthusiasts who "think snow" seven months of the year and spend the other five months preparing for the next winter. Tell it to the little parka-clad boy walking along the icy village road eating his ice cream cone. (Alaskans are said to have the highest per capita consumption of ice cream in the United States — and, yes, Eski-

Preceding pages; a totem face; an Eskimo in fur-lined garb; Mount Brooks; a living glacier at Tracy Arm; gold miner's cabin in the Wrangells; celebrating tradition with the blanket-toss; men survey the mountain scenery; skiers express their Alaskan indomitability. Left, icy moustache of a mountaineer. Right, mountain coiffures with the help of a friend.

mos *do* buy refrigerators!) Tell it to the dog musher waiting for good trail conditions so he can train his team for the impending race season. Tell it to anyone who has felt every sense come alive in the crisp pure air of an Alaskan winter, who has known the undercurrent of excitement that accompanies a hike at 50 below.

For those whose reaction to winter is less fervent, there are fortunately three other seasons, brief but vivid. The indescribable summer, when all of Alaska seems to live feverishly out-of-doors — hiking, biking, fishing, running, sailing, gardening, camping — gives way to a mellow autumn, coming early but with glory.

Only springtime, with breakup, flooding and new potholes, loses out on seasonal

Collecting Superlatives

Alaska offers countless examples of the most, the highest, the longest, the largest. Some figures, while impressive, are not necessarily the stuff of which boasts are made. No one rushes to claim credit for having had the most powerful earthquake ever recorded in North America (between 8.4 and 8.6 on the Richter scale in 1964 in south-central Alaska), nor to admit that the state has one of the highest cost of living in the country (although it should be added that this is offset by high levels of income).

It is much more satisfying to think instead about things like the world's longest sled dog race — the internationally famous Iditarod run annually over an arduous thousand-mile

beauty prizes, but in typically enterprising fashion Alaskans by the thousands relieve the stress of late winter's stubborn weeks by betting on the exact minute when the breakup of the ice on the Nenana River of the Interior will signal spring's official arrival.

In the uniquely Alaskan town of Talkeetna, the old-timers who live virtually in the shadow of Mount McKinley enjoy the relaxed weeks of late winter before spring brings the climbers who headquarter here regularly and the tourists who search the horizon for the outline of the famous mountain. Hundreds attempt to climb McKinley each year; many succeed, many give up, some occasionally do not return from its heights.

trail between Anchorage and Nome. It is more interesting to consider that Alaska is known as the flyingest state in the nation, with six times as many pilots per capita as the average in other states, and where residents of bush villages are often more familiar with air travel than with cars.

Trivia buffs can tuck away the little-known fact that the last shot of the Civil War was fired off the coast of Alaska, nearly two months after the official end of that war. And our Aleut friends know from bitter experience that their part of Alaska was the only U.S. territory ever occupied by enemy forces, for they were there on Attu during World War II when their island was invaded, their homes destroyed, and they were shipped off to concentration camps.

A generation ago a common question among non-Native Alaskans was, "Where are you from?" Today, the increasingly heard answer is, "I was born here." Many of the early "sourdoughs," seeking their fortunes, settled down and established homes and families. Some Alaskans came originally on military assignment, recognized Alaska's unique offerings, and put down roots.

Many residents of the Matanuska Valley came during the bleak days of America's Great Depression, founding farms, families and communities. Modernday gold-seekers arrive steadily, lured by tales of oil wealth and high wages. Some, unable to adjust to the extremes of weather and the demand for self-reliance, soon depart, empty-handed

live here; the adversities are matched only by the rewards of fulfillment and self-discovery which personal resourcefulness bestows. It is a make-or-break kind of place. And it is not for everyone.

Extremes of climate and imposing statistics make for interesting letters to the folks back home, but the true measure of a place lies not in its highest or largest or longest or farthest, but in the intangible essence which draws and holds its people. This essence creates the mood and the magic of a place and the attitudes of those who choose to call it home. Alaskans are an independent breed, and their definitions of what their state is all about are as varied as their own backgrounds. Northland poet Robert Service said it best when he wrote of "the freshness,

and disillusioned, for more predictable climes.

As in any frontier society, a certain number of people exist always "on the edge" — the reclusive, the individualists, the radicals and those who stay a scant step ahead of the law. Those who come to escape from their pasts or from themselves may find their problems do not disappear but instead magnify in this larger-than-life land. There is a sense of returning to the basics in coming to

Left, a string of fish caught in Prince William Sound. Right, cheery climbers defy the cold.

the freedom, the farness" and "the stillness" that filled him with peace.

These elements of the dream that has long brought dreamers to the North and claimed their labor and their loyalty are the basic ingredients of the Alaskan way of life. The last frontier is fast disappearing in the face of modern technological society, and the sourdough's vision is fading from the eyes of today's youth, but Alaska's taiga and tundra are broad, its mountains are many and high, and dreams will always live on in those who come seeking intangible treasures. Those whose vision remains clear and whose reach extends beyond the limits of things material will find that living in the land of superlatives is, in a word, superlative.

ALASKA NATIVES: THE 'FIRST PEOPLE'

Vsitors to Alaska have found the Alaska Native to be not what they expected. They do not live in igloos, dress only in the skins of animals, share wives or rub noses with everyone. Except for the ancestors of one native group, most of them never looked or acted this way. So what is an Alaska Native?

An Alaska Native is a reindeer herder in Mekoryuk, a fisherman in Kodiak, a public health employee in Ketchikan, a woman living in a garage in Fairbanks while she attempts to earn a living sewing skins, an executive in a regional organization based in Anchorage. The term "Alaska Native" is misleading, used for only convenience. Alaska's native people are as diverse as the geography of the state and more so, because different languages are often spoken among tribes in areas with a common culture.

What Alaska Natives do have in common is the fact that their people have been in Alaska since before time was recorded. For the most part, Natives share a love for the land, and a fear that their way of life and the teachings of their ancestors will die out. Together they struggle for balance, trying to keep their own culture intact as it meets modern society, with a foot in both worlds.

It is believed that the first inhabitants of came from Asia over a land bridge between Siberia and Alaska. Today, they are divided, for convenience, into three main groups: the Eskimos, the Aleuts, and Alaska's Athabascan and Southeast Coast Indians.

Eskimos include the Inupiat speaking people of the north and the Yup'ik people of the south. The Aleuts occupy the Aleutian chain of islands and the Gulf Coast. Although the various Aleut languages have led anthropologists to classify them technically as Eskimos, they prefer a separate grouping based on culture differences. The third category includes the Athabascans of the Interior and Cook Inlet; and the Tlingit, Haida, and Tsimshian Indians of Alaska's southeast coast. Language differences are common within many subgroups, for instance, the Aleut language may vary from village to village around the gulf, and 11 different

Left, a Nulato boy in warm parka.

languages are spoken by the Athabascans.

The first Alaskans lived by hunting and gathering. All used waterways and some kind of boat for transportation. With a few exceptions natives lived in permanent dwellings and moved to summer camps to collect seasonal food like the salmon and caribou.

Using what materials were available, homes were usually dome-shaped structures with a frame of driftwood, whalebone or sticks that supported moss and turf and/or animal skins. Floors often were below ground level, with entrance through a narrow tunnel or a hole in the roof. Where wood was available it was used not only for construction but for fuel and light, but in areas without trees the oil of sea mammals was used for both heat and illumination.

Many native religions featured a belief in afterlife and a respect for the spirits of food animals. Groups relied on a shaman, or medicine man, to interpret the supernatural and to cure illnesses. Their ceremonies included song and dance, and stories were told by every group. These stories were of warfare and raiding, and myths involving animals, especially tales about the Raven.

Raven was the first creature. He married a lovely white swan and they spent a happy summer in the North. But soon the swan had to fly South with the rest of her kind.

"I must remain here to look after my kingdom," said Raven, but he loved her so much that when she left he tried to follow her. Soon Raven was far behind the graceful swans and his wife's attempt to carry him on her back was of no use.

"I can go no farther," cried Raven in despair, "Goodbye," and he plummeted to a small rock in the ocean below. There he sat, wet, cold, lonely and miserable.

Just then a baby whale flipped in the water. Raven pulled it gently onto the rock and played with it until the angry mother whale arose from the sea.

"Give me back my baby," she ordered.

"No," said Raven, who had a crafty thought. "I will return your baby if you will bring me rocks from the bottom of the sea,"

The whale agreed and brought rocks as the Raven demanded, and then mud and gravel to fill in the cracks. After the baby had returned to the mother, Raven arranged seaweed around the rocks. Soon lichens, mosses and willows grew. Raven caught seeds from the wind. He planted them along the south east coast and they grew into big trees.

Raven was very proud of his new land, and although people and animals were attracted there, he always thought it was his. To this day he considers himself King of Alaska, and swans return each year as loyal subjects.

Eskimos, Aleuts and Athabascans

Life for the early Eskimo was a constant struggle against hunger and the cold. Seasonal food was stored against future shortage and the long dark winter; and even though his own family might be wanting, a hunter always divided a fresh kill evenly throughout the community. Because food was a primary concern, status within a village was determined by hunting ability.

served in skin containers or baskets.

Umiak were the Eskimo boats used to hunt larger sea animals, and *kayak*, a smaller one-man craft. These were made of wooden framework, covered with skins or hides. Sleds and dog teams were used for winter travel, and during the summer dogs were used as pack animals.

Women were skilled in basketry and sewing. They stitched and fitted waterproof garments of animal intestine and fish skins. Everyday clothing of trousers, boots and coats were sewn with skins and fur, sometimes in complex geometric designs. The coats, called parkas, featured an attached hood and ruff and are worn today, in brightly

colored fabrics with decorative trim.

The Eskimo are reputed for their fine carving, especially in the production of small ivory pieces. In early times household utensils and weapons were beautifully ornamented. Using wood, bone, baleen, walrus ivory and fossil mammoth tusks they crafted small sculptures and game pieces, ceremonial masks, goggles to protect eyes from glare, dishes and knives, oil lamps, and, in fact, every object needed for living and transportation. The *ulu*, or woman's knife, can be found in tourists shops today and is appreciated by contemporary cooks for its beauty and useful shape.

Village sites were chosen according to availability of food sources. Western Eskimos subsisted on salmon and seal meat. The Arctic coast people depended on seal, walrus and whale, while the inland Eskimo lived on caribou, birds and other small game animals. Eggs were gathered by all, and berries, roots and wild greens were eaten fresh or pre-

A recent find at Barrow has given archaeologists new insight into the world of the northern Eskimo before their contact with Europeans in 1826. This find was unique: a family frozen in time, buried by an enormous piece of ice rafted in from a stormy sea. Besides numerous artifacts, inside the wood and sod house were the remains of five people. Autopsies of the bodies revealed the effects of seasonal starvation and accumulated soot inside their dwelling. A 42-year-old woman was found to have survived bacterial pneumonia, an infection of the heart valves, arthritis, trichinosis, and blood poisoning. She had also recently also given birth.

For survival it was necessary that Eskimos summed up by the Koniag saying, "When the tide goes out the table is set." With this bounty; however, came a legacy of unpredictable weather: earthquakes, high winds, stormy seas, and blinding rain that contrast with a clear day of breathtaking beauty.

Aleuts wore little clothing indoors and during the summer. When weather made it necessary, hoodless skin parkas were worn that reached to the knees, and in cold weather Aleuts donned knee-length skin boots. Waterproof overgarments made from the intestines of sea lions were also worn, some designed to fit over the opening in a skin boat to keep a hunter dry.

Aleut women were able to develop skill in

develop great ingenuity and resourcefulness. In a barren waste where temperatures are seldom above zero small mistakes take on life-or-death significance. Courage was also necessary: courage of the kind that led the Eskimo, in his search for food, to take on an animal the size of a whale in a fragile skin boat and armed only with a harpoon.

The Aleut people are best remembered for their tie to the sea. The people of the Aleutian Chain, and the Koniag, Chugach and Eyak in the Gulf of Alaska all enjoyed a lifestyle

Right, Yup'ik Eskimo basket weavers. Left, Yup'ik dancers from Tunanak.

basketry because of a ready supply of grass in the summer, and are known for this expertise. Coiled baskets were crafted by the early Eskimo, but the Aleut basket was made by tiny stitches, so closely woven that the resulting container would hold water. Mats and clothing were also crafted the same way.

Aleut fishing technology included fish spears, weirs, nets, hooks and lines. Various darts and nets were employed to obtain seals, sea lions and sea otters. Whales were killed with a poisoned, stone-bladed lance. After the spear was embedded in the whale the lance head became detached. When the poisoned tip worked its way to a vital spot the whale would die, usually within three days, and the carcass would drift to shore.

The one- and two-man skin boats used by the Aleut were called "bidarkas" by the Russians. Because of their dependence on the sea, these people seldom went over a mile inland, but they did develop a clever method of transportation over snow. Aleut skis were made by drying hair-seal skins over wooden frames. When the traveller went uphill the hair would dig into the snow and act as a brake, and would lie flat to provide speed when going downhill.

Among the Koniag people of the Kodiak archipelago each group had a leader for a specific area of expertise, like seal hunting,

rior Athabascan Indians were people of the rivers, hunters and inland fishermen. Most lived in small nomadic bands along rivers. Like the Eskimo, theirs was a difficult life that required tenacity; they travelled for days without food and existed in temperatures of -50 degrees F (-46°C) or colder without shelter or fire. Endurance and physical strength were prized; game was often run down on foot over difficult terrain.

Athabascans hunted salmon, rabbits, caribou, and bear, using bows and arrows, snares and clubs. Abundant birch trees provided materials for canoes, containers, snowshoes and sleds, even cradles. Clothing was of animal hides with porcupine quills colored

warlike activities, or boat-building. In these societies, ridicule was a major instrument of discipline; good things in life were shared, and deviant behavior harmful to others was viewed as insanity. Community life of the Natives depended on two larger structures, called the "kashim" and the "banya." The kashim was used for formal activities, usually by the males. The banya, or steam bath, was the center of the community and was frequented by all, equally. Here friendships were made and cemented, and news and gossip exchanged.

The Southeastern tribes and the Athabascans have significant differences. The inte-

with plant dyes. After traders introduced colored beads to the Athabascans, their women began to produce beadwork sewn on skins to make numerous decorated items.

Athabascan bands were strongly protective of their hunting territory, warfare, however, was not as common to them as it was to the peoples of the Southeast.

The most flamboyant Alaska Natives were those of southeastern Alaska. A milder climate with more available food sources allowed these people time to devote to social pastimes, travel and trade. They developed a standard of currency, and were expert navigators and superb craftsmen. While living in a complex society, they practised religion based on mythology that united them with nature. They enjoyed ceremony and drama, and the habit of reciting family history kept an accurate account for generations.

These peoples were also able to refine a distinctive style of design which they applied to everything created, including everyday utensils, clothing, masks, canoes, tradegoods, ritual objects, and the characteristic totems that marked family residences. The remarkable painted designs of the Southeastern Indian feature abstracted fish and animals, often in bold patterns of black and red.

Before Europeans discovered this land, trading went on for years between groups

The Tlingit and Haida lived in tight family groups. Households of clan or blood relations contained as many as 50 members. Every household and every clan had their own history, traditions, and animal crest.

These peoples believed the world was alive with supernatural spirits, and this made them one with their environment. Everything has spiritual power whether it was a rock, a lake, a tree or a man. It was believed that fish and animals gave themselves willingly to man for his needs, and must be treated with respect. A bear killed for meat might be brought to the house, greeted with a welcome speech and placed in a seat of honor for a day or two. The bones of a con-

along the Pacific Northwest coast and parts of Southeastern Alaska. The Tlingits were known to travel over 1,000 miles (1,600 km) to the south for this purpose. In early times, the standard of currency was "blanket value," based on blankets made of cedar bark, dog and goat hair. After white men began trade in the area, the Hudson's Bay Company was established and blankets of wool became its medium of exchange. A canoe, for example, was at one time worth 700 blankets and a sea otter robe, 30.

Right, wise Native face from Aniak village. Left, Athabascan boys share a smile.

sumed salmon were always returned to the river where it had been caught to allow reincarnation. Any bones missing would then create a deformed fish.

Each household owned economic goods, while the clan owned religious titles and objects. The whole group or sections within the group might own the right to perform a certain dance or practice a profession like seal hunting. Individuals within the group usually owned weapons and clothing, and anything they had made themselves.

In the social organization of the Tlingit and Haida, status was determined by wealth. Ownership of goods, privileges such as the right to light ceremonial fires or dance a certain dance, and prestigious family background were all important in achieving status as a noble. In order to maintain position, a person of power demonstrated wealth by giving a ceremonial "pot-latch." Here, usually men would give away, destroy, or cause to be consumed, vast stores of possessions. Those who received goods at one potlatch were expected to reciprocate and "better" their host at another. The exact meaning and purpose of this potlatch has been the subject of lively debate among anthropologists for the past few decades.

In the early 1900s the potlatch was banned by the United States, whose European colonists were opposed to the practice. A few potlatches were held secretly and in 1951 the law was repealed, but the damage had already been done. Without the repetition of family background (something central to the ceremony) histories of tribes, families, and individuals were lost forever.

these influences. The Chilkat, a subgroup of the Tlingits, used musk ox and caribou skins for armor, obtained from the Athabascans, who were themselves familiar with tobacco and tea that had come their way from Siberia.

Later European and American contact had differing effects on Native populations. Some starved when food sources were depleted, or when drinking the trader's whiskey took priority over hunting. Others were decimated by epidemics of disease. Value systems were lost as luxury articles became essentials, and culture died as a foreign way of life penetrated. Missionaries and schools discouraged Native background, replacing Native beliefs and language with their own.

Contact and Change

Before European discovery, Alaska's Natives traded over a large area, drawing from Siberian Natives across the Bering Strait and Indians of the Pacific Northwest. Their culture was constantly changing from

Most abused were the Aleuts, who were enslaved or killed outright by Russian fur traders. In the first 50 years of Russian influence the population in the Aleutian Islands went from 10,000–20,000 to 2,000. During World War II they were further depleted as many were killed, taken to Japan by the Japanese, or evacuated to Southeast Alaska by the Americans.

Least affected were the Indians of the Southeast whose culture was familiar with trade and whose strength in war was respected. The Tlingits were always quick to defend what was theirs; in 1799 they wiped out a Russian trading station, and a century later sent two war canoes to Seattle to demand return of a totem pole taken by tourists. After Alaska's purchase by the United States from Russian, Tlingits were the first to take advantage of the U.S. system of government and education, and have provided important native leaders for the state.

In 1966 all Alaskan Natives united to claim title to their lands. They began to participate in state and local government and to be recognized for their voting impact. When interest in Alaskan oil development was blocked by the unsettled land claims, the oil companies added strength to Native urgency. As a result, in 1971 Natives were awarded $1 billion and 40 million acres (16

million hectares) of land. With the settlement, Natives found themselves thrust into the 20th century. Traditionally a hunting and gathering society, they now had to deal with large sums of money and to develop a financial mentality overnight. As a result, Natives were organized into regional profit-making corporations and administered the settlement themselves. Native stock was placed in a trust for 20 years to allow the youngest stockholders to grow up. What the natives

Left, a Native fiddler entertains during the long winter. Right, craft shop proprietor models a Yup'ik squirrel coat.

lacked in the agreement, however, was their sovereignty and right to govern themselves, like other aboriginals in the United States.

The settlement plan has been a failure in the eyes of the Natives. Several corporations have gone bankrupt due to mismanagement and greedy business groups have taken advantage of the Native's plight, siphoning off millions. In many cases, the Natives have ended up land rich and cash poor.

It should not be assumed that because of the land claims settlement the Alaskan Native is rich; so far little money has reached Native hands. In spite of better communications systems, health care, education, housing, and the addition of electricity to remote villages, the standard of living is comparatively low. Alcoholic-related tragedies are common, among them a growing number of suicides among the young.

Today, a Native family who lives almost entirely off the land and speaks the old language resides in a wooden frame house. Outside, racks of drying salmon are suspended over various possessions that include a wooden boat and a snowmobile. Under her fur-trimmed parka the mother wears a western dress obtained through a mail-order catalog. Her whaler husband and friends will track the movements of their prey with a short wave radio, and when the meat is consumed raw, as in the old days, they will wash it down with canned pop.

1991 marks yet another era for the Alaska Native. A provision in the 1971 Claims Settlement Act allows Natives to sell their corporate stock and land to the public, as long as a majority of the corporation's shareholders approve. Journalist June Degnan, daughter of the first Yup'ik Eskimo elected to the Territorial Legislature in the 1950s, felt this may spell doom for her people. Once native landownership ceases, the people will lose their culture entirely, she predicts. The result will be that the Natives will make a mass exodus from their rural villages into the large urban areas. And this tragedy will impact upon everyone, Degnan says.

Yet, today in Alaska there is heightened pride in Native birth and a revival of Native culture. Native language and skills are now taught in the schools and the Native voice is growing stronger in Alaskan politics. This is a period of great change for Alaska Natives, and for many, the future holds promise.

ALASKA, THE GREAT LAND

Alaska is more than a place, it's a state of mind. A passenger flying overhead caught a bit of this mentality as she gazed below at Anchorage, wrapped in winter's cold, "Brr, Alaskans are tough." Most Alaskans would agree. They are indeed tough. And adventurous, romantic. hard-working, but not necessarily in traditional ways. Some Alaskans deliberately seek the last frontier, preferring to pit their wits against the challenges of the Bush. Others, ordinary middle-class Americans, partake of the Alaskan experience in Anchorage, the state's only connection with urban America.

All come seeking riches. Some hope for wealth of the pocket: gold, oil, fish, construction. Others search for riches of the spirit: freedom, experience, opportunity. Alaska has its own charisma, its own pride, its own language. To be an Alaskan means to be something special. In earlier times Alaskans were few. Even today transients from just about everywhere overwhelm those born in the north. Though the numbers have increased, the feeling of being different, of being special, remains.

Geologic Formation

Even from a satellite orbiting high above the earth Alaska stands out. More than 1,400 miles (2,250 km) north to south and 2,400 miles (3,860 km) east to west, Alaska is one-fifth the size of the entire United States. This great chunk of North America sits at the top of the Pacific Ocean where her 591,004 sq miles (1,531,000 sq km) stretch from a longitude on line with New Zealand in the west to the Canadian border on the east. Her north boundary follows the coast of the Arctic Ocean. The Chukchi and Bering seas combine to limit her western reach, and waves of the Gulf of Alaska and Pacific Ocean shape her southern fringes.

Mount McKinley, known as Denali to many Alaskans (or just "The Mountain") but still officially named for the former United States President, surveys this expanse from its summit at 20,320 feet (6,195 meters), highest point on the continent. Alaska claims many superlatives: the biggest, the widest, the longest. But all this

Preceding pages: Mount McKinley, highest peak in North America. Left, poplar trees grace the Parks Highway near Fairbanks.

bigness had to come from somewhere, and well back in geologic time Alaska came together in a giant shuffle.

According to scientists, Alaska is made up of bits and pieces of the earth's crust, some from far to the south, others from the polar reaches of prehistoric Canada. The theory of plate tectonics holds that the earth's crust floats on a molten mantle surrounding the planet's core. This molten material leaks from the mantle through huge rifts that split the ocean basins. The crust, in giant pieces known as plates, drifts away from these rifts. Millions of years ago through slow but inexorable movement, this drifting brought about a rearrangement of continental land severing some and amalgamating others.

As plates underlying the northeastern Pacific Ocean bumped into those of continental North America, they slid northward, propelled by movement along the San Andreas and other faults. In the meantime, a distant piece of land in the northernmost reaches of North America began a gradual swing to the west, still hinged at one end to the continent but sweeping farther and farther into the Pacific. About 80 million years ago, by some estimates, the northern landmass completed its swing and bridged the North American and Asian continents, thus forming the foundation for northern Alaska and northeastern Siberia.

Some time later, the plates slipping northward along the west coast collided with this land bridge. Something had to give. In a process known as subduction. the Pacific plate dove under the continental plate. Some scientists speculate that this subduction may not have occurred until more than 200 miles (320 km) inland from the present coast of southcentral Alaska. The tremendous forces caused by subduction of the oceanic plate may explain the precipitous rise of the central Alaska Range, home to Mount McKinley, Mount Foraker and their towering neighbors. In any event, the landmasses riding on the oceanic plate now make up parts of southern Alaska.

Volcanic Activity

To the west, activity in the Aleutian Island arc provides a textbook example of subduction and its more spectacular surface manifestation, volcanoes. The Pacific is famed for its ring of fire, the series of volcanoes and associated earthquakes which surround the earth's largest ocean. Alaska contains at least 10 percent of the world's identified volcanoes, and the Aleutians are notorious for their volcanic activity. Most of the state's active or more recently active volcanoes occur in a 1,600-mile (2570-km) arc from Mount Spurr west of Anchorage across Cook Inlet down the Alaska Peninsula and out to near the western tip of the Aleutians. When the oceanic plate dives beneath the continental plate at the Aleutian Trench in the Pacific just south of the island chain, it carries ocean-bottom sediments with it. Exposed to extreme temperatures deep within the earth, the sediments and bits of crust melt and become magma. This magma seeks escape along fractures in the crust, and when

shifted laterally, blown itself up, been resurrected, and become home to colonies of seabirds and sea lions. Scientists still keep an eye on Bogoslof, today about a mile (1.6 km) long and more than 300 feet (984 meters) high, just waiting for the next act in this spectacular performance.

With the pieces of prehistoric Alaska generally in place, it was left to the great ice sheets of the Pleistocene epoch, which ended about 10,000 to 15,000 years ago, to sculpt the landscape of much of the state. Extensions of continental ice masses centered near Hudson Bay in Canada, the Pleistocene ice sheets generally reached from the Alaska Range seaward, covering the southern third of the state. The tremendous weight of the ice scoured the landscape,

it finds a weak point, it bursts to the surface, either oozing out along cracks or erupting as volcanoes. Major volcanic activity occurs yearly in the Aleutians or neighboring Alaska Peninsula, although some eruptions remain unreported because of poor weather and the low population in the region. In clear weather, airline passengers headed for Cold Bay near the tip of the Alaska Peninsula need only look out the window at steaming Mount Pavlof or Mount Veniaminof.

Every once in a while, volcanic activity presents Alaska with a new island. The magic of Bogoslof on the Bering Sea side of the Aleutians has intrigued visitors for two centuries. Known by various names, the island has risen from the sea, subsided,

gouging out deep fjords and shearing off highlands.

Much of northern Alaska, however, except for the Brooks Range and portions of the Seward Peninsula, escaped this icy tomb. And because the ice sheets acted like sponges, soaking up great quantities of water to support their massive bulk, sea levels were lowered. This exposed Beringia, or the Bering Land Bridge, the corridor by which prehistoric peoples are supposed to have populated the Americas. Just how and why ancient man made his way to the western hemisphere is much discussed.

Evidence indicates that much of northern and western Alaska was similar in climate and habitat to the steppes of Siberia. Many animals which foraged in Siberia also thrived in Alaska. Early hunters may have been simply following game and crossed the land bridge in their search for food. Sea level at this time fluctuated, rising and falling in conjunction with advance and retreat of the ice sheets. While some hunting parties made their way across the land bridge, others were blocked when rising sea levels inundated their path.

The Earliest Alaskans

Throughout the centuries, those early people who did reach North America made their way to the heart of the continent as the Pleistocene came to an end. Some became ancestors to Athabascan Indians of Alaska's

scendants occupy today: Inupiat Eskimos in the north and northwest; Yupik Eskimos in the west; Siberian Yupiks on Saint Lawrence Island; Aleuts in the Aleutians and portions of the Alaska Peninsula; Athabascans in the Interior and Eyak in the Copper River Valley; Tlingit, Haida and Tsimshians in Southeast; Chugach, and Koniag in Prince William Sound, Kodiak archipelago and Alaska Peninsula.

In 1741 the first Westerners arrived in Alaska when Vitus Bering, a Dane sailing for Peter the Great of Russia, sighted the mainland coast from his ship cruising in the Gulf of Alaska. After sailing east from the Siberian coast about the beginning of June, the crew of the *Saint Peter* spotted the lofty summit of Mount Saint Elias the following

Interior, others to the Tlingit, Haida and Tsimshian Indians of southeastern Alaska. Later arrivals migrated down the Bering Sea coast of western Alaska to become the Aleuts of the Aleutian Islands and lower Alaska Peninsula. Probably the last to reach North America were the predecessors of modern Eskimos who spread their various cultures as far as Greenland.

Thus, by about a millennium ago, prehistoric Alaskans had established the broad boundaries for the regions which their de-

Left, the Knik Glacier from the air. Right, these lands were freed of glacier ice only during the last 200 years.

month. Rising to more than 18,000 feet (5,500 meters) and second only to Mount McKinley in Alaska, the peak crowns the mountains of the same name, highest coastal range in the world. Turning westward, Bering's vessel anchored off Kayak Island while crew members went ashore to explore and find water. Georg Wilhelm Steller, ship's naturalist, hiked briskly along the island, taking notes on plants and wildlife. Here he first recorded for science the striking blue-and-black jay which bears his name. Bering was anxious to return to home port before bad weather blocked his passage, so once again he put the *Saint Peter* on a westward heading, unaware of the magnificent country lying beyond the coastal mountain barrier.

SOUTHEASTERN: ALASKA'S PANHANDLE

Southeastern Alaska, simply Southeast or "The Panhandle" to many residents, extends from Dixon Entrance on the Canadian border north to Icy Bay. The 1,000-plus islands of the Alexander Archipelago and a narrow coastal strip of mainland from the crest of the Coast Range to the sea make up the bulk of Southeast.

Water binds this region of islands, ice and forests. The lush green of Tongass National Forest carpets Southeast, creating scenes of unimaginable beauty and providing the foundation for a sometimes shaky timber industry.

The forests shelter black bears and their larger cousins, brown bears. Wolves inhabit the Glacier Bay area, the Yakutat Forelands, and portions of southern Southeast; red foxes are found in the northern reaches of the region. Furbearers—marten, weasels, mink and river otters—occur throughout Southeast, while their ferocious relative, the wolverine, sticks primarily to the mainland and some of the smaller islands. Sitka black-tailed deer are synonymous with Southeast, and moose, largest members of the deer family, forage in coastal areas south of Yakutat and in the Chilkat Valley north of Haines. Agile mountain goats, whose thick hair provides the raw material for the famous Chilkat Indian blankets, feel right at home in rocky crags that wall much of the region. Southeast waterways harbor an abundance of marine mammals. Sea otters, sea lions, fur seals and harbor seals feed in the rich marine environment. Most spectacular of Southeast's marine fare are the great whales, particularly humpbacks and killers.

Rivers of Ice

Where there are no forests, there is ice. A chilly cap rides the crest of the Coast Mountains, sending glaciers inching downward toward the sea. Atop this cap sit the Juneau and Stikine icefields which together harbor thousands of square miles of glaciers just in Alaska, to say nothing of their icy expanse into Canada.

Left, Francis Seward persuaded the U.S. Congress to "buy" Alaska from the Russians. Right, "Red Leggings," an Alaskan Native.

Mecca for all true glacier-watchers lies about 50 miles (80 km) from Juneau in the ice-shrouded fjords of Glacier Bay National Park and Preserve. North of Glacier Bay lies a wilderness with few breaks in its rugged coastline. Several glaciers calve into the T-shaped fjord of Lituya Bay.

The isolated fishing community of Yakutat, on Yakutat Bay, is the only outpost in this remote northern corner of Southeast. Magnificent Yakutat Bay is surrounded by some of the tallest mountains on the continent, fed by active rivers of ice, and flanked

by Malaspina, the largest piedmont (at the foot of a mountain range) glacier in North America.

Southeast brings to mind Christmas card images: waves rhythmically lapping the sides of a fishing boat, gentle snows whitening a thick forest, shy deer peeking out from shelter, sleek furbearers scurrying across a beach. But the region has another side. Fierce storms sweeping unhindered across the breadth of the Pacific buffet the coast. Rain drenches the region. The fishing port of Ketchikan makes the most of its annual rainfall, pointing with pride to its soggy statistic as one of the wettest spots on the continent. Upper Southeast communities lie in a rain shadow, protected by high peaks which block moist air from the nearby Pacific Ocean.

A Land of Boats and Floatplanes

For years water transportation was the only way to get around Southeast. Few rivers breach the Coast Range, and until recently only two roads connected the region with the rest of the continent. From Stewart, Alaska—along the Canadian Border—a spur joins the Cassiar Highway which eventually connects with the continental road system.

In the north, scenic Haines Highway climbs out of the lush Chilkat Valley to cross the high country of extreme northwestern British Columbia and southwestern Yukon

perhaps nothing stranger than the 500 reindeer which were driven up the route to feed residents of Dawson City. Only 114 survived the trek to the gold fields.

For decades business and government leaders have complained about the lack of road access to Juneau, state capital and the region's largest city. Various proposals including bridging Lynn Canal and building a road up the Taku River Valley have been suggested as the panacea for Juneau's access problems. But the rugged terrain of Southeast has stood its ground, not giving an inch to the dreams and schemes of modern man.

The Alaska Marine Highway, a fleet of ferries, provides public transportation for Southeast. Major airlines call at Juneau, Sitka and Ketchikan; commuter lines handle

Territory to Haines Junction on the Alaska Highway. In the late 1970s, a mostly gravel road, now designated the Klondike Highway, was punched through from near Whitehorse on the Alaska Highway to Skagway at the head of Taiya Inlet, an offshoot of Lynn Canal.

The Chilkat Valley route through Haines has been used for centuries as a transportation corridor. Interior Indians traded with the powerful Tlingit of the coast through the valley. When Jack Dalton arrived in the area in the late 1800s, he saw the potential for profit and laid a toll road from Lynn Canal to Fort Selkirk at the junction of the Yukon and Pelly rivers in Yukon Territory. The trail carried a lot of traffic to the Yukon, but

traffic for smaller fishing ports and timber towns. Floatplanes are likely to be found in any quiet cove, and boats from cruiseships and freighters to kayaks patrol among the islands.

Early Discoveries

Lt. Alexsei Chirikof, commanding the second of two vessels under Vitus Bering in 1741, became the first Caucasian to report sighting the Alexander Archipelago. Other countries, seeking a water route from the Atlantic to the Pacific across North America, sent explorers to study the northwest coast. In 1785 French King Louis XVI sent Jean François de Galoup de La Pérouse to explore the coast. The French scientist made landfall in Lituya Bay in 1786, claimed the territory for his king, and headed south, passing Alexander Archipelago on his way to California. La Pérouse perished before he could reach his homeland, but his detailed studies were carried overland by a messenger and published in French and later in English, adding to the growing knowledge of the Alaskan coast.

Spain did its bit by sending Alessandro Malaspina, an Italian sailing under the Spanish flag, to search for the fabled Northwest Passage. Malaspina struck land in the vicinity of Baranof Island in 1791 and continued north to explore Yakutat Bay. He, too, failed to find the water route to the Atlantic, but one of the largest glaciers in North America bears his name.

It was left to the Russians to make the most of the natural bounty of Southeast. Reports of Chirikof's adventures brought the abundant sea mammal populations to the attention of ever-eager fur hunters and traders. Dreams of riches drew hunters to the Aleutians where they quickly decimated the sea otter herds. The Russians expanded to the mainland, to Kodiak, and finally to Sitka.

In 1795 Alexander Baranof decided that Sitka was a good site for a trading post and fort. Four years later, the post rose from the forest north of present-day Sitka. Tlingits of the region were divided on just how to handle the Russians. In 1802 they overcame their indecision and destroyed the post. Baranof, away on Kodiak Island at the time of the attack, was determined to carry out his plan.

Two years later the Russian returned, this time with a warship. He engaged the Tlingits in battle, drove them away, and once again set about building a post. By 1808, long before San Francisco blossomed from the prosperity of the gold rush, New Archangel (Sitka) was made capital of Russian America and headquarters for its commerce.

A New American Territory

Decline of the fur trade due to over zealous harvesting of sea mammals, difficulties of supplying and protecting such a distant colony, and affairs of state closer to home eventually brought about a waning of Russia's interest in its American territory.

Left, miners trudge up treacherous Chilkoot Pass on their way to the Klondike gold fields. Right, a miner's camp.

Nearly six decades had passed since Baranof had raised the Double Eagle high atop the hill overlooking beautiful Sitka harbor. The Russians thought that perhaps this was a good time to sell their North American interests to a growing United States. In 1867, the U.S. Congress, at the urging of Secretary of State William Henry Seward, passed legislation calling for the purchase of Russian America for $7.2 million, just under 2 cents an acre.

In 1880 hired prospectors found gold along Gastineau Channel and founded Juneau. Miners headed up the Inside Passage, and with them came merchants and traders. And Juneau boomed. Alaska-Juneau Mining Company's mill at the coast processed mountains of rock. Hotels, res-

taurants, a hospital, newspapers, all the commerce of a thriving community sprung up along the shore. Juneau citizens, enjoying employment in fishing and lumbering as well as mining, took an active interest in their political future, and the territorial capital was transferred there from Sitka in 1906.

Mining ended during World War II, but by then government offices and commerce had put Juneau on a solid footing. When Alaska became a state in 1959, Juneau continued as its capital. In the 1970s, Alaskans voted to move the capital to a more accessible site in the southcentral part of the state, but votes to fund the move were rejected and the capital remains in Southeast.

SOUTHWESTERN ALASKA:
ON THE EDGE OF TOMORROW

A delta, basin, peninsula and island chain make up Alaska's Southwest. South of Unalakleet the land flattens out into the Yukon-Kuskokwim delta, one of the world's largest. Centuries of river deposits have built out the delta more than 200 miles (320 km) into the Bering Sea. River channels meander through the muck; ponds are everywhere. Villages settle on high spots near sloughs or along the coast. A few hills rise near Saint Michael, a few more near Cape Romanzof. Nelson Island fits neatly into a gap in the delta, and here there is some elevation. Not far offshore, Nunivak Island provides a home for the Eskimos of Mekoryuk and a grazing range for musk oxen.

South of where the Kuskokwim River enters the Bering Sea, the mountains reappear, not towering giants but peaks of 5,000 feet (1,500 meters). The heights separate delta country from the Bristol Bay basin, home to giant runs of sockeye salmon in one of the world's richest fishing grounds. Islands along the bay's north shore host thousands of male walrus. Inland, tundra and forested hills interlaced with clear streams and backed by a mountain vanguard, the Aleutian Range, characterize the basin. Lake Iliamna, by far the state's largest, descends to great depths at its eastern end and shelters a small group of freshwater harbor seals.

On the south begins the long arc which eventually reaches the edge of tomorrow at the western tip of the Aleutian Islands. A continuation of the Aleutian Range whose sharp peaks form the backbone of the Alaska Peninsula, the chain separates the Pacific Ocean from the Bering Sea in a 1,100-mile (1,770-km) curve of more than 270 islands.

About 200 miles (320 km) offshore, three widely separated island groups rise from the shallow Bering Sea. Largest of the these and home to Siberian Yupiks is Saint Lawrence. Even more isolated Saint Matthew and Hall islands lie in the eye of a controversy between oil companies and those who would prefer the islands remain a wilderness segment of Alaska Maritime National Wildlife Refuge. Smaller Saint Paul and Saint George islands, the Pribilofs, have the world's largest Aleut community as well as

breeding colonies of northern fur seals. The history of seals and Aleuts is intricately intertwined in the chronicle of the Pribilofs.

About 50 Yupik Eskimo villages spread out on the delta, the greatest concentration of native communities in the state. Bethel, largest community in western Alaska, is the commercial center for this network.

Huge Yukon Delta National Wildlife Refuge takes in much of this valuable breeding area, sheltering eggs and nestlings for many birds. In summer, shorebirds outnumber the waterfowl with numbers in the millions.

Offshore on Nunivak and other Bering Sea Islands, hundreds of thousands of seabirds find a niche on the cliffs to lay their eggs. The delta lacks suitable habitat for large land mammals, but the smaller furbearers— beaver, mink and muskrat—find this watery world to their liking. Reindeer used to be important here, and some village elders still remember their days as herders. Today reindeer remain only on Nunivak.

Primarily, however, this is fish country, from the world's largest sockeye runs to substantial numbers of king, chum, silver and pink salmon. For sport anglers there are rainbow trout, grayling, pike, Dolly Varden, whitefish, arctic char—the list is long and enticing.

Left, bearded sourdough sounds a welcoming bugle. Right, one of the first settlers in front of his supply tent.

The Alaska Peninsula has more to offer in the way of large mammals. And it has bears, lots of them. Becharof National Wildlife Refuge can boast perhaps the largest concentration of brownies in the state. Except for foxes, Alaska's major land mammals seem to reach their limit at Unimak, first of the major Aleutian Islands when heading out the chain. Seabirds and marine mammals, in some of the largest congregations known, take over in the Aleutians.

An Unexplored Land

The watery maze on the delta kept westerners from exploring Southwest Alaska for years. The Russians had a post at Saint

delta suddenly acquired formal ownership to millions of acres of land and received $165 million in cash. Modern times had hit the delta. Efforts to manage this new wealth were shaky at first, but slowly the regional corporation has grasped the fundamentals of modern business and looks forward to a profitable future.

British explorer Capt. James Cook first noted the Bristol Bay shore, naming the mud-lined bay after a British admiral. Cook continued on his way in 1778 and left the area to the Russians. In the second decade of the 1800s, the Russians built a fort at Nushagak. Trade flourished here for some time, but declined when silt infiltrated the harbor and better ports opened up on the Kuskokwim. A Finn and a Russian were

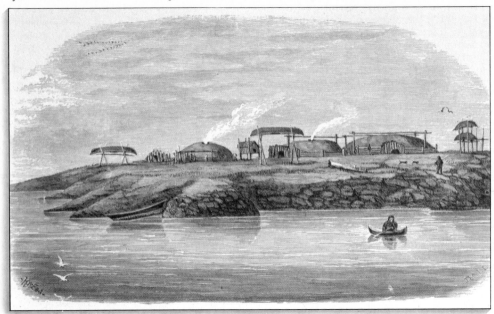

Michael near the mouth of the Yukon but seldom penetrated inland. A short-lived trading post was established at Russian Mission on the Yukon, and another on the Kuskokwim, but Russian influence did not go far.

Even World War II didn't stimulate much activity in the delta. Times were tough. When the fish didn't come, the people starved. Disease was rampant; education poor. Not until the area caught the attention of politicians from the Lower 48 in the 1960s was there a concerted effort for change on the delta. Disciples of poverty programs had a perfect place to test their theories. With passage of the Alaska Native Land Claims Settlement Act in 1971, the people of the

sent to map the shores of the bay, but shallow waters kept them at length. The area was still generally unknown to westerners at the time of United States purchase in 1867.

Except for establishment of a mail run from Saint Michael to Nushagak, and then to Southeast by water, little happened in the bay until a way was found to exploit the immense runs of salmon. Arctic Pack Company established a cannery at Nushagak in 1883. Two years later Alaska Packing Company opened a cannery across Nushagak Bay which operated until the end of World War II. Modern-day Dillingham got its start from a cannery set up there in 1886. By 1908 10 canneries ringed the bay.

But the Interior remained a mystery. A

few explorers entered the area. Some survived, some didn't, but a written record of their exploits remained non-existent. Lake Clark, the huge lake north of Iliamna, was only a vague rumor until an expedition from Frank Leslie's Illustrated Newspaper finally pushed through to its mountain hideout. Meager attempts by government and private citizens to open the area proved fruitless. The bay wasn't about to turn loose of its remoteness. Steamer service across Cook Inlet to the Iliamna shore, plans for a railroad and other hopes for a string of roadhouses all came to naught.

The salmon industry was suffering hard times. Overfishing and a poor market had taken their toll. A ban was placed on power boats, and fleets under sail went after the

ters depended on the individuals involved. Some were friendly and peaceful, others less so. As word spread of the riches in furs to be had, competition among Russian companies increased and treatment of the Aleuts deteriorated.

Catherine the Great became leader of the Russians in 1762. She proclaimed goodwill toward the Aleuts and urged her subjects to treat the Natives fairly. But the Czarina was thousands of miles away, and the hunters' all-consuming quest for furs caused them to overlook Aleut welfare. Hostages were taken, families split up, individuals forced to leave their own villages and settle elsewhere. Open conflict broke out in 1763. Aleuts won initial victories, but the Russians retaliated, killing many Natives and destroying boats

fish. Population had always been low in the bay, but a series of epidemics didn't help. Development was stymied, if indeed it ever had gotten started. The 1960s and 1970s saw the most progress in the basin. Bay communities organized a borough, formed a solid school system, sought government assistance for some of their economic and social needs, and with money from the land claims settlement set about improving and diversifying their economy.

In the early years of expansion into the islands, the tenor of Aleut/Russian encoun-

Left, an Eskimo village in fall. Right, harbor scene on Unalaska Island.

and hunting gear, their means of survival.

About this same time, the British were continuing their search for the Northwest Passage. Capt. James Cook sailed to the islands in 1778. The Russians tried to impress him with the extent of their control over the region; but Cook was a crafty, intelligent explorer who had seen much of the world. He understood the situation in the Aleutians with his own eyes as well as from information supplied by the Russians. Cook's expedition spurred the English to increase their sailings along the northwest coast. In turn, the Spanish stepped up their interest in the area.

All this activity convinced Russian leaders to solidify their position in the New World.

One way to do this was to grant official sanction to the monopoly over fur trade which Grigori Shelikof wanted for his Russian America Company. In 1787 Shelikof took control of the Kodiak trade. By 1804, Alexander Baranof, manager in Alaska for the Russian American Company, had consolidated the company's hold on fur trade activities in the Americas. If the Russian American Company was willing to hold the land for the Czar, Emperor Paul was willing to grant the monopoly.

With the official charter came responsibility for health, education and religious well-being of the Aleuts. Schools and hospitals were opened. Russian Orthodox clergy were now in the Aleutians; Father Ioann Veniaminof, famous throughout Russian

fur seal and sea otter to survive, and American hunters had decimated these stocks as much if not more that had Russian hunters. Marine mammal skins provided the coverings for Aleut boats. Without the boats, Aleuts couldn't hunt. They were becoming malnourished.

New Economic Ventures

Finally the federal government took action to cut back on the slaughter. Warships were sent to patrol the region, and poachers were prosecuted. The United States, Canada, Japan and Russia agreed to a treaty for distribution of fur seal pelts from the legal harvest in the Pribilofs. Steps were taken to

America, developed a dictionary and grammar for the Aleut language. Life improved for the Natives: better education, wages and management positions in the company for those with some Russian blood. And slowly the population began to grow. But by the mid-19th Century the fur trade had declined severely, and the cost, in both money and diplomacy, of maintaining the colony was becoming a burden. In 1867 the United States took over, and the Aleuts had to adjust to new masters.

The federal government paid almost no attention to the chain. A deputy marshal was appointed to the area in 1884 to maintain order under the laws of Oregon. The Aleuts were suffering, however. They needed the

protect sea otters which were almost extinct. Most of the central and western chain became a wildlife reservation.

By the turn of the century commercial fishing was gaining a foothold in the islands. Packing houses salted cod and herring. Salmon canneries were opened. Experiments in livestock raising were imaginative but financial failures. A shore-based whaling station at Akutan held on until World War II, rendering carcasses of whales into dog food and fertilizer.

Fox farming proved the most lucrative of commercial enterprises tried in the Aleutians before World War II. Russians had imported the blue color phase of arctic fox, known as blue foxes, to the Aleutians.

44

Aleuts paid little attention to foxes, but toward the end of the 1800s, Americans began raising blues for their pelts. But the Depression years brought an end to fox farming.

Japanese expansion in the Pacific and the attack on Pearl Harbor brought the Aleutians out of forgotten isolation. Even though many military planners did not see the strategic value of the island chain which reaches within a few hundred miles of the Japanese home islands, Col. Simon Buckner did what he could with limited funds to prepare the Aleutians for war. Working under the guise of various fish packing companies, Buckner built a base at Cold Bay, Fort Mears at Dutch Harbor, and Fort Glenn on Umnak Island.

mained throughout the war. After some discussion at the military high command about just what to do with Kiska and Attu, officials ordered the Navy and Air Force to bomb the enemy out.

Aleuts from the Pribilofs and Aleutian villages were evacuated to southeastern Alaska. In fall, 1942, the Navy began construction of a base on Adak from which to strike the western Aleutians. Today, Adak remains the largest community in the chain and a major military base.

After the war, Attuans who returned from Japan were resettled to Atka, the federal government explaining that their home village was too remote to defend. Times were bleak for returning Aleuts, although during recent years life has improved somewhat.

The Navy was slow in coming to the islands, but by the time of Pearl Harbor, they were setting up a major base at Unalaska. Good thing, too, because on June 3, 1942 the Japanese attacked Dutch Harbor. On June 6, the Japanese landed on Kiska in the western Aleutians, defended only by a 10-man station of weather observers. The next day the Japanese took Attu, overwhelming Attu village and killing the white schoolteacher, Charles Jones. The villagers were later taken to Japan where they re-

The military controls Adak and Shemya. The Coast Guard has a loran station at Attu. The Fish and Wildlife Service manages most of the remaining central and western islands as a wildlife refuge. Atka remains remote, but villagers are getting new houses and an improved runway. The Unalaska/Dutch Harbor complex has grown into a major fishing port. Fish processors again operate along the region's shores. Land claims money has helped the Aleuts gain the threshold of economic security. But modern developments haven't lessened the chain's remoteness, and the marine life and seabirds that have claimed the islands since before the earliest Aleuts still watch the sea sweep the land.

Left, interior of the orthodox church on St. George Island. Right, Russian church at Ninilchik on the Kenai peninsula.

SOUTHCENTRAL: URBAN ALASKA

Southcentral Alaska is home to two-thirds of the state's population, with more than half of the total living in Anchorage, Alaska's largest city. From her birth as a railroad construction camp to her burgeoning growth as a center for oil development, transportation, communications and commerce, Anchorage takes her position as the state's largest metropolis and hub of Southcentral.

Lying south of the Alaska Range, east of the Aleutian Range, and west of the Canadian border, Southcentral looks to its strategic location as gateway to the northern, western and interior regions. Two great indentations of the Gulf of Alaska, Prince William Sound and Cook Inlet, moderate temperatures for coastal regions, while a transition climate inland brings greater temperature extremes and less precipitation.

The Isolated Coast

Few Alaskans or visitors ever tread the isolated Gulf of Alaska coast from Icy Bay to Prince William Sound. As recently as the beginning of the 20th Century, Icy Bay didn't exist. Today the glaciers have retreated more than 25 miles (40 km), leaving four newly exposed fjords in their wake.

At the tiny settlement of Yakataga, less than a dozen people stick it out through the winter. At the turn of the century, a couple hundred miners walked the area's beaches, but word of the big strike at Nome caught their imagination and most left: Yakataga returned to its isolation. In summer a young couple operate a small lodge at Cape Yakataga, serving hunters and occasionally state forest service workers. The state owns much of the timber along this stretch of the gulf coast, and in recent years logging operations have been harvesting trees from Icy Bay west.

West of Yakataga, the granddaddy of all North American glaciers makes its way to the sea from the Bagley Icefield. Bering Glacier's icy mass covers more than 2,000 sq miles (5,180 sq km). The glacier's terminus doesn't quite reach the sea, however, and icebergs calving from the glacier's face ground on a series of lakes at Bering's lower end.

The Chugach Mountains take over where the Saint Elias leave off, rimming much of the gulf coast, and blending with the Kenai Mountains on the Kenai Peninsula south of Anchorage. Only one river breaches this mountain bulwark, the rushing, silty Copper River.

East of the Copper and beyond the coastal mountains spreads an immense wilderness, Wrangell-Saint Elias National Park and Preserve, largest in the nation. With Kluane National Park just across the border in Canada, the two make up a World Heritage Area as designated by the United Nations. The formidable Saint Elias range consists of row upon row of snow-covered peaks, and not more than 30 miles (48 km) distant, Mount Logan, at more than 19,000 feet (6,200 meters) is the highest point in Canada.

A little more accessible than the main body of the Saint Elias and just as enchanting are the Wrangell Mountains. The Copper River skirts the western end of the Wrangells, and travellers on the Richardson Highway from Valdez to Delta Junction can enjoy stunning views of the great volcanic cones of Mount Drum, Mount Sanford and Mount Wrangell.

Prince William Sound

The Chugach Mountains cup Prince William Sound, an island-studded wonderland that rose to prominence in the early part of this century, then languished in the backwater of Anchorage's growth, only to reemerge as the southern terminus for the trans-Alaska pipeline.

The great earthquake of 1964 struck hard at the sound, destroying towns and ports, tilting islands, uplifting some lands, sinking others. The uplift destroyed salmon streams because the fish could no longer negotiate the falls and other obstructions to reach their spawning grounds. The village of Chenega was wiped out, most of its inhabitants killed. Ports at Valdez and Cordova were destroyed. What land and mud slides didn't claim, fire did. A ship of the Alaska Steamship Company fleet had the ride of its life when a huge wave carried the ship over the docks, then out to sea. Most hands survived, as did the ship, but those on shore who viewed the spectacle claimed they could see daylight all the way under the ship at one point. Old Valdez was abandoned. The town moved a few miles away to rebuild in a zone supposedly free from earthquakes.

Eighty years ago Cordova was battling Katalla for supremacy of the lower Copper

River region. Cordova won. To the victor went copper, and the Copper River and Northwestern Railway. The building of the railroad is a classic example of frontier ingenuity and enterprise, and the power of big bucks. The Guggenheim and Morgan Alaska Syndicate supplied the capital, Michael J. Heney supplied the know-how, energy and enthusiasm. Builder of the White Pass and Yukon Route, out of Skagway and over the mountains to Whitehorse, Yukon Territory, Heney already knew just what the Alaskan wilderness could throw at him.

Desire for an all-American route to the gold fields of the Interior had brought all manner of men to the gulf coast in the late 1890s. Heney's White Pass route would take miners to the Klondike, but mostly across Canadian soil. The rich copper lodes of the Wrangells had yet to be discovered when the government sent an army captain to the port of Valdez to explore for a route to the Interior. Valdez had a good, deepwater port, and it was possible, although difficult, according to the captain's staff, to build a road north through the mountains. But what

Above, snowy mountains provide backdrop for Matanuska Valley farm.

would the train haul? There would be no freight to fill the rail cars, only desperate miners anxious to find their fortune.

By 1900 copper had been found, as had deposits of high-grade coal needed for fuel near the Bering River and oil at Katalla east of the Copper River delta. But the port at Katalla was poorly protected, and fierce storms often swept in from the gulf. Cordova, on Prince William Sound west of the delta, had a good port. Thus the stage was set for Heney to head up the Copper. The railroad reached Kennecott, headquarters for the copper mines, in 1911. For nearly the next three decades, before the copper ran out and the mines were closed down, the Copper River and Northwestern Railway provided access to the Copper River Basin.

Kenai Peninsula

Across the sound, the Kenai Peninsula reaches into the Gulf of Alaska. Connected to the rest of the state by a narrow isthmus at Portage, the peninsula's eastern side carries the spiny backbone of the Kenai Mountains. The 1964 earthquake was felt here too. Only a few broken and weathered cabins remind visitors of early Portage, where miners somehow managed to cross the Kenai Mountains and make their way to the head of Turnagain Arm, an offshoot of Cook Inlet. The quake caused land here to subside. Incoming salt water from Turnagain Arm killed the trees and the cabins slowly began sinking into the mud.

Athabascan Indians gathered long ago to trade at the mouth of the Kenai River. When the Russians came, they built their second permanent settlement on the bluff overlooking Cook Inlet near the river's mouth. After purchase by the United States, the small community of fishermen, miners, trappers and homesteaders grew slowly. The Sterling Highway was pushed through across the lowlands to Kenai after World War II, but not until discovery of oil in the Swanson River Field in the 1950s did the area see sustained active growth.

Today industry, chiefly oil and some fishing, fuels the economy of Kenai and neighboring Soldotna. Kenai is a major supply point for the Middle Ground Shoals oil field offshore in Cook Inlet. One of the first of the modern oil discoveries in Alaska to go into production, the offshore field has several platforms pumping oil and natural gas through pipes to a transfer facility on the west shore of Cook Inlet.

Kachemak Bay

Early Indians, Eskimos and Aleuts knew of the riches of Kachemak Bay. And it didn't take the Russians long to find out; they built a trading post at Port Graham south of the bay. As usual, dreams of riches lured the first Americans to the Homer area. But when word came of big strikes elsewhere, their dream took them onward. The first visitors who stayed for any length of time were convinced that coal was the way to wealth. They built their tiny post at the end of the spit and made plans to mine the coal.

continued its dominance of local commerce with well developed fish processing facilities and an active fishing fleet. But once again the great quake stepped in, destroying the harbor at Seldovia and leaving its fishing industry in shambles. Today Seldovia continues as a quiet fishing community with a budding tourist industry. Homer, on the other hand, has become the preeminent community on Kachemak Bay.

A state park and state wilderness park share the lower peninsula with Kenai Fjords National Park. The peninsula's outer coast is a rugged fjordland subject to the full fury of the open Pacific. Less than a handful of hardy Alaskans live year-round on this entire stretch of coast. They fish, trap, or just live, being mighty careful that the restless

This dream died too, and the town slowly fell into ruin.

Later arrivals built a new town site on the benchlands above the spit, and their views of reality were a little more practical than those of the get-rich-quick schemers. Homesteaders and farmers eked out a living. With rising fur prices, fox farming flourished. In the 1930s great herring runs increased the income from fishing, and Halibut Cove on the south side of the bay became a center for herring fishing. The Sterling Highway reached Homer in the 1950s, and growth picked up some. But the town still took second place to its rival across the bay.

Seldovia, on the south side near the junction of Kachemak Bay and Cook Inlet,

sea doesn't take them.

Charter operations out of Seward on Resurrection Bay take travellers to the fjords for close inspection of the glaciers, the seabird and marine mammal colonies, and perhaps, for the fortunate, a glimpse of baleen whales, fin, humpback or gray, which pass by. The Chiswell Islands shelter the Kenai Peninsula's largest seabird colonies. Rhinoceros auklets, horned and tufted puffins, murres and kittiwakes crowd the rocky crags.

Kodiak Island

If ever an artist needed a model for a rocky shoreline, he couldn't do better than to head for Kodiak. The island is cut by so many bays that nowhere is it possible to be more than 15 miles (24 km) from tidewater. The Kodiak archipelago is an extension of the Kenai Mountains which descended into the sea when they reached the tip of the Kenai Peninsula. Fifty miles (80 km) to the southwest the mountain ridge surfaces to become the Kodiak Mountains, backbone for an archipelago of 16 major islands.

Koniags and even earlier prehistoric cultures were the first to make use of the marine mammals which have sustained Kodiak's human inhabitants ever since. The Russians, following the sea otters and fur seals in their thirst for more and more pelts, established the first foreign settlement on the islands at Three Saints Bay in 1784.

navy and army base for defending the Aleutians, and the sleepy islands really came alive during the war years. After the war, the fishing industry grew. The Wakefield family developed a procedure for canning king crab, and things looked promising for Kodiak. Then disaster struck. On Good Friday, March 27, 1964, a tsunami from the great quake centered in Prince William Sound roared into the archipelago, wiping out the villages of Afognak, Old Harbor and Kaguyak and damaging other communities.

Today Kodiak and outlying villages still look to the sea for their livelihood. Fishing and processing of salmon, halibut, crab and shrimp sustain the economy. Shellfish stocks have been depleted in recent years, and ongoing efforts to determine why keep

(Other Russians had attempted to get a foothold on Kodiak earlier, but the wary Koniags drove them off.)

Kodiak's first canneries were built in the late 1800s when word of phenomenal fish runs became widespread. Rumors of being able to cross streams on the backs of salmon drew fishermen from far and wide, and the Karluk is still considered one of the finest salmon rivers around.

World War II brought a break in the dominance of fish. Kodiak became a major

Left, Eskimo in traditional waterproof skin canoe. Right, the Columbia Glacier in Prince William Sound.

fisheries researchers busy. Many have placed future hopes on development of a bottomfish industry. Foreign fleets harvest tons of bottomfish in Alaskan waters, and officials seek to encourage local use of that resource.

Tourism and sport hunting and fishing bring some income to the island group. Much of Kodiak Island is home to the Kodiak brown bear, a huge mammal which captures the imagination of any would-be or real hunter. Native to the island group, these huge bears stick primarily to the interior highlands except when they come to the lowlands to feed on returning salmon. Several other species have been introduced to the islands: mountain goats, Roosevelt elk, Sitka black-tailed deer and numerous smaller mammals. Offshore, the rich marine life, which first lured the Russians and then was hunted out, is coming back. Sea otters, sea lions and harbor seals find the islands' extensive coastlines to their liking.

Volcanic Explosions

Two national parks ride the crest of the Aleutian Range on the west side, Lake Clark and Katmai. Beauty seems to be Lake Clark's chief claim to fame. Towering mountains, jade-colored lakes, dense forests and coastal lowlands give the park about every kind of environment found in Alaska. A few communities along the shores of Lake Clark serve outdoor enthusiasts, but wilderness prevails with good hiking and river running. Bush planes, either on floats or wheels, provide access.

Quick thinking by a mail clerk on the steamship *Dora* recorded the cataclysmic eruption of Mount Katmai, one of the largest volcanic explosions recorded in North America. In 1912, the *Dora* was steaming for Kodiak when it was covered by a thick layer of ash. Before light was obliterated and day turned to a premature night, *Dora* crewmembers took a bearing on the smoking mountain, thus pinpointing the source of the ash. When scientists visited the area after the explosion, they found a large valley covered with a thick deposit of ash and still steaming from numerous vents. They named the area the Valley of Ten Thousand Smokes, and Katmai National Monument was set aside to preserve this geologic phenomenon. The smokes have declined since 1912, and recent legislation has changed the monument to park status, but hikers can still study the groved formations of ash deposits hundreds of feet thick.

Ports and Railways

Like Cordova and Valdez, Seward got its start as a shipping center when it became southern terminus for Alaska Central Railroad in 1902. The railroad had a rough time getting started, went bankrupt, and came back in 1909. By the time the railroad reached infant Anchorage, Seward was a thriving port. All that changed in 1964 when the great earthquake struck another blow for Mother Nature. Seward's port was destroyed, as was 90 percent of her economy. It took years for the town to recover. Tourism and fishing contributed to summertime revenue, but winter brought severe unemployment. Recent efforts to build a stable year-round economy have focused on an industrial park, ship repair facility and transhipment of bulk raw materials, such as coal, from the Interior to ports in the Lower 48 and the Orient. The town's location at the southern terminus of the Alaska Railroad and the Seward Highway seems to secure her position in future ocean shipping.

Except for special charters, the Alaska Railroad only carries freight between Seward and Portage. At Portage, a short spur brings passengers from Whittier on Prince William Sound. The train continues north to Anchorage. Passengers and freight can ride the rails north, past the Matanuska Valley and up the Susitna Valley, over the Alaska Range, down to Nenana on the Tanana River and on to the northern terminus at Fairbanks.

Fertile Valleys

North of Anchorage two large river valleys, Matanuska and Susitna, make up the fertile lowlands of interior Southcentral Alaska. From Anchorage the Glenn Highway takes traffic to near Palmer where the George Parks Highway begins its run north to Fairbanks through the Susitna River Valley. The Glenn continues east, follows the winding course of the Matanuska River to its headwaters, then climbs out of the valley and crosses to Nelchina Basin to Glennallen on the Richardson Highway. The Susitna River heads in the Alaska Range, winds through the Talkeetna Mountains, and then enters a broad lowland on its way to Cook Inlet.

Palmer began as the center for the Matanuska Valley Colony, an agricultural project sponsored by the federal government during the Great Depression. The community has retained much of its small town charm. Its bustling neighbor on the Parks Highway, Wasilla, is typical of suburban American.

The Mat-Su is Alaska's breadbasket and one of two major agricultural areas in the state. From here come cabbages, pumpkins, zucchini, broccoli, radishes, potatoes, lettuce and a variety of other vegetables and berries. Good soil and near 24-hour daylight combine to produce giant specimens.

In years past, dairying was important in the valley, but in recent decades, fewer and fewer farmers have been able to successfully compete with dairy products shipped in from the Lower 48. To stem their tide, the state has sponsored the Point MacKenzie dairy project. A lottery was held for parcels of state land which had to be developed into dairy farms. The state provides financial and technical assistance, and although there are grumblings that some regulations are unrealistic, the state has taken steps to encourage the rebirth of dairying. One hoped-for side benefit of this program is that the expanding dairy herds will generate an Alaska market for barley grown as the state's other major agricultural effort, the delta barley project in the interior.

Water and Power

The upper Susitna Valley with its unofficial headquarters at Talkeetna is laced with fine fishing streams and lakes and carpeted with dense stands of birch. With sharp peaks of the Alaska Range towering to the north and rounded humps of the Talkeetnas rising

rapids agitate its flow into a stretch of world class whitewater. Kayakers world-wide know of Devil Canyon. They gather here to take on the Susitna, although not until the 1970s did the first kayaker survive the 15-mile (24-km) challenge.

The same canyon that gives kayakers such thrills also has the requirements of a suitable hydroelectric site. Here and farther upstream officials propose to build two giant dams which they say are necessary to meet future demands for electricity. Opponents say the project is too costly, and that scaled-down dams would be more practical. Others wish that the Alaska Power Authority and its legions of planners and surveyors would just go away.

to the east, this is picture postcard country. Many Alaskans think so also, and homesteads dot the hills and lake shores.

But the area's proximity to state population centers and to Alaska's number one tourist attraction, Mount McKinley, brings potential disruption to this serenity. The biggest dispute, at least in terms of cost and project size, revolves around efforts to dam the Susitna River for hydroelectric power.

A narrow canyon constricts the river where it passes through the Talkeetnas, and

Above, a remote cabin in the Alaska Range.

Mount McKinley and the increasing numbers of visitors that come to Denali National Park every summer present another problem. There's only one road into the park, on the north side. From the end of May until mid-September the National Park Service provides shuttle bus service to prevent congestion and disturbance to the park's wildness. But before Denali officially opens and after it closes, visitors can take their vehicles in at will. This has caused problems for wildlife and lessened the wilderness experience for some visitors. Proposals to build a second road and visitor's center on the south side of the park have also upset local ideas of peace and quiet.

BUSH ALASKA: THE INTERIOR

Interior, northwestern and southwestern Alaska most commonly conjure up images of wilderness living, although "The Bush" is technically defined as those areas beyond the state's road system. There are various levels of living in the Bush. In some areas, the reality means isolation and an almost total dependence on one's own ingenuity. In other areas it means groceries come by barge to the village store a short walk down the beach. Many say Bush Alaska is the real Alaska. Perhaps. A century ago all of Alaska was the Bush, but the times, they are changing.

The Great Interior

North of Southcentral, Alaska's great Interior lies sandwiched between the Alaska Range on the south and Brooks Range on the north. From the Canadian border west to an indeterminate and sometimes shifting line separating the cultures of the Athabascan and the Eskimo, the Interior sprawls across the heartland of Alaska. Great extremes of temperature alternately warm and cool the land. The Yukon River and its major tributaries, the Porcupine, Tanana and Koyukuk cleanse the region, carrying ice and debris downriver each spring at breakup.

Since prehistoric times rivers have been main arteries for travel through the Interior. The Athabascan Indians, who claim the Interior as their homeland, settled along the rivers, paddling up and down the waterways in canoes, taking their sustenance from the yearly return of salmon to spawning streams. In winter travel still followed the rivers, only this time by dogsled or snowshoe.

The white men kept to the rivers also. Early explorers and traders went along major watersheds in their first reconnaissance of the region. In 1847 the Hudson Bay Company built a post near Fort Yukon at the confluence of the Porcupine and Yukon rivers to take advantage of thriving fur-bearer populations on the Yukon Flats.

Interior Alaska remained little touched by Russian excursions along the coasts, although one Russian scout did explore the Yukon as far as the mouth of the Nowitna

looking for potential trade. Few white men had penetrated the region before Robert Kennicott led his surveying crew to Nulato on the banks of the Yukon in 1865. Western Union had decided to lay a telegraph line across Alaska to Bering Strait where it would connect with an Asian line. Kennicott was put in command of the effort in Alaska, but he died the following year at Nulato. Among Kennicott's contingent were several scientists, and upon his death, William H. Dall took charge of scientific affairs. The Western Union expedition conducted the

first scientific studies of the region and produced the first map of the entire Yukon River. That same year, workers finally succeeded in laying an Atlantic undersea cable, and the Alaskan overland project was abandoned. Dall later returned to Alaska many times, recording names and giving names to many geographical features. Dall sheep and Dall porpoise bear the name of this distinguished scholar.

Missionaries, Miners and Traders

After the United States purchase of Alaska territory in 1867, officials determined that the Hudson Bay Company post at Fort Yukon was on American soil. An Army

Left, two-storey cabin built in the early 1900s. Right, grave of a pioneer along the Yukon River.

captain was sent to inform the traders and they withdrew to Canada. In the last decades of the 1800s, Alaska Commercial Company began building trading posts along the rivers. One by one, small parties of trappers and traders entered the Interior. During this time the federal government appropriated little money to officially explore the region, but every once in a while an Army officer would broadly interpret his orders and do a little reconnaissance on his own.

In a four-month journey, Lt. Frederick Schwatka and his party rafted the Yukon from Lake Lindeman in Canada to Saint Michael near the river's mouth on the Bering Sea. Lt. Henry T. Allen made an even more remarkable journey. In 1885 Allen and four others left the Gulf of Alaska following

the years just after the turn of the century, Archdeacon Hudson Stuck mushed his dogs thousands of miles throughout the region on behalf of the church. He also found time to be the first to climb to the summit of Mount McKinley.

The Golden Dreams

Even with these efforts, the Interior was still generally unexplored. Not until cries of gold rang from the wilderness was the region invaded with the first wave of fortune seekers. The Klondike was in Yukon Territory, Canada, not Alaska, but hopeful miners from the south cared little about geographical distinctions. Those who didn't make their fortune at Dawson City, and

the Copper River, crossed the mountains, went down the Tanana River to the Yukon, portaged to the Kanuti, then to the Koyukuk River. Allen went up the Koyukuk, then back down to the Yukon, crossed over to Unalakleet on the coast, and then made his way to Saint Michael. All in all Allen explored about 1,500 miles (2,400 km) of virgin Alaska in an effort to open up the territory.

Men of the cloth were busy in the Interior at this time also. Archdeacon McDonald of the Church of England, with his headquarters at Fort Yukon, ministered to the Indians of the upper Yukon for five decades. Representatives of the Episcopal and Catholic faiths set up missions along the Yukon. In

there were many, spread out across the north, spilling over into Alaska in pursuit of their dreams.

Eventually the Tanana Mining District out of Fairbanks became the biggest gold producer. But there were strikes elsewhere, in the Fortymile, at Wiseman, Ruby, Circle, Livengood and many others.

Ruby, today the only town on the river between Calena and Tanana on the central Yukon, got its start in 1907 when gold was discovered at Ruby Creek. The initial discovery didn't yield much color, and miners who had hurried to the area soon left. Three years later another find on creeks south of town brought a larger and more stable population.

Newcomers arrived from up and down the river, some by small riverboats, others on the large paddlewheelers. The big woodburners had been chugging along the river since 1869, carrying passengers and freight from Saint Michael to Dawson City. The steamers required several cords of wood daily to keep them moving, and residents along the river supplemented their trapping and fishing by maintaining woodlots.

The paddlewheelers brought in heavy equipment needed to thaw the frozen ground out along the creeks. The first year or so individual miners had to provide the back-breaking labor needed to retrieve the gold. By 1912 steam-operated machinery did much of the heavy work, and the take from the creeks increased substantially. In 1917 at

took over. The dogs started their runs as soon as river ice was thick enough to support them. Every 30 miles (48 km) of the 1,600-mile (2,575-km) run between Dawson and Nome, teams and drivers changed.

World War I took many of the miners from Ruby. Some claims lost so many workers they had to shut down. Life at Ruby slowed considerably, but in 1922 the Guggenheim Syndicate acquired claims in the neighboring Flat Mining District. The purchase stirred a new influx of miners. Through the early and mid-1930s miners in the Flat District held their own, while depression struck the Lower 48. Planes, modern equipment and bulldozers all helped to ease the miners' day. World War II brought a halt to all mining, and Ruby drifted into

the height of the rush, creeks south of Ruby yielded $875,000.

Ruby grew from a tent city in 1911 to a bustling river port. With running water in summer months, a theater, several shops and cafes, Ruby sought to have all the amenities of its upstream rival, Fairbanks, and the two competed to be queen of the Interior.

During summer, river traffic moved travellers, freight and mail. When the boats were forced off the river by ice, dog teams

Far left, placer mining along the Klondike. Left, a miner guards his claim. Right, a deserted gold mine in the Wrangells.

lethargy, not quite a ghost town but definitely not the bustling river port of earlier days.

Fairbanks

In the half decade from the time Felix Pedro announced his strike on Pedro Creek, opening up the Tanana Mining District, Fairbanks grew from an outpost in the middle of nowhere with lots of supplies and no customers to become the largest town in Alaska. Today Fairbanks is the state's second largest city and commercial hub of the Interior.

An unusual combination of fortune and misfortune caused the paths of miner Felix Pedro and entrepreneur E.T. Barnette to cross. For several years the Italian miner had been prospecting in the Tanana Hills, searching for a rich creek he had stumbled upon years earlier. At the end of summer, 1901, just as the miner was about to run out of supplies and set out on a 165-mile (266-km) walk across the hills to Circle City for another grubstake, Pedro spotted smoke coming from the banks of the Chena Slough.

The smoke was the final chapter in the failed effort of E.T. Barnette to get thousands of dollars of supplies up the Tanana River to Tanana Crossing, a point on the proposed Valdez to Eagle trade route. Barnette had convinced the captain of the steamer *Lavelle Young* to take him, his wife, his partner and supplies up the Tanana against the captain's better judgment. The

supplies and amazed to see his first customers come walking out of the wild.

The following July, 1902, Pedro made his find, and Barnette's outpost in the wilderness was on its way. Fairbanks grew as more miners and new businesses came to the Chena. Public services, libraries and hospitals all eased the early days in Fairbanks. True, the town had shanties along its fringes, but city center offered many of the conveniences of Lower 48 communities. Traffic came and went on the river. An overland route to Valdez which became the Richardson Highway cut days off a trip to the Lower 48.

When gold mining slowed, construction of the Alaska Railroad with its northern terminus at Fairbanks picked up the slack. A

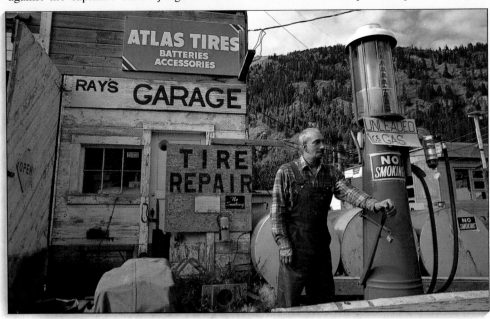

skipper agreed to haul the party upstream to where the Chena River entered the Tanana. Captain Adams would take Barnette farther if he could work the *Lavelle Young* through the shallow river channel, but if he couldn't, Barnette and his party agreed to be put ashore wherever upstream progress was halted.

Barnette didn't anticipate disembarking on a slough off the main Tanana River in the middle of a total wilderness, but that's where he was when Felix Pedro spotted smoke from the *Lavelle Young's* boilers. Pedro and his partner made their way to the Chena riverbank, anxious to buy more supplies and happy to be saved the long walk to Circle City. Barnette was delighted to sell some

college was founded which later became the University of Alaska. Huge dredges were brought in to sift from the hills the gold that escaped individual miners of earlier years. Airplanes came with their speed and ability to reach far corners of the Interior: Fairbanks became headquarters for bush aviators.

Oil and Advancements

World War II gave the Interior and all of Alaska a giant shove. Japanese attacks on the Aleutians brought visions of waves of Oriental soldiers marching toward the United States from the north. Alaska was isolated and vulnerable. The Army Corps of

Engineers was assigned the formidable chore of building a road from the Lower 48 to Alaska across Canada. Beginning at Dawson Creek in northeastern British Columbia, the engineers pushed 1,500 miles (2,415 km) north to Fairbanks. Ladd Field, now Fort Wainwright, at Fairbanks served as interchange point for Lend Lease planes going to Russia, while at Eielson, a little farther out from town, the Air Force operated a major base.

In the 1960s, as the 100th anniversary of Alaska's purchase approached, city fathers conceived of a park and major celebration in honor of the event. Mother Nature conceived of a flood which inundated "Alaskaland" and much of Fairbanks. Nenana, downriver at the confluence of the Tanana

Camp in the Brooks Range.

The Trans-Alaska oil pipeline extends 800 miles (1,288 km) from Prudhoe Bay to Valdez on Prince William Sound. The line passes near Fairbanks and generally follows the Richardson Highway south to Valdez. Oil development brought a tremendous influx of people and money to Fairbanks. With new construction, new services and new opportunities, the city was fairly bursting at its seams. Fairbanks survived the onslaught of oil, and today thrives as a transportation, shipping, military and educational center.

Woodlands—white spruce, birch, aspen, cottonwood in river lowlands, and black spruce in bogs—cover much of the Interior. Tundra blankets higher elevations and exposed ridges. Although Alaska's forest in-

and Nenana rivers, was also badly damaged by the flood.

Oil ruled the 1970s in Fairbanks and elsewhere in the Interior. Fairbanks became the headquarters for oil pipeline and haul road construction. Now named the Dalton Highway, the North Slope Haul Road officially begins near Livengood, about 70 miles northwest of Fairbanks. The road follows the pipeline corridor north across the Yukon Basin, through the Brooks Range and on to Prudhoe Bay on the arctic coast. Travellers without permits can only drive to Dietrich

Left, a Chitina garage complete with gravity-fed gas pump. Right, man and women work alongside the latest in pipeline technology.

dustry concentrates in Southeast where huge expanses of evergreens carpet the land, the Interior actually has far more acreage classified as commercial forest. But the timber in Southeast is readily accessible to the coast where it can be floated to processing facilities. The lack of access and the low rate of regeneration once trees are cut hinder commercial harvest of timber in the Interior. Some forests are cut for local use as house logs or firewood.

Portions of Denali National Park and Preserve and Gates of the Arctic National Park and Preserve lie within the confines of the Interior, as do several national wildlife refuges and a national recreation area and a national conservation area.

THE HIGH ARCTIC

North and west of the Interior the domain of the Inupiat Eskimos spreads across the top of Alaska and down to Unalakleet on the Bering Sea coast. The High Arctic descends from the crest of the Brooks Range to a broad coastal plain. In the west the De-Long Mountains, an arm of the Brooks Range, reach the Chukchi Sea at Cape Lisburne, separating the coastal plain from the great river valleys and Kotzebue Basin to the south. Below the basin, the Seward Peninsula reaches toward Asia. At Bering Strait, no more than 60 miles (96 km) separate North America from Asia. The tiny outposts of Big Diomede Island in the Soviet Union and Little Diomede in the United States ride the international date line. Halfway down the coast of Norton Sound the village of Unalakleet marks the southern boundary of the Inupiat world. The Arctic Ocean forms the region's northern boundary, and waves of the Chukchi and Bering seas wash its western shores.

Alaskans refer to the arctic coastal plain as the North Slope and that's just what it is: a great, sloping plain cut by north-flowing rivers and covered with tundra. The low relief makes river bluffs, pingoes and the few other heights even more remarkable. Beneath the tundra, perpetually frozen ground, permafrost, reaches to depths of more than 1,000 feet (300 meters). Permafrost blocks drainage of the soil, thus rainfall that would only support a desert in other parts of the globe creates a huge marsh with countless shallow lakes and ponds. Low relief enables waterways to escape confining valleys and spread out in wide, braided channels.

Tussocks, the scourge of hikers, cover the terrain. These bumps, sometimes knee-high, twist, turn, stretch and wiggle whenever an unsuspecting foot is placed on their rounded surface. Each bump seems to have a life of its own and hikers fall off in all directions, only to stand up, try the next tussock, and have the same thing happen all over again. In between the bumps are tiny channels, in random order, fit only for the foot of an elf. Anyone else gets his foot squeezed in the too-small pathway and once again topples. The northern portion of the slope near the

coast wears a necklace of shallow, oval lakes. Some, with outlets to the sea, have whitefish and a few dog salmon.

Flying overhead, areas of the North Slope give the impression that someone with a giant ruler had been at work on the land. Outlines of geometric shapes stand out on the ground's surface. Polygons develop in fine sediments when freezing causes the ground to crack. Ice forms in the cracks and as it expands, it pushes up the soil creating the geometric outlines.

Pingoes, small hills rising from the tundra,

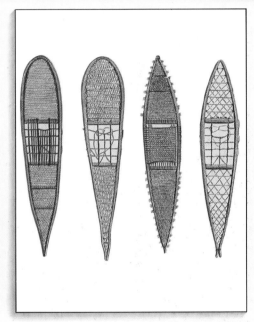

develop when ice lenses beneath the ground grow, forcing up the overlying ground. Sometimes drier, better drained soils develop on a pingo's flanks and support an entirely different community of plants than those found on wetter lowlands.

In summer the tundra is ablaze with colorful wild flowers. Insectivorous butterwort eat mosquitoes which plague hikers. Moss campion seek drier sites to spread their cover of pink. White puffs of cottongrass stick up from marshes.

The Arctic Coast

Arctic National Wildlife Refuge encompasses portions of the eastern Brooks Range

Left, a Hooper Bay girl. Right, a variety of traditional snowshoe styles.

and coastal plain. A tribute to the efforts of Olaus and Margaret Murie, early-day Alaskans who knew the value of this high arctic wilderness, the refuge takes in some of the wildest and least disturbed land on the continent. Oil threatens the refuge today as big companies push for exploration in the coastal portion.

Beyond the refuge's western boundary, the hand of man lays everywhere on the tundra for this is oil country. Ancestors of the Inupiats knew of the oil beneath the tundra from seeps along the coast. They collected chunks of oil-soaked tundra to take to their houses for use as fuel. British explorer Sir John Franklin was the first westerner to visit the area. In 1826 he travelled along the coast and named the bay that would

World War II once again brought it to the minds of government officials. The war ended before extensive exploration could be undertaken, but the government kept geologists in the field until the early 1950s.

Oil Fields And Tradition

In 1957 oil discoveries at the Swanson River fields on the Kenai Peninsula focused attention on Alaska once again. Ten years later oil company drillers pierced the Sadlerochit Formation and located the 5 to 10 billion barrels of oil lying beneath Prudhoe Bay. Neighboring Kuparuk field and other smaller fields are also being explored and developed along the arctic coast. Offshore, artificial islands have been built as a founda-

become the eye of the hurricane of future oil development.

To Ernest deKoven Leffingwell goes much of the credit for detailed knowledge of the arctic coast. The geologist explored the area from 1906 to 1914, much of the time by himself, from his headquarters on Flaxman Island west of Barter Island. Leffingwell conducted some of the first studies of permafrost, and named the Sadlerochit Formation, reservoir for the Prudhoe Bay oil field. In the 1920s, the U.S. Navy set aside an area of the North Slope south of Barrow as a petroleum reserve. Government geologists canvassed the area to determine the extent of any oil deposits. The area lay out of the mainstream of government attention until

tion for rigs drilling beneath the Beaufort Sea in the ongoing effort to find oil and natural gas.

Near Point Barrow, northernmost tip of Alaska's North Slope, the largest Inupiat community in the state spreads out along the shore. Headquarters for a vast region, Barrow is a study in contrasts. Modern glass-sided office buildings with elevators rise next to small houses made of bits of this and that. Snowmachine parts and walrus heads with the tusks still attached are stacked in the yard. Fish and animal skins hang to dry on

Above, skiers cross the Bering Sea near Nome.

wooden racks or perhaps from the house roof. Modern health facilities serve a community in which permafrost hinders construction of a sewer system. Restaurants, a hotel, shopping center, even a suburb, Browerville, bring touches of the Lower 48.

Settlement of native land claims in 1971 brought millions of dollars to Alaska's Natives, including the Inupiat. And Barrow has money. Construction booms. Oil at Prudhoe Bay brings tax revenues to the borough headquartered at Barrow. Some residents have adopted modern ways wholeheartedly; others seek a balance between traditional and contemporary. Whaling crews still gather on the ice in spring and fall to hunt the bowhead. When emperor geese fly by the point each fall, the guns are waiting. Caribou hides protect just as well as the most modern fabric when winter winds send the chill factor to 100 degrees below zero.

Bowhead whales, those great, lumbering, oil-rich behemoths of northern seas, led the parade of early-day seamen to the High Arctic. Following routes they had used since the end of the Pleistocene, the bowheads migrated twice yearly through Bering Strait on their run from the southwestern Bering Sea wintering grounds to summer feeding areas in the Beaufort. Weighing a ton per foot and reaching lengths of 60 feet (20 meters), the huge mammals filter their food through large plates of baleen and carry huge quantities of oil in their tissue. Whalers sought the baleen and oil and pursued the bowhead to the edge of extinction.

Charles Brower came north in the 1880s, having already survived at 20 years of age a lifetime of adventures on the high seas. Reports of coal seams near Cape Lisburne north of Point Hope had caught the attention of whaling company officials in San Francisco. (Coal fueled the whaling fleet.) The Pacific Steam Whaling Company brought Brower north and he stayed, for nearly six decades, as trader, fur buyer, postmaster and commissioner. To Brower fell the task of rushing, in August, 1935, to a lagoon south of Barrow where Eskimo friends had reported a plane had gone down. As commissioner he was in charge of sending the bodies of Will Rogers and Wiley Post south.

Gates of the Arctic

South of the mountain barrier, great rivers flow into Kotzebue Sound, draining much of northwestern Alaska. Noatak National Preserve encompasses much of the watershed of the unsullied Noatak, a 400-mile (640-km)

ribbon of crystal water in a pristine land. Only one village casts the hand of man upon the Noatak.

To the south, the Kobuk Valley has for centuries been a major artery for people moving from the coast to the Interior. Several villages scattered along the banks and tributaries of the Kobuk River rely on fishing, trapping and hunting for their livelihood. A bit of the Sahara touches the river's banks in Kobuk Valley National Park. The Great Kobuk Sand Dunes cover several square miles on the river's southern flank where they slowly move, driven by the wind, and overtake surrounding forests.

Headwaters of both the Noatak and Kobuk lie within the mountain fastness of Gates of the Arctic, a wilderness in the central Brooks Range. When forester Robert Marshall came to Alaska in the 1920s and 1930s, he wound up in the village of Bettles in the Interior and headed north toward the Brooks Range. He came to a pass between Frigid Crags and Boreal Mountain that he christened Gates of the Arctic. The name stuck and expanded to include much of the central range which now is Gates of the Arctic National Park.

Commercial hub for this rich region is Kotzebue, largest Inupiat village in northwestern Alaska and for centuries a center of trade. The Russians across the Chukchi long knew of the rich, forested lands on the eastern side of the great sea. But westerners exploring the coastline seemed to miss the basin lying between Cape Espenberg and Cape Krusenstern. Not until 1816 when Otto von Kotzebue sailed around Espenberg and met several Natives in skin boats did the two cultures have their first official encounter. About this same time Americans were also cruising the coast, seeking trade and the ever-elusive Northwest Passage. American excursions into these waters spurred the Russians to even greater efforts at exploration. G.S. Shishmarev sailed along the coast in 1820, but like his predecessors, he received a less than friendly reception.

Sir John Franklin's exploration efforts in the Canadian Arctic and along the northern coast of Alaska brought British seamen to the northwest coast to rendezvous with Franklin's men. F.W. Beechey sailed into Kotzebue Sound in 1826, had several skirmishes with the Natives, sailed away and returned the following summer. Relations with the Natives had not improved, and Beechey finally had to fire his guns in earnest, killing one Eskimo. By 1848 the whaling fleet was heading north and the British Admiralty had ordered several ships to the

Chukchi to search for the missing Franklin party.

Coastal Eskimos had a taste of western culture, but inland Natives didn't have their first encounter with white men until Lt. George M. Stoney and Lt. J.C. Cantwell pushed up the rivers and into the mountains on the region's boundaries. Even the missionaries seemed to overlook the basin until 1897. Traders slowly followed.

As in many other regions of Alaska, the call of gold drew miners to the river valleys just prior to the turn of the century. This rush didn't make the splash of those in the Klondike or at Nome, but gold brought more people to the region, more commerce and more services.

Kotzebue was growing. In 1960 the first bank opened. A barge service provided lighterage for supply ships that had to anchor far offshore because of the shallow harbor. Scheduled air flights brought tourists. Native leaders from the Kotzebue area were elected to the state legislature. With settlement of land claims and formation of NANA regional corporation, Inupiats of northwestern Alaska can now manage their own resources and look forward to prosperity without forgetting the heritage of their ancestors.

With a View of Asia

South of Kotzebue Basin, a mountainous finger points towards Asia. Forests cover eastern portions of the Seward Peninsula, tundra the west. From Little Diomede Island to Cape Prince of Wales at the finger's tip lies a mere 25 miles (40 km). On a clear day, when fog lifts from Bering Strait, the two Diomedes and miles and miles of the Siberian coast are visible from the summit of Cape Mountain.

More than 250 years ago Vitus Bering sailed the waters of Bering Strait and the northern Bering Sea under orders from the Czar to determine if Asia and North America were connected. Fog and bad weather prevented Bering from officially sighting the North American mainland, but he did come upon a large island to the southwest which he named Saint Lawrence, because the day of discovery coincided with that saint's day in Russia.

A few other explorers skirted the peninsula's coast, but as in much of Alaska, it took the cry of gold to bring the people. In 1898 miners, stormbound along the coast, discovered gold in gravel of nearby river bars. They staked claims on creeks flowing into Norton Sound and headed south for the

winter. When word got out of their find, miners headed for the peninsula. The following year gold was found in beaches near Cape Nome, and by 1900 the rush was on. Contraptions of all kinds guaranteed to retrieve the yellow metal from its resting place lined the beaches. By this time though, gold readily accessible on the beaches had already been taken. However, prehistoric beaches, now rising from the tundra as benchlands back from the shore, also held the precious metal. Mining the frozen gravels of the benchlands required different techniques and much more money. Syndicates were formed with investors from the Lower 48, pipes heated by steam crisscrossed the ground, and huge floating dredges followed behind the thaw fields to scoop the

newly released gravels. The town of Nome itself grew as a supply center, feeding the gold fields and villages spread along the peninsula's shores.

The lifestyle of Seward Peninsula's villages resembles that of most other Native communities. Subsistence and seasonal government work sustain their economy. Modern-day subsistence here revolves around reindeer, although some villagers continue to hunt marine mammals and fish the streams. Moose and bear roam the inland hills, but it is the great herds of reindeer which provide the cash. The peninsula is divided into territories for several large, native-owned herds. Each summer the deer are herded off the tundra by helicopters to corrals where their antlers are clipped, and sold to Oriental buyers who process them into medicinal compounds. For several years the price of antlers brought substantial income to the villages. Lately, however, competition from other markets such as the red deer of New Zealand have affected earnings from the peninsula's herds.

Life in the North Country

The daily activities of modern-day Inupiat villagers are a blend of modern and traditional. Many houses, built by the federal government under a Bureau of Indian Affairs program, are unsuited to the northern environment. Constant winds sweep sand into cracks in the house, covering ev-

matic clothes washers—but must lug water from springs in the hills in huge metal washtubs. More and more villages now have water storage tanks and washeterias.

The villagers' diet is also a blend of old and new. A harpooned seal rests in a bucket of water on the back porch. Pieces of muktuk (layers of skin and blubber) from a recently taken beluga are passed around the table. Walrus meat and fish hang to dry on wooden racks.

Supplies from the village store also reach the table. White bread and canned peaches, fried chicken, sugar, tea and coffee blend well with the food of the land. If the village is on the coast, the supply barge comes once or twice a season, weather permitting. Food, fuel, building supplies, furniture, VCRs,

erything with grit. The heater must be turned on high, even in mid-summer, or the insulation will rot from constant moisture brought in from the sea. Plumbing has been installed but running water is not available. Honey buckets are emptied every two or three days, and garbage is sacked and placed on the beach to be carried away when the ice goes out in June or July. (Natives speak euphemistically of this practice as sending presents to Russia.) There is electricity in most villages—and some families have auto-

Left, a Native woman and her child ice-fishing. Right, careful etching technique on a whale's tooth results in scrimshaw art.

snowmachines and every once in a while a vehicle find their way to Arctic Alaska. Perishable items or those with immediate demand come by bush plane. Some villages have telephone systems, others have one phone that may not work much of the time. Satellite television provided by the state is available in most villages. Since passage of a state law requiring construction of high schools in the Bush, children are no longer sent to high schools far away or in the Lower 48. Village elders speak their native tongues and may switch to English if they feel like it; younger villagers rely on English. In some areas bilingual education is encouraged, but the successful blending of old and new is an ongoing challenge.

PLACES

Alaska is, above all else, a land of remarkable diversity. With an average of about 1.2 square miles (three km) of land for each resident, this huge state possesses an abundance of distinct places: the confluence of two tiny streams, the migratory paths of a caribou band, a rural village, or a few square blocks of a major city.

There's urban Alaska: usually described as Anchorage, but often enlarged to include Fairbanks and, occasionally, Juneau. There's rural Alaska: villages scattered throughout the land, mostly along major rivers or near the coast. And there's wilderness Alaska, vast regions of relatively untouched ground–ground that knows only the whims of nature.

Communities have their attractions to be sure, but it is the wilderness that calls one to Alaska. Where else in the world can you climb the highest of peaks, tread softly along an unexplored river bank, chill refreshments with ice broken from a glacier, or view hundreds of square miles of untrampled wildflowers, all with little more formality than a passport check when stepping from an airliner?

Almost every city or town has one or more businesses designed to provide access to the wilderness. Charter air services, outdoor expedition ventures and a host of other related industries exist as a means of taking travellers into remote regions, and, not incidentally, provide methods for earning a living in the wilderness.

Each Alaskan enjoys his or her own "special place," almost all of which are in the wilderness. Visitors to Alaska should make the effort to spirit themselves away from civilization and seek that special place of their own. Ask those who have been to Alaska whether it was a picture of a glacier or a picture of a city that lured them north. From the answers to such questions come the first blushes of wisdom about Alaska–the Great Land.

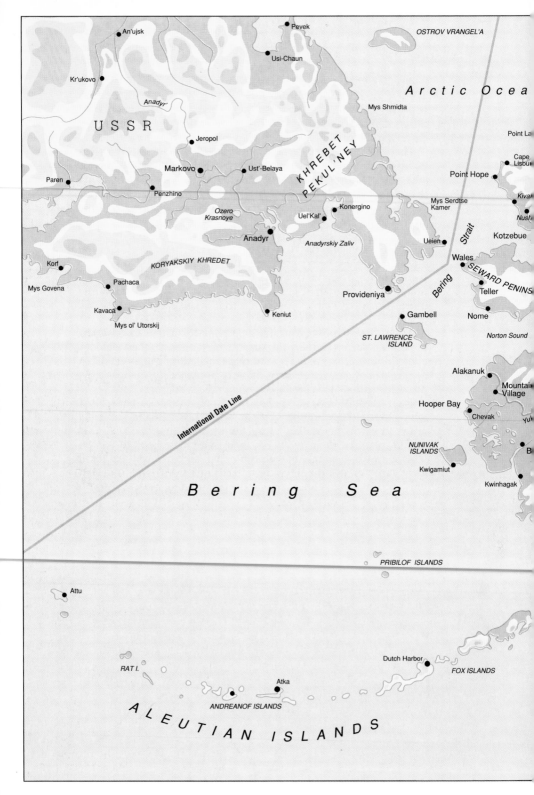

An'ujsk
Pevek
OSTROV VRANGEL'A

Usi-Chaun

Kr'ukovo

Arctic Ocea

Mys Shmidta

Anadyr'

U S S R

Jeropol

Point La

Cape
Lisbu

Markovo
Ust'-Belaya

Point Hope

*KHREBET
PEKUL'NEY*

Kival

Paren

Penzhino

Mys Serdtse
Kamer

Nusf

*Ozero
Krasnoye*

Konergino

Uel'Kal'

Strait

Kotzebue

Anadyr

Anadyrskiy Zaliv

Ueien

Wales

KORYAKSKIY KHREDET

SEWARD PENINS

Korf

Bering

Teller

Mys Govena

Pachaca

Providencia

Nome

Kavaca

Keniut

Gambell

Norton Sound

Mys ol' Utorskij

*ST. LAWRENCE
ISLAND*

Alakanuk

Mountain
Village

Hooper Bay

Chevak

Yu

International Date Line

*NUNIVAK
ISLANDS*

B

Kwigamiut

Kwinhagak

B e r i n g   S e a

PRIBILOF ISLANDS

Attu

Dutch Harbor

RAT I.

FOX ISLANDS

Atka

ANDREANOF ISLANDS

A L E U T I A N   I S L A N D S

70

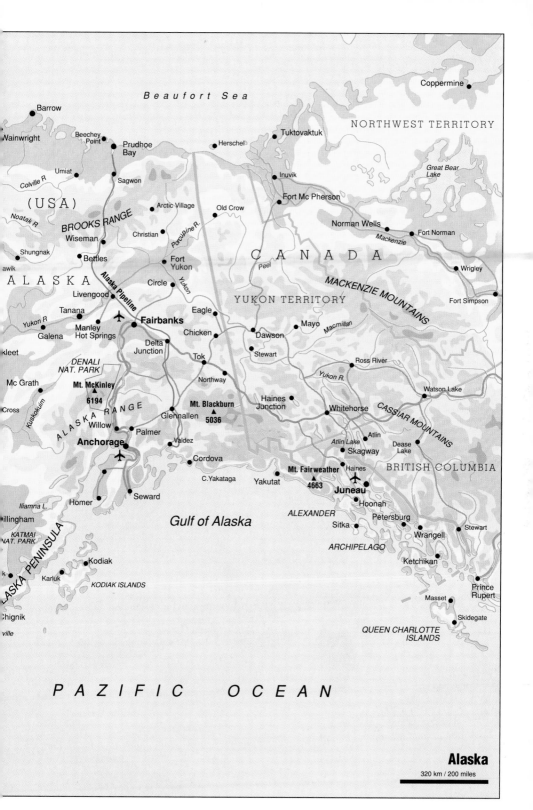

Coppermine

Beaufort Sea

NORTHWEST TERRITORY

Barrow

Wainwright

Beechey
Point

Prudhoe
Bay

Tuktovaktuk

Herschel

Umiat

Sagwon

Great Bear
Lake

Colville R

Inuvik

(USA)

Arctic Village

Old Crow

Fort Mc Pherson

Noatak R

BROOKS RANGE

Norman Wells

Fort Norman

Wiseman

Christian

Mackenzie

Shungnak

Bettles

Fort
Yukon

C A N A D A

Wrigley

awik

ALASKA

Circle

Peel

MACKENZIE MOUNTAINS

Fort Simpson

Livengood

Alaska Pipeline

Eagle

YUKON TERRITORY

Tanana

Yukon

Fairbanks

Chicken

Dawson

Mayo

Macmillan

Yukon R

Manley
Hot Springs

Delta
Junction

Stewart

Ross River

Galena

Tok

Watson Lake

kleet

DENALI
NAT. PARK

Northway

Yukon R.

Mc Grath

Mt. McKinley

Haines
Junction

Whitehorse

CASSIAR MOUNTAINS

Cross

6194

RANGE

Mt. Blackburn

Atlin

Kuskokwim

ALASKA

Glennallen

5036

Atlin Lake

Skagway

Dease
Lake

Willow

Palmer

Anchorage

Valdez

Haines

BRITISH COLUMBIA

Cordova

Mt. Fairweather

Iliamna L.

C.Yakataga

Yakutat

4663

Juneau

illingham

Homer

Seward

Gulf of Alaska

Hoonah

KATMAI
NAT. PARK

ALEXANDER

Petersburg

Sitka

Wrangell

Stewart

ALASKA PENINSULA

Kodiak

ARCHIPELAGO

Ketchikan

k

Karluk

KODIAK ISLANDS

hignik

Prince
Rupert

Masset

ville

Skidegate

QUEEN CHARLOTTE
ISLANDS

PAZIFIC   OCEAN

Alaska

320 km / 200 miles

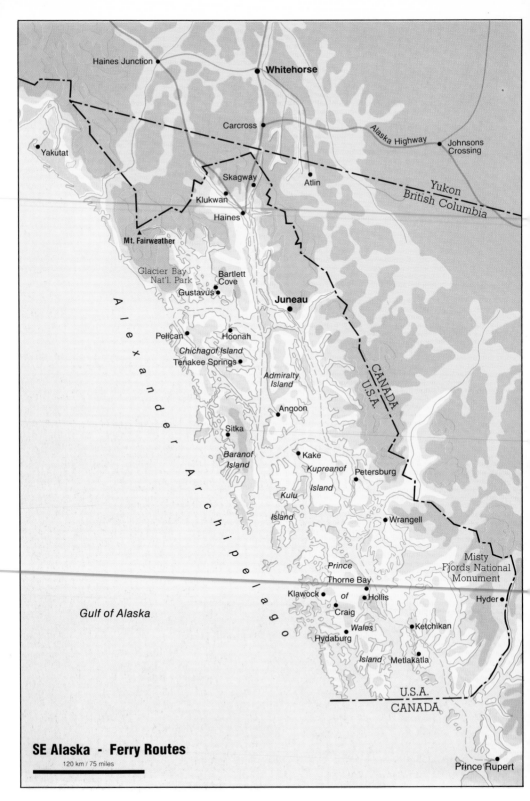

SE Alaska - Ferry Routes

120 km / 75 miles

AN INSIDE PASSAGE TOUR

Ever since it emerged from the melting of the last great Ice Age–some 15,000 years ago, give or take a millennia or two–the great island-studded, 1,000-mile passage of water that stretches from present lower British Columbia to the top of the southeast Alaska panhandle has been one of earth's treasures. Well, not quite for everybody. The first out-of-towners to visit a portion of what is now called the Inside Passage got an unfriendly reception from the locals, they were taken prisoner by the Indians 248 years ago and they haven't been heard of since.

The occasion started out happily enough. In 1741 Alexei Chirikov, captain of the good ship *St. Paul*, set sail for Czar Peter of Russia. With his commander, Vitus Bering (who also was captain of the vessel *St. Peter*), he had left the Russian Kamchatkan Peninsula in Siberia and had headed east on a voyage of exploration and discovery.

What Chirikov and Bering were looking for was North America, which everyone knew was out there someplace (after all, Columbus had established that definitely back in 1492) but which Bering and his colleagues had only shortly before determined was not connected to Siberia and the European-Asian land mass. Alas for the Alaska seekers, the two sailors were separated in a storm which struck soon after leaving port. They never saw each other again. Bering, in fact, died after being ship-wrecked on his voyage home.

To Chirikov goes the prize for seeing North America first. His crew sighted the high wooded mountains of what we now call Prince of Wales Island in southeast Alaska on July 15, 1741. Two days later he dropped anchor probably near the present-day vicinity of Sitka. It was there that tragedy struck–a tragedy recorded by Lieutenant Sven Waxel, a Swede who served as first mate and pilot aboard the *St. Peter*. The following account is his story:

The ship went to anchor a good dis-

tance from the shore and, being short of water, Chirikov decided to send a boat ashore. To command it he chose an officer called Avraam Demetiev, a very capable man, and gave him a crew of the best man he had. They were all equipped with guns and ammunition and also had a metal cannon with appurtenances. They were also given a signaling system and complete instructions how to behave and act in the event of the unexpected happening. Besides all this, they were supplied with provisions to last several days.

The boat pulled away from the ship: they watched it disappear around a headland and some while later noticed various signal flashes corresponding with the orders given, so that they had every reason for thinking that the party landed safely. However, two days passed and then a third day, and still the boat did not come back.

Nevertheless, they could see the whole time that the signal fires continued to burn and so they began to think that perhaps the boat had been dam-

Preceding pages: rail-train near near Denali; cruiseship at sunset; view of the inlet near Haines; climber atop McConnell Ridge in Glacier Bay Park. Right, the willow ptarmigan, Alaska's state bird.

aged on landing and that the party's return was being delayed by having to repair it.

They then decided to send the little jolly-boat ashore with carpenters, calkers and all that they might need, so that the boat could be repaired if that should prove necessary. No sooner said than done. Six men were ordered into the jolly-boat, equipped with guns and ammunition and well supplied with everything else they might need. They were to search out the boat and give all help that might be called for when they found it, after which both boats were to return to the ship immediately.

Next morning two craft were seen coming out from the land, the one slightly larger than the other. Naturally it was assumed that these were the long-boat and the jolly-boat and very glad they were to see them. They began to get the ship ready to put to sea again... But then, as the two craft drew near the ship, they discovered the truth was the exact opposite of what they had thought.

These were American boats and they were filled with savages. They approached to within three cable lengths of the ship. Then, seeing so many on deck, they turned back towards land. Those on board the ship had no boat left in which they could have put out after the Americans, and they had just to draw the melancholy conclusion that both the long boat and the jolly-boat were lost along with their entire crews.

These days, it is rare indeed when a visitor to the Inside Passage fails to return to ship. And on those infrequent occasions when that happened, it is likely the person simply lost track of time in the search for culture at the incredible provincial museum in Victoria, in the quest for adventure on a hike to the top of Deer Mountain in Ketchikan, or in the pursuit of pleasure at the Red Dog Saloon in Juneau.

Cosmopolitan Cities and Indian Villages

For certain the sites and sightings along the Inside Passage are never

Totems at Ketchikan's Cultural Heritage Center.

boring–and they are surprisingly varied. One of Canada's–and North America's–largest, most cosmopolitan, cities is located along the way. There are, likewise, tiny Indian villages where food on most residents' tables still depends on the hunter's, trapper's or fisherman's skill. There are two capital cities along the length of the passage, one Canadian and one American, where life and lifestyle revolve around lusty politics and bureaucratic doings and the strange machinations of government. There are other communities in both countries where jobs and ways of living are spawned from the more basic harvest of sea, land and forest.

There are homes and condos and highrise hotels as modern as can be found in any of the communities of the world, and there are tiny, hand-built cabins and camps which may be spotted–briefly, on a cruise or during a fly-by–in isolated wilderness settings far from roads, stores, television stations, or daily newspapers.

The geography and the geology of the Inside Passage varies greatly as well. At its southernmost, the passage is protected by Vancouver Island, a large and elongated landmass that begins near the northern border of the United States and stretches nearly 300 miles (482 km) northwesterly, nearly half the distance up the British Columbia coast to southeast Alaska. Then comes the seaward protection of the Queen Charlotte Islands, not as large as Vancouver Island but a number of them–especially Graham and Moresby islands–are sizeable nonetheless. And finally, about where U.S. jurisdiction, and southeast Alaska begins, there's the Alexander Archipelago. (For the purpose of this book, only destinations within Alaska's national boundary are covered.)

This is a 400-mile-long (643 km) maze of 1,000 massive and miniscule isles that, along with a 30-mile-wide (48 km) silver of mainland, makes up the southeast Alaska panhandle.

If the size and national colors of the islands of the Inside Passage vary, there is this commonality all along the way:

Russian dancers at Sitka.

lush green forests of hemlock, cedar, pine and other conifers cover whole islands and mountains except for snow-capped peaks and gravel beaches. Generous bays and exquisite little coves rival one another for exposure in visitors' cameras and memories. And major rivers course through great glacier-carved valleys, while waterfalls plunge from mountainside cliffs to the sea.

And everywhere–absolutely everywhere–along the way there are watercraft: seineboats with crews of half a dozen or more; small trollers and gillnet fishing craft with a skipper and, maybe, a single helper; tugs pulling rafts of logs or barges or commercial goods; exotic yachts and simple open boats; cruiseships; state ferries; freighters; supertankers; even sailboats and kayaks.

The reason for this concentration of watercraft, of course, is protection from the elements. The same islands which provide near-continuous evergreen beauty to visitors along the way provide buffers from North Pacific winds and weather that could otherwise threaten all but the toughest vessels.

The islands afford protection and nurture for a wide variety of wild creatures. Ashore, and beyond the gaze of spectators, thousands of animals make their homes within the forests and even atop the mountains of the southeast Alaska panhandle. Charter a light aircraft at Yakutat, near the very top of the panhandle, and you'll likely see moose and perhaps brown bear as well. Near Juneau or Ketchikan or any of the other cities in the region, and the opportunity to spot whole herds of glistening white mountain goats is almost assured.

Take one of the kayak excursions in **Glacier Bay National Park**, located also in the northern panhandle, and as you paddle alongside forest or beach you just might see the rare "Glacier Blue"–a subspecies of black bear. Cruise or fly to Pack Creek on **Admiralty Island** during the salmon spawning season and you can easily view and photograph dozens of huge, lumbering brown bears. Throughout the panhandle, and down the coast of British Columbia as well, Sitka blacktail deer

are extremely numerous. Indeed, this is one species of land animal you may see along the beaches from a cruiseship.

If critters on land are not that commonly seen from a cruiseship, sea mammals are an entirely different story. Humpback and killer whales, cavoting porpoises by the twos and fours, and sea lions by the dozens are frequently seen and always appreciated by vessel-borne visitors along the Inside Passage.

Symbol of the States

And eagles are everywhere–the white headed, white tailed bald eagle which is the symbol of the United States. You see them diving and swooping from the heights to grab unwary fish swimming near the water surface, you witness the strength of their powerful talons as they rip salmon carcasses to shreds alongside spawning streams, and you view them high in the spruce trees, standing guard over tons-heavy nests which are lodged in the forks of great branches.

Besides the eagles, there are huge

Left, Alaskan State ferry travels up Lynn Canal. Right, window at "Dolly's House" Museum in Ketchikan.

black ravens, tiny gray wrens and black-capped Arctic terns (who come each year, to the northern climes from as far south as Antarctica), plus hundreds of other kinds of waterfowl, shorebirds and upland species.

And the fishing here is world-class. Perhaps your goal is to haul in a lunker king salmon of 50 pounds or more. Or maybe you want to test your skill against diving, dancing and frothing steelhead trout. Whatever your angling heart's desire, the fishing in this region is simply unexcelled anywhere else. In addition to kings and steelheads, there are coho (silver) salmon–considered by many to be, pound for pound, the fightingest, gamest fish in salt water–plus sockeye, halibut, rainbow trout, Dolly Varden and eastern brook trout (these latter two actually chars). With this concentration of fish, furry creatures and scenic beauty, it's not hard to imagine why increasing numbers of people choose to live in this region. Big cities and small can be seen all along the way.

Ketchikan, which Alaskans call "the First City" because it is the first major Alaskan community encountered on a journey north, is famous for at least three things: totem poles (more of them are located here, in fact, than anywhere else in the world); salmon (caught in considerable numbers both by sport and commercial fishermen); and it is the jumping-off place (as well as cruising-off or flying-off place) for **Misty Fjords National Monument**, which in recent years has come to be appreciated as one of the mountain and maritime scenic wonders of Alaska. Ketchikan is also known as a place where it rains a lot, although that is true of almost anywhere along the Inside Passage.

Wrangell is a town by passed by most cruise boats and most tourists. This is a pity, because it is a small untouristy patch of authentic Alaska. The fishing is excellent, the people are genuinely anxious to help you enjoy their town. A local museum and an easily accessible totem park (on **Chief Shakes Island**) are well-worth a visit. A boat trip up the nearby **Stikine River**

Shore and peaceful village at Petersburg.

is a time capsule voyage back into Alaska's unspoiled past. The forested scenery around the town is likewise spectacular–except for some big, ugly clearcut logging scars on the side of some mountains, but that's part of what Alaska is all about these days.

Petersburg, across the Stikine to the north and just a few minutes by plane from Wrangell, is likewise bypassed by most tour ships and visitors. Again, a pity–for this spick-and-span little city of Norwegian descendents offers still another opportunity for the unstructured visitor who enjoys poking around on one's own.

There are ancient Indian petroglyphs to be seen on the beaches, a small but tasteful museum offers a lot of insight into the history and art of fishing, and simply wandering the docks and wharves of the community gives the visitor a view of the largest home-based halibut fishing fleet in Alaska.

Sitka, as the well-read history buff may know, dates back to 1799 when the Russian trader and colonizer Alexander Baranov established his headquarters there. Actually, Tlingit Indians had been there centuries before, and near the site of present day Sitka were fought two of the bloodiest battles in Alaska's recorded history. The Indians won the first round, but the Russians, utilizing cannons as well as guns, won the second encounter. Today, the city is a pleasurable blend of Indian, Russian and American culture. The Russian Orthodox **Cathedral of St. Michael**, with its priceless icons and other religious treasures is reason enough to visit this city. Additional reasons include excellent fishing, the **Sitka National Historical Park** (located at the site of the second battle), and mountain-water-island scenery on a grand scale.

Juneau is a port of call for virtually every cruiseship, ferry and airline that comes to southeast Alaska. (This capital city is covered in detail in the following chapter of this guide.)

Haines, 80 air miles (130 km) north of Juneau, is the northern co-terminus (along with Skagway) of the southeast

Packing house amid spectacular mountains, near Haines.

segment of the Alaska state ferry system. From here you can drive the 150-mile (242-km) Haines Highway to Haines Junction (Canada) on the Alaska Highway to the interior of the state. But do not leave for the Interior until you have seen what this community offers.

Old **Fort William Henry Seward** with its massive turn-of-the-century officers homes and command buildings still surrounding the old rectangular grounds. The biggest hotel in town is located in two of these buildings.

And in the fall the world's greatest gathering of bald eagles–over 3,000 of the winged creatures, many of them coming from home territories hundreds of miles away–flies to a nearby river and woods to feast on a late run of salmon in icefree waters.

Skagway is the northernmost of all the communities usually visited on a cruise or ferry tour of the Inside Passage. (See "Skagway, the Fun City" chapter in this guide.)

In addition to the major communities along the Inside Passage, there are

throughout the region countless other settlements, Indian villages and fishing camps equally worth a day's or a week's visit. Near Ketchikan, colorful old **Waterfall Cannery** has been converted into a what the owners call "the most civilized resort in Alaska"; it's within easy access to some of southeast Alaska's hottest salmon angling. Similarly superlative fishing can be experienced near the Indian villages of **Angoon, Kake** and **Hoonah**, all of which offer modest but tidy tourist accommodations. Small commercial fishing centers, like **Elfin Cove, Tenakee Springs** and **Pelican**–though never touted as tourist towns–nonetheless provide do-it-yourself, arrange-it-yourself visitors with indelible memories of a very happy and contented portion of Alaska.

How to get around amongst all this wonderful wildlife, fabulous fishing, glacier grandeur and mountain-shrouded seaways? It's easy and the options are wide. There are posh cruise-ships, some drive the family buggy aboard ferries of the Alaska state "marine highway" system, getting off and exploring big towns and small villages along the way. Still others jet from Seattle to Ketchikan, Wrangell, Petersburg, Sitka and Juneau. Those who are really tough paddle their own canoe or kayak–but watch it…crossing Queen Charlotte Sound in such little craft can be deadly).

Once you've arrived the options are even broader. Big and little yacht excursions are available at every turn. Alaska's famed bush pilots, some on wheels and others on floats, will take you wherever you want to go. Hiking trails fan out from every settlement.

Few indeed–with the possible exception of Chirikov's hapless kidnapped sailors of 1741–are the visitors who are not more than satisfied with an Inside Passage sojourn. And southeast Alaskans, never hesitant to tout the attractiveness of their place on the planet, speculate that *maybe…just maybe* having sampled life ashore in this lush and bountiful land, those Russian visitors decided on their own they really didn't want to leave.

Left, a line of Dolly Varden trout caught near Glacier Bay. Right, a radio-tagged eagle is to be released.

JUNEAU, STATE CAPITAL CITY

The going had been slow, sweaty, frustrating—plodding upstream beside the forest-rimmed waterway. Thick entangling underbrush, huge grasping devil's club plants (with thousands of tiny needles on every stalk and leaf), and great boulders in and alongside the stream . . . these obstacles and more had hampered the party's progress every step of the way. Then it got even worse, and the five men—two white prospectors who were guided (some would later say all but carried) by three natives—had to abandon the stream entirely. They were forced literally to climb the mountain beside them in order to get to the gulch they sought. But as they descended from the mountaintop into the watershed the labor was well worth the effort. And a great deal more!

Before they even got to the mouth of the gulch, they took samples from the quartz lodes that cropped out of the mountain. And they were incredulous at what their pounding hammers yielded. One of the men recorded the experience in his journal thus:

"We knew it was gold, but so much, and not in particles; streaks running through the rock and little lumps as large as peas or beans . . . I took the gold pan, pick, and shovel and panned $1.20 to $1.30 to the pan . . ."

The two men were Joe Juneau and Richard Harris. The year was 1880. The place was Silver Bow Basin. And out of their discovery came a camp that became a town that became the capital city of Alaska.

City of Gold, Glaciers, Government

Juneau today is a far cry from the wilderness site that Joe Juneau and Dick Harris encountered. It is, instead, a delightful modern city of complementary contrasts. About 30,000 Alaskans—whites, Native Tlingit Indians, other ethnic groups—call the community home. The overwhelming majority of Juneau's folk either live off the government (state, federal, or local) or live off the civil servants who do. The town is as modern as a state-of-the-art computer center in the S.O.B. (for "state office building") and as old-fashioned as the plantation-style turn-of-the-century Governor's Mansion a couple of blocks down the street. It is as cosmopolitan as a local World Affairs Council which meets to discuss the weightier matters of international geopolitics and as down-to-earth as a lobby group of Alaskan Mothers Against Drunk Driving who want to get dangerous inebriates off the road.

The town is as sophisticated as a surprisingly talented symphony and as earthy as the Red Dog Saloon or the equally frontierish Alaskan Hotel bar next door. (At either of these two watering holes it would not be out of character, on any given rehearsal night, to find musicians letting down after their music making—arm-wrestling, perhaps, to see who picks up the beer tab.) The town is as urban as highrise office buildings and high comfort hotels, and it is as rugged as the northern wilderness of thick, lush forests, glacial ice and saltwater which surrounds the city. The wilderness begins literally where the houses stop.

By stateside standards, Juneau is a

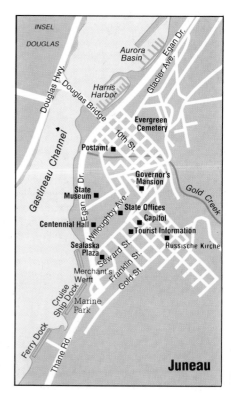

Left, banners welcome visitors at the Juneau waterfront.

small town in terms of population (about 30,000)—but in square miles it is the biggest town in North America and second biggest in the world. More about that later, but first some additional data about how the city came to be.

Gold Fever

The town was first named Harrisburg—some say because Harris, unlike his partner Juneau, was able to write and recorded it that way. The name didn't stick, however. After news of the gold strike spread to Sitka and elsewhere, and nearly 300 prospectors swarmed to the scene during the following year, the miners decided to rename the place Rockwell. Shortly thereafter it became Juneau. By whatever name, the camp was bustling with gold fever and, soon, gold production. It didn't take long for simple goldpans, pickaxes and human labor to be replaced by miles-long flumes and ditches, carrying water to massive hydraulic earth moving and sluicing operations. Within a decade of the Juneau/Harris discovery, wagon roads penetrated the valleys behind the camp-turned-town—roads you can drive or hike on to this day.

Juneau is, of course, on the North American mainland. Across Gastineau Channel, on **Douglas Island**, even more furiously paced development took place. By 1882 the world famous Treadwell Mine was operational and expanding. Near it, the proud community of **Douglas** grew up, and indeed rivaled Juneau in population, industry and miners' baseball for a good number of years. Eventually, more than half a century later, the two towns would merge, but the Douglas community and Douglasites remain distinct and still-prideful to this day, sort of the way Alaska is part of, but somehow set apart from, the rest of the United States.

Early on, politics assumed considerable importance in Juneau. The future state's first political convention was held there in the summer of 1881. The camp became a first-class municipality under the law in 1900 and in 1906 the district government of Alaska transferred there from Sitka.

In 1913, Alaska's first Territorial legislature convened, in what is now the Elks Hall on Seward Street. Near-life-size photo murals of that distinguished

Native artifacts in the Juneau Art Museum.

group can be seen today on the first floor of the state capitol building. The all-male representatives and senators in the pictures look like what they were, rugged frontier types, most of them probably uncomfortable in the stiff collars and ties they were forced to wear on the floors of their respective houses.

As the city grew and prospered, such additional enterprises as fishing, sawmilling and trading became important in Juneau's economic scheme of things: important but never paramount.

Compared to mines and minerals they were the Avis industries of their day—trying hard, but never Number One.

Gold was what Juneau was all about.

Gold was not only practically everyone's vocation, it was the avocation of choice as well. Miners labored daily within miles and miles of tunnels that honeycombed the mountains both on the mainland and on Douglas Island. For recreation on days off they scoured the wild country beyond the urban centers, digging, panning, hoping against hope that they, too, might strike it rich like Juneau and Harris. (Juneau and Harris, like many gold locators the world over, never really realized much from their discoveries. Juneau, in fact, died broke in the Canadian Yukon and a collection had to be taken up to send his body home for burial in the city he co-founded.)

A Frontier Government

As the years passed there were ups and downs (definitely down when in 1917 major portions of the Treadwell tunnels beneath the waters of Gastineau Channel caved in and flooded) but gold remained Juneau's and Alaska's mainstay, until relativley recent times. Came World War II, however, and the government closed down the massive AJ gold mine and milling operation as a manpower conservation matter. There hasn't been any sizeable mining activity in the area since.

But even with the mine closure things didn't go too badly. By the time the 1944 shutdown came about, the city was experiencing something of a war boom, and with war's end there came a gradual but continuous rise in Territorial government activity and employment.

By 1959, when Alaska became state number 49, government had all but filled the economic void left by mining's demise. And in the years since, Juneau has grown from an ingrown waterfront community hovering beneath the skeletal remains of the old AJ millsite to a gregarious upreaching outreaching city spread for miles both north and south.

The city's size was established in the mid-1960s when the then-city of Juneau, the then-city of Douglas and the Greater Juneau Borough (county) were unified by a vote of the people into the City and Borough of Juneau. Since then, at least two additional communities in Alaska (Anchorage and Sitka) have consolidated their city and borough governments, but none have come close to ending up with as much territory.

The city is spread so many miles, incidentally, that it is the biggest town, in size, in all of North and South America. In the international bigness sweepstakes, in fact, Juneau's 3,108 sq miles (8,050 sq km) are exceeded only by the city of Kiruna, Sweden, which boasts 5,458 sq miles (14,136 sq km) within its borders.

With that much land under its collective belt, it's little wonder that visitors

A prospector contemplates his future riches.

to Juneau find lots to see and do in Alaska's capital community.

Glaciers—Up Close

From Juneau, a number of impressive glaciers can be reached by auto, by trial, or viewed by airplane or helicopter. Best known of Juneau's great rivers of ice is the **Mendenhall Glacier** which can be seen, and photographed, quite easily from a U.S. Forest Service information center about 13 miles (21 km) north of town. The glacier begins about 12 twisting, meandering miles (19 km) "upstream" from the information center and the nearby frigid lake into which it calves icebergs both large and small. The glacier's source is 1,500 sq miles (3,885 sq km) of ice and snow called the **Juneau Ice Field**.

Dozens of glaciers flow down from the ice field, creating Mendenhall, Eagle, Lemon and Herbert glaciers, to name only a few.

Mendenhall is unquestionably among the most visited and photographed glaciers in the world. (Hint: mornings and late afternoons render the most satisfactory pictures. Dramatic shadows which give depth and definition to the blue ice river are missing when photographed near noontime.)

There are several options for exploring the glacier. Choices range from just sitting in a car or bus in the parking lot and taking in the glacier's incredible mass and majesty to hiking several trails around it, actually hiking on it (at least two local outfitters offer package tours complete with crampons, ice axes and other gear) or floating past it in rubber rafts before "running" the Mendenhall River from the glacier almost to the saltwaters of Gastineau Channel.

Perhaps the most exciting way to savor the glacier and its originating ice field is to take a "flightseeing" excursion with one of several air charter companies or the helicopter carrier that offers 45 minutes or so over the great white deserts of snow. The copter ride includes not only flying *over* the icefield, it includes a landing right smack dab *onto* the surface itself. There's time to take pictures, walk around on the hardpacked snow, even kneel down to take a bone-chilling drink from a puddle of cold water—the temperature of which is only a fraction of a degree or

Whale-theme weathervane graces a Juneau rooftop.

two above freezing.

If Mendenhall Glacier and the Juneau Icefield are, collectively, Juneau's best known visitor attraction, the **Alaska State Museum**, within walking distance of downtown hotels and shopping, is a close and highly regarded second.

To visit the museum is to visit, in a real sense, all of Alaska. Eskimo culture is represented in the form of small, intricate ivory carvings and a huge 40-foot (12-meter) *oomiak*, or skin boat, of the type used for whale and walrus hunting on the ice floes of the Arctic Ocean.

Southeast Alaska's ancient Indian way of life is reflected in the recreation of an authentic community house, complete with priceless totemic carvings, living utensils, and even a figure of an Indian woman busily engaged in weaving a much-valued Chilkat Indian blanket.

Alaska's Interior Athabascan Indians, too, are represented with displays of a birch bark canoe, weapons and the bead-decorated moosehide garments for which these people are renowned. Goldrush memorabilia, natural history

The Alpine Forget-Me-Not, Alaska's state flower.

displays (including ancient mastodon and prehistoric musk ox skulls) are on display, as are contemporary mounts of deer, moose, wolves and a rich variety of birdlife. Nor is Alaska's pre-goldrush Russian heritage ignored. Orthodox religious exhibits include precious coins, priest's raiments and the first American flag to be flown at Sitka when Russian-America became American territory on October 18, 1867.

Most notable of all the museum's exhibits is probably the "eagle tree," encountered just inside the front entrance of the building. There, in the middle of a spiraling staircase, a towering spruce tree rises from ground level almost to the ceiling at the second floor. About three-quarters of the way up, in a natural fork of massive branches, is a huge, flat, very authentic nest on which a six- to eight-week bald eagle fledgling sits awaiting its parents. At the edge of the nest a large adult eagle—its magnificent five-foot (1.2-meter) spread of wings outstretched—has just landed. There are other eagles in the tree, and beneath its branches stand two brown bears, a mother and her cub.

To the museum's credit, the bears are

mounted in a normal, standing-on-all-fours position, as they would likely be seen in real life. Frequently, bear hunters and taxidermists like to mount the creatures standing on back feet, with teeth ferociously abred and front claws outstretched and ready to do combat.

Most of Juneau's other visitor attractions can be encountered in a walking tour along the community's docks and among its meandering, frequently narrow streets and alleys. For starters there's **Marine Park**, overlooking the city's dock and wharf area. It's small, but a pleasurable place of green grass, benches and shade trees situated near the ramp where cruiseship passengers land after being lightered from ships at anchor offshore. This is where it seems half of Juneau eats its lunch, especially on sunny days. Street vendors in the vicinity offer entrees, literally *a la carte*, that range from halibut to hot dogs to tacos and Vietnamese spring rolls.

Nearby are shops that feature Alaskan ivory, jade, totemic wood carvings and leatherwork. Nearby, too, are art galleries, bars (yes, the **Red Dog Saloon** and the **Alaskan Hotel bar** really are worth a visit, even if you don't imbibe),

seafood and regular restaurants, and, of course, the city's standard assortment of merchants and professional offices.

Juneau's visitor information office—a re-creation of the town's first log church, which later became a brewery—is located on Seward Street, uphill three blocks from Marine Park and on the way to tiny **St. Nicholas Russian Orthodox Church**. This, surely, is one of the most picturesque houses of worship in Alaska.

The onion-domed, octagon-shaped church, located on Fifth Street, was constructed in 1894 at the specific request of Ishkhanalykh, the then principal chief of the Tlingit Indians of Juneau. It is the oldest original Orthodox church in southeast Alaska and one of the senior parishes of the entire state.

Downhill on Fourth Street is the **State Capitol Building** where tours are conducted daily in the visitor season. The capitol was built in the 1930s and many of its halls and offices have recently been refurbished to reflect that era. You can see where the Alaska House and Senate meet during sessions; it's well worth a stop, as is a stroll through the sky-lighted great hall of the **State**

Left, a curious owl. Right, the Mendenhall Glacier near Juneau.

Office Building on Fourth Street. S.O.B. visitors on Friday, at noon, can enjoy a special treat. A giant old Kimball theater organ, a magnificent relic of Juneau's silent movie days, has been relocated in the atrium of the building; visiting organists and local musicians joyously celebrate T.G.I.F. at the end of each workweek by playing its pipes from 12 to 1 p.m.

Two blocks beyond the State Office Building is the **Governor's Mansion**. Although you cannot enter the house, you can take pictures of its exterior. Recently the state spent $2 million restoring it to the glory of its 1913 opening—at which time it was built and furnished for a grand total of $40,000.

Beyond the Governor's Mansion and across **Gold Creek**—where Joe Juneau and Dick Harris panned their first gold in the area—you come to a cemetery where the two lie buried.

Their burial monuments are not overly impressive but the partially wooded cemetery is a popular place for visitors to stroll, for residents to walk their dogs, and for youngsters from the nearby high and middle schools to sneak cigarettes and a host of other forbidden substances.

Perhaps the memorable thing about Juneau for outdoorsy folk is the rich variety of hiking trails which can be reached within minutes even from dockside. The **Mt. Roberts Trail** takes off from a trailhead on Fifth Street, practically downtown. The starting point for the somewhat gentler **Perseverance Mine Trail** is only a few blocks further; for the history buff the reward on this path is the chance to see and explore the mountainside ruins of early mining sites.

For the experienced, and thoroughly fit hiker, **Mount Juneau's** steep trail provides perhaps the community's grandest, most panoramic view to be had with two feet planted on the ground. Mainland Juneau and Douglas Island are laid out below—3,500 rather precipitous feet (1,066 meters) below—and the twisting, glistening channel of saltwater called Gastineau seems to go on and on forever.

The scene is classic southeastern Alaska: woods, waters, snowcapped peaks and solitude. It's what visiting southeast Alaska, and living there, is all about.

A magnificent bull moose.

Skagway, The Fun City

The old sounds are everywhere. You hear them all the time in **Skagway**. Especially on a calm midsummer night when the sun has just skipped behind the last peak, you can't help but hear them coming from behind those false fronts as you walk up the boardwalk on Broadway. They're the sounds of a not-too-distant era: ragtime pianos, whooping cancan girls, ringing cash registers, gay songs and laughter. Happy sounds of gold fever run rampant at the start of the trail. They're still heard in Skagway today nearly 90 years since the great Klondike Gold Rush. Here you'll find the rollicking past preserved. But if you stop at a corner, let your imagination wander and listen carefully, you can hear other sounds too: horses slogging through mud, whips cracking backs, hammers striking rail spikes, and the faint moans and cries of broken men. These unpleasant sounds of the gold rush aren't really heard anymore nor recreated. They're just sensed when an unexpected gust of wind comes howling around the corner of an old building.

Skagway's Rich Past

There's no town in Alaska quite like Skagway when it comes to blending history with natural beauty. Situated at the northern end of southeast Alaska's Inside Passage, Skagway was and always will be the natural jumping-off point for anyone taking the shortcut over the Coastal Mountains into Canada's Yukon. In 1897-98 stampeders took to the trail, and a town of 10,000-20,000 sprouted. Today many of the old buildings still stand and the town's 600 residents cater for the needs of more than 150,000 tourists who hit the trail every summer in cars, campers, buses, bikes, or as in the old days, on foot.

When you approach Skagway from the south–by Alaska ferry, cruise ship or air taxi–you see a tiny town at the base of a river valley surrounded by mountains. The mountains range in height from 5,000 to 7,000 feet (1,500 to 2,100 meters) above sea level, rising almost straight out of the salt water fjord. To look at the closed-in valley, you would not expect to find a pass, but there is one–the White Pass. The first white man to discover it was Captain William Moore, a member of an 1887 Canadian survey party. Moore, who had captained steamboats on rivers all over the Western Hemisphere, was a professional dreamer. At the spry age of 65, he came across the wooded tideflats of "Skagua" (Tlingit Indian word meaning "windy place") and visioned a lively port with a railroad heading across the pass into the Yukon. The railroad would haul miners in and bring gold out, he dreamed, and he would make the most of it. Moore and his son Bernard staked their claim, built a cabin (still standing), constructed a wharf, and waited for the rush to come. It was a long wait.

The big strike in the Yukon did not occur until August 1896, and word did not reach the rest of the world until *Portland*, the steamship with the fa-

Preceding pages, patriotic colors and flags adorn all-terrain vehicle in a Skagway parade. Below, a gold-rush style one-armed bandit.

mous "ton of gold," cruised into Seattle harbor about a year later. Twelve days later, the first of many hundreds of steamers brought men and supplies in Skagway. Captain Moore was in for a rude shock. The early miners preferred the old name to the one Moore had given: "Mooresville." They added a "y" at the end to make it "Skaguay." The U.S. Post Office later went with a simpler pronunciation, and replaced the "u" with a "w." The change caused quite a stir around town, but the official name exists, however, a few local businesses harken back to the old days and display the "u" proudly in their logos. Skagway boomed overnight in the fall of 1887. Miners literally pushed Moore aside, setting up their own system of streets (one going right through the Captain's home), and "gave" the old man five acres (two hectares) of the 160 he and his son had originally claimed. Moore protested, moved his building and watched the excitement pass him by.

Pony-drawn cart down Skagway's main street.

When Skagway's first newspaper was published in October, 1897, it re-ported 15 general stores, 19 restaurants, four meat markets, three wharves, 11 saloons, six lumber yards, eight pack trains, and nine hotels. Three other newspapers would join in the competition by the summer of 1898. The stampeders arrived in Skagway with lots of money to tie up in supplies and in various distractions made available to them by Skagway merchants.

As the town grew, so did its bad reputation. With no law to speak of, Skagway was ripe for con artists. Jefferson Randolph "Soapy" Smith, a master of the shell game who had been chased out of Colorado, set up his gang in Skagway. For nine months under the guise of a civic leader, he won the allegiance of not only prostitutes, gamblers and saloon keepers, but also bankers, editors and church builders. But Soapy's downfall was quick once things got out of hand; one of his men robbed a miner, and Soapy refused to bow to vigilantes and return the gold. He died in a shootout trying to break up the lynch mob.

Skagway was not alone at the top of

the Inside Passage in its quest to become the "Metropolis of the North." **Dyea**, a city on the bay 10 miles (16 km) to the west, sprang up as well. It sat at the foot of the Chilkoot Trail, an established Indian route that was shorter but steeper than the White Pass Trail. Dyea and Skagway competed bitterly for every stampeder heading into the interior, each boasting the better trail.

The biggest liars were in Skagway, because the White Trail was far more treacherous, nicknamed "Dead Horse Trail" for the 3,000 pack animals that perished in the canyon. But Skagway won the battle for survival with Dyea. The White Pass and Yukon Route railroad laid its first tracks up the middle of Broadway in May 1898, and by 1900 the narrow gauge line was completed, 100 miles (177 km) to Whitehorse, future capital of the Yukon Territory. An easy route to the gold fields was established, and Dyea became a ghost town.

The Klondike rush had subsided by 1900, but Skagway was set up for life as the port for Yukon. Its population fluctuated between 400 and 3,000 in the years since, due to the North's continuous boom and bust cycle. Food, fuel, war supplies, minerals and tourists have all been hauled by the railroad in various volumes. More volume meant more trains running and more people employed. According to the railroad's owners, there was not enough volume of anything, even tourists, to meet rising costs at the end of the 1982 summer season. The railroad "suspended operations" at that time, however, service was reinstated in the summer of 1988.

Riding the narrow gauge train over the White Pass is the best way for visitors to get a feel of the gold rush. Travel in turn-of-the-century parlor cars, pulled by steam or diesel engines, which seem to cling to the small cut in the mountainside. Hundreds of feet below are the still visible remains of the old trails. Excursions are available to White Pass Summit or passengers may book a one-way ticket from Skagway to Fraser, British Columbia, where they can continue to Whitehorse by motorcoach.

An antler-bedecked facade.

Visitors can also drive the Klondike Highway, completed in 1978, which climbs the opposite side of the canyon from the railroad. It is paved from Skagway to the junction with the Alaska Highway near Whitehorse. The three-hour drive gives you much the same scenery viewed on the railroad: **Skagway River Gorge, Pitchfork Falls, White Pass Summit** (3,290 feet/1,000 meters), and the beautiful lake country of British Columbia and the Yukon.

The center of activity in Skagway is along **Broadway Street** in the Historic District, where over 60 gold-rush era buildings still stand. After its creation in 1977, the Klondike Gold Rush National Historical Park took over ownership of many of these buildings and has since spent millions of dollars in their restoration. Private restoration has also taken place, breathing life into old structures that surely would have fallen down in time. Occupying the old buildings are curio shops, restaurants, saloons, hotels, art galleries, ice cream parlors, and other businesses creating a carnival-like atmosphere in a gold rush setting.

It always helps to know what you're seeing, and Skagway has a number of options for the interpretive traveller. Cheapest among then is the free walking tour of the Historic District given by the National Park Service. The tours are conducted three times a day and begin at the Visitors Center in the restored WP & YR depot building. More mobile and interesting tours of the district are given by pony-pulling hacks, which also take you to the **Trail of '98 Museum, Reid Falls** and the **Gold Rush Cemetery**, where Soapy Smith is buried.

Skaguay in the Days of '98, recreates the Soapy Smith tragedy nightly at the **Eagles Hall**. This one-hour historical drama follows an hour of live ragtime music and gambling. The dealers are cast members and the money is phony, and some of the tables date back to the gold rush. The show's popularity has kept it going since 1925, and residents affectionately refer to it as "the longest running show on Broadway."

If you're in reasonably fit, own a

A marching band, Skagway style.

backpack, and have time, hiking the **Chilkoot Trail** is the most adventurous option for tracing the route of the gold seekers. Managed by the park services of the U.S. and Canada, the trail extends 33 miles (53 km) from old Dyea to Lake Bennett, British Columbia. Most hikers allow three to five days to fully capture the scenery and explore the thousands of gold rush relics left behind during the stampede. As you approach the base of the **Chilkoot Pass** and look up at the steps carved in the snow by the day's hikers, one can't help but visualize what passed there before. Fortunately, it was captured in photographs and on paper.

Edwin Tappan Adney recorded the scene for *Harper's Weekly* in September, 1897: "Look more closely. The eye catches movement. There is a continuous moving train; they are perceptible only by their movement, just as ants are. The moving train is zigzagging across the towering face of the precipice, up, up into the sky, even at the very top. See! they are going against the sky! They are human beings, but never did men look so small."

Alaska's Fun City

Skagway has the reputation for being a party town, especially in summer. Ask any Yukoner who bolts for the coast on weekends. Skagway people are fun-loving and seem to bask in the attention, but by the time fall rolls in, they are ready for the quiet months ahead.

The best weather is in spring. Skies are clear, the sun is hot, and the snow's still deep on White Pass until mid-May. Cross country skiers and snow-mobilers drive to the top of the highway, jump on their gear and go all day. Later in the summer after the snow has melted, hundreds of small ponds form on the moon-like terrain. On hot days, the ponds warm up to about 80 degrees F (27°C)–the next best thing to a hot tub! Other good picnic spots are at Dyea; among the ruins there, **Yakutania Point, Lower Dewey Lake**, and **Pullen Creek Park**, where pink and silver salmon run in August and September.

Historic train.

98

When the fish aren't biting, Skagway's saloons are hopping, especially on days when the larger cruise ships are in town. Jazz musicians off the boats frequently jump ship in Skagway for a few hours to attend jam sessions. They say it's the only day of the cruise that they don't have to play "old folks music." If business is good, the bars stay open till 5 a.m., the official closing time.

Visitors are welcome to join several official town-wide parties in Skagway throughout the summer. Featured in May is the *Gold Rush Stampede*, with gambling night, a softball competition, and a candlelight parade. Late June's *Summer Solstice Party* is an all-night event, with band performing in parks.

A traditional gold-rush style Independence Day is celebrated on July 4th, complete with parades, races and contests of all kinds. Four days later, on July 8th is *Soapy Smith's Wake*, a grave yard party and champagne toast to Skagway's notorious con-man.

The "Hugs and Kisses" Road Run in August is open to all who want to run the 10 miles from Dyea to Skagway. Everyone who finishes gets a hug and kiss from costumed guys and gals.

The party to end all parties is a *Street Gala* held in September. A relatively new tradition, these festivities are held on blocked-off Broadway complete with buggy rides and roving musicians.

Skagway's award-winning Bigger Hammer Marching Band, who won grand prizes in four southeast Alaska State Fairs is usually present. Dressed to fit the day and theme, this kazoo-blowing band of Skagway's least respected civic leaders will parody anything remotely political that is blowing in the wind, be it rail closures or the nuclear age. Bigger Hammer's motto is: "In Skagway, we take humor seriously."

A more direct route to the interior of Alaska from the panhandle is through **Haines**, an hour south on the ferry from Skagway. Haines is a community rich in Tlingit Indian culture and is best known for its majestic mountain scenery, king and sockeye salmon fishing, native art and dance, and the newly created **Chilkat Balk Eagle Preserve**.

The Haines Highway follows the Chilkat River, a rich stream that stays ice-free in late fall and early winter, supporting salmon runs and the world's largest concentration of bald eagles. November and December are the best months to view eagles in the Haines area. Over 3,000 bald eagles congregate in the area, feeding off the spawned-out salmon in the river.

Since the opening of the Klondike Highway out of Skagway, more and more travellers have opted to drive the "Golden Horseshoe" route to include both Haines and Skagway on their way to or from the Interior. Driving up the Alaska Highway from the south, you can cut off to Skagway on the Klondike, put your car on the ferry for the short ride to Haines, and then proceed north over the Chilkoot Pass till you meet the Alaska Highway again at Haines Junction. Drivers see Haines first, and Skagway second, if they choose this route on the way south. Either way, the two towns and the two mountain passes are worth seeing in one trip.

Rugged Alaskan in saloon-girl garb, complete with parasol.

PRINCE WILLIAM SOUND

Few slide shows present pictures of rain in **Prince William Sound**. Rather, viewers see sunshine flickering in water cascading from the flukes of a breaching humpback whale. Kayakers wearing T-shirts are silhouetted in front of a brilliant white glacier. Sea otters float atop their glossy reflections and munch on Dungeness crab they have plucked from the ocean floor.

But all those pictures are taken on clear days which many people consider mythical. The cameras are brought out during the times visitors call Prince William Sound a backcountry heaven.

While some may regard a slide show which depicts sunny scene as meteorologically deceptive, it would be similarly inaccurate, in the wake of the 1989 *Exxon Valdez* oil spill, to limit a presentation on Prince William Sound to pictures of oil-stained beaches, coated sea birds and crews of cleanup workers scouring blackened rocks.

The fact is, most tourists will be hard-pressed to observe any of the 10.8 million gallons of crude which spilled when the tanker ran aground on Bligh Reef between the port cities of Valdez and Cordova in the north end of the sound, says Gary Kranenburg, executive director of the Valdez Convention and Visitors Bureau.

Kranenburg, along with U.S. Coast Guard authorities who supervised the massive cleanup operation immediately after the disaster and during the following summer, report that only remote stretches not commonly visited by tourists still bear signs of the sticky oil which washed along more than 1,100 miles of Alaskan shoreline.

Those willing to charter boats or floatplanes to isolated locations – primarily the Barren Islands between the Kenai Peninsula and Kodiak Island, hundreds of miles southwest of Cordova – no doubt would be able to return with photographic evidence of the disaster. But most visitors to Prince William Sound will come back with pictures of the aformentioned kayakers in T-shirts, and even sea otters and whales.

And each year those pictures, along with stories told by the travellers who took them, draw more people to see the sound's wonderful natural displays of animals, ice, forest and mountains.

Yet rain is the rule in this watery wild country southeast of Anchorage, where coastal peaks form a cloud-stopping arc from Whittier to Cordova. Here, precipitation is measured in feet, not inches. Much of that moisture, driven into the sound by the Gulf of Alaska's wicked winter storms, pours onto maritime rain forests. Even more precipitation falls as snow and adds substance to the sound's numerous glaciers. Come summer the rain hardly falls. Then moisture, too thick to be called fog, hangs between gray-green glassy salt water and clouds the color of concrete.

Often enough the clouds seem as durable as concrete, apparently anchored in place by gray, rocky peaks and black, green and gray forests of Sitka spruce and western hemlock. Horizons close in and the spirit of the sound plays games with visitors. Newcomers camping in this cloud-shrouded funereal world often feel tension build. Many get depressed and sometimes desperate too.

But frequent visitors aren't particularly bothered by the rain. They overcome the weather by laughing a lot. They recognize that rain accounts for much of the sound's mystique, and they relish telling weather stories.

"I've never had a problem getting wet out there," says Kelley Weaverling, a bearded, gangly kayaking guide. "On the other hand, I've had some real problems getting dry."

During one "good weather" summer in the sound, Weaverling took a group through 13 consecutive rainy days. He prides himself that he accomplished the task without having anyone become violent from a build-up of stress. He did it – and kept dry, too – with the help of an umbrella.

"Rough, tough woodsmen might laugh at the idea of carrying an umbrella," Weaverling says, "well, let 'em.

Left, flukes of a humpback whale.

Laughter's good for the soul."

When the umbrella wasn't keeping rain off his head, it was engaged in a Charlie Chaplin routine he'd perfected over many years of practice.

Weaverling also is one of the few who, under the protection of his umbrella, has taken pictures in the rain.

But it was a geologist new to the sound, a woodsman who'd never carried an umbrella, who one day conveyed the eerie quality that cloudy, rainy weather imparts to the region. The geologist, Ben Porterfield, and a partner were drinking beer at the Sportsman's Inn in Whittier. They couldn't very well work. Clouds boiled across the glaciated mountains that shoulder up to the community's concrete buildings. Wind grabbed waterfalls pouring off invisible ice sheets and torqued them into horizontal jets of spray.

Porterfield told a story about weather and bears. One day he and his partner were working their way down Fish Creek drainage, taking sediment samples from the stream for study by the government. The high overcast was standard cement as they descended through spongy alpine tundra. But the clouds dropped with them as they approached brush line, where they faced dense tangles of alder interwined with thorny devil's club.

Down a Brown Bear's Trail

The geologists' mood plummeted. They became only a little happier when they found a trail packed by brown bears, the large grizzlies of Alaska's southerly coasts. The trail obviously was well used by brownies commuting to the steam's lower reaches for a steady supply of spawning chum salmon. Still, it was a route through the thickets.

The first paw prints the geologists saw were big as a magazine cover but full of rain water – at least several hours old. The two talked loudly and sang songs. They weren't about to vacate the trail, but they didn't want to interfere

Forest Service cabin in remote Prince William Sound.

with any fellow travellers, either.

A bit farther down they came across a pile of fresh, rank scat. At that point, Ben checked his shotgun. His partner slipped the government-issue .44 magnum from its shoulder holster. The two talked more and sang louder.

The brush finally gave way to hemlock forest. Tall trees formed a canopy over an open carpet of light-green moss that completely covered the ground. Moss covered fallen rotting trees, and even many of the live trees. It hung in tendrils from branches, and it dripped.

Safe for the steady drone of stream, the forest was silent. Only the bear trail wasn't covered with moss. It was almost a trench of slick, soft soil. And on the trail they saw urine steaming in a foot-print that dwarfed the others. The claw marks were well-defined points far in front of the imprint of the pad.

Around a bend and across a moss-covered deadfall, 50 feet above the stream, a fresh salmon lay on the trail. The strong smell of dead fish came from a clump of nearby trees. Brown bears smell like dead fish when they gorge on salmon. Now, the geologists didn't say anything. Porterfield and his partner stood and held their guns like a couple of cowboys expecting a bandit. But the bandit never showed.

The two tip-toed to the stream. Porterfield stood guard while his partner collected a final handful of gravel. Then they waited in a sopping meadow for their helicopter to arrive.

Only after the geologists were listed away did they feel silly about the melodrama. It was the gloom, Porterfield says, the Twilight Zone atmosphere of the forest, that got to them as much as the perceived threat of a bear attack.

So too figures Lynn Mitchell, a district ranger for the U.S. Forest Service, the agency that manages much of the land throughout the sound.

"The bears are very real, but they tend to leave people alone, so long as you don't startle them or bother them," Mitchell says. "It's a rich environment. The bears have plenty to eat without going after campers. Just be sure they don't get at YOUR food."

Visitors can savor the atmosphere of the sound simply by crossing it on a ferry or tour boat. Passengers travelling by boat between Whittier and Valdez sometimes see bears and occasionally, goats balanced on high cliffs. Humpback and killer whales frequent the route, and Dall porpoises surf the bow wake. Seal lions haul out on rocks, and harbor seals rest on chunks of ice that drift with the wind and tide away from the glaciers.

It's a stop at one particular glacier, the Columbia, that passengers remember most about their boat trips.

Columbia Glacier is the largest among 20 that drop from the Chugach Mountains into the northerly fjords of Prince William Sound.

Fortunately, the enormous sheet of ice is situated almost due north of the spill site, upwind and upstream, so none of the black oil fouled the glacier's dazzling blue-white face. Fed each year by enough snow to bury a five-story building, Columbia Glacier covers an

A secluded inlet, reachable only by floatplane.

area the size of Los Angeles. It flows more than 40 miles (64 km) from the mountains to Columbia Bay, where its four-mile-wide (6.4-km) face daily drops hundreds of thousands of tons of ice into the sound.

The glacier's output of ice increased in 1983, when it began a rapid retreat. Now, glaciologists estimate that 50 cubic miles (210 cu km) of icebergs could be released during the next half century.

So much ice has filled the bay in recent years that boats can't approach the glacier as closely as they could in the past, when passengers routinely were provided a close-up view of massive flakes peeling from the 300-foot-high (90-meter) wall.

When the flakes come down, the harbor seals resting on bergs in the bay are rocked by the resulting swells. They don't even look up. Meanwhile, gulls and other birds swarm around the glacier face; the plunging ice has stirred the seafood-rich water, bringing shrimp and other delicacies to the surface for their consumption. Thus, the glaciers are a part of the life cycles of Prince William Sound.

Earthquakes and Tidal Waves

The land is also shaped by forces other than slow-moving glaciers. Earthquakes cause sudden, dramatic changes in the lay of the country. On March 27, 1964 – Good Friday – bedrock shifted just west of Columbia Glacier. The shock waves, registering between 8.4 and 8.6 on the Richter Scale, were the most intense ever recorded on North America. In just a few minutes, extensive new beach lines emerged as the land rose. The most dramatic geological adjustment occurred at the south end of **Montague Island**, which tilted upward 38 feet (11.5 meters).

But most damage was done by undersea landslides that generated enormous tidal waves. **Valdez**, to the east of the earthquake epicenter, was destroyed,

Worthington Glacier, near Valdez.

and had to be rebuilt at a different site.

Whittier, to the southwest, was hit by three successive waves, one of which crested at 104 feet (32 meters). A lumber mill was demolished and 13 people were killed, but the port was left relatively undamaged.

The worst human disaster was at **Chenega**, a village of 80 on an island south of Whittier near the western edge of the sound. A wave enveloped all the buildings but the school and one house, and swept away 23 residents. Only recently have the survivors and their offspring returned to rebuild.

Many hard rock and placer claims are buried under rock slides and fast-growing alder and hemlock. In a few places, like the Beatson mine on **Latouche Island**, piles of tailings stand out, along with a few unstable and old buildings, rust-red lengths of steel pipe and pumps, and stripped trucks whose tires have been eaten by porcupines.

The sound is still rich in copper and gold, molybdenum, tungsten and silver. However, low mineral prices mean those resources will be left in the ground for at least the next decade, according to executives with Chugach Alaska Corporation, a major private land owner in the Prince William Sound basin.

Miners initially came to the sound at the turn of the century to reach Valdez. From there they intended to take the Richardson Trail to Interior Alaska's gold fields.

The spirit of the sound is powerful indeed. But perhaps it isn't as powerful as the human spirit. A story is told of a prospector who fell into a crevasse while crossing **Blackstone Glacier** northwest of Whittier. Wedged between the tapering walls, he felt the ice sap his body heat. The prospector realized his partners couldn't rescue him. He called up to them and asked that, some day, they retrieve his gold poke and send it to his wife.

Like Valdez, **Cordova** also became a transportation center shortly after the turn of the century. But there, the important mineral was copper. The deposit, the richest in the world, was at **Kennicott**, 200 miles (320 km) up the Copper

and Chitina rivers, and transportation was by rail.

Cordova, still an attractive community of brightly painted, woodframed houses, was turned into a railroad town with the arrival of a shipload of men and equipment April 1, 1906. The railroad was the brainchild of Michael J. Heney, an engineer who pushed the White Pass & Yukon Railway through the Wrangell-Saint Elias Range.

Heney was too well-known for anyone to say it out loud, but quite a few folks considered him an April Fool.

Yet for the next half decade, Cordova was the operations center for the the the Copper River & Northwestern Railway construction project. The CR&NW was an undertaking which, along with the oil pipeline, ranks among the greatest engineering achievements in the history of the world.

Heney had to contend with temperatures of minus 60° F (-50° C), wind that knocked boxcars off the tracks, drifting snow that buried locomotives, rampag-

ing floods, and a fast copper River current that sent massive icebergs crashing into footings of a crucial bridge.

On April 8, 1911, the first train returned to Cordova with ore from the Kennicott mines. The ore was almost pure copper, and it made the fortunes of the railroad builders. The unfortunate Heney, though, had died of exhaustion a year before the railroad's actual completion. By the mid-1930s the price of copper had dropped drastically and the high-grade ores had been mine. In 1938 the railroad was abandoned.

Fashionable Fur

The mineral industry isn't the only one that has declined. Fur harvesting also disappeared early in the century. Foxes, richly fed on salmon, were "farmed" for great profit on various islands in the sound until the fashion industry shifted away from those pelts.

Sea otters, whose thick, warm fur originally attracted Russian and American colonists to Prince William Sound, were hunted to the brink of extinction.

Now protected by law, those animals had proliferated until thousands perished in the spill. Cleanup workers collected the bodies of 1,016 sea otters and figure at least that many bodies disappeared at sea.

While wildlife officials have reported seeing the animals back in the sound in 1990, the long-term consequences on the sea otter population are unknown. And while commercial fishing remains the major source of income for the 5,000 people who live along the sound, the spill has contaminated numerous shellfish beds containing such native delicacies as the Alaskan king crab. State health authorities have advised against eating shellfish from polluted areas but following extensive tests report there is no evident danger in consuming finfish.

Now, however, the sound's most promising resources are its wilderness and its visitors. Many visitors moor their boats in Prince William Sound's

Harbor seals at the Columbia Glacier.

coves and sleep on board. Kayakers and others often pitch tents on beaches, where they can avoid boggy ground.

The increase in requests for cabin-use permits is one sign of a growing number of visitors to the sound, according to the Forest Service. And after Rex Beach documented construction of the Copper River & Northwestern Railway in his bestseller *The Iron Trail*, Cordova and its nearby glaciers became one of the greatest visitor attractions in Alaska.

Whittier has recently developed into an important visitor point. Historically, the site of that community was a resting place for Native and Russian traders portaging their wares between the Sound and Cook Inlet. Later, gold miners and mail carriers crossed Portage Pass to reach the Iditarod Trail, which led to Alaska's far-west gold fields. But Whittier didn't really develop until World War II, when the Army decided to use its ice-free harbor for a strategic fuel dump. Troops blasted two tunnels through the Chugach Mountains to connect Whittier with the Alaska Railroad depot at Portage.

A large marina and residential area are being planned for **Shotgun Cove**, an isolated area east of Whittier. Farther out, near Columbia Glacier, Chugach Alaska Corporation is considering a lodge and other facilities to serve boaters and cruise ship passengers.

But plans for those developments were little more than concepts in early 1985. George Cannelos, Vice President of tourism for Chugach Alaska, said the corporation wants a firm understanding of the visitor market before committing itself to a particular design.

That's a philosophy reiterated by Forest Service Officials and by the Alaska Division of Parks, which has planned a for-now undeveloped series of parks on its land throughout Prince William Sound.

Whatever developments come about as a result of recreational visitors, it's a sure bet they'll be designed to keep rain off and spirits high.

KODIAK, THE CITY AND THE ISLAND

A shift of the wind can change **Kodiak Island** from a desolate, windswept, rain-pounded rock isolated from the rest of the world by fog to a shimmering emerald of grass, spruce trees and snow-capped mountains glowing pink in the sunrise. But while the winds may shift, they remain predominantly from the north, which along with the tide carried oil spilled from the *Exxon Valdez* in Prince William Sound to Kodiak's northeast-ern shores.

Eighteen months after the disaster, most of the visible oil on Kodiak has been either removed by cleanup crews hired by Exxon or scoured by the same buffetung wind and waves which brought it there.

Biologists fear that much of the oil remains saturated in the intertidal zone, which poses a more insidious long-term threat to wildlife and marine life because for many species this is where the food chain starts. Both the island itself and the city of Kodiak are places whose characters change with the weather, the seasons and the observer.

A popular T-shirt carries the slogan "Kodiak – It's not the end of the world but you can see it from here." At first glance the city of **Kodiak** might seem to be somewhere near world's end, a town of 8,000 people perched precariously on a small ledge of land between ocean swells and mountains. A look into Kodiak's economy reveals a major fishing port (one of the top three in the United States) and the center of Alaska's developing whitefish industry. Kodiak is home to a multimillion dollar fishing fleet which ranges from the Pacific Northwest to Norton Sound.

Like the waves which bring the sea's debris to Kodiak's shores, 200 years of recorded history have swept across Kodiak in waves, each wave leaving traces of its passing. Artifacts of the indigenous Koniag culture surface near remnants of the Russian period or World War II bunkers, derelict whaling stations, collapsing herring rendering plants, or fish processing facilities.

Just under the top soil is a layer of volcanic ash which covered the town in 1912 and still drifts about leaving a coating of fine, white dust. White spruce tree skeletons guard the salt marshes, monuments to the land subsidence which occurred during the 1964 earthquake and tidal wave.

At the Kodiak International Airport, Lear jets and DC-3s sit on one side of the fence. On the other side bears and foxes roam, while eagles ride the wind.

In restaurants residents talk of trips to the Orient to negotiate fish or timber sales, riding out storms at sea and running traplines for fox and otter. Many residents live simultaneously in the world of international business and subsistence hunting and fishing.

From the air Kodiak Island seems an empty wilderness, 3,588 sq miles (9,293 sq km) of rugged mountains deeply indented by bays. The north half of the island is covered with spruce trees, the south half with grass.

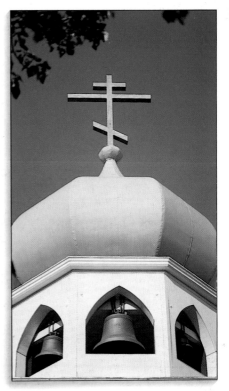

Preceding pages; Steller sea lions, Kenai Fjords. Left, brown bear in the midst of a salmon run. Right, Russian church, Kodiak.

Foresters say the spruce forest is advancing down Kodiak Island at the rate of one mile a century.

Landing in Kodiak can be an adventure. As the jet approaches the airport, it drops lower and lower over the water until its landing gear seems to skim the waves. Just beyond where the runway seems to emerge from the water the plane sets down. At the other end of the runway sits **Barometer Mountain**, so called because the peak is only visible in good weather.

"The scariest landing I ever made in Kodiak" or "Is the approach into Kodiak more frightening than the approach into Juneau" is cocktail party talk.

The airport is about five miles from Kodiak city. Spruce trees cast shadows across the highway to town, then the road wends its way in sharp turns around Pillar Mountain. In the winter bald eagles, sometimes as many as 10 to a tree, perch in cottonwoods above the highway. The road then dips down and slips into Kodiak's back door.

The sea is Kodiak's front yard. Fifteen fish processing plants line the city's waterfront. Their names and signs, "We buy halibut" or "Herring wanted," face the sea, visible to passing fishing vessels. Flocks of sea birds bob on the swells and in the spring, bald eagles wheel overhead. The salt-tanged smell of fish announces that this is Kodiak, a fishing port producing fish and shellfish for markets around the world. The blue onion dome of the Holy Resurrection Orthodox Church announces that this is Kodiak, the first Russian settlement in Alaska.

The Russian Legacy

Drawn by his search for sea otter pelts, Grigor Ivanvich Shelikof arrived in Three Saints Bay on the southeast corner of Kodiak Island in 1784 with two ships, the *Three Saints* and the *St. Simon*. A third ship, the *St. Michael*, left Russia under Shelikof's command, but overwintered near Unalaska Island so

Early tribes trading for oil.

TUSKI AND MAHLEMUTS TRADING FOR OIL.

the crew could repair the vessel. When the *St. Michael* sailed from Unalaska it hit a reef and sank.

The indigenous Koniag did not welcome Shelikof, but proceeded to harass the Russian party. Shelikof, who needed the Koniags to hunt sea otters, responded with what today would be considered appalling force.

"They said Shelikohov (sic) loaded two bidarkas (skin boats) with his people…and with the armed band murdered about 500 of these speechless people; if we also count those who ran in fear to their bidarkas and trying to escape, stampeded and drowned each other, the number will exceed 500. Many men and women were taken as prisoners of war. By order of Mr. Shelekohov, the men were led to the tundra and speared, the remaining women and children, about 600 altogether, he took with him to the harbor and kept them for three weeks. The husbands who succeeded in escaping the murder began to come. Shelekohov

"City of the Wild Ram," a drama performed in Kodiak.

returned their wives to them, but he retained one child from each family as hostage," wrote Ival Peel, acting governor-general of Irkutsak and Kolyvan, to the Russian ruling senate in 1789.

Having established his authority on Kodiak Island, Shelikof founded the first Russian settlement in Alaska on **Three Saints Bay**, built a school to teach the Natives to read and write Russian, and introduced the Russian Orthodox religion.

In 1791 Alexander Adrevich Baranof arrived at Three Saints Bay to take over leadership of the Russian settlement. He moved the colony to the northeast end of the island where timber was available. The location was also closer to the resources of Cook Inlet and Prince William Sound. The site chosen by Baranof is now the city of Kodiak.

Russian members of the colony took Koniag wives and started family lines whose names still continue – Panamaroff, Pestrikoff, Kvasnikoff, Chichenoff…names which now represent

clans and families. Russian heritage in the city of Kodiak is also found on its street signs: Baranof, Rezanoff, Shelikof, Purtov and Delarof.

In August, residents recall their Russian heritage with an outdoor pageant, *The Cry of the Wild Ram*, written by Alaskan Frank Brink. The audience sit on wooden benches in Frank Brink Theater, a natural outdoor amphitheater. As the sun sets in Monashka Bay, the tale of one man's effort to turn a wilderness into a community unfolds – a story of determination, adversity, treachery and love, complete with pyrotechnics and local residents playing the characters. August nights are cool. Viewers usually take a thermos of hot coffee, sandwiches, cushions and warm clothing or blankets.

Much of the rich culture of the Koniags was absorbed by the Russian culture and can only be guessed at through artifacts and the diaries of the early Russian settlers. The **Baranof Museum** across from the ferry dock in downtown Kodiak, contains displays of Koniag artifacts and clothing as well as items from the Russian and early American periods. The small, homelike museum is located in the **Erskine House**, designated a National Historic Landmark in 1962.

A facsimile Russian well was recently constructed near the **Shelikof Lodge** on the site of one of the wells used during the Russian era. Recently archaeologists unearthed a Russian brick kiln. The bricks which formed the kiln arches were moved to the Baranof Museum for eventual reconstruction on the museum grounds.

When the United States purchased Alaska from Imperial Russia, the Russian citizens left, but the Russian Orthodox church remained. The two blue onion domes of the **Holy Resurrection Church** are the town's most outstanding landmarks. The church is still a significant part of Kodiak's religious community, and the predominant religion in the six villages in the Island area.

A colorful mural celebrates the Alaska bear.

In 1974 the **St. Herman Orthodox Theological Seminary** was relocated to Kodiak. (The seminary's white buildings stand near the church.) Father Herman was canonized in Kodiak in 1970, the first Orthodox canonization to take place on American soil. Saint Herman arrived in Kodiak in 1794 and settled on **Spruce Island**, when he established a school and became renowned as an ascetic and miracle worker. The Russian Orthodox faithful make an annual pilgrimage to his shrine on the island.

The Russian Orthodox Church follows the Julian calendar, making Kodiak a town of two Christmases, December 25 and January 7, and two New Years, January 1 and January 14.

Treasures of the Holy Resurrection Orthodox Church include many brilliantly colored icons. Visitors are welcome to attend services in the church.

During World War II, Kodiak served as a major supply center for the Aleutian campaign. Military personnel and construction workers changed the city from a fishing village of 500 residents to a boom town of 4,000 people with another 20,000 in nearby areas. The U.S. Navy built a major base on the site, which is now used as a U.S. Coast Guard facility. Residents who lived in Kodiak during the war tell tales of sailors on liberty, submarine nets stretched across the Kodiak-Near Island channel, the difficulty of obtaining fishing supplies. Today all that remains of those years are silent, moss-covered bunkers.

Fort Abercrombie, a state park with limited camping facilities four miles (6 ½ km) from the city of Kodiak, is dedicated to the memory of World War II. A large bunker and the remains of gun implacements overlook the sea from a cliff. Other bunkers can be found by walking through an alpine meadow and along the cliff edge.

There are also bunkers on **Pillar Mountain** behind the city. Hikers working their way through the alders and spruce forests along the tops of

Picking salmonberries, Kodiak Island.

shale cliffs often find other bunkers.

Kodiak's U.S. Coast Guard facility is the largest in the United States. Its cutters and C-130 airplanes keep track of the foreign fishing fleets working off the coast. For locals, the Coast Guard facility is the home of "angels" who arrive in helicopters to pluck men off their sinking vessels or search the coastline for survivors of a marine tragedy.

Natural events have left indelible marks on Kodiak Island. Twice in the 20th Century the landscape on the island has been altered, first by a volcanic ash fall in 1912 and again in 1964 by an earthquake and tidal wave.

Humus has covered the ash that fell June 6, 1912, when Mount Katmai on the Alaska Peninsula exploded, but where roads have cut into the mountains the white layer of volcanic ash is visible under the soil's surface. Kodiak residents may exaggerate, but they say the volcanic ash still seeps in through every crack. In places the ash from Mount Katmai's 1912 eruption drifted several feet deep. Small lakes vanished. Wildlife died, and much natural vegetation was destroyed. Five hundred residents were evacuated on the revenue cutter *Manning*, and the town choked by ash.

The March 27, 1964, earthquake which devastated much of central Alaska also set off a tidal wave which swept into the city of Kodiak and destroyed the downtown buildings, canneries and docks.

Many Kodiak residents fled up Pillar Mountain and watched helplessly while the sea ran out, leaving the harbor dry, and then rolled back in across the land. Those who didn't reach high ground were swept away.

Although a few fishermen managed to take their boats to sea – and safety – before the tidal wave hit, boats left in the harbor were pushed into town by the wave. The 100-ton power scow *Selief* ended up a half mile inland, still with 3,000 king crab in its hold. Along the shore the land and seabed dropped or subsided by as much as five feet (1 ½ Fossil Beach.

meters). Forested areas turned into salt water marshes, now identifiable by the still standing skeletal trees.

After the tidal wave, most of downtown Kodiak was redesigned and rebuilt. Fish processing companies sent in floating processing plants to can king crab and salmon until new plants could be built. Old-timers play their own version of trivia games, pointing out where roads used to be and where buildings stood "before the tidal wave."

Residents who lived through the tidal wave and stayed to rebuild the town have a special bond formed during the difficult post-tidal-wave years. Though the tidal wave was a tragedy, it left behind a feeling of unity which still pervades the community.

A Thriving Fishing Industry

Kodiak's economic dependence on the sea has never changed, but the species of fish and shellfish on which the town's economy is based has changed repeatedly. The Russians built Kodiak as a base for harvesting sea otters; salmon and herring fisheries have Kodiak an economic base after the sea otter trade died out.

Catches of both these fish have dropped precipitously in Kodiak after the spill, but the exact extent of the losses remains the subject of considerable debate, reports Chuck Meacham, fisheries program manager for the Alaska Department of Fish and Game.

Meacham said lawsuits filed by fishing interests against Exxon challenge the oil companies claims minimizing losses.

Kodiak is home to one of Alaska's three principal fishing ports affected by the spill, the others being Prince William Sound and Cook Inlet.

Meacham said the 1990 harvest of fish has been mixed. "There was an all-time record harvest of pink salmon, between 43 million and 45 million, in Prince William Sound," he said. Meacham noted that most of those fish,

Left, the remote Pribilof Islands. Right, bald eagles in Kodiak.

though, were of hatchery origin, with catches of wild salmon being "very weak."

The proliferation of hatchery salmon resulted from a record release of fish before the spill, so it wasn't something planned by the department to counter anticipated losses, he said. "It was just a fortuitous situation," Meacham said. But while Prince William Sound was reporting bountiful catches, the other two prime fishing areas showed major losses, he said.

"In Lower Cook Inlet there were very dismal returns, and in the Kodiak there were also poor returns," Meacham said.

Meacham also echoed the comments of state tourism officials, that the casual visitor to Alaska would not be aware of the spill.

What's more, "There are very few closed areas (to fishing) associated with the spill," he said.

The city of Kodiak provides moorage and services to more than 2,000 fishing boats a year. Fishermen deliver up to $100 million worth of fish and shellfish annually. Small skiffs, medium-sized salmon seiners, big shrimp trawlers, crab boats and 100-foot-plus midwater draggers steadily steam in and out of the harbor bringing back king crab, snow crab, Dungeness crab, shrimp, red salmon, pink salmon, chum salmon, silver salmon, herring, halibut, black cod, Pacific cod, pollock, flounders and flat fish.

Ask a Kodiak resident what season it is and, if it is summer, he's likely to answer, "Salmon season." Fall is king crab season; winter is season of the Tanner crab, marketed as snow crab. Spring is herring season, and halibut and black cod are harvested in spring and summer. Whitefish species are harvested most of the year.

Kodiak's fishermen proudly call themselves diversified fishermen – fishermen who work year round, switching from fishery to fishery as the seasons change. Between seasons the waterfront throbs with activity. Crane trucks and flatbeds move 500-pound steel crab pots from storage to the boat and back to storage. In spring, herring seines and gillnets are stretched out on the docks where crew men with shuttles can attach float and lead lines.

A truck goes by loaded with fluorescent pink balloons? No, crab buoys that mark where a baited crab pot has been dropped to the sea floor, baited to attract crabs into its funnel-shaped opening. The buoy is attached to the pot by a line long enough to reach the surface.

Visitors are welcome to wander down the ramp behind the **Harbormaster Building** and walk along the floats in **St. Paul Harbor**. Across the channel is **St. Herman Harbor**, on **Near Island**. A bridge between Kodiak and Near Island was begun in 1983, but until the bridge is complete, access to St. Herman Harbor is via the free shuttle ferry. Directions to the shuttle ferry can be obtained from the harbormasters office.

In St. Paul harbor there are two loading docks where skippers load gear onboard their boats – crab pots may swing at the ends of booms or seines may be lifted to the deck. Just before a fishing season it seems there are more boats in a hurry to load than dock space for loading. Fishing boats line the loading docks – the ferry dock, the city dock and the Sea-Land dock where a huge crane is used to lift Sea-Land vans off barges.

At any time a vessel may be sitting on the harbor grid, a sloped ramp. At high tide the skipper runs his boat up the ramp and when the tide goes out the vessels hull is exposed for painting or repairing. When visitors wander down the floats, skippers with time to talk may nod "hello" which is an invitation to stop and visit.

On processing-plant docks heavy cranes lift bathtub sized totes filled with fish or shellfish out of a vessel's fish holds. Forklifts carry the totes into the plants where machines peel or fillet or skin products for the cookers or freezers. The plants are not open to visitors. However, it is possible to watch a boat being unloaded by standing on the southwest corner of the ferry dock and looking across to the All Alaskan Seafoods dock. All Alaskan Seafoods oper-

Right, a sturdy beaver dam.

ates out of a World War II ship, *Star of Kodiak*, which was converted for fish processing and permanently run aground.

Visitors expect to come to a major fishing port and eat seafood. Although most of Kodiak's fresh seafood is in refrigerated vans waiting to be loaded onto barges for shipment, the local supermarkets offer fresh seafood in season and some restaurants include fresh seafood on the menu. Kodiak's fishing industry is geared to large volume production and sales, which has made it difficult for small, local buyers to establish a steady source of supply.

Like its fishing industry, Kodiak's population is diversified. Filipinos began coming to Kodiak to work in the processing plants in the 1970s, and stayed to establish a strong community. Japanese and Korean technicians are assigned to processing plants to oversee the preparation of products destined for their countries. The southern drawls of fishermen, who found Alaska a better place than the Gulf of Mexico, mix with the accents of Oregon and Washington, Maine and Massachusetts.

Touring Kodiak Island

The populated portion of Kodiak Island is confined to the road system, 55 miles (90 km) of road around five coastal villages on the island. Visiting a village is rather like visiting a private home and should be done only after prior arrangements are made through the village tribal council. The rest of the island remains a mountainous wilderness belonging to bears and foxes, rabbits and birds, muskrats and otters. Two-thirds of Kodiak Island is a national wildlife refuge.

Most visitors find all the wilderness they want along the road system. It takes about an hour to drive to road's end at Fossil Beach. The road heads out of town past the **Buskin River** where the headquarters for the Kodiak National Wildlife Rufuge is located. (The headquarters includes a Visitor's Center.) The Buskin River is a popular sportfishing stream for salmon and steel-head. The road continues past the airport, the Coast Guard base, the fairgrounds, the community of **Bells Flats**, and then climbs headlands, curves around bays and crosses rivers.

In summer salmon can be seen jumping in the bays and swimming up the rivers. July and August are the best months for salmon watching or fishing. Occasionally sea lions come into the bays to feed on salmon. It is tempting to stop at every twist of the road and perfectly permissible to explore the beaches, walk in the forests, climb the mountains, and smell the wildflowers.

Eventually the road comes to a "T." To the left is the community of **Chiniak,** like Bell Flats a "suburb" of Kodiak. To the right the road travels through cattle country where Kodiak's ranchers run about 2,000 head of beef cattle. The cattle assume they have the right of way and drivers who assume otherwise may have that assumption corrected rather unpleasantly.

Ahead the ocean comes into view again by **Pasagshak**, a popular river for fishing silver and king salmon. The road continues past a sand-duned, surf-beaten bench and ends at **Fossil Beach** where fossil shells lay loosely in the clay and rocks. During the fall, gray whales pass Pasagshak and Fossil Beach on their migration to California from the Bering Sea.

Kodiak's bears are legendary – the largest grizzlies in the world. But the best place to see the Kodiak bear is at the airport, the First National Bank of Alaska or the Baranof Museum. Each has a stuffed bear behind glass where its teeth and claws can be leisurely contemplated. Wilderness hikers, however, must walk noisily through Kodiak's back country to reduce the chances of any confrontations with bears.

During the salmon season, bears appear along the streams and beaches. (During the fall of 1984 one unwelcome bear hung out around the school bus stop in Bells Flats.) As well as berries and salmon, the Kodiak bear enjoys calves, much tot he dismay of local ranchers, and deer, much to the dismay of hunters.

121

KENAI PENINSULA

It's often said that Alaska is too big to see and do in a single lifetime, let alone a single vacation. But there is one place where one can sample most of the best of Alaska, and do it in a few weeks. That place is the **Kenai Peninsula.**

The entire peninsula is within easy driving distance of Anchorage. In fact, people in the "Big Town" like to refer to the Kenai as their backyard. But please, don't use that line on the peninsula. That one phrase is more likely than any other to dry up local hospitality.

Assuming that critical *faux pas* is avoided, visitors will find that most peninsula residents are quite friendly. And they are the best source of information when it comes to getting the most out of your visit.

On a map of the state, the Kenai Peninsula looks deceptively small. It's worth remembering that the peninsula covers 9,050 sq miles (23,000 sq km), making it larger than the combined areas of Rhode Island, Connecticut and Delaware. It is bordered by Prince William Sound and the Gulf of Alaska on the east and Cook Inlet on the west, and attached to the mainland of southcentral Alaska by a narrow mountainous neck of land at the north.

The peninsula has a reputation as one of the most conservative areas of the state, and perhaps in the nation. A large part of that reputation is due to the political prominence of several members of the Libertarian party who live on the peninsula. (Libertarians believe that government should interfere as little as possible in people's lives, and many of their efforts are directed at preventing new programs from being created, or at dismantling those already in effect.)

Many of the people living on the peninsula moved there to go away from modern society, and the Libertarian philosophy seems especially appealing to them.

But the peninsula is also home to one of Alaska's more artistically inclined cities, Homer, and a thriving school system that's considered a standard-maker for the nation. For every development-minded resident, you'll find another who belongs to an environmental group. Some belong to both camps, which is part of what makes the peninsula a lively place.

The peninsula's history is also one of many contrasts. Kenai, the largest city, is also its oldest, founded by Russian priests in the late 1700s.

Kenai's next door neighbor, Soldotna, is number two in size, but is a relative newcomer in terms of its age – it was founded by homsteaders after World War II.

Seward, founded in 1903, was for years the leading port city of Alaska. It was eventually eclipsed in that role by Anchorage, and the 1964 earthquake devastated the economy. Twenty years later, it began to regain its financial legs and is once again a thriving port.

The peninsula was originally home to Denai'na Indians, a branch of the Athabascan family, and to Eskimos. Their descendents still live here, mostly in small, remote villages, and today they account for less than 10 percent of the borough's population. Western ways have long since replaced those of the Natives; they speak, dress and act like their white neighbors, donning their traditional dress and customs only on special occasions.

The Russians were the first whites to establish permanent communities on the peninsula. From their base on Kodiak Island, they sent out missionaries to found churches all along the eastern shore of Cook Inlet. The town of Kenai began as a Russian settlement in 1791. Other Russian-founded communities include Seldovia, which also dates to the 18th Century, and Ninilchik, founded in the early 1800s. Seward didn't yet exist as a town, but the area around Resurrection Bay was used as a shipbuilding site for the Russian America Company. Early Russian influence is still to be seen in the onion-domed churches, and heard in the Russian names of places and people.

Driving from Anchorage, one crosses into the peninsula just south of **Portage**,

Preceding pages, carved Eskimo figures overlook Kachemak Bay. Left, loading king crab at Homer.

a town which sat at the eastern end of Turnagain Arm, the thin finger of Cook Inlet that separates the peninsula from the Anchorage Bowl. Portage was destroyed by the 1964 earthquake, and only a few ruins remain. Almost immediately after passing the wreckage of Portage, one begins to climb through the Kenai Mountains, maximum elevation about 3,500 feet (1,050 meters).

Mileage along the Seward and Sterling highways is measured from Seward. At about Mile 70 is the summit of **Turnagain Pass**, elevation 988 feet (296 meters). It's a popular spot for winter recreation, primarily cross-country skiing and snowmachining.

The pass and much of the area along the highway, are part of the **Chugach National Forest**, Creeks, lakes and campgrounds are scattered through this area. The camps' opening dates vary with the weather, but generally they are open from Memorial Day through Labor Day. Fees are charged for camp use. Facilities often include tables, fire grates, tent pads and some type of water and sanitary facilities. While fires are usually allowed, one might want to consider carrying a small camp stove instead. If you do decide to light a fire, take care to extinguish it properly, and try to restore the area before moving on.

The Forest Service does operate some cabins on the peninsula, most of them located along the **Resurrection Trail**. Cabins must be reserved in advance. Most have bunk space for six and wood stoves. If a cabin is on a lake, it usually has a row boat and oars. Campers must bring their own food, utensils and sleeping bags.

The first town one encounters on the peninsula is **Hope**, a mining town of about 200, founded in the late 1890s. A trip to Hope requires a detour onto the Hope Cutoff, Mile 56 of the Seward Highway, but it's well worth the time.

Hope is the site of the oldest school house in Alaska – a red, one-room school still in active use. Other facilities in Hope include two stores, two cafes, a bar and one lodge.

An ideal site for pink salmon fishing, moose, caribou and black bear hunting,

Hope also is the head of the Resurrection Trail, one of the most popular hiking areas on the peninsula.

The trailhead is located at Mile 3.5 of the Resurrection Creek Road. The entire trail is 38 miles (60 km) long, and hikers emerge at **Schooner Bend**, Mile 52 on the Sterling Highway. An option is to turn off the Resurrection Trail at Mile 20 and take the 10-mile (16-km) **Devil's Pass Trail**, which emerges at Mile 39 of the Seward Highway.

Because of the route's popularity, it is wise to make cabin reservations well in advance. Reservations can be made up to six months in advance by writing to: United States Forest Service, 201 East 9th Ave., Suite 206, Anchorage, AK 99501. A payment of $15 per night is necessary to confirm reservations and hikers should provide alternative dates. Depending on the endurance and interests of the hikers, the Resurrection Trail takes two to four days to cover. Trout fishing is possible in the several lakes along the trail. It also provides spec-

Daring windsurfer is dwarted by a passing cruiseship.

124

tacular scenery for the photographer. People who don't want to hike the entire route can take a wonderful day hike, starting at either end.

The Seward Highway

Upon leaving Hope and rejoining the Seward Highway, the next decision for the automobile traveller is whether to go west or south at the Seward Junction at Mile 40. To the south lie Moose Pass and Seward; to the west Cooper Landing, Soldotna, Kenai and Homer.

Heading south, the first community is **Moose Pass**. This is a quiet village of less than 400 people. Residents enjoy hiking, fishing and biking – the town has one of Alaska's few bike trails. One of the highlights of the year is the annual Summer Festival, held to celebrate the solstice. The date changes from year to year, but is always held on the weekend with the most total hours of sunlight. Activities include a barbecue, carnival, softball games and an auction.

Iceboating on Kenai Lake.

To the south, a few miles outside of Seward, is Exit Glacier Road. The glacier is part of the **Kenai Fjords National Park**, and is the most easily accessible point of the **Harding Icefield**, a remnant of the Ice Age that caps a section of the Kenai Mountains.

The glacier itself lies about two miles past the car parking area at the end of the road; cross the bridge at the parking lot and head up the trail.

It's possible to hike to the face, although the approach up the loose moraine below the glacier can be tricky. The park staff schedules ranger-led hikes and campfire programs. It's also alright to hike in on your own. The elderly and handicapped also can visit the glacier via a shuttle on the vast Sunday of each summer month. (For further information, contact the park office in Seward at 907-224-3874.)

Turning back onto the highway after a visit to the glacier, one heads south into **Seward**. The city has about 2,000 residents, and there are many things to see and do. The city offers a full range of services, including a hospital.

One of the main attractions of the area is **Resurrection Bay**. Charter boats for sail or power excursions on the bay are available at the city harbor. Boats can be hired for sightseeing or fishing. The state ferry system also has a dock in Seward, offering trips to Kodiak and the Prince William Sound areas.

Visitor information is available at the Chamber of Commerce railroad car, located at Third and Jefferson streets. Other sites downtown include the city museum, located in the basement of city hall, and the town library. The museum is dedicated to Seward's past and features displays recreating rooms from early settlers' homes, old copies of newspapers, and equipment from ships which operated in the area. The library features a film of the 1964 earthquake in Seward. Hours at the museum and library vary with the season and day of week. Information on operating hours is available at the Chamber of Commerce.

Another interesting stop is the **Institute of Marine Science,** operated by the University of Alaska. Tours are available week day afternoons, except on holidays.

The highlight of the year in Seward is undoubtedly the annual Fourth of July celebration. This festival includes an all-town barbecue, a parade, acrobatic fliers, fireworks and the Mount Marathon foot race. Racers make a mad scramble up one side of a mountain located behind town, and then take a wild slide down the mountain's back.

Another special event is the annual Silver Salmon Derby, a week-long fishing contest that offers more prize money than any other fishing derby in Alaska. The derby begins on the second Saturday of August.

Driving north out of Seward, it's time to make the drive west on the Sterling Highway. Turn left at the junction; the road is marked as Alaska Route 1.

Heading west toward **Cooper Landing**, one enters an area that's been closed to Dall sheep hunting. As a result, it's a good area to spot them. Look for white specks high up on the peaks. A spotting scope or powerful zoom lens is a big help for this pastime.

Cooper Landing is a community of about 300, spread out along the headwaters of the Kenai River. Here the river is a beautiful turquoise color, and in the winter the open stretches of water are a prime feeding ground for bald eagles.

Fishing, hunting and tourism are the area's main industries, although the town began as a mining area. The mining legacy lives on at the **Charley Hubbard Museum**, open during the summer. Watch for a sign on the highway that points the way to the museum.

At nearby **Kenai Lake**, one can fish for Dolly Varden, lake trout, rainbow trout and whitefish. In the Kenai River are trout, king, silver and red salmon. Rafting is another popular activity on the river, and several local business offer fishing and float trips.

Hunting and fishing regulations vary with different areas and with the species. Complete game regulations are available free from the state Department of Fish and Game. Many sporting goods shops and tourist businesses also offer copies of the regulation manuals.

Continuing west, just outside of the Cooper Landing area, is the turnoff to the **Russian River Campground**. The campground is easy to spot in the summer, as it's usually overflowing with visitors. The Russian is the largest freshwater fishery in Alaska, and it draws about 60,000 fishermen, each year, all hoping to catch a red salmon.

Heading west past the Russian, one leaves the Chugach National Forest and enters the **Kenai National Wildlife Refuge**, which has different regulations and is in a different state game management area. Refuge regulations, as well as information about things to see and do in the refuge, are available from the unit's Soldotna headquarters, phone 907-262-7021.

Among the major recreational areas in the refuge is the **Skilak Lake Loop**, which intersects the Sterling Highway at two points. This road not only takes one to **Skilak Lake**, but also provides access to several other smaller lakes, streams and trails in the area.

Skilak itself has a surface area of 24,000 acres (57,600 hectares). It is prone to sudden and violent storms – boater warning signs should be taken very seriously. The lake offers fishing for salmon, trout and Dolly Varden.

Sterling is a community of about 2,000, based at the confluence of the Kenai and Moose rivers. It's a very popular salmon fishing area, and is the main access point to the Swanson River oil field and an endless string of lakes that are excellent for canoeing.

An unusual attraction of the area is the **Izaak Walton Recreation Site**, which contains an archaeological dig. It is believed the area was an Eskimo village more than 2,000 years ago. Several depressions mark the sites of ancient houses.

Sterling is also the site of the Moose River Raft Race, an annual event that is on the weekend after the Fourth of July. Area businesses construct rafts in a variety of categories, then race down the Moose River to the Kenai River.

Heading on past Sterling, one comes to **Soldotna**, seat of the borough government and home of 3,600 people.

With its central location at the intersection of the roads to Kenai and Homer, Soldotna has become the hub of the central peninsula. Here on will find a hospital, a detachment of the Alaska State Troopers and the headquarters of the Kenai National Wildlife Refuge.

Soldotna is a popular spot to meet up with professional fishing guides, most of whom specialize in helping their clients find king salmon.

The amount of traffic on the Kenai River has become the subject of state-wide controversy. Twenty-five years ago, only a handful of locals fished on the river for sport. Now the Kenai River system is the most popular fishing area in the state. A special panel is studying the use of the river and may recommend some major changes to protect it. Consult local Fish and Game or state parks officials for the most up-to-date information on the river use.

Visitor information is available at a log cabin operated by the Grater Soldotna Chamber of Commerce. The cabin is located at the corner of the Sterling Highway and Binkley Street. Information also is available at the wildlife refuge headquarters, located at the top of Skihill Road, which intersects the Sterling Highway at the Kenai River bridge. The headquarters includes a visitor's center complete with audio/visual wildlife displays, and the refuge offers the most complete collection of maps and outdoor advice books on the peninsula. Free wildlife movies are also shown on weekends.

Soldotna's festivals include Progress Days, held the last weekend in July, a winter sports festival and the state sled dog racing championships in late February. Because of its location near the coast, Soldotna doesn't receive enough snow to cover the sled dog course. For that reason, the city usually stockpiles snow scraped off the city streets, saving it over the winter to spread over the course a few days before the races.

Located on the southwest edge of Soldotna is the **Kenai Peninsula**

Kenai Peninsula view.

Community College. Among its major programs is petroleum technology, reflecting the area's tie to the oil industry.

Kenai

Heading west from Soldotna on either the Kenai Spur Highway or Kalifornsky Beach Road, one comes to **Kenai,** the oldest permanent settlement on the peninsula, and its largest city.

Kenai is home port to a good share of the peninsula's drift-net fishing fleet. In the summer a parade of boats can be seen coming in and out of the mouth of the river in their quest for red salmon.

In 1990, there was a record salmon catch in Prince William Sound to the north of Kenai, but fishermen who ventured up the Lower Cook Inlet or off Kodiak Island came back with sparse catches. During the spring, the flats along the mouth of the river are temporary nesting group for thousands of snow geese. They stay in the area for about two weeks and are a popular subject for early-season photographers.

Kenai is also home of the peninsula's largest airport and has the most regularly scheduled flights. Airlines also fly in and out of Soldotna, Seward and Homer, and charter flights can take one almost anywhere else.

One of Kenai's main attractions is the area known as **Old Town,** which includes the **Fort Kenay Museum,** the Russian Orthodox Church, chapel and rectory, and several old residential buildings, most of them abandoned. Tours of the Russian church, which is still used by the local parishioners, are conducted by the resident priest. He lives in the rectory building, located across the street from the church and next to Fort Kenay.

Special events include the Fourth of July parade and the "Christmas Comes to Kenai" celebration on the weekend following Thanksgiving. That fete includes a fireworks display at about 4 p.m. Since the peninsula has very long days during the summer, the people of Kenai hold off on fireworks until November, when they can easily be seen against the black afternoon sky.

Continuing north of Kenai on the Spur Highway, one comes to the **Nikiski** industrial area. There are: a large chemical plant, two oil refineries and a natural gas liquification plant. The plants aren't open to the public.

The area north of Kenai has several names. Some call it simply "North Kenai," while others say "Nikishka," "Nikiska," or "Nikiski." The latter name won a recent popularity vote in the area, but when discussing "that place" with a local, it's best to listen carefully to what he calls the area, and use that term while you talk.

North of the refineries is the **Captain Cook State Recreation Area**, a popular spot for hiking, camping, fishing, and snowmachining.

Much of the view across the inlet is part of the **Lake Clark National Park**. Charter flights to the park can be arranged in Kenai. Returning to Soldotna and turning south, an interesting stop at Mile 111 is the **Crooked Creek Salmon Hatchery**. This state-run hatchery is open to the public.

Farther south, the highway begins to parallel Cook Inlet and runs by some fine clamming areas in the aptly named **Clam Gulch**. Clamming requires patience, practice and a fishing license. But for those who like to eat the mollusks, a day in Clam Gulch could well be one of the highlights of their visit.

At Mile 135 is **Ninilchik**, a fishing village founded by the Russians more than 100 years ago. There are 750 residents, most of whom live in recently constructed homes along the highway. The original village, open to visitors, sits on the inlet at the mouth of the Ninilchik River. On a hill above the old village is the town's Russian Orthodox church, not open for tours but still used by the parish. The modern community of Ninilchik hosts the Kenai Peninsula's fair grounds. The fair is held on the third weekend in August.

Continuing south, one comes to **Anchor Point**, the most westerly point in North America that is accessible by continuous road system. The 2,000-member community hosts a king salmon derby from Memorial Day weekend through the third weekend in June. In addition to kings, the area is a popular fishing spot for silvers, steelhead and trout.

Still farther south is **Homer**, the southern terminus of the Sterling Highway. Homer sits on the shore of **Kachemak Bay**, famed for the variety of its marine life. Major attractions are chartered tours of the bay, and halibut fishing trips.

Another attraction is the **Pratt Museum**, a natural history museum that focuses on Kachemak Bay. The museum is surrounded by a flower garden, and among the exhibits are skeletal remains of a whale and a live octopus.

Homer is also the jumping-off point for trips to the other side of the bay, including Kachemak Bay State Park and the town of Seldovia. The state ferry service links Homer to Seldovia, Kodiak and Seward during the summer.

Seldovia is accessible only by air and water. One can bring a vehicle on the state ferry, but a car isn't really necessary; all of the town is within easy walking distance.

Seldovia is home of yet another of the peninsula's historic Russian Orthodox churches. Like its sisters around the peninsula, it also is still the home of an active parish. Seldovia's Russian history predates the church, however. It was the site of one of the Russians' first coal mines. By the 1890s, it had become a fishing and shipping center.

Unfortunately, much of the town's boardwalk area was destroyed during the 1964 earthquake. Town residents can show visitors where things were before the ground dropped. Today, Seldovia's largest celebration is on the Fourth of July, famous for its seafood dinner, which all visitors are welcome to enjoy. Seldovia also has a winter carnival, which brightens up a peaceful, quite winter. With the bulk of visitors gone and with plenty of nearby trails for hiking and cross-country skiing, winter is one of the nicest times to venture over to the southern shore of Kachemak Bay.

The port of Homer, with its mountain views.

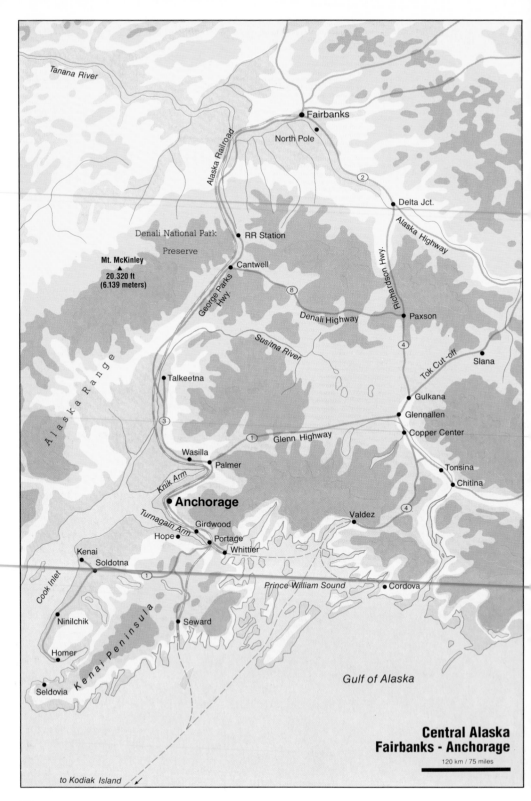

Tanana River

Fairbanks
North Pole
2
Delta Jct.
Alaska Highway

Denali National Park
Preserve
RR Station
Cantwell
Mt. McKinley
20.320 ft
(6.139 meters)
George Parks Hwy.
Alaska Railroad
8
Denali Highway
Richardson Hwy.
Paxson
4
Tok Cut-off
Slana
Talkeetna
Susitna River
3
Gulkana
Glennallen
1
Glenn Highway
Copper Center
Wasilla
Palmer
Tonsina
Chitina
Alaska Range
Knik Arm
Anchorage
Turnagain Arm
Girdwood
Hope
Portage
Whittier
4
Valdez
Kenai
Soldotna
1
Prince William Sound
Cordova
Cook Inlet
Ninilchik
Seward
Homer
Kenai Peninsula
Seldovia
Gulf of Alaska

Central Alaska
Fairbanks - Anchorage
120 km / 75 miles

to Kodiak Island

ANCHORAGE, BIG-CITY IMAGE

Imagine you're a passenger aboard one of the many domestic and international air carriers serving **Anchorage** daily. About three hours out of Seattle, the pilot announces you'll be landing in Anchorage in a few minutes. You've been peering out of the window ever since your plane took off from the Seattle-Tacoma airport, and except for when you flew by the coast of British Columbia, you've seen darn few signs of civilization. Just as you're beginning to wonder if the pilot has lost his way, you see Anchorage.

Plopped down on a point of land that sticks out into Cook Inlet, with Turnagain Arm bordering the southwest shore and Knik Arm the northwest, the city of Anchorage sprawls out over a 10-mile (16-km) length, seeming to spread over most of the available land between the inlet and the Chugach Mountains to the east.

With almost a quarter of a million residents, Anchorage is the largest metropolis and the commercial center of the state. This port city didn't get a good purchase on life until 1915, but in the 70 years since, has grown from a railroad tent camp to one of the fastest growing cities in the nation.

The broad peninsula between Turnagain and Knik Arms was probably used by Eskimos from about A.D. 1000 until 17th or 18th Century, when they were driven out by the Tanainas, a tribe of nomadic Athabascan Indians. It was the Tanainas Natives who traded furs and fish with Captain James Cook, the British explorer who sailed into Cook Inlet in 1778. Cook, who was looking for a Northwest Passage to the Atlantic, noted the Indians carried iron and copper weapons, evidence of trade with the Russians who had set up trading posts in lower Cook Inlet and at Kodiak. Other Russian influence can be seen today at Eklutna, a Tanaina village inside the northern boundary of the municipality of Anchorage.

When Cook found no way out of the arm of Cook Inlet to the south of Anchorage, he ordered his ships, the *Resolution* and the *Discovery*, to turn about, hence the name "Turnagain." Knik Arm gets its name from the Eskimo word for fire, *knik*, which was used in reference to the Tanaina people and their villages.

After Alaska was purchased from the Russians in 1867, gold seekers worked the land along Turnagain Arm and at Crow Creek and Girdwood, which is now the southern boundary of the municipality. The gold rush spread north and across Knik Arm. The old mining supply center of **Knik**, located across the inlet from downtown Anchorage, is the starting point of the Iditarod Trail Sled Dog Race from Anchorage to Nome.

During its short history, Anchorage, where half the state's residents live, has reverberated from the sounds of several major construction booms: laying track for the Alaska Railroad, building two adjacent military bases during World War II, discovery and development of the Cook Inlet and Kenai Peninsula oil fields, and construction of the 800-mile (1,290 km) trans-Alaska oil pipeline from Prudhoe Bay to Valdez.

Three other events have had significant impact on Anchorage. The first was the federally-sponsored agricultural colonization of the Matanuska Valley by 204 families from the Midwest. Anchorage residents met the newcomers in 1935 with typical frontier hospitality: they threw a wild-game dinner with all the trimmings. Statehood in 1958 opened up new vistas for the territory that had for too long been under federal dominion.

The Good Friday Earthquake

The Good Friday earthquake of 1964, which measured 8.7 on the Richter scale was the most powerful earthquake ever recorded in North America, brought Alaskans together to work for a common cause. While the quake devastated many homes and businesses in Anchorage and in other communities, the reconstruction generated a miniboom and Anchorage emerged a new city.

Preceding pages, Anchorage vista.

Quakes still shake Anchorage and South Central Alaska occasionally. Reporters in the *Anchorage Times* newsroom have a guessing game every time a noticeable quake shakes the building. The contest is to see who can forecast the correct Richter magnitude–before the official word comes from the Alaska Tsunami Warning Center in Palmer.

During the last decade Anchorage has strived to overcome the consequences of its boom-and-bust economy–unemployment, out-migration, poverty, to name a few. The city is in an extreme financial bind and the picture looks bleak. Many residents say that the present situation could have been avoided had the state spent its oil monies wisely; and one bumper sticker reads, "God, if you give us another oil windfall, we promise not to piss this one away."

Where Rugged Individualism Lives

Alaska's population is highly transient, with few people making it home for more than three years. The majority are lured by the promise of high paying jobs. The days of the trans-Alaska pipeline (the 1970s) saw salaries for construction workers in six-digit figures. More recently, people flocked into the state when they heard that Alaska was willing to share its oil profits with residents. Since 1982, the state has paid an annual dividend from oil revenues. The first year of the program resulted in $1,000 to each man, woman and child. And subsequent years have seen the dividend range from $300 to $800.

A few people move to Anchorage, because they want the adventure of living in the "last frontier." Anchorage is a city where one needs only to walk out their backdoor to find the wilderness. Many residents find no need to jump in the car to get away for the weekend–especially when it is common to view a moose right out a living room window or see a bald eagle fly overhead. Wildlife is so common that no one even blinks an eye when they see a moose grazing on the median between the lanes of the New Seward Highway. The Anchorage president of the Safe Home Program for school children recently cited the only hazardous incident she could recall for the year: one morning a Safe Home mother looked out of her window and saw a moose and calf approaching 10 children waiting at the bus stop. The woman quickly threw on her housecoat and led the children into her house. Her main concern was not that the moose would attack, but that the children would try to pet them.

Discovering the City

Most visitors to Alaska find their way to or through Anchorage. Anchorage is the air crossroads of the world with 17 major airlines offering direct flights from 39 cities. Anchorage is as close to Houston as it is to London or Tokyo. Over 100 flights arrive daily at the Anchorage International Airport.

There are numerous activities within the city limits and the surrounding area offers an endless array of opportunities

Omnibus in downtown Anchorage.

to experience Alaska. Like most American cities, the best way to see Anchorage is to rent a car and explore it on your own. There are several car rental firms in town: Avis, Hertz, Budget and Rent-a-Wreck. There is a bus system, the People Mover, but its routes cater to the local residents versus the visitor and due to the economic downturn, its schedule is limited. The transit center is located on 6th Avenue between "G" and "H" streets.

Local tour companies offer half day and full day tours of the city and surrounding area. Try Alaska Sightseeing Tours or Gray Line of Alaska.

If you are staying downtown, you can easily explore this section of the city on foot. Start at the **Visitor Information Center** at 546 West 4th Avenue. Built in 1954, the log cabin is surrounded by flowering foliage in the summer. Here visitors can get information and talk to volunteers representing the Anchorage Convention and Visitors Bureau.

Next to it is the **Old City Hall**, a classic 1930s construction. A gallery on the main floor features a changing display of historic Anchorage photographs.

This is the older section of town, but the city itself is in its infancy compared to other cities in the world. Anchorage's first wood frame house, on Second Avenue near Elderberry Park, has been completely restored and is open to the public. It belonged to **Oscar Anderson** and his family and was built on one of the first lots sold by the Corps of Engineers in 1915.

Also near Elderberry Park on Second Avenue is the start of the **Costal Bike Trail**. The municipality has over 120 miles (190 km) of bike trails through downtown and the outskirts of the city. The Costal Trail is 11½ miles (19 km) long and parallels the Knik Arm and then continues past Westchester Lagoon, ending at Kincaid Park. Bicycling is a unique way to experience the city; and offers great views of the city and waters of the inlet, where migrating Beluga whales are often seen. Ask at the log cabin about bicycles that are on free loan during the summer. Maps of all

Skyline from Cook Inlet.

trails are also available.

For a better understanding of Alaska and its history, stop at the **Anchorage Museum of History and Art**. The museum has recently been renovated and expanded with money from Projects 80s. There is an excellent permanent collection of Native art displayed in skylit galleries, and artifacts from Alaska's past. The museum shop sells books, prints and Alaska Native crafts.

Another Projects 80s site is the **Alaska Center for the Performing Arts**. This building is viewed by some as a monstrosity and by others as architecturally innovative, richly adding to the beauty of the downtown area. The building is sandwiched between the glass-towered office buildings and ground-level older, wooden frame houses, which are sporadically placed on high-valued land.

The Alaska Center is a hub of activities for the arts. Performances by the **Anchorage Symphony Orchestra** and the **Anchorage Concert Association** begin in the fall. The Concert Association each year presents two series—one music and one dance—of world class performers. Check the local newspapers and visitors guides for a schedule of events.

Around the corner from the arts center is the **Alaska Experience Theater and Museum**. The theater features the film, *Alaska the Greatland*, shown on a 180 degree screen.

For a firsthand look at the effects of the quake, visit **Earthquake Park** on the west side of the city. Here you will see how the land shifted and view an interpretative display of the '64 quake. The park, now deserted land, was once a residential neighborhood.

Downtown also has several shopping malls and major department stores that feature sections selling Alaskan souvenirs. Alaskan jade and gold nugget jewelry are popular buys. Or pick up an Alaskan T-shirt at **Petee's Quality Alaskan T-shirts** on 6th Avenue.

For Alaskan art, visit the non-profit **Alaska Native Arts & Crafts Association** located in the Post Office Mall at

Eskimo Blanket Toss is popular at the Fur Rondy.

136

333 West 4th Avenue. Other shops also carry Alaskan Native art, which are generally purchased directly from the Natives. Artists make an array of carved walrus ivory, soapstone and horn. Native women are known for their excellent basket weaving skills, so look for their intricately made works. Authentic Native-made handicrafts are indentified by a tag. There are two different designs: one has a silver hand and the other states "Authentic Native Handicraft." All other Alaskan artists works are identified by a tag with a "silver map" symbol.

Local artists specialize in Alaskan-influenced paintings and photographs. Galleries offer a variety of these artists' works. Try **Artique, Ltd. Gallery** on "G" Street, or **Stephan Fine Arts Gallery** on Sixth Avenue Alaskan-influenced paintings and photographs.

Downtown has several outstanding restaurants, however, you need to be aware that wherever you eat prices are steep. Services in Alaska are costly and most foodstuffs must be flown in.

For excellent seafood and a view of the inlet, try **Simon & Seaforts**. The neighboring **Kayak Club** also has a view and good food. **Saks Cafe**, **Zeppos** and **Center Stage Cafe** offer an intimate atmosphere and good lunches and dinner. Don't miss trying the Alaskan specialities like baked halibut or salmon and steamed crab.

For an evening out, try **The Marx Brothers Cafe** or the **Corsair**. **Josephines** in the Sheraton and the **Crows Nest** at the top of the Captain Cook, offer gourmet cuisine and a formal atmosphere. For a hardy Alaskan-style breakfast, try **Gweenies Old Alaska Restaurant**. The crab omelet served with homemade bread is excellent.

Anchorage has a variety of plush accommodations. The **Sheraton**, the **Anchorage Hilton**, **Hotel Captain Cook** and the **Westmark** are among the largest. There are also many smaller hotels and motels. The **Voyager Hotel**, located in the heart of downtown, has a quaint atmosphere and is economical. There are also over 100 bed and breakfast facilities. For more details contact **Alaska Private Lodgings**, 1236 W. 10th Avenue, Anchorage, AK 99501, (907) 258-1717.

Organizations and businesses planning conventions will be pleasantly surprised to find two excellent facilities in the city. Funded by the Projects 80s money, the **William A. Egan Civic and Convention Center** is located downtown on 5th Avenue. This 10,000 sq feet (930 sq m) facility has a capacity of nearly 3,000. The lobby is decorated with Native art, including "Eskimo Spirit Carvings" and "Volcano Women" sculptures. The **George M. Sullivan Sports Arena** on Gambell Street hosts larger affairs such as major sporting events and entertainers on the concert circuit.

For a taste of nightlife in the last frontier, you can try **Chilkoot Charlies**. Don't bother with a coat and tie, this is where Alaskans go in their boots and jeans. The **Fly By Night Club** and **Midnight Express**, also offer a taste of what life is like for the hardy. All clubs are located in Spenard, known to attract the adventuresome.

Around Anchorage

If you want to experience the Alaska outdoors, try fly-in fishing or a flight-seeing trip. Excursions can easily be arranged by flight operators at **Lake Hood** or at **Merrill Field.** Not far from downtown near the international airport, is **Lake Hood Air Harbor**, the busiest seaplane base in the world. On most summer's days, there is an average of 800 take-offs and landings. Channels on Lake Hood and Lake Spenard provided the runways for these seaplanes. Alaskans fly into the bush for fishing, hunting, hiking and a myriad other activities. It is almost as common for an Alaskan to have a pilot's license as it is to have a driver's license—one out of 45.

On the southern edge of town, visitors can view a variety of waterfowl at **Potter Point State Game Refuge** (locally known as Potter Marsh). The area is the nesting ground for migratory birds during summer. Bald eagles, Arctic terns, trumpeter swans and many species of ducks are commonly spotted. Canada geese and mallards raise their young here. From the boardwalk above the channel, huge red salmon are visible from mid-July to September as they return to spawn in nearby Rabbit Creek.

Not far from Potter Marsh on the Seward Highway, visitors have a chance to view larger wildlife. During spring and summer it is common to see mountain sheep peering over the rocks of the adjacent cliffs at passing motorists. Several turnouts on this road allow visitors to watch the waters of the Turnagain Arm for white Beluga whales. Stop at **Beluga Point Interpretive Site** in spring and fall. Here you will find spotting scopes, benches and interpretive signs describing the surrounding area.

And if you want to contemplate the beauty and absolute mammoth size of Alaska, you can grab a takeout lunch in town and picnic at nearby **McHugh Creek Picnic Area**, located just a few miles down the road from Potter Marsh. Here you can see miles and miles down

the inlet and view the majestic mountains located on the other shore. Or you can take a short hike on the trail.

At Anchorage's backdoor to the east is **Chugach State Park**, the park headquarters are located across from Potter Marsh in the **Potter Section House Historic Site.** Here you will find a railroad museum and an old rotary snow plow on the track behind the house.

The park covers 495,000 acres (200,500 hectares) and offers visitors a wide variety of opportunities to experience the Alaska outdoors without being too far away from civilization. Between June and September, the park rangers lead nature walks to various parts of the park. Each walk is about two hours and focuses on a specific activity, like wildflower observation or bird watching. For a recorded message call: 694-6391.

The park also has a second headquarters is at nearby **Eagle River**, north on the Glenn Highway from Anchorage. Only a 20-minute drive (14 miles/23 km) from downtown Anchorage, Eagle River is a popular suburbia. The drive

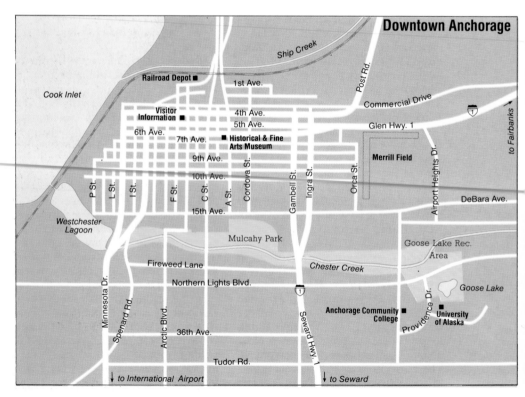

Downtown Anchorage

through the lake-dotted valley is worth the trip itself, however, once at the center you are likely to see Dall sheep and possibly a bear or two. During August the berries are plentiful and cross-country skiing is a popular winter activity.

Winter Activities

Winters are long in Alaska, but this is a special time of the year for visitors. Each weekend following Thanksgiving in November, the University of Alaska, Anchorage hosts the **Great Alaska Shoot-Out**, an invitational college basketball tournament. Eight major college basketball teams from across the United States come to Anchorage to compete in the tournament. The tournament has gained national prominence and is televised via satellite.

The university is located on several acres of wooded land in the city. The four-year old institution recently merged with the community college and now enrolls over 10,000 each year.

After the holiday season, Anchorageites prepare for their own 10-day carnival in February–**Fur Rendezvous** or as the locals call it, "Fur Rondy." (It is rumored no one could spell rendezvous!) It starts on the second Friday and ends on the third Sunday. This annual festival celebrates Alaska's frontier past, when fur trappers meet to sell and trade their goods. Many came by sled dog over miles of frozen terrain to trade furs, tell tales and have a little friendly competition.

Today the Anchorage Fur Rondy features over 150 events, ranging from the famous World Championship Sled Dog Race to the annual snowshoe softball tournament on the downtown 9th Avenue park strip. Competition is held for the best snow sculpture and the fastest canoe in the Downhill Canoe Race. Other events include the traditional Eskimo blanket toss and the largest outdoor public fur auction in the United States. The highlight of the carnival is the **World Championship Sled Dog Race**. For three days competitors run heats totaling 75 miles. The racers start on 4th Avenue downtown, and continue

on the city streets to the outskirts of town where they circle back. Dog mushing is the official state sport and competitors come from all over.

At the conclusion of Fur Rondy the **Miners and Trappers Ball** is held. This is not a black tie affair and everyone in the city is invited, however, tickets must be purchased in advance. Held in a huge warehouse, people arrive in every conceivable attire. There is even a contest for the most unusual costume.

Fur Rondy is a great time to experience what life is *really* like in Alaska. It is a time of camaraderie among the local people and they welcome the chance to share the love of their land with visitors. As the event is becoming more popular with visitors, it is best to book reservations well in advance. The Anchorage Convention and Visitors Bureau can be contacted for the date of the festival.

The last great race on earth–the **Iditarod Trail Sled Dog Race**–starts on the first Saturday in March. From downtown Anchorage competitors race to Nome, a distance of 1,049 miles

Dogteam crosses downtown Anchorage during the Iditarod Race.

(1,750 km). Generally the race takes about two weeks, but Susan Butcher, a three-time consecutive winner, has set a record breaking time of 11 days. Mushers compete with a team of 12 to 18 dogs against themselves, each other and the wilderness. Butcher's incredible winning streak has originated a T-shirt which reads, "Alaska, where men are men and women win the Iditarod!"

The race started in 1973 to commemorate the 1925 event, when 20 mushers rushed life-saving serum to Nome, which was fighting a diphtheria epidemic. Today, the race receives television coverage and residents line the streets to cheer on the competitors.

The **Knik Museum and Sled Dog Mushers Hall of Fame** is 40 miles (63 km) from Anchorage in Wasilla. Open between June and September, the museum displays the history of the Iditarod Trail and Alaskan mushers.

In Girdwood visitors can join the **Glacier Valley Tour** and experience the excitement of riding in a dog sled. The run passes scores of ancient, hanging glaciers and stops in the wilderness for a homemade lunch. Visitors even have a chance to "mush" the dogs and snowshoe during the lunch break. For information contact **Chugach Express**, P.O. Box 261-VG, Girdwood, AK, 99587, (907) 783-2266.

Downhill and cross-country skiing in Anchorage can be found in **Russian Jack Springs Park** and **Centennial Park**, both have gentle slopes and rope tows for beginning skiers. **The Hilltop Ski Area** has a chairlift and is an excellent facility for beginning skiers. It also has night skiing and is accessible by public bus. For advanced skiers, **Alpenglow** at **Arctic Valley Ski Area** offers more challenging slopes. Two chair lifts, T-bar and three rope tows service the area which has over a 1,000 feet drop. Trails can be very steep and maintenance is sometimes questionable.

Alaska's most popular ski area–**Alyeska Resort & Ski Area** is 40 miles (64 km) south of Anchorage in Girdwood. With a vertical drop of over 2,800 feet it caters to all levels of skiers

Kayak races at Anchorage.

and is a full service resort with both day and night skiing. The area just installed a quad chair lift in addition to four other double chair lifts. Accommodations are available at the lodge and there are several excellent restaurants in the area.

For the cross-country skier, Anchorage offers 141 miles (230 km) of trails. **Kincaid Point** in Campbell Park on Raspberry Road, has 18 miles (26 km) of Nordic ski trails with five being lighted. **Russian Jack Springs Park** has four miles (7 km) of lighted trails. Near Service High School and Hilltop Ski Area, another trail is lit for skiers.

In Chugach National Forest over 200 miles (234 km) of hiking trails which extend from Anchorage to the Kenai Peninsula are open to the cross-country skier. The trail at the top of Upper Huffman Road offers breathtaking views of the city and is manageable for skiers of any level. Take the Seward Highway to the O'Malley turnoff going east. Continue towards the mountains turning on to Hillside Drive, and making a left on Upper Huffman to the trailhead.

Each year the **Nordic Ski Club of Anchorage** offers several one-day ski train trips beginning in February. The train leaves the Alaska Railroad terminal in the morning and heads south past Portage into the Chugach Mountains and Grandview Glacier, where it stops and skiers head out over unspoiled snow. The train heads back at 5 p.m. On the way back weary skiers make a comeback in the polka car which gyrates as wall-to-wall bodies bounce to the rhythm of the live band. For scheduled ski train dates, contact the Nordic Ski Club, P.O. Box 103504, Anchorage, AK 99510, (907) 561-3141.

An hour's drive north of Anchorage is an excellent cross-country ski area with a historical flavor. **Hatcher Pass** is at the heart of the majestic Talkeetna mountains off the Glenn Highway on Fishhook Road. At the turn of the century **Independence Mine** was a hub of gold mining activity. Today it is a state historic park and its abandoned buildings and old mining machinery have become landmarks of the past. The area has miles of treeless groomed ski trails and on a clear day you can see all the way down the valley to the city of Palmer (20 miles/134 km). Accommodations are available in the small lodge at the entrance to the area. For more information call (907) 745-5897.

Heading South

With only two roads leading in and out of Anchorage, selecting a day trip is easy. You either head north or south.

Heading south on the Seward Highway, pay a visit to Girdwood, Crow Creek Mine and Portage Glacier. The drive parallels the **Turnagain Arm**, an extension of the Cook Inlet. Numerous turnouts along the 40 mile (66 km) drive to Girdwood offer spectacular views of both scenery and wildlife. Lookout for Dall sheep, moose and beluga whale.

Girdwood is a quaint community which sees an influx of tourists in the summer and skiers in the winter. A ride up the Alyeska Ski Resort chairlift on a clear day, provides an incredible view of the surrounding mountains and the inlet. The town has a variety of shops offering traditional Alaskan souvenirs.

Outside of Girdwood, three miles up Crow Creek Road, is **Crow Creek Mine**. The placer mine and its eight original buildings are listed on the National Register of Historic Sites. They represent the first non-Native settlement in the area. Visitors can pan for gold in this scenic setting. For the robust type, nearby Crow Pass Trail climbs through beautiful mountain valleys. Be sure to have some basic hiking gear before attempting any hike. Weather in Alaska can change dramatically and hikers should always be prepared.

Continuing down the Seward Highway, at **Twenty Mile River**, visitors can see Arctic terns, bald eagles, mew gulls and moose from the observations platform. Plaques on the platform have information on the various species.

About 10 miles (16 km) past Girdwood is the turnoff for Portage Glacier. On the right side of the road is **Explorer Glacier.** The turnout has an excellent photography vantage point. Stop at the bridge over Williwaw Creek to observe salmon spawning from late July to mid-September. At the end of the road is the **Begich Boggs Visitor Center**. Be prepared for a dramatic view, as Portage Lake with its mammoth floating blue-icebergs seems to appear out of nowhere. The center has an interpretative display on how glaciers are formed. It even has an iceberg on display so visitors can touch the ancient ice. Due to the slow formation of the glacial ice, it also melts very slowly. During the summer, it is common to see campers pluck out ice chunks for their coolers. At the center, you can view a film on wildlife and the geology of the surrounding area.

There are several glaciers in Portage Valley with numerous trails where visitors can view a variety of glacial features including wild flowers and plant life. Take the short walk into **Byron Glacier**. Signs near Portage Glacier Lodge mark the road to the trailhead. Black bears are commonly seen in the area. Portage Glacier is the turnaround point for this trip to the south. However, visitors with more time may want to head for the Kenai Peninsula and Seward or Homer. Each is only a four-hour drive from Anchorage (see Prince William Sound and the Kenai Peninsula).

On the way back to Anchorage stop at the **Bird House Bar** (near Bird Creek), a small sinking log cabin with its walls plastered with business cards and some unmentionables. Ptarmigan, the state bird, are commonly seen, so be sure to ask the bartender to point one out.

Heading North

Travelling on the Glenn Highway north of Anchorage on a day trip, visitors have an opportunity to observe cultural remnants of Alaska's past and also to enjoy several scenic areas in Palmer and the Matanuska Valley.

In Eagle River, stop at the **Eagle River Visitor Center** in Chugach State Park. Continuing on the Glenn you will see beautiful **Mirror Lake Wayside** area on the right. Here you can swim in the icy water on a warm day or ice fish in the winter. A mile further takes you to the entrance of **Thunderbird Falls**

Trailhead. This is a pleasant one-mile walk to the rushing falls.

Eklutna Lake is Anchorage's largest lake. There is a campground and several trails to **Eklutna Glacier**, whose waters feed the lake. There is good wildlife viewing and berry picking in the area.

Anchorage's oldest building may be the **St. Nicholas Russian Orthodox Church** on the Eklutna turnoff, off the Glenn Highway. It was built with hand-hewn logs and the surrounding spirit houses represent the interaction between the Natives and the Russians.

This was the site of the first Tanaina Indian settlement east of the Knik Arm, around 1650. The "spirit" houses show how the Indian beliefs were mixed with Russian orthodoxy. Spirit houses were placed over traditional graves and contained personal items to help the spirit in the next world. A three-bar orthodox cross was placed at the foot of the grave. Small spirit houses indicate the resting place of a child and a large house with a smaller one inside means a mother and child were buried together. A picket fence around a spirit house means the deceased was not a Tanaina Indian.

Further down the Glenn is the **Eklutna Flats**. Moose are often spotted grazing in the area. This is the entrance to the Matanuska Valley, the breadbasket of Southcentral Alaska. Wheat, barley and oats are grown. Local markets sell Mat Valley carrots, cabbage and potatoes. Here you will find the fabled cabbage weighing over 80 lbs displayed at the Alaska State Fair. Large-sized produce are a result of the area's maximum 19½ hours of daylight in the summer.

To really get a feel for the valley and a unique Alaskan experience stop at the **Matanuska Riding Stables** (907) 745-3693. Make a left off the Glenn towards Wasilla and take the first right on Trunk Road and follow the signs. Here you can savor the beauty of the area while riding through the Bradley-Kepler Lakes system. All trips are guided and range from 1½ to 3 hours. For information write Matanuska Riding Stables, HCO-1 Box 6156, Palmer, AK 99645.

In Palmer stop at the **Visitor Information Center and Museum**. Over

200 local artists have their works on assignment here. This small town of 3,000 residents is located in a majestic rural setting and reminiscent of what many visitors visualize Anchorage to be. Palmer is the site for the **Alaska State Fair**. The fair features the famous valley produce and the largest cabbage wins the blue ribbon. A cabbage must weigh at least 75 lbs to enter the competition. Displays also include farm animals and locally handmade items. A carnival operates and foodstalls line the runway so visitors can literally eat their way from one end to the other. The 11-day event attracts over 200,000 people a year and shouldn't be missed.

North of Palmer is the turn off for Hatcher Pass and Independence Mine. A mile after the turn off is the **Musk Ox Development Corporation Farm and Gift Shop**. Here are the world's only domesticated musk-ox. In the summer, visitors can watch the newborns romp with their parents in the pasture. The coats of these shaggy animals produce *qiviut*–a rare musk oxen wool. The material is used by the Alaska Natives to hand-knit hats, mittens, gloves and scarves in traditional patterns. The *qiviut* is sent to villages around the state and then returned as finished articles to be sold. It is believed that *qiviut* is the warmest material in the world. The **Oomingmak-Musk Ox Producers Co-op** in downtown Anchorage on "H" Street, also sells *qiviut* products.

Beyond Anchorage

For visitors wishing to get off the beaten track, a day trip on the **Alaska Railroad** is just the answer. The railroad offers excursions to Talkeetna or Seward and longer packages to Denali National Park and/or Fairbanks. The depot is located on the northeast corner of Second Avenue and "E" Street.

The Alaska Railroad has been operating for over 65 years and runs from Seward on the Kenai Peninsula to Fairbanks in the Interior. Travelling by rail takes the visitor through areas that are not accessible to other modes of transportation. Besides carrying passengers, the railroad brings goods from food and fuel to sled dogs and building materials to those living in the bush.

The Alaska Railroad is the only one in the United States to provide flag stop service. This means passengers may flag down the train anywhere and also alight anywhere along the line. This is an invaluable service for people living in the bush, and it also offers the visitor a unique opportunity to see the Alaskan outback.

Packages include a day trip to **Talkeetna**, a three-hour ride through valleys and spectacular gorges. A 10 minute walk will get you from one side of town to the other. Stop at the **Fairview Inn** for a drink with the locals and hear some great Alaska tales. Talkeetna is the jumping off spot for climbers to Mt. McKinley in the summer. Women may want to peruse the "bachelors' book" to see the local offerings. Or better yet, single women can attend the annual bachelors ball held the first weekend in December where eligible men auction themselves off to the highest bidder for an evening of dancing. For more information, contact the Talkeetna Bachelors Society c/o Fairview Inn, Talkeetna, AK, (907) 733-2423.

Another one-day excursion offered by the Alaska railroad is to **Seward**. This four-hour trip parallels the Turnagain Arm for 60 miles (100 km) and then cuts into the heart of the mountains. The tracks traverse deep valleys and come to within a half a mile of both Spencer and Trail Glacier before descending to Seward on Prince William Sound. Overnight trips are also available which include a cruise of Kenai Fjords National Park and lodging.

Visitors with a few days to spare can take the railroad trip to Mt. McKinley or Fairbanks. Packages are available for a minimum of one overnight which include round trip rail transportation from Anchorage, lodging in Denali National Park and a bus tour of the park. Extensions to Fairbanks can be made. For more information contact Alaska Railroad Corp Passenger Services, Pouch 107500-VG, Anchorage, AK 99510, (907) 265-2494.

FAIRBANKS AND THE INTERIOR

"Gold!" The cry has lured men and women to the Interior for nearly a century. At first, the passionate quest, the lust, the hunger was surfeited by a stampede and a handful of nuggets. The golden never-dreams are history now, but the Siren of the Interior still summons the adventurer, entices the wanderer, beckons to the daring spirit. It whispers yet of gold; those who listen to it and enter the Interior are forever haunted, because they have found truth in these promises. There *is* gold in the Interior, gilding every aspen leaf in the autumn explosion of color, glancing off the wingtips of geese, shimmering in the river current as it flows into a blazing sunset. Gold? It splashes across the midnight sky as the aurora and dances as moonlight over the hulking white shoulders of mountain peaks. And for a few days each spring, this gold lies strewn like nuggets, captured for a moment in a carpet of wildflowers.

Those who linger, even momentarily, in the Interior find that even its people are a part of this extraordinary wealth, possessing what can only be called "hearts of gold." Many an ill-equipped gold miner would have suffered horribly had it not been for the Athabascan Indians who unquestioningly provided food and shelter for these explorers, then quietly moved on as the rush for riches intensified. Folks in the Interior carry on this tradition of caring and generosity, and their warm-heartedness calls the traveller back again and again to the edge of the frontier.

Land of Great Contrasts

The Interior of Alaska, that one-third of the state north of the Alaska Range and south of the Brooks Range, is an area of stark contrasts. Denali (Mount McKinley), "the Great One," 20,320 feet (6,195 meters) and snow-capped year-round, towers above the Tanana and Yukon river valleys where summer temperatures can reach 100 degrees F (38 degrees C). The Alaska Range is girdled with miles of glaciers, while in the valleys below rolling hills of white spruce, bitch and aspen fold into scraggly stands of black spruce, willow tangles and muskeg.

Three hours and 42 minutes of sunlight is a meager wage for those who winter in the Interior. Temperatures plummet to -30 and -40 degrees F (-40 degrees C), with the average December temperature registering -14 degrees F (-26 degrees C) in Fairbanks. An unpleasant side effect of temperatures below -20 degrees F (-29 degrees C) is ice fog, which hangs in the still air. The fog results from a temperature inversion trapping ice crystals, smoke and exhaust in a blanket of cold air close to the ground.

But then there's summer, with daylight lingering for up to 22 hours. In July, when the average temperature in Fairbanks can be more than 61 degrees F (16 degrees C), it is hard to recall the cold winter nights when the aurora borealis screamed across the clear, crisp sky and everyone huddled by the wood stove for warmth and reassurance that he was not alone in the dark.

Fairbanks International

Welcome to the **Fairbanks International Airport.** Before descending the

Preceding pages; Fairbanks at noon in January, −41° through ice fog! Below, gold miners.

escalator to claim your luggage, study the panoramic photo-mural overhead. The reproduction makes you feel as if you can almost touch the behemoth machine that helped extract the gold from the hills around Fairbanks.

The Fairbanks Airport offers all standard airport services less one. Be prepared to handle your own luggage; there is no porter service. Don't be dismayed; it is only a short scrape to the doors and transportation to town. Take a moment to survey the other luggage being off-loaded in Fairbanks. Backpacks, bicycles, folding boats, dogs, dry fish and the old Alaskan travel favorite, the cardboard box, will be present.

A full range of transportation possibilities awaits to whisk you to your destination. Many hotels and motels offer free transportation for their guests and will send a vehicle if called. Taxis are usually plentiful and limousine (actually a van) service is also available.

At the Heart of Downtown Fairbanks

Now that you are settled, where to begin? Without hesitation, head for the site from which **Fairbanks** erupted, near the corner of what is now Cushman Street and First Avenue. This is the heart of downtown Fairbanks, the center of a borough that includes 60,000 people and the towns of North Pole, Fox, Ester and Salcha.

If you are visiting the Interior in summer, try conjuring up an image of winter in this spot, low light reflecting blue off the snow-covered riverbed. Summer weather is as glorious as winter weather is unbearable, with temperatures as high as 96 degrees F (36 degrees C). (No, this is not a misprint.) Travellers may even experience some difficulty sleeping with all the light. The most practical advice is don't sleep until you're tired. Enjoy the late evening light — this is the season that makes the cold dark winter worth enduring.

You will also discover that the later evening is a wonderful time for photography. Light of this quality is experienced at lower latitudes for only a few moments around sunrise and sunset. In Alaska's Interior, the special glow hovers for hours, casting gigantic shadows and ethereal reflections.

Left, songsters at the Malemute Saloon. Right, a Fairbanks street.

The Founding of Fairbanks

E.T. Barnette was not enjoying the summer weather on August 26, 1901, for his string of bad luck had on this day placed him in a dire predicament. Barnette had just been deposited, along with his 130 tons (130,000 kg) of equipment, into the wilderness, on a high wooded bank along the Chena River. How did this river boat captain, dog musher and aspiring enterpreneur manage to become marooned on this desolate piece of real estate? The answer has all the ingredients of a true Alaskan story …

Barnette journeyed to the Klondike in 1897, taking what was considered the rich man's route. He sailed from Seattle to St. Michael, then was to travel by sternwheeler to Dawson. But when he arrived in St. Michael, the sternwheeler had already departed. Undaunted, Barnette and several others bought a dilapidated sternwheeler, elected Barnette captain, and set off for Dawson. Barnette piloted the craft to Circle and finally arrived in Dawson via dogsled, after freeze-up. He prospered that winter selling much-needed supplies to men in the gold fields, but the Klondike was too tame for the likes of this man.

During the winter of 1901, Barnette travelled south to Seattle, arranging the coup that he speculated would make him a rich man. He and a partner purchased $20,000 worth of equipment to outfit a trading post, not in the Klondike but at the half-way point on the Eagle-to-Valdez trail. Barnette considered this to be a strategically sound location upon which to create the "Chicago of the North," the industrial hub of the territory. At this point, the trail crossed the Tanana River, and he would accommodate the overland as well as the river traffic (if there ever was any).

Barnette shipped the equipment to St. Michael and departed for Circle to purchase a sternwheeler. He arrived in St. Michael without incident, but there Lady Luck abandoned the entrepreneur. The sternwheeler struck a submerged rock, and the bottom was torn from the boat. Imagine Barnette at this point more than 1,000 miles (1,600 km) from his destination with 260,000 pounds (120,000 kg) of equipment, including a horse and food, no ready cash and a worthless sternwheeler. It was

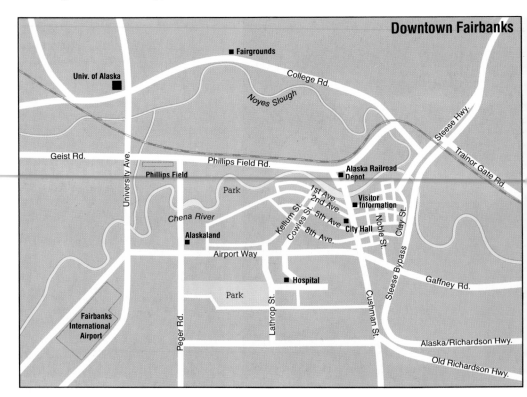

time for another partner. He convinced the customs agent in St. Michael to co-sign notes and made him a full partner.

Barnette struck a deal with the captain of the sternwheeler *Lavelle Young* to take him to Tanacross (Tanana Crossing). The fine print on the contract stated that if the *Lavelle Young* went beyond the point where the Chena joined the Tanana River and could go no farther, Captain E.T. Barnette would disembark with his entire load of supplies, no matter where they were.

As destiny would have it, the *Lavelle Young* could not float through the Tanana shallows called Bates Rapids, so the captain steamed up the Chena River, convinced by the desperate Barnette that it would join again with the Tanana River. It did not.

The scene was set on August 26, 1901. Captain Barnette off-loaded his full kit on a high bank with a good stand of trees. It seemed that his string of ill-luck could get no worse.

"No-Credit" Purchases

Two down-and-out prospectors watched the spectacle of the stern-wheeler in the Chena from a hillside, now called Pedro Dome, about 20 miles (32 km) north of Fairbanks. The miners had found some "color" but no major strike, and were faced with the frustration of a 330-mile (530-km) round-trip hike back to Circle City to replenish much-needed supplies. The prospectors, Felix Pedro, an Italian immigrant, and Tom Gilmore eagerly set off for the stranded boat, hoping to purchase necessities.

Barnette was shocked to see the prospectors and pleased to sell them anything. Nonetheless, he was furious about his dilemma and Isabelle, his wife, was distraught. Still possessed by his wild scheme to establish a trading post at Tanacross, Barnette sent for Frank Cleary, Isabelle's brother, in Montana. Frank was to guard the caché of supplies while Captain and Mrs. Barnette returned to Seattle to obtain a boat capable of travelling the remaining 200 miles (320 km) up the Tanana to Tanacross. Cleary's orders were simple, "No credit." The Barnettes departed for Valdez and points south in March 1903, braving the -40 degree F (-40 degree C) temperature.

High noon and sub-zero temperatures during winter.

Upon arriving in Seattle, Barnette began with singleminded determination to raise the necessary cash to buy a boat and more supplies. Meanwhile, back at camp, brother-in-law Cleary broke the only rule, "No Credit." Frank decided to outfit Felix Pedro again, on credit this time because Pedro had no collateral. Frank's decision changed the history of the Interior; just three months later, Pedro quietly announced to Cleary that he had struck pay dirt.

The Barnettes returned to the Chena camp six weeks later and immediately abandoned all thoughts of moving to Tanacross. Here was Barnette with two shiploads of supplies in the midst of the next gold rush. There was money to be made. The rush was on!

Hundreds of gold-hungry prospectors swarmed out of Circle City, Dawson and Nome, scurrying to the new and, they were told, the richest gold fields in the north. By the time they arrived, much of the promising land was already staked, most of it by "pencil miners" like Barnette who secured the claims only for the purpose of selling them later. These clever businessmen staked as many as 100 claims of 20 acres (eight hectares) each, thus controlling vast amounts of potentially rich ground. Regardless out of control, the stampede continued.

On the return trip from Seattle, Barnette had spoken with Judge Wickersham about naming his little settlement. The judge offered his support to Barnette if he would use the name "Fairbanks," after Senator Charles Fairbanks from Indiana who later became Vice-President of the United States under Teddy Roosevelt. Fairbanks it was.

The community of Fairbanks in 1903 consisted of Barnette's trading post, numerous tents, a few log houses and wooden sidewalks where the mud was particularly deep. What a fine tribute to the senator from Indiana.

Past Meets Present

A stone monument near the **Fairbanks Convention and Visitors Bureau** marks the place where Fairbanks was born. This is an appropriate beginning for present-day explorers also. The building at 550 1st Ave. (907-456-5774), is an invaluable source of information. River rafting.

The center is open 8:30 a.m. to 5 p.m. everyday during summer, and Monday through Friday during the off-season. Besides offering hundreds of brochures on Alaskan attractions, experts provide two additional services: a free one-hour guided walking tour of downtown Fairbanks (highly recommended); and a visitor information telephone number, 907-456-INFO. The recorded message is available at any hour, is updated daily, and may include information on events as diverse as an evening opera performance or the starting time of a dog race. The bureau also provides a well-written, free, multilingual brochure printed in English, Japanese, German and French. The booklet contains sections dedicated to transportation, accommodations, attractions, annual events and a host of other topics.

Stroll Through Town

Several commercial sightseeing outings of Fairbanks' downtown area are available. The free junket sponsored by the Visitors Bureau is by far the most reasonably priced, but why not design your own tour?

The Chena River in downtown Fairbanks.

Start at the Visitors Bureau on 1st Avenue for the information you may need and a peek at the well-constructed log building. Notice the monument to E.T. Barnette and the obelisk that marks Milepost 1,523 (2,450 km) of the Alaska Highway. The Milepost is hidden behind posing tourists most of the summer. Even with the completion of the Dalton Highway to Prudhoe Bay, Fairbanks has, since World War II, been touted as the end of the highway. Fairbanksans like to say that this is where the road ends and the wilderness begins.

Amble west along the **Chena River** for a walking tour of Fairbanks, crossing Cushman Street at the lights. The first stop is **St. Matthew Episcopal Church** at 1029 1st Ave. The land between Cushman and Cowles was the site of E.T. Barnette's trading post, sawmill and home. The log building on the corner of Cowles and 1st Avenue was built in 1909 as the first library in Fairbanks.

The altar of St. Matthew was carved from a single piece of wood, but no one is quite sure of the origin of the huge chunk. The stained glass windows are of special interest; they portray images of

Jesus, Mary and Joseph with dark hair and Alaskan Native features.

Retrace your steps for a scant two-and-one-half blocks and turn onto Wickersham, continuing south until 4th Avenue. Wickersham Street is named for Judge Wickersham, who "suggested" the name Fairbanks to E.T. Barnette. Turn left on 4th Avenue, walk one block, then cross Barnette Street. It's a congested thoroughfare now, but perhaps Barnette's sighs can still be heard above the whir of his city.

The next block of 4th Avenue between Barnette and Cushman was known as **The Row.** To ensure that no one unwittingly wandered into this sinful area, the booming city of Fairbanks erected tall, Victorian, wooden gates at both ends of the avenue. Both sides of this scandalous boulevard were lined with small log cabins housing prostitutes. The Row is gone now, replaced by the downtown post office, Woolworths, the Elks Club and a parking lot.

Cross Cushman Street again and continue on 4th Avenue for one more block to Lacey Street. Are you curious where the names Cushman and Lacey originated? Judge Wickersham, always alert for an opportunity to win political friends, requested that the streets be named for Congressmen Francis Cushman of Tacoma and John F. Lacey of Iowa.

The "Ice Palace"

On the block bounded by Lacey and Noble streets and 3rd and 4th avenues towers the "Ice Palace." Officially the **Alaska National Bank Building,** most Fairbanksans call it the Northward Building. This, the first steel-girded skyscraper built in the Interior, became the inspiration for Edna Ferber's novel *The Ice Palace.* (The Ice Palace in the novel is a modern skyscraper built by a ruthless millionaire named Czar Kennedy.) Locals also recognized in Czar Kennedy the reflection of prominent businessman, developer and politician Captain Austin E. Lathrop.

Turn north (toward the river), walk two blocks to 2nd Avenue, turn left, and head toward Cushman Street. Urban renewal has taken its toll here, with the remaining storefronts protruding like the teeth of a Halloween jack-

Contestants in a "Pedro Look-a-Like" contest.

o'lantern. The block between 2nd and 1st Avenues is the proposed site of a new luxury hotel.

The next stop is **Coop Drug Store** at 535 Second Ave. Of 1927 vintage, this building was Captain Lathrop's gift to the people of Fairbanks. Before then, the structures in Fairbanks were built of wood because, it was believed, no other material could withstand the test of a -60 degrees F (-51 degrees C) winter. This concrete affair was originally the Empress Theater, outfitted by Captain Lathrop with 670 seats and the first pipe organ in the Interior. A common cry in Fairbanks is "Meet me at Coop," so be sure to take a look. People visiting Fairbanks from the villages often shop here and eat at the snack bar.

During the mid-1970s, while the Trans-Alaska Oil Pipeline was under construction, 2nd Avenue was the scene of incessant activity. Bars were packed at all hours, and the reputation of the avenue rivaled The Row of gold rush days. Workers flew to town during rest periods from remote construction camps only to spend most of their time (and money) along 2nd Avenue.

An Old Courthouse and the Oldest National Bank

The **Old Federal Courthouse** is just south of the intersection of 2nd Avenue and Cushman. When Judge Wickersham officially moved the Federal Court to Fairbanks in 1904, he built the courthouse on this piece of real estate, donated by E.T. Barnette, securing the future of the young settlement. The original wooden structure burned, and the present building was completed in 1934. It included the first elevator in the Interior. Federal offices soon required more space and were relocated, leaving the building open for tasteful remodeling into office space and shops.

The **First National Bank** at the corner of 2nd and Cushman was started on that very site in June 1905. "Square Sam" Bonnifield and his brother John founded the bank, now the oldest national bank in Alaska. "Square Sam" was given his nickname because he had been an honest gambler in Circle City, and miners could turn their backs while Sam weighed a poke of gold.

Turn toward the river and stroll across the Cushman Street Bridge.

Bearded miner forms logo for an Alaskan airline.

pausing perhaps for a momentary glance into the Chena. The **Immaculate Conception Church** stands directly across the river from the Visitor Information Bureau. The church, interestingly enough, originally stood on the opposite side of the river at the corner of 1st and Dunkle. In 1911, Father Francis Monroe decided the church should be closer to the hospital on the north side of the Chena. Many good Catholics pitched in to move the building across the frozen river. Visitors are welcome inside to enjoy the stained glass windows and the pressed tin ceiling paneling.

One-half block north on the opposite side of the street is the *Daily News Miner* building at 200 N. Cushman St. The *Daily News Miner* publishes seven days a week, carrying on a long newspaper tradition. Judge Wickersham published the first newspaper, headlined the *Fairbanks Miner*, on May 9, 1903. All seven copies sold for $5 each, making the first edition one of the most expensive in the world.

Fairbanks offers a cornucopia of perfect gifts for the traveller. Gold-nugget jewelry, always a favorite, is priced by the pennyweight (dwt) with 20 dwt equal to one troy ounce (1 dwt=1.555 grams). Remember, nuggets used in jewelry command a premium price above raw gold.

Native handicrafts from the Interior are also treasured souvenirs. The Authentic Native Handicraft Symbol assures visitors that they are buying the genuine article, handmade by an Alaskan Native. Favorite items include beaded slippers, beaded mittens or gloves, birch bark baskets, porcupine quill jewelry and fur dolls.

The Alaskan Interior produces some of the finest lynx, marten, wolverine, fox and wolf fur in the world. Fairbanks is the place to purchase raw or tanned furs and fur coats, jackets and hats. Be aware of customs regulations if you are taking these items out of the States.

A Wildlife Trail within the City

Save a little shoe leather for a very special wildlife trail situated within the city limits of Fairbanks. **Creamers Field** at 1300 College Rd. was originally a homestead until Charles Creamer set up a dairy farm in 1920. The 250 acres (101

Cabin at Alaskaland.

154

hectares) remained in active production until it was purchased by the state and was set aside as a waterfowl refuge in 1967. While hiking the nature trails you can see many species of animals, including diving ducks, shore birds, cranes, fox or even a moose. The real show, however, is in late April/early May and again in August/September when the sandhill cranes, Canadian honkers and ducks congregate in the field.

Alaskaland, a 44-acre (18-hectare) city park at the corner of Airport Way and Peger Road, is a snapshot of life in the Golden Heart of Alaska. The park is open year-round with summer hours from 11 a.m. to 9 p.m. daily. Summer shuttle bus service leaves frequently from downtown to the park; telephone 907-452-4244 for information.

The **Mining Valley** on the west end of the park contains many machines used in the hills around the area to extract gold. Sluice boxes, dredge buckets, a stamp mill and other equipment lend an air of authenticity to the display.

Be sure to stroll through the **Mining Town,** which includes an assortment of original structures rescued from the boom-town period. Every building is a piece of history, including Judge Wickersham's home, the first frame house in Fairbanks built by the Judge in 1904 as a surprise for his wife. It is a rather melancholy reminder of life in early Fairbanks, as the bedridden Mrs. Wickersham spent most of that summer sleeping in a tent; fresh air was thought to aid in the cure of tuberculosis.

Even the building now housing the **Park Office** had a spicy past as a brothel in Nenana. The **Gold Rush Town** is packed with small shops containing a delightful array of unique crafts.

The **Sternwheeler Nenana** is listed in the National Register of Historic Places because so few of these vessels remain. It was a classic paddlewheeler with a colorful history on the waterways of the Interior. Imagine leaning back in the captain's chair, with its commanding view of the river, the stack belching sparks, and the crew scurrying about the deck as you maneuver the craft through the Yukon River.

Along the Chena River within the park you'll find the **Alaska Native Village** display, where artifacts are on display as well as demonstrations of crafts still used in remote parts of the Interior.

Snowmobiles ready to race to the finish line—97 miles distant.

If you get hungry, follow your nose to the **Alaska Salmon Bake** (5 p.m. to 9 p.m. daily, June 1 through September 1), a great value for a tasty Alaskan meal. King salmon, halibut and ribs are grilled over an open alder fire for that special flavour. After dinner, saunter over to the **Palace Saloon** and enjoy your favorite beverage and the cancan girls.

University Pursuits

The **University of Alaska Fairbanks** (UAF) is located on a bluff overlooking Fairbanks and the Tanana Valley. Established in 1917 as the Alaska Agricultural College and School of Mines, the UAF is the main campus for a system that operates four-year satellites in Anchorage and Juneau. Emphasis on high latitude and Alaskan problems have earned the UAF an excellent reputation.

The 2,500-acre (1,000-hectare) campus is a town unto itself, complete with its own post office, radio station, TV station, fire department and the traditional college facilities. A trip to the UAF campus is worthwhile if only to relax at the turnout on Yukon Drive and absorb the view of the Alaska Range in the distance. The large marker, complete with mountain silhouettes and elevations, assists you in identifying all those splendid peaks fringing the southern horizon − yes, including Denali.

The **Otto William Geist Museum** on the UAF campus is a must for visitors to the Interior. Displays include prehistoric objects extricated during mining operations from the permanently frozen ground. One recent addition is a 36,000-year-old bison carcass found near Fairbanks, preserved in the permafrost, complete with skin and flesh. The Native Cultures displays are an educational introduction to the Athabascan, Eskimo, Aleut and Tlingit cultures. The collections date back to 1926 when the president of the school assigned Geist the task of amassing Eskimo artifacts.

During summer, free guided tours of the museum are available Monday through Friday; telephone 907-474-7505 for information. Tours are also provided at the **Geophysical Institute** during which a spectacular film of the aurora borealis is shown.

Left, advertisement for a unique Alaskan product. Right, chain-saw carving produces a wooden miner.

Two free UAF off-campus tours are offered, both unique to the Interior. The first site is on Yankovich Road about one mile (1.6 km) from Ballaine Road at the **Large Animal Research Facility,** formerly known as the Musk Ox Farm. These woolly prehistoric creatures graze in research pastures together with moose, reindeer and caribou.

The second tour, no less unusual, offers an opportunity to enter the **Permafrost Tunnel,** which was bored into the frozen ground near Fox. In this natural icebox, the temperature remains below freezing year-round. The one-eighth mile (.2 km) cave was constructed to test drilling machinery in cold weather. Numerous prehistoric bones were discovered during excavation. The tunnel is not wet, but it is dusty and those with respiratory problems should take precautions. Telephone the UAF Geology department to arrange a tour.

River transportation in the early days.

Wheel into the Past

Riverboats have never been far removed from the history of Fairbanks, since E.T. Barnette's load of supplies was put ashore. Jim and Mary Binkley continue the tradition with river tours aboard the *Discovery I* and *Discovery II.* The four-hour excursion begins at 8:45 a.m. and 2 p.m. each day, covering 20 miles (32 km) on the Chena and Tanana rivers. The Binkleys' narration brings history to life along the river banks. To reach the sternwheelers' port of departure at the landing off Dale Road, take Airport Way toward the airport, turn onto Dale Road, and watch for the signs. Reservations are recommended; telephone 907-479-6673 or write to Riverboat Discovery P.O. Box 80610, Fairbanks, Alaska 99708.

As you float by the **Pump House Restaurant,** take note for later. Excellent family-style meals, mining decor and turn-of-the century atmosphere combine to create a noteworthy dining experience. This historical site was built by the F.E. Company to supply water to diggings in Ester.

The gold dredges in the Fairbanks area have been mute since 1966 and now stand like aging, silent dinosaurs with necks outstretched, waiting. The dredges, like so many pieces of Fair-

banks history, are strewn about the hills waiting for the traveller's quest. Beware of the danger of becoming involved with this history, for many have been swept up in the search for gold.

The easiest gold dredge to visit is **Dredge Number 8,** rusting at Nine Mile (15 km) Old Steese Highway, ironically only 200 yards (183 meters) from the Trans-Alaska Oil Pipeline. The five-deck ship is more than 250 feet (76 meters) long and displaced 1,065 tons (1,065,000 kg) as it plied the gold pay dirt of Goldstream and Engineer creeks. Tours of the dredge are available all summer and may be arranged any time by phoning 907-456-6058. The nominal admission fee includes gold panning; keep what you pan.

If you admired the photograph of the gold dredge in the International Airport, you may want to visit Mile 28.7 (46 km) Steese Highway. Walk on the easy trail through the dredged tailings (piles of crushed rock) opposite the **Chatanika Roadhouse** for a topside view.

Only the true dredge aficionado will care to explore the other three dredges in the area. The one on **Nome Creek** off 57 Mile (92 km) Steese Highway requires a long hike before reaching the dismantled piece. The site resembles a complete inventory of the disassembled behemoth spread over about three acres (1.2 hectares). The second dredge is off Two Mile (3.2 km) Murphy Dome Road, but on the other side of the valley. The final apparatus is off Six Mile (9.7 km) Murphy Dome Road on **Nugget Creek.** Prepare for a strenuous hike made even more difficult by blood-thirsty mosquitoes.

The Big Ditch

Large-scale mining demands water, lots of water. J.M. Davidson, to bring water from the Chatanika River to the diggings on Fox, Cleary and Goldstream creeks, proposed building an 80-mile (130-km) water system composed of 72 miles (116 km) of canals and seven miles (12 km) of huge pipes that created siphons to raise the water over the hills. A 5,000-kilowatt power plant was erected, as well as six or seven dredges and shops and camps to maintain the equipment and house the crews.

Musk oxen, traditionally raised for their luxurious warm undercoat.

During construction of the **Davidson Ditch,** portions of the Steese Highway were built to facilitate access. The "Ditch" was completed in 1930 and was capable of carrying 56,000 gallons (254,500 liters) of water per minute. After the dredges were put to rest, this system continued to generate electricity until the Flood of 1967 destroyed it.

Remnants of the Davidson Ditch are visible along the Steese Highway in several places. One of the most accessible is at 57 Mile (91 km), where a turnout guides you within a few feet of a decaying siphon.

Over the River and Through the Woods

Outdoor adventure is the glue that binds people to the land in the Interior. The mountains, rivers and valleys offer unparalleled opportunities for hiking, canoeing, hunting and fishing.

Three excellent sources of information you should not ignore when planning a hike in the Interior are the State Division of Parks, the Bureau of Land Management (BLM) and the United States Geologic Survey map distribution center in the Federal building in Fairbanks. Armed with these sources, hikers can head for the hills well-informed. One stimulating trek, the **Pinnell Mountain National Recreation Trail,** a 24-mile (38.6-km) spine connecting 12 Mile Summit and Eagle Summit on the Steese Highway, is a challenging example. The trail is defined with rock cairns along mountain ridges and high passes. Caribou migrate through here in summer, and an occasional moose or bear may claim the path. The trail promises stunning vistas of the Alaska Range, the White Mountains and the Tanana Hills. Due to the elevation, 3,600 feet (1,100 meters) at Eagle Summit, hikers are treated to nearly 24 hours of daylight during the summer solstice.

The usually blue skies of summer coupled with hundreds of miles of wild and scenic rivers make water travel a natural pastime. Canoeing offers an idyllic opportunity to observe game animals undisturbed as the boat slips silently past. You couldn't manage to cram your canoe into the suitcase? Never fear. Several rental establishments have anticipated your needs. In Fairbanks, try **Canoe Alaska, Beaver Sports**

Furs for sale at a trading post near Fairbanks.

or **Charley River Canoe Sales.**

For the novice, the **Chena River Floats Co.** rents inflatable two-person canoes at Alaskaland in which to take a sinfully lazy float to the Pump House, where paddlers can "deflate" and catch the borough bus back to town.

With the entire Interior river system at your paddle tip, deciding where to explore depends on ability and time. The Chena and **Chatanika Rivers** offer a multitude of easily accessible possibilities for day trips. If time can be stretched, one might attempt the clear waters of the **Birch Creek** at 94 Mile (150 km) Steese Highway or a five-day sojourn on the broad sweep of the **Tanana River** from Delta to Fairbanks.

Those fortunate enthusiasts with a month or more could paddle away from Fairbanks and float into the Tanana and Yukon rivers. This expedition is more than 1,000 miles (1,600 km) of wilderness river without a portage. Portions of the easily accessible **Nenana River** contain Class IV and V rapids (not suitable for an open canoe), and should be reserved only for experienced kayakers able to perform the Eskimo roll. If contemplating the Nenana, select one of the many guided raft tours available at Mile 239 (385 km) on the Parks Highway.

The water level of the Nenana varies with the temperature. It is a glacier-fed river and will run in torrents if several days of warm weather produce ideal melting conditions.

The aforementioned rivers are all conveniently accessible by road. If the traveller owns a collapsible kayak, myriad remote rivers can be reached by airplane.

Happy Hooking

The Interior is a fisherman's promised land, and the Arctic grayling its manna. The flash of the strike and the fight of the silver streak on light tackle is a treasured memory — not to be hauled out again and again when swapping fishing tales, but to be savored nonetheless. All clear-flowing creeks and rivers in the Interior are suitable grayling habitat. The Clearwater, Salcha, Chantanika and Chena rivers are superior grayling producers and are accessible by road. Northern pike, rainbow trout, burbot and lake trout abound in the clear, cold waters

throughout the Interior.

Experience unrivaled fishing in the remote lakes and rivers. Chartered airplane operators can be contacted in Fairbanks, North Pole, Delta and Tok. Fly-in fishing is an expensive proposition, but the spectacular scenery and bountiful catches make it a good value.

The fall hunts in August and September attract avid trophy hunters to the Interior. Guided hunts are available into the Alaska and Brooks ranges, with most hunters hoping for a Dall sheep, moose or caribou. Make arrangements for guided hunts far in advance.

Special Events in Fairbanks

The winter carnival spirit has been revived in Fairbanks and is now called the **Ice Festival,** celebrated during the second and third weeks of March. Fairbanks has traditionally hosted the **North American Open Sled Dog Championship** during this time. The North American, as locals refer to it, is not to be missed. The sprint race is run on three consecutive days, with the start/finish line in downtown Fairbanks on 2nd Avenue. It attracts the finest sprint dogmushers

Leaping skills are part of the annual Eskimo Olympics.

from the States, racing teams of up to 20 dogs.

Another sled dog race, not a sprint, has been added to the Ice Festival. The **Yukon-Quest,** a grueling 1,000-mile (1,600 km) race between Whitehorse, Canada, and Fairbanks, ends in Fairbanks in odd-numbered years and runs in the opposite direction in even-numbered years. The Quest challenges the sturdiest of long distance mushers, who finish the arduous journey during the Ice Festival.

A full slate of events continues throughout the festival including, of course, Ice Sculpting. The Festival of Native Arts also takes place, along with Native-style potlatches.

Fairbanksans do not allow the Summer Solstice to slip by uncelebrated. The Fairbanks Gold Panners baseball team plays a game at Growden Field with the first pitch crossing the plate at 10:45 p.m. — under natural light.

Boating fanatics endure competition of another sort. Sleek racing boats propelled by twin 50-horsepower outboard motors zoom down the Chena, Tanana and Yukon rivers to Galena, returning at breakneck speed to Fairbanks and the finish line at Pike's Landing. The Yukon 800 tests both machine and man.

Felix Pedro sported a beard. And so does almost everyone else during the third week of July when Fairbanks celebrates Golden Days. One event is a Felix Pedro look-alike contest, so men allow facial hair to grow unchecked. The largest attraction of the week-long celebration is a parade through downtown Fairbanks complete with antique cars, clowns, marching bands and Felix Pedro himself dragging his reluctant mule through the streets. Beware of the roving jail, for those not true of heart and dressed as an early miner could be incarcerated for the short time it takes to bribe the jailkeeper.

For those in Fairbanks during July, the **World Eskimo-Indian Olympics** are a must. Among Alaskan Natives, great value and respect have always been awarded to physical fitness. The wide variety of games and contests have become traditional Native pastimes. Many of the games require excellent coordination, quickness of hands and eye, and great personal strength.

The list of games includes the ex-

Worker along the pipeline road.

The list of games includes the expected and also some surprises. The blanket toss competition is fun to watch, as is the Native Baby Contest. The Knuckle Hop, Ear Pulling and Ear Weight competitions seem excruciatingly painful. The Muktuk (whale meat) Eating, Fish Cutting and Seal Skinning competitions are opportunities to learn more about the Native cultures. The World Eskimo-Indian Olympics is a time for Natives to display crafts for sale, including beadwork, baskets, mukluks, skin garments, masks and carvings, and a unique opportunity for travellers to buy arts and crafts directly from Native artisans. For specific dates about the Olympics write W.E.I.O. Office, Box 2433, Fairbanks, AK 99707.

Although officially called the Alaska State Fair on even years and the Tanana Valley Fair on odd years, most everyone uses the latter name every year. The fair, held at the College Road fairgrounds during the second or third week of August, has grown to be the most popular event in the Interior, with attendance of more than 100,000. The prime attraction for travellers is the Harvest Hall filled with colossal vegetables. See what the long days can produce in the Interior, including huge radishes and 70-pound (32-kg) cabbages.

The Fringe

"So the stranger stumbles across the room, and flops down there like a fool.
In a buckskin shirt that was glazed with dirt he sat, and I saw him sway;
Then he clutched the keys with his talon hands – my God! but that man could play."

The sawdust floor and sourdough bartenders pushing beer across the bar mingle in a frozen moment when past and present swirl into one, as the deep-voiced rendition of Robert Service's *The Shooting of Dan McGrew* silences even those vivacious cheechakos (newcomers to the north) near the door. To enjoy this trip back in time, head for the settlement of **Ester,** seven miles (11 km) from Fairbanks off the Parks Highway. To the outsider, Ester is just another quiet, faded mining community, but during summer months, the **Malamute Saloon** swings open its doors to evening readings of Robert Service and vaudeville shows. Locals hang around the **Red**

Garter, and everyone enjoys the **Cripple Creek Lodge and Restaurant.** The rest of the year, the 200 residents of Ester sink into the solitude of small-town Alaska.

Home of Santa Claus

Yes, there is a Santa Claus. His home is located 14 miles (22.5 km) east of Fairbanks in, of all places, the **North Pole.** Other people have moved in around him; a few were even there before Santa handhewed the logs for his first **Santa Claus House.** With urban renewal and all, Santa had to move closer to the highway, where he's situated today. **Santaland** is a thriving commercial enterprise on the Richardson Highway, and perhaps it gives the visitor an idea of the enterprising types who homesteaded this area during the 1930s and 1940s. They were a new wave of pioneers who found Fairbanks already too crowded and who didn't mind living in this low-lying basin where winter temperatures are severe enough for the nickname "North Pole" to stick.

Presently, North Pole, an incorporated city within the North Star

Left, finding the elusive rainbow among the mountains. Right, ballooning.

Borough, is home to 940 folks and a surrounding population of 13,000. Land parcels are still available, and some of the homesteads remain intact, although most have been subdivided to ease the craving for land and housing. No longer a little sister to Fairbanks, or that swampy outpost between the city and Eielson Air Force Base, North Pole operates with its own utilities, brand-new shopping malls and thriving real estate businesses.

There's no mad stampede, no gold rush. But there is a bit of black gold flowing through North Pole. Daily, 45,000 barrels of crude oil are diverted from the Trans-Alaska Pipeline to North Pole Refining. Fifteen thousand barrels of home-heating oil and jet fuel are distilled and the rest returned to the main pipeline.

Another form of refining is going on in North Pole, at the sod-roofed KJNP (King Jesus North Pole) radio and television station on Mission Road.

With its 50,000 watts of broadcasting power, KJNP sends messages out to Bush Alaska. This service, aptly labeled *Trapline Chatter,* has saved lives, ended relationships, and eased the loneliness for many a bush dweller.

One young trapper, after tuning in 1170 AM night after night at 9:20 sharp to eavesdrop on his northern neighbors, fell so deeply in love with the soothing voice of the announcer that he returned to civilization in spring and married her.

Trails, like the threads of a spider's web, spun into Fairbanks from every direction in the early 1900s. The more popular routes were eventually transformed from dogsled tracks to the paved and gravel roadways that link the rest of Alaska to Fairbanks, the commercial hub of the Interior. The first trail-cum-highway in all of Alaska, the **Richardson,** was originally a pack trail between the then-bustling mining settlement of Eagle and Valdez. Following the gold rush, the trail was extended to Fairbanks, linking the Interior to an ice-free port. E.T. Barnette and company made many a trip on this path. Today, the Richardson joins with the Alaska Highway for the 98 miles (157 km) between Fairbanks and Delta Junction.

As surely as there is gold in the hills, there are buffalo and barley in **Delta Junction,** or is that buffalo IN the barley? The **Tanana Valley** is one of the

An Alaskan Malemute.

largest agricultural areas in the state, with most of the farming centered in the Delta area. Despite the typical Interior winter climate, the valley supports the Delta Barley Project, a state-sponsored attempt to introduce large-scale grain production to the Interior. Now at 90,000 acres (36,450 hectares), this farming venture, begun in 1978, is another example of the exuberant pioneering spirit in the Interior.

But what of hirsute bearded beasts? Although they could be the spirit watchers of the shaggy bison who ranged the Interior millennia ago, this herd was actually imported from Montana and introduced to the area specifically as a game animal. The original 23-member herd now numbers 400, and is the largest free-roaming buffalo herd in North America. These woolly wanderers have even been granted their own 90,000 acres (36,500 hectares) which in no way discourages them from haunting the barley patch. For a glimpse of the Delta buffalo, most people pull over at Mile 241 on the Richardson Highway and scan the country across the Delta River.

Fairbanks or Bust

"Once is Enough" declares the mud-splattered bumpersticker. Inside the vehicle is another *cheechako*, as a first-time visitor to Alaska is called, and this one is probably fresh off the **Alaska Highway,** that infamous 1,500-mile (2,415-km) stretch of road paved with curses and windshield chips. Bulldozed through the wilderness in 1942 as part of the war effort, the "Alcan" literally rose from the permafrost and slid down mountainsides as the U.S. Army Corps of Engineers frantically battled mud, mosquitoes and time. Much of the road from Dawson Creek in British Columbia, Canada, to Fairbanks is now paved, easing the perils of the odyssey, but not diminishing the thrill of arrival.

State Highway 3, alias the George Parks Highway – alias the Anchorage-Fairbanks Highway, and locally referred to as the "Parks" – does, ironically, lead to Denali National Park, although the roadway was named in honor of a governor, not the park. While still in the rolling hills of the Tanana Valley, the Parks passes through the town of **Nenana,** located 64 miles (103 km) southwest of Fairbanks.

Nenana, Railway Town

Nenana, an Athabascan word meaning "between two rivers," is situated at the confluence of the Tanana and Nenana rivers. Always one of the main river-freighting centers in Alaska, life in Nenana changed with the completion of the Alaska Railroad in 1923.

Folks in Nenana remember the stifling hot day of July 15, 1923, when President Warren Harding drove the golden spike signifying completion of the federally owned railroad. The original tracks stretching from the seaport of Seward to Nenana were later extended to Fairbanks. During construction, Fairbanks breathed softly. It appeared in 1920 that Nenana would become the major city of the Interior. All danger has apparently passed, as the population currently hovers around 500,

The railroad, constructed with excess equipment from the Panama Canal Project, made headlines again in January 1985 when it was purchased from the U.S. government by the state of Alaska. As in 1923, the celebration was held in Nenana, with the townspeople serving up moose stew for the dignitaries, sightseers and old-timers on hand to witness or relive a bit of Alaskan history. Losing its status as the only federally owned railroad in the country has not changed the Interior's love affair with this slow-moving apparatus. The train chugs along at about 50 mph (80 kmph) and still makes flag stops. Travellers can board in Fairbanks for the rolling trip south.

Nenana is also the terminus port for tug and barge fleets that service villages along the Tanana and Yukon rivers, loaded with supplies, fuel and tons of freight. For a closer inspection of an old tug, look up the refurbished **Taku Chief** behind the Visitor Information Center.

Although not yet the Monte Carlo of the north, Nenana is known far and wide for the **Nenana Ice Classic,** one of those annual events held only in the land of snow and ice and cabin fever. Cash prizes are awarded to the lucky souls who guess the exact time – to the minute, mind you – of spring breakup on the Tanana. Breakup is that moment when suddenly there's more water than ice on the river, when massive blocks of ice rip and surge, grind and groan against one another. But at that exact moment, ticket holders are more concerned with the time than with the spectacular release of winter energy.

The Tanana River again becomes the focal point a month or so later with **River Daze,** celebrated during the first weekend in June. One event is the raft race down the Tanana from Fairbanks to Nenana. Not an ordinary race, it's permeated with typical Alaskan inspiration and humor of latter-day Huck Finns who create a variety of floating contraptions and boldly enter them as "rafts." Anything goes, providing it floats and utilizes only "natural" power. All in good fun.

Whether one arrives in Nenana by highway or railroad, he is ultimately drawn by the wide sweep of the river to stand close to the bank, fix an eye on the river, and listen for the imagined slap of the sternwheeler or the swish of a canoe paddle.

Off to the Gold Fields

To drive the **Steese Highway** is to travel with the spirits of the miners who worked the many creek beds prospecting for gold. The road angles to the northeast for 162 miles (260 km) before ending at the Yukon River. First stop is on Haegelbarger Road at 3.6 Mile (six km) for a scenic wide-angle view of Fairbanks and the Alaska Range. Back out on the Steese, don't accelerate too much. The best look at the Trans-Alaska Pipeline is right up ahead at 8.4 Mile (13.5 km). Resting on vertical support members (VSMs) and bound in a sleeve of insulation, the pipeline parallels the Steese Highway above the permafrost-rich ground. Farther on at 11 Mile (18 km) is the community of **Fox,** an early mining encampment which took its name from a nearby creek. The community is most famous now for its excellent spring water. The symmetrical piles of gravel surrounding Fox are the dregs of the mighty earth-eating dredges. The piles lie like great loaves of bread, browned on top and awaiting the next course.

The **Monument to Felix Pedro** at 17 Mile (27 km) is a modest reminder of the Italian immigrant who was the first to strike it rich in these valleys. Gravel in the creek on the opposite side of the road has been known to show some "color," so practice your panning skills here.

The next three miles (five km) of road gradually ascend to **Cleary Summit,** named for Frank Cleary, Barnette's brother-in-law. The sister – or should it be brother – peak is **Pedro Dome,** the hill from which Felix Pedro spotted the sternwheeler *Lavelle Young* grounded in the Chena River. Cleary Summit offers a panoramic view of the Tanana Valley, the White Mountains and the Alaska Range.

The Story of a Bandit

Back in 1905, the legendary "Blue Parka Bandit" found this encompassing lookout quite handy for his trade. Charles Hendrickson, engineer-turned-robber and terror of the trails, haunted these bold granite crags, pinching the pokes of unsuspecting gold miners. Armed and masked, he demanded gold, occasionally tarnishing his ignominious reputation with Robin Hood tactics; like the time he detained the Episcopalian Bishop and his entourage. The episode concluded when the Bishop convinced the bandit to give him all the gold pokes. Fans of Alaskan gold rush lore will not want to miss **Fairbanks Creek Road.** Leave the Steese Highway

Low winter sun silhouettes a refinery at North Pole.

and Cleary Summit and travel south along the ridgeline for eight miles (13 km) to **Alder Creek Camp.** Beyond this, be prepared for a one-mile (1.6 km) walk to **Meehan,** an abandoned machine shop area where maintenance was done on mining equipment. History hangs heavy in the air here; rusted equipment can be found strewn along the trail.

Fairbanks Creek Camp is an additional two miles (3.2 km) below Meehan. Dredge Number Two met an untimely end in 1959 along this creek when a deck hand decided to use dynamite to open an ice-blocked hole. The dredge quickly sank! Fairbanks Creek relinquished many tusks, teeth and bones of Pleistocene mammals during stripping operations. One of the most famous fossils is a well-preserved baby Woolly Mammoth found in 1949.

Hot Baths for the Miners

The old Circle District is not devoid of gold yet or the miners who search for it. Some of them live in **Central,** a small mining community strung out along the Steese Highway and described by locals

A hard-hatted oil worker.

as "three miles long and one block wide." An active winter population of 100 swells to more than 800 during the summer months when miners and vacationers return. With the addition of a permanent school in Central in 1981, more and more "summer people" are staying on late into fall. A worthwhile detour on your way to the hot springs [eight miles (13 km) up the road] is a stop at the **Circle District Historical Society Museum** located in Central. The museum's grand opening was celebrated in July 1984 with the unveiling of a mining equipment attraction, a display featuring the hardy alpine wildflowers found on Eagle Summit, and a period cabin containing authentic artifacts. The museum is open noon to 5 p.m. in summer and upon request in winter. Overnight accommodations, camping facilities and general "pitstop" services are available in Central.

Gold nuggets weren't the only pleasures that warmed the miners' souls during the rush. Imagine the heartwarming experience of William Greats, who, back in 1893, crept into a small valley for a closer look at the steaming witch's cauldron he had spotted. He must have been a popular fellow for a time when he led his cohorts to the mineral springs he'd discovered.

Many areas are abandoned after a rush, but never a hot spring. Visitors do not have to reenact days of old when ice was chipped from tent flaps to enter the bathing houses. The **Arctic Circle Hot Springs** has been spruced up, and now offers a 1930s hotel refurbished with Victorian decor, an ice cream parlor, family-style restaurant and the Miners' Saloon. The hotel offers an upstairs hostel and a campground with hiking and skiing trails. But those are places and activities to investigate after your body has withered beyond recognition and your rubbery legs can no longer propel you to the edge of the open airpool. There's really nothing quite like dangling from an innertube in 109-degree (43 degrees C) mineral water, completely enveloped in a cloak of mist as the water condenses in the -40 degree (-40 degrees C) air.

The summer experience is equally pleasurable after the 130-mile (210 km) trip up the Steese. **KAK Tours** (907) 488-2649 provides scheduled small van service from Fairbanks in summer. Scheduled commercial flights are available since 1984, the Steese Highway is maintained everyday except Monday and Tuesday during winter. Call ahead for overnight reservations and road conditions. No advance notice is necessary to use the pool.

Circle City

All roads end some place. For the Steese, it's all over at **Circle City,** a small community 50 miles (80 km) south of the Arctic Circle, poised along a bend in the Yukon River. This is the same Circle of gold rush days with an 1890s population of 1,000, that has dwindled down to 71 friendly folks.

Once the largest gold mining town on the Yukon, Circle was nearly abandoned after the gold strikes in the Klondike and Fairbanks areas. Gone are Jack McQuesten's two-story log store, two dozen or so saloons, eight dance halls, theaters and the music hall of the Circle City that was called the "Paris of the North." In their places reign a modern-day trading post with a motel, cafe, general store, bar and gas station. Tourist facilities are definitely geared for the summer visitor. Chartered "flight-seeing" trips are available, but boat rentals are not.

There's usually plenty of waterfront activity in this popular "take in" and "take out" place for canoeist and rafters travelling the Yukon River. One popular river trip begins in either Eagle or Circle and terminates at Fort Yukon or farther downstream under the pipeline bridge.

Circle, so named because early miners thought they were camped at the Arctic Circle, still teems with activity. Fishwheels smack the water as they turn in the current, flat-bottomed boats zoom up and down the river, and barges still make their way to points upriver. River travellers could easily miss all of this; the "land" in front of Circle is actually an island concealing another channel of the mighty Yukon.

Gamblers gained notoriety in the saloons of boom and bust towns like Circle City. One who went on to national fame was Tex Richard. He was 24 years old in 1895 when he trekked into Circle and found a job in Sam Bonnifield's gambling saloon. Impressed by the honesty of his boss, for the rest of his life, it is said, he gambled "as if Sam Bonni-

Alaskan pipeline zigzags across the state.

168

field were looking over his shoulder." His claim to fame was not made in Circle City, however, but a bit later when he built Madison Square Garden in New York City. He was also well-known as a promoter for the heavyweight boxing champ of the world, Jack Dempsey. You just never know who you're going to meet in the Interior!

Historic Eagle

"Sam. We left 'round midnight. Dried out, canoe patched. Meet ya in Circle or Fort Yukon. Gene and Doreen."

Not an uncommon message to be left fluttering on the bulletin board outside the U.S. Post Office in **Eagle,** a popular jumping-off place for Yukon River paddlers, as well as an official stop for river explorers floating from Dawson City. As the first city on the U.S. side of the silty Yukon, Eagle's Post Office is where river travellers check in with U.S. customs.

Life in Eagle has all the pleasurable ingredients of a river village as well as the advantages of an "end-of-the-road"

Hydraulic mining to reap Alaska's natural riches.

community. It is situated 161 miles (260 km) from Tetlin Junction at the terminus of the Taylor Highway, a mixed blessing since the road closes when winter snow isolates the community.

"People of the River," or the Han Athabascans, were the original inhabitants of this area. Chief John, of legendary fame for crushing the cheap glass beads offered to him by early white traders, left his impression; and, for quite a time, Eagle was known as John's Village.

Perhaps the spirits of those first white traders still linger in the back streets of Eagle, whispering revenge on John's ancestors. An uneasiness has settled over Eagle, most perceptibly in the white community and Native populations separated by a three-mile (4.8-km) gravel road and an invisible barrier not yet completely hurdled by either group.

The Eagle visited by travellers today had its beginnings in 1874 when the far-reaching and powerful Northern Commercial Company (NC) stretched its commercial fingers along the Yukon River and established a trading post at this site. Gold seekers followed fur traders and, within 24 years, Moses Mer-

cier's tiny outpost was transformed into a brazen mining town of 1,700. Seized by gold fever, thousands more, digging in every tributary of the Yukon, swept through Han territory.

By 1898, the city was renamed for the eagles who stake their claim on the bluffs along the river. A post office was established, along with an army post, saloon and dressmaker; and entrepreneurs flourised, including a piano player.

History was being made at the turn of the century, and Eagle was host to its share.

Judge Wickersham wintered here in 1900. The incredible Valdez-to-Eagle telegraph line spun out a most interesting message in 1905 when Roald Amundson, passing through after his successful expedition into the Northwest Passage, made his announcement to the world from Eagle.

Eagle paid its dues in the boom-and-bust cycle of the gold fields. By 1910 the muckers had vanished, trekking after even richer dreams near Fairbanks. They left behind 178 people, about the same population as today. But the buildings still stand and Eagle has

undertaken a program to restore many of its fine older structures.

During summer, the Eagle Historical Society conducts a free walking tour, which includes **Judge Wickersham's Courthouse,** built by fines he imposed quarterly on gamblers and prostitutes in the rowdy mining town. Inside are the Judge's desk and an early map of the country constructed of papier-mâché and moose blood. Also open for inspection is **Fort Egbert,** established by the U.S. Army, but abandoned in 1911.

Summer visitors will find the basic necessities — laundry, restaurant, lodging, groceries, gas station, gravel airstrip and mechanic shop. For those who are inclined to go further "upriver," a daily commercial cruise motors between Eagle and Dawson City. Gone, though, are the sternwheelers plying the muddy Yukon between Dawson and the Bering Sea, bringing to Eagle the gold dust and sweeping away discarded dreams. Today, Eagle "feeds" the Yukon in another way. The insatiable appetite of the river current crumbles the high bank, devouring chunks of the city's real estate with each season and causing

Packhorses —one way to savor the backcountry.

a stir each time the "river viewing" bench is moved back a few feet.

Another Hot One

A jog to the right at 5 Mile (8 km) and Steese sends you rollercoasting through the countryside on Chena Hot Springs Road. This paved beauty is only 56 miles (90 km) long, passes through the middle of the 254,000-acre (103,000-hectare) **Chena River Recreation Area,** and terminates at the gates to the privately owned and publicly adored **Chena Hot Springs Resort.** The place is commercially equipped with all the necessities for an extended visit, but more alluring are the steaming hot-water ponds scattered throughout Monument Creek Valley, and the indoor swimming and soaking facilities.

The four major highways in the Interior extend out of Fairbanks like the arms of a lopsided windmill. To the northwest is the **Elliot Highway** and, continuing beyond, the Dalton Highway. The Elliot branches off the Steese 11 miles (18 km) north of Fairbanks and winds through 152 miles (245 km) of gold-mining country trimmed with broad valleys, bubbling creeks, blueberries and poppies, homesteads and mining camps.

Livengood, near the junction of the Elliot and Dalton highways, had secured the "end-of-the-road" position. Here, a jog to the left terminates in either the Athabascan Village of **Minto** on the Tolovana River or at **Manley Hot Springs,** another mining center, farther on. Livengood, however, experienced an invasion in the mid-1970s when it was transformed from an isolated "mind-your-own-business" neighborhood to a pipeline construction camp.

Black Gold

Three million man-hours, five months of intensive labor, and millions of tons of gravel equal one 416-mile (670-km) service road paralleling one of the most ambitious projects ever undertaken in the North American Arctic — the **Trans-Alaska Pipeline.** This service road-cum-state highway, officially dubbed the **Dalton Highway** but known simply as the "Haul Road," opened up thousands of acres of wilderness terri-

Hunters show off their catch.

tory which can now be explored from the comfort of a vehicle. The road is maintained from Livengood to Prudhoe Bay, but privately owned vehicles are allowed only as far as **Disaster Creek** near Dietrich Camp, about 280 miles (450 km) north of Fairbanks and 200 miles (322 km) south of the Arctic Ocean. Travel beyond the Dietrich checkpoint is reserved for industrial traffic, by permit.

A journey north on the Dalton, above the Arctic Circle, through the land of sheep, bears, wolves and foxes can be the ultimate coup of your trip, but beware. Rental cars cannot be driven up the road. Conditions are hazardous; the roadway is rough and dusty in summer and slippery in winter. Because this is primarily a service road, heavily loaded 18-wheelers rule the route. If you can't resist going, plan as you would for a wilderness camping trip, but take your wallet; automobile towing charges can cost up to $5 per mile (1.6 km). Service station facilities and emergency communications are available at only two locations, the Yukon River crossing at Mile 56.6 (91 km) and Coldfoot at Mile 173.6 (280 km). For road conditions, telephone 907-451-2294.

Into the Bush

What is beyond Pedro Dome, Cleary Summit and the White Mountains? What is it that the Chena, the Chatanika and the Tanana rivers are drawn toward? Not unlike explorers of yesterday, visitors to Fairbanks often feel a gentle urge to soar over the mountain peaks or float with the river current to its mouth. Beyond, north of Fairbanks, is the **Yukon River,** seemingly with a magnetic force of its own. If Fairbanks is the heart of the Interior, then the Yukon is surely a life-supporting artery.

Centuries before European explorers spread out over the land, the Yukon River and its many tributaries were a common link in the survival of the nomadic Athabascan tribes living in the Interior. Ironically, the Yukon became the means of intrusion as sternwheelers labored upriver from St. Michael on the Bering Sea to the fur country and gold fields.

When explorers, missionaries and fortune hunters penetrated this wilder-

An inland cowboy.

ness, the Athabascans were living as they had for generations, subsisting on salmon, moose or caribou, berries and water birds. They were survivors in a harsh and unmerciful land. With the arrival of outsiders, the Natives congregated into small communities.

Along the Yukon, scattered like knots on a kite string, are the Athabascan river villages. Dozens of tiny settlements still exist, sharing this inhospitable northern country with the rivers. The historical perspective of each community varies, but, remarkably, they remain part of 20th-Century Alaska, silent tributes to the Athabascans of the past.

Present-day Village Lifestyles

It would be naive to believe that the villages exist in a totally virgin state, untouched by the modern world; conversely, it would be presumptuous to assume that the villages continue to provide a viable lifestyle due only to space-age technology (e.g. satellite telephones). Generally, villagers maintain a subsistence lifestyle, hunting, fishing, trapping, gardening and gathering ber-

Mountain vistas abound in the Interior.

ries. Daily life embraces the rhythm of the seasons; and, often, survival demands adjusting to weather conditions and the unpredictable cycles of wildlife.

Elementary schools, many containing the most modern educational equipment available, are a part of every village. Since 1976, many villages offer a high school education to its young people. The typical village teenager, however, carrying all the dreams of his ancestors, is spiralling into the 20th Century, often at a crossroads both personally and culturally.

The village elders, those "keepers of the culture," go on dispensing wisdom daily as did their grandmothers and grandfathers a century ago. Village pride reached new horizons in the 1980s when influences from the "outside" pressed an ever-tighter fist into the core of Athabascan strongholds. Almost forgotten dialects now roll easily from the lips of youngsters. Ancient drumbeats and dances are as popular as are the howl of today's "rockers." The village is a microcosm of contrast, evoking a strong sense of the past and surging into the present, welcoming the traditional and grappling toward the future.

175

NOME AND THE REMOTE WEST

"I've never been to Nome and not had a good time," says one Alaskan who has visited the city six times in the past dozen years. His words, directly and indirectly, capture the spirit of this most remote of Alaska's major cities. **Nome** has long been known as the city that wouldn't die, although it has had more than enough reason to disappear many times since its founding in 1899.

Nome has been burned to the ground; pounded by relentless gales (including one that left the city looking like it had been "shelled by a hostile fleet," according to a survivor); decimated by flu, diptheria and other maladies; and almost starved out of existence. Yet, through it all, the city has always rebuilt and always struggled on.

It was gold, discovered in 1898, that brought men, and later women to this wind-swept, wave-battered beach on the Seward Peninsula, 75 or more miles from the nearest tree. Of all the Alaska gold rush towns. Nome was the largest and the rowdiest. 1900 was the big year in Nome. Best estimates put the population in excess of 20,000 people by the end of the summer, but nobody knows for certain–there was no way to make an accurate count.

By the time gold-bearing creeks around the area were discovered, claim jumping and other less-than-ethical mining practices were well advanced in Alaska. Claim jumping was so rampant that it probably took a dozen years or more before everything was straightened out. By then the boom was dying and Nome boasted little more than 5,000 residents. Over the years the permanent population has shrunk to as low as 500. It has more or less stabilized in recent years at about 3,000 residents in the immediate area.

Nome hosted a whole series of gold rushes, each almost blending into the other. The first gold came the traditional way–it was found in the streams flowing into Norton Sound. The thousands

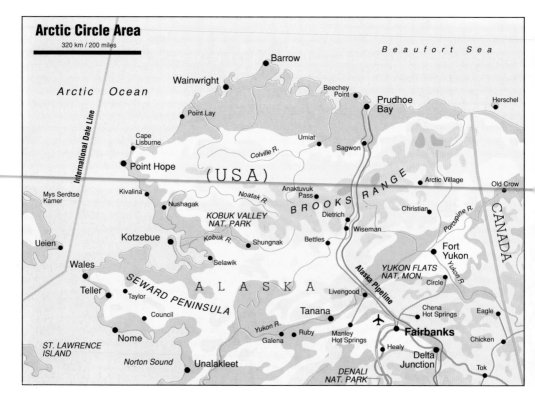

who rushed to Nome set their tents on the beach and explored the nearby gullies, little realizing that all they had to do was sift the sand that was their floor for the precious yellow metal.

The famed black sand beaches of Nome count as the "second" gold rush. Since nobody could legally stake a claim on the beach, a man could work any ground he could stand upon near the shoreline. The sands were turned over dozens of times and yielded millions of dollars in gold.

Then geologists pointed out that Nome had more than a single beach. Over the centuries, as rivers carried silt to the ocean, the beach line had gradually extended out to sea. These geologists predicted early on that under the tundra a few yards back from the water, miners would find an ancient beach and, with it, more deposits of gold. And so it was that later years saw yet a third gold rush as ground behind the sea wall was dug and redug to extract the gold.

Today, fortune seekers still sift the sands in front of Nome. During the summer of 1984, a Nome resident out for a walk along the beach reached under a piece of driftwood and picked up a gold nugget weighing over an ounce. Such are the rewards of fresh air and exercise.

The beach at Nome is still open to the public. Anyone with a gold pan or a sluice box and a tent to camp in can search for gold along the waterfront. It's hard, back-breaking work, but then riches have never come easy for miners. Perhaps the only ones who found easy money were the gamblers and the tricksters who made their living relieving miners of their hard-earned gold.

The shifty-eyed characters who learned their crafts in the boom towns of the wild west converged on Nome as practiced, professional con artists—men like Wyatt Earp, famed frontier marshal, who arrived in Nome as a paunchy, 51-year-old saloon keeper. (In Nome he was frequently at odds with the law.)

Yet Nome's gold rush years spawned a hero or two amid the unscrupulous. Shortly after Earp arrived, a family named Doolittle moved to town. One

Preceding pages, Unalakleet from above. Below, welcoming words to Polar Circle visitors.

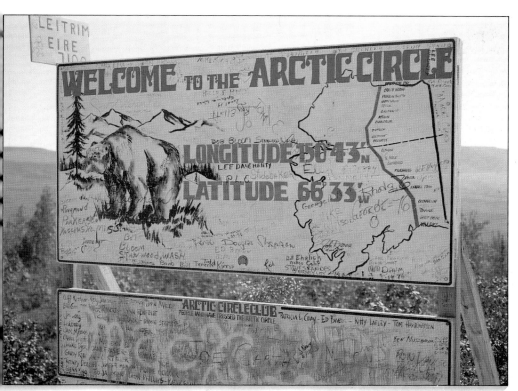

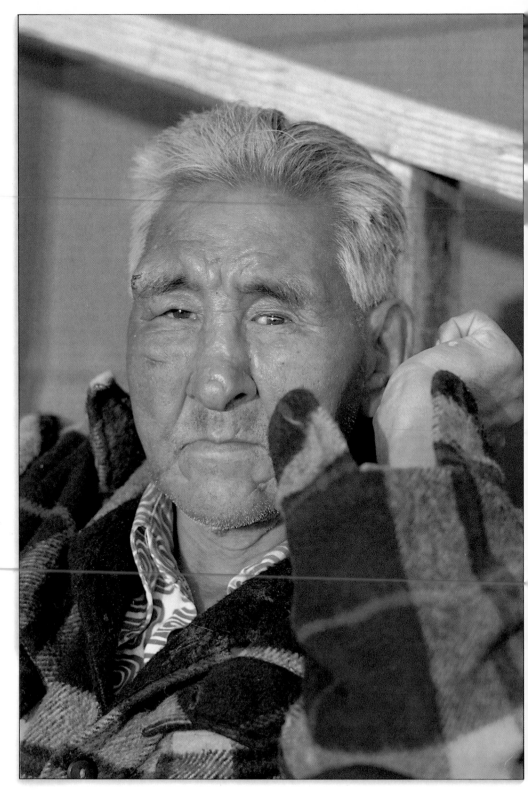

boy, Jimmy, never very tall, delivered newspapers for the *Nome Nugget*, the oldest continually published newspaper in Alaska. Jimmy grew up to lead "Doolittle's Raiders," the daring group of Army pilots who launched their oversized, overloaded bombers from the pitching decks of a Navy aircraft carrier in the darkest days of World War II.

Energetic Celebrations

The ability to face all comers, whatever the odds, is what makes Nome the rollicking place it is today. Nomites bring a special energy to almost every project they take on. After all, in western Alaska you sometimes have to make your own fun.

The combined Midnight Sun Festival/4th of July celebration is a good example. Up until a few years ago these were two separate events. But, by lengthening one party and starting the second one a few days early, Nome gave itself an excuse for a week-long bash beginning about the 28th of June.

As with with most civic celebrations. there's a parade. There are hardly any spectators: most of the local residents are in the parade. If you walk down to the starting point, you'll find those scheduled to march last in the parade watching the leaders start out. At the finish line, all those in the early part of the parade get to watch the stragglers finish. Thus everybody gets to be part of the parade and watch part of it too.

Then there's the Nome River Raft Race. The only rule seems to be that there are no rules. Any contrivance that floats and carries a significant quantity of beer or wine for the riders is deemed to be in the race. Few participants can be considered sober when they lurch from the water at the finish line.

And what would the 4th of July be without fireworks? In the early 1980s Nome's city council wanted to stop such devices within the city limits because of the fire hazard–burning down the whole town gets old after you've done it a few times. This particularly affected the mayor, one of the largest fireworks dealers in the area. He solved

the problem by setting up his firework stand a few steps outside the city line and gleefully sold all manner of pyrotechnics to the people, who then immediately took the goods to their homes in town. Thus there's still plenty of noise, fire and smoke for the Fourth of July, and the mayor needs not worry about being jailed for breaking the law.

Nome loves to party–almost any excuse will do. Take June of 1981, when a U.S. Coast Guard icebreaker with a crew of about 150 men anchored offshore. Early that afternoon the skipper made his way into Nome's police department to warn the cops that he was giving half his crew liberty at 4 p.m. He was worried lest any of his men be jailed, and offered the services of his officers should any problems arise.

News travels fast in rural communities and by the time the Coasties hit the beach a few hours later. Nome was ready. Modern-day hucksters were trying to sell illegal walrus ivory to gullible sailors–$60 and two drinks for a whole tusk. The bars were doing a booming business and Front Street was jumping all night.

And the cops filled up the jail. But when things calmed down and the jailer took a head count, there were no Coasties behind bars. All those incarcerated were locals caught trying to show the Coast Guards how to party. So much for the rumors about sailors on liberty. And, mysteriously enough, few of those jailed saw a judge the next morning. When they sobered up the doors were opened and the party-goers made their way home. There are advantages to living in a remote frontier town.

Those advantages show themselves in other ways. Nome is a close community, almost anyone is available to lend a hand. Consider Christmas. Christmas trees are traditional decorations in local homes just as elsewhere in the United States. The problem with this arises when one realizes that the last ship of the season usually departs in October, Just before Norton Sound freezes. Trees can be flown in, but that's expensive. However, about 80 miles (129 km) to the east is a forest, and in the weeks

A Kotzebue man.

before Christmas residents band together and dispatch truckloads of volunteers along a bone-crunching road leading to the forest. The trucks are filled with small spruce trees, enough to insure that every home can have a tree. These aren't the magnificent Douglas firs favored in the Lower 48. Instead, they're scraggly tundra spruce trees, but they are adequate for the task.

The Great Race–by Dogsled

After Christmas, there's one more high point in the long winter, the combined Spring Carnival and Iditarod Trail Sled Dog Race. The Iditarod commemorates the frantic race to get diptheria serum to Nome in 1925. The town was teetering on the verge of an epidemic and the only possible way to get the serum to Nome was overland by dogsled. The serum was taken by train to Nenana and from there experienced mushers ran their sleds and teams in relays, round the clock, to get it to Nome. A trip that normally took a month or more was completed in a matter of days.

Today, the Iditarod is a sporting event billed as "The Last Great Race on Earth." About 65 racers bring their teams to the starting line in Anchorage on the first Saturday in March. The winners reach Nome about two weeks later, having travelled an actual distance of about 1,049 miles (1,678 km) on the grueling trail. All manner of hostile terrain–and the elements–batter the racers from start to finish.

In the 1985 race, Susan Butcher, leading the pack a couple of days out of Anchorage, tangled with a moose. Before things were sorted out in the dark, the moose had stomped and kicked her dog team out of the race. Later the race was halted twice for bad weather. And finally, in an act of considerable courage–some say foolhardiness–Libby Riddles, a quiet, blue-eyed blond from Teller, a small village northwest of Nome, headed out of a checkpoint into the teeth of a howling gale only a couple hundred miles from the finish line. No other musher would risk travelling in

Early dogsledders.

DOG-DRIVING NEAR THE VESOLIA SOPKA.

180

the storm. But the few miles she made that night before being forced to make camp and sit out the storm gave Libby the extra edge needed for victory, and she became the first woman to win in the 13-year history of the event.

Susan Butcher made an incredible comeback in 1986, winning the gruelling race in a record time of 11 days. She continued on through 1988 to be the only person to win three consecutive races. What was once considered only a man's domain has recently been dominated by women.

Nome is today the transportation hub of western Alaska. It has a major airport with daily jet service to and from Anchorage and provides commuter plane service to almost every other state. Almost anyone touring western Alaska must at least pass through Nome.

Superb Fishing

Unalakleet, an hour by air southeast of Nome on the eastern edge of Norton Sound, is a pleasant Native village with good schools, churches and probably the best-kept secret in Alaska. The Unalakleet River, which runs through town, supports a large run of king salmon in late June, and the angling is superb. And, unlike most king salmon sport fisheries, bag limits are generous. Six fish per person per day has been the rule in recent years. Most other major fisheries only allow anglers a single king salmon daily.

Travel agents in Anchorage can set up a stay at a full-service fishing lodge on the Unalakleet River for those who wish to battle the giant salmon. Such a tour is not cheap: $300 to $500 a day or more per person. But, a couple of days fishing in the Unalakleet River when the kings are in is probably the experience of a lifetime for most fishermen.

North of Nome lies **Kotzebue**, a large, predominantly Eskimo community. Kotzebue is also served by daily jet service out of Anchorage.

Kotzebue is the headquarters for NANA, one of the regional Native corporations established in 1971 with pas-

Iditarod sled racer nears Cape Safety.

sage of the Alaska Native Claims Settlement Act. That act granted Alaskan Natives nearly $1 billion in cash and title to some 44 million acres (18 million hectares) of land: the money and the ground were divided up by 13 Native corporations formed to manage the sudden wealth. NANA's share was significant and it is believed to be one of the more successful of the 13 corporations.

NANA is actively involved in the reindeer industry, which is restricted by law to Alaska Natives. Several other business ventures of a more contemporary nature round out NANA's holdings. The company is providing jobs to its shareholders and is a significant economic force in western Alaska.

The big up and coming economic development of the mid-1980s in western Alaska is the development of a world-class zinc mine just a short distance northeast of Kotzebue. Cominco, a Canadian-based mining concern, is developing the roads and other infrastructure necessary to support the venture. The state of Alaska guaranteed a $150 million dollar loan in the spring of 1985 for the road system. The Red Dog Mine project is expected to provide 400 or more full-time jobs in the region, a tremendous economic impact for such a sparsely populated area. Zinc deposits are expected to last 20 years or more once the mine reaches full production, and recoverable quantities of silver, lead and other minerals have been detected in the same ground.

At the same time, however, Kotzebue is traditional. Fishermen still tend nets in Kotzebue Sound and nearby streams. Walrus, seal, whale and polar bear hunters still brave the elements in pursuit of their quarries. Kotzebue is a unique combination of the old and the new, and one of the few places where traditional and contemporary lifestyles are blending together in reasonably good harmony.

Wilderness Adventures

Kotzebue is also the jumping-off point for those seeking wilderness ad-

Nome schoolchildren prepare to welcome Iditarod winners.

venture in the **Noatak National Preserve** and **Kobuk Valley National Park**. Also accessible from Kotzebue are **Cape Krusenstern National Monument** and the **Bering Land Bridge National Preserve**. These lands were all set aside as part of the 1980 Alaska National Interest Lands Conservation Act, known to most Alaskans as simply "d-2."

There is no easy way to get to these remote parks and preserves. There are no roads. Charters airplanes from Kotzebue, starting at about $200 an hour, are about the only means of access. Before chartering to any of these areas, however, check carefully with the National Park Service office in Kotzebue. Various activities, such as reindeer herding, are allowed to take place on portions of these lands. Those planning a wilderness adventure to seek solitude would probably be disappointed to land in the middle of a commercial reindeer drive.

One Kotzebue attraction that shouldn't be missed is the **NANA**

Museum of the Arctic. Tours include a two-hour program with a diorama show that is unequalled anywhere in Alaska. It is a splendid introduction to the land and the traditional Native culture of the region.

There's also a superb city museum, **Ootukahkuktuvik**, which means "place having old things." Among the articles on display are a raincoat made from walrus intestine and a coat created from bird feathers.

The biggest summer celebration in Kotzebue is again the 4th of July. But here it's a little different. Instead of the routine games found at most such festivities, Kotzebue awards prizes for traditional Native games, the largest beluga whale killed by hunters, a *muktuk* eating contest and seal-hook throwing events.

The week following the 4th of July celebration features the Arctic Trades Fair. People from all over the region come to trade handicrafts and participate in traditional dances and feasts.

For wintertime travellers, the week

The waterfront at Kotzebue.

between Christmas and New Years brings the preliminaries for the annual Eskimo Olympics. Events include one- and two-legged high kicks, knuckle hops, ear pulls, blanket tossing, finger pulling and greased pole walks. Sports fans will find these events refreshingly different and interesting, and some- times a bit painful for the participants.

Another western Alaska destination that should rate high with history buffs is **Saint Michael** on the south shore of Norton Sound. Saint Michael was the major trans-shipment point for freight going to the Klondike gold fields at the turn of the century.

Almost everybody who has read of the Klondike Gold Rush (often called the Alaska Gold Rush although the Klondike was in Canada) knows about the struggles of the miners to hike the Chilkoot Pass out of Yukon River. Lesser documentation tells of the thou- sands of miners who reached the same destination by travelling in relative comfort abroad sternwheelers plying the Yukon River. Saint Michael, near the mouth of the Yukon River delta, was the base for the river steamers. Ocean steamers transferred cargoes bound for Dawson and other upriver points to the river boats at Saint Michael. Bits and pieces of old river steamers can still be found along the waterfront. Other than the gear miners carried on their backs over the Chilkoot Trail, most of the heavy equipment, food and freight that eventually reached the Klondike gold fields came through Saint Michael on Alaska's remote western coast.

Islands off the western coast of Alaska include the **Pribilofs**, nesting grounds for hundreds of thousands of sea birds of 191 different species, and the breeding grounds and summer home of the Pacific fur seals. There's a small hotel in **Saint Paul** (population about 600) and two small restaurants. Sched- uled air service is available from An- chorage to Saint Paul.

In the 1990s, the oil industry is ex- pected to base several exploration ac- tivities in the Pribilof Islands. The bot- tom of the Bering Sea north and west of the island is believed to shelter millions,

maybe billions of barrels of oil, and many of the industry's giant companies are beginning to seriously investigate the region.

Today, the fishing industry is being developed as Saint Paul's main eco- nomic support. Past revenues were generated by the annual fur seal harvest and various government doles. With the discontinuation of the fur seal harvest, the community was forced to find other means of support. Saint Paul's newly completed harbor is a boon to local fishermen, who have had no safe haven for their boats, and is expected to attract industry to the island.

For the adventuresome traveller, a trip to Alaska's West Coast can be as thrilling as finding gold on the beach, or as daring as competing in the grueling Iditarod race. The region's residents are fun-loving and hospitable—and some- times unconventional. With a colorful past and a resource-rich future. Alaska's West Coast offers a look at the traditional way of life in the language of today.

Below, an Eskimo of delicately- carved ivory; left, Eskimo boys at Kotzebue.

CAPE KRUSENSTERN

It's hard to imagine a less likely place for buried treasure. There's nothing particularly conspicuous about **Cape Krusenstern**, no towering mountains, magnificent waterfalls, verdant forests. Only a low, ridged spit with deep furrows, it's dotted with countless ponds, and bordered by a relentless sea on one side, while a large lagoon on the other greets the visitor's eye. Resembling a giant scythe clipping the waves of the **Chukchi Sea**, Cape Krusenstern stretches into polar waters in northwestern Alaska. Hidden beneath beach ridges on the cape is an archeological treasure reaching back at least four thousand years. This chronicle of early man in Alaska brought about the establishment of 560,000-acre (226,600-hectare) **Cape Krusenstern National Monument** in 1980.

Charter planes and boats headquartered in **Kotzebue** take visitors to the monument, 10 miles (16 km) northwest across Kotzebue Sound at its southern border. The small village of **Kivalina** stretches out along the Chukchi shore north of the monument, and to the east across the Mulgrave Hills lies the village of **Noatak**. Kivalina and Noatak have airstrips although most visitors arrive via Kotzebue, which has jet service from Anchorage and Fairbanks.

Cape Krusenstern is a bring-your-own-shelter monument, and that goes for stove, food and water also. Highlands beyond the beaches have fresh water streams, but it's still best to carry water along. The National Park Service has built no shelters, and there are no campgrounds. (Cabins and tent platforms are off-limits to the public.) The Krusenstern tableau is waiting, but come prepared to be self-sustaining.

Planes can land on some beaches of the monument, and floatplanes put down on nearby lagoons. Many beach areas are privately owned; visitors should check with monument headquarters staff in Kotzebue for specific locations of private property. No signs mark private areas. Travellers are free to explore archeological zones, but no digging for artifacts or other disturbance is allowed.

Winds sweep almost constantly across the lowlands of Cape Krusenstern. In winter they bring instant freezing to an already-cold land. In summer fog blankets coastal areas, although temperatures warm from 40 to 65 degrees F (four to 18°C). Inland, the skies are often clear in June and July, but visitors should always carry rain gear and be alert for hypothermia, the severe lowering of the body's core temperature.

Formation of the Cape

The cape at Krusenstern didn't always exist. In fact, as recently as about 10,000 years ago, the coastline angled straight southeast from Point Hope, skirted a small mountain, and turned east. Kotzebue Sound was mostly a giant sandy lowland and not the busy waterway it is today. During the Pleistocene epoch, about 2 million to 10,000 to 15,000 years ago, great ice sheets covered much of the northern hemisphere. These ice masses absorbed water, causing sea level to recede. As the sea shrank away from the shore, it exposed a land bridge connecting North America and Asia. At the end of the Pleistocene, when the ice sheets melted,

Preceding pages, migrating sandhill cranes; below, an archeological dig.

sea level rose once again and covered the land bridge.

Sweeping down the newly aligned coastline, prevailing winds from the northwest propelled waves, which carried bits of gravel in their churning surf, down the beach. When the waves hit the turn where the coastline swung east, they dropped the gravel offshore. Every so often, usually in the spring, the winds shifted to the southwest. Great chunks of ice were driven onshore, but not before the ice scooped up gravel from shallow offshore beds and deposited it on the beach beyond the surf. Ridge after ridge built up on the outer shore of the cape.

Slowly the cape pushed seaward. Hardy beach plants colonized the ridges, their root systems helping to stabilize the gravels. Year after year the birth and death of beach plants built up a thin layer of soil, creating suitable habitat for other plants. Throughout the centuries, a carpet of green followed the shoreline, advancing seaward, until 114 ridges lined the two-to-four-mile-wide (3.2-to-6.4-km) spit. Lt. Otto von Kotzebue, sailing for the Imperial Russian Navy, gave geographical recognition to the cape by naming it Krusenstern after the first Russian admiral to circumnavigate the globe in 1803-04.

View of Tunanak.

Arctic Archeology

Not until the late 1950s was the significance of the beach ridges correlated with the history of early man in Alaska. Professor J. Louis Giddings, anthropologist and archeologist, unlocked the treasure chest buried in the frozen beach gravels and began a new chapter in arctic archeology.

Giddings had sought signs of ancient man at several sites in northwestern Alaska prior to coming to Krusenstern in 1958. In 1948 he had uncovered artifacts from the Denbigh Flint people at Cape Denbigh in Norton Sound to the south. These ancient Alaskans left their calling cards—tiny chipped flints—in the soils of prehistoric Alaska about 4,000 years ago. (The discoverer placed the date at about 5,000 years ago, but more recent studies lead scientists to think 4,000 years is closer to the mark.) Archeologists view these discoveries as the first from the Arctic Small Tool tradition which eventually

spanned the top of the continent from the Bering Sea to Greenland.

At Krusenstern, Giddings probed the ridges back from the shore to discover artifacts related to the succession of early man in northwestern Alaska and probably the entire northern portion of the continent. Laid out in order of their occurrence along the series of beach ridges were the remains of houses or hunting camps for every ancient man culture known to northwestern Alaska. Excavations during several years opened the prehistoric record, ridge by ridge, of the ancestors of modern Eskimos and those cultures which preceded them across the land bridge from Asia to arctic North America.

From the ninth to the 19th ridges, Giddings and his assistants unearthed bits of pottery, ivory and whalebone harpoon heads, snow goggles and other tools of a coastal dwelling lifestyle. Carvings and other decorations on these items pointed to the Thule culture which spread along the northwestern arctic coast about 800 A.D. Scientists have concluded that the Thule people are the first of the early cultures which can definitely be linked with modern Inupiat Eskimos of northern Alaska.

Giddings continued poking among the beach ridges, and at a large ridge extending much of the length of the cape he came upon artifacts of the Ipiutak people, a highly artistic prehistoric culture dating to about 2,000 years ago. First discovered when archeologists uncovered remnants of a huge village near Point Hope, 100 miles (161 km) to the northwest, the Ipiutaks carved elaborate designs on bone and ivory and fashioned fanciful items whose practical use has remained a mystery. At burial sites, the scientists came upon a wealth of artistic treasures: eyes of ivory and pupils of jet staring up from skeletons, elaborately carved coverings for openings of the body, instigated perhaps by the belief as recounted by Eskimo elders that evil spirits entered through body openings.

Tragedy struck prehistoric man even as it does today; at one site Giddings and his assistants meticulously unearthed the skeletons of an adult woman and two children who had perished when their house burned two millennia ago.

Moving inland once again, Giddings

Cleaning salmon for the drying racks.

190

came upon a more moist habitat. Here pottery decorated with waffle-like rectangles provided the clue to the early residents of the next series of beaches. Unknown to the Ipiutaks and unlike pottery of more recent peoples, pottery of the Norton culture lay scattered over nine ridges that guarded six centuries of this prehistoric culture.

Earlier in the archeological parade came the Choris people, first discovered on the Choris Peninsula of southern Kotzebue Sound. Identified by their large oval house depressions, the Choris people left no signs of permanent houses at Krusenstern. But tiny flakes lying exposed on early beach ridges led scientists to the hearths of temporary hunting camps set up by Choris people about 1,000 B.C. At one prized find, the scientists chanced up a bounty of flints, flaked diagonally, and including a single blade nearly seven inches (18 cm) long.

The Old Whalers

Every once in a while the continuity of the archeological record was broken when scientists unearthed artifacts from a culture that did not fit in the spectrum of early man in northwestern Alaska. One such find was the record of Old Whalers on the beach ridge inland from Choris remains. These prehistoric people who lived for a brief time at the cape year-round sometime between 1,800 to 1,500 B.C. relied almost exclusively on the sea for sustenance. Their record indicates a greater use of whales than either preceding or subsequent cultures. Modern observers are uncertain where the Old Whalers came from, or where they went. But they left their legacy on beach 53 at Cape Krusenstern.

The cape still had more to offer. On the innermost ridges beyond the Old Whalers and adjacent to the lagoon, Giddings came full circle, back to the prehistoric people he first encountered a decade earlier at Cape Denbigh. Beaches a mile and a half from the current Chukchi coast yielded hearths with bits of charcoal, burnt stones and tiny chips—remains of the earliest inhabitants of the beach ridge system, the Denbigh Flint people.

The archeological treasure chest buried in the beach ridges had now been opened, but there remained one final

Strips of dried salmon to fill winter stores.

chapter to write in the story of ancient man at Krusenstern. **Ingitkalik Mountain**, whose prehistoric ancestor guarded the Pleistocene coast before the beach ridges formed, rises across the lagoon at the beginning of the benchlands above Cape Krusenstern. At several elevations on the mountain's slopes Giddings found signs of ancient man's presence even older than those of the beach ridges below. Not until excavation of the vertical stratigraphy at the **Onion Portage** site in the Kobuk Valley, east of Kotzebue, were scientists able to confirm that the Palisades findings of the benchlands above Krusenstern were indeed older than any of the artifacts found buried in the beach ridges.

Giddings and others had now exposed the archeological treasures of Krusenstern and added to our knowledge of ancient man in Alaska. Man had subsisted at Krusenstern for thousands of years, as he does today.

The Cape Today

Each spring, rivers and streams of Kotzebue basin cleanse themselves when snow melt fills the channels which dump their load into Kotzebue Sound. Whitefish join this migration, leaving their inland wintering grounds and moving into summer feeding areas in coastal estuaries. This annual flooding acts as a catalyst for one of the region's major subsistence hauls.

As the flood waters fan out into Kotzebue Sound, several species of whitefish swarm into sloughs along the Krusenstern coast, fattening throughout the summer in the brackish waters. Local residents congregate at the sloughs each fall when ground swells from the Chukchi Sea push gravel and sand across the channels by which the whitefish exit the saltwater areas on their return migration. Residents harvest the fish, now trapped in the sloughs, to add to their winter staples.

Subsistence controls the lifestyle of Krusenstern residents today as in ancient times. Only the commercial fishery for chum salmon each July and August in Kotzebue Sound contributes much to the cash needs of area residents. Travellers should take extra care not to disturb fishing nets, boats or other gear on which local residents rely.

The tundra, northeast of Nome.

Also crucial is the six-mile (10-km) flatland at the monument's southern tip—**Sheshalik**, "Place of White Whales." Several families maintain year-round homes at Sheshalik, traditional gathering place for hunters of beluga, a small, light-colored, toothed whale.

Life at Sheshalik revolves around stockpiling the meat, fish, berries and greens that see these familes through nine months of winter.

When snow and cold blanket the region, families keep busy ice fishing and trapping for small furbearers. In spring, marine mammal hunters take to the ice in search of seals which they kill by spearing them as they come to their air holes to breathe. When leads open in the sea ice, belugas become the quarry. For centuries, hunters have gathered at **Sealing Point** on the narrow isthmus separating the Chukchi from the inner lagoons. Returning, their boats loaded with sea mammal carcasses, the hunters portage the isthmus and continue their southerly journey over calm lagoon waters rather than fighting waves of the open sea.

In May waterfowl return from their winter sojourn and head for Krusenstern where snow melt has weakened the ice and open water spreads early throughout the lagoons. Several species of geese and ducks nest on the ponds, joined by their cousins on stilts, the sandhill cranes.

Later in the summer residents harvest salmonberries, cranberries and blueberries. Women pick greens, preserving some in seal oil for later use. Fish—grayling, arctic char, whitefish—hang to dry on wooden racks. Chum salmon are taken for subsistence as well as for the commercial fishery in Kotzebue Sound.

After waterfowl leave in the fall, hunters turn to caribou, ptarmigan and sometimes walrus, or rarely bear. Black bear and brown bear have been found in the monument; polar bear roam offshore ice at certain seasons. Agile arctic fox follow behind these northern barons, ready to inspect any tidbit left by the bears. Onshore, elusive furbearers—wolves, wolverines, red fox, lynx, mink, short-tailed weasels, snowshoe and tundra hare, and arctic ground squirrels—patrol the tundra. Hunters take moose in low-lying areas or Dall sheep in the Igichuk Hills. A small group of musk ox, descendants of shaggy mammals which once roamed all arctic North America but were wiped out by hunters in Alaska in the mid-1800s, thunder across the tundra of the Mulgrave Hills.

Other species, generally not part of the subsistence catch, share Krusenstern's bounty. Lesser golden-plovers, western and semipalmated sandpipers, whimbrels, Lapland longspurs and Savannah sparrows add their beauty and song. Arctic and Aleutian terns float gracefully above the tundra, ready to defend their nest from the purposeful forays of glaucous gulls and jaegers. An Asian migrant, the handsome yellow wagtail, builds its nest in tiny cavities in the beach ridges. Overhead, rough-legged hawks soar from their nests in the highlands to hover over the tundra, piercing eyes searching for voles and lemmings.

The ambience at Krusenstern is understated, but for the curious and the thorough, the history of early man in the north and its modern translation in the subsistence world of local residents are only a step away.

An arctic tern hovers over Cape Krusenstern.

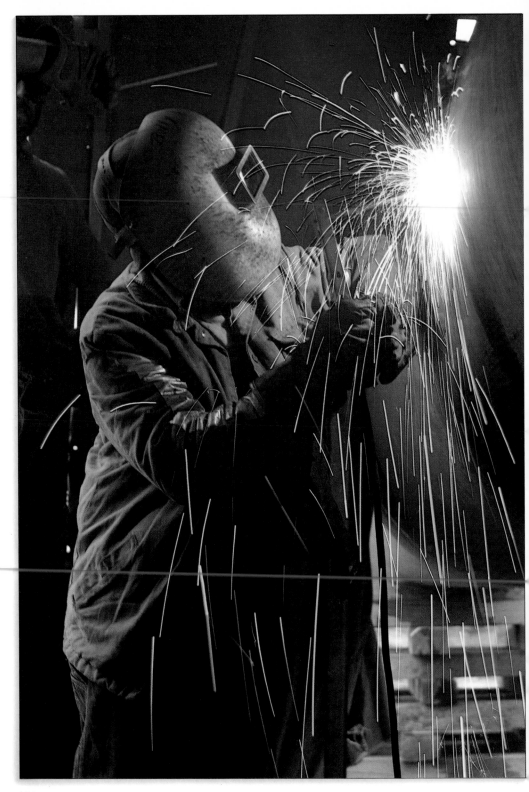

THE NORTH SLOPE

Bush pilots on Alaska's north coast have little use for aerial charts. There are few usable landmarks that can be depicted on a map to aid a pilot in this world of myriad tiny lakes and meandering rivers. Pilots plot their positions by counting the number of rivers crossed from a known starting point.

Rivers flow from south to north on the North Slope, a vaguely defined but huge chunk of territory that includes everything north of the summit of the Brooks Range. Once a pilot locates a particular river by flying east or west, he turns inland toward terrain with more features, the treeless northern side of the mountains about 100 miles (160 km) to the south.

Most people fly bush planes or helicopters in these latitudes. There are no roads and few means of overland travel except dogsleds and snow machines in the winter.

Hidden Riches

There are, however, exceptional map readers who can chart a course across Alaska's northern fringe. Union Oil Company geologist Norm Kent — not a flier but riding in the copilot's seat — can read a map better than most people can read a book. When his company is paying $500 an hour and up to rent a helicopter for oil exploration, he knows where he is every second of every flight.

Kent flies out of the coastal oil production zone into the Brooks Range, seeking clues that might lead to oil. His clues are the rocks and fossils laid down in a bygone age and thrust upwards when the Brooks Range was born. The same rock strata that underlie the mountains also underlie the North Slope oilfields; the varied terrain in the mountains, however, allows that strata to be seen and evaluated. The next rock Kent cracks with his hammer, seemingly in the middle of nowhere and maybe during a lunch break, could eventually lead to an oil strike worth millions, even billions of dollars.

Map reading problems aside, a constant fog is the next biggest problem facing pilots navigating visually along the coast. A 1,500-foot-thick (458-

meter) cloud of mist blankets the north coast of Alaska most days of the year. It usually stretches inland about 20 miles (32 km); most of the airports are hidden in the fog. Helicopter pilots, who rarely fly on instruments, roar along at 120 mph (200 kmph) through the perpetual mist. Just inches above the ground, they can usually only see objects within a quarter-mile of their cockpits. Helicopter pilots joke that the only navigational hazard on this flat landscape is a caribou that suddenly stands up. A haunted look in their eyes after such a flight dampens laughter the remark might otherwise elicit.

When ferrying a geologist such as Kent, the pilot flies south, out of the fog, then lets the passenger do the navigating. Usually geologists are heading for the foothills of the Brooks Range, a different world but still considered part of the North Slope.

Stark, trackless beauty and the undisturbed miracles of nature surround the fragile helicopter. The country is so remote that Alaskan law requires firearms be carried aboard aircraft for use in possible survival situations. Aircrews forced down in the northern Brooks Range may have to survive for weeks on only their wits and the gear they have aboard the aircraft. A gun is handy for killing food animals or defending against marauding bears.

Lighter Moments

But there are lighter moments. A sack lunch on a 6,000-foot (1,830-meter) ridge overlooking a glacier is one. Discovering a bushel-basket full of 300-million-year-old fossils under the helicopter might be another. These moments are there, and more.

Almost every stone or fossil is a clue to the varying layers of rock underlying the flat coastal plain, a clue that can lead to the eventual discovery of oil. And every clue is zealously guarded by the company that finds it, for finding and developing oil is the name of the game on the North Slope. Initial explorations by geologists are just the first move by the players.

Alaska's economy floats on an ocean of black gold, most of it pumped from beneath the tundra on the North Slope. Oil generates 85 percent of the state's income and a large transient population of oil-industry workers on the Arctic

A pipeline welder works on the North Slope.

coast.

Prudhoe Bay is a working person's world. Several thousand people live and work at Prudhoe Bay strictly for the money – there are no schools, no public roads and few entertainment facilities. The workday is 12 hours long, seven days a week. The pace, though, is temporary. After two or three weeks on the job, workers are flown to Anchorage, Fairbanks or even Dallas, Texas, for a week or sometimes two of vacation. It's not uncommon for a worker on the slope to make $75,000 a year for only 26 actual weeks on the job.

The larger oil companies house and feed their staffs, at no expense to employees. Meals are more than just sustenance. Common Friday night entrees are steak and lobster, all you can eat of either or both. Ice cream, sweet rolls, pies, cakes, cookies and a host of other snacks are available at all hours. But other than a movie or exercising in a weight room, there's little else to do besides work, eat and sleep.

Few Slope transient workers see more than the inside of the housing building, work station and air terminal. For them, Prudhoe Bay is the latest example of U.S. technology transplanted into a frozen wilderness. Little outside their doors interests them; it's only frozen tundra and fog. Frozen it may be for most of every year, but people have called Alaska's Arctic coast home for centuries.

North Slope Native Life

Nuiqsit, west of Prudhoe Bay and east of Barrow, is geographically between big oil and tradition. Unlike most northern communities, it is several miles inland from the coast, at the apex of the Colville River delta, about 60 miles (100 km) from Prudhoe. Eskimo men still hunt whales off the coast, as well as polar bears and seals. Although most still lead a traditional lifestyle of hunting and gathering, a few jobs are available, mostly in government. But for those who still venture onto the frozen sea in search of food and skins, their safety is less in the hands of chance these days. If they are late returning to their modern frame houses in the village, one quick telephone call launches a helicopter to search the coastline near the delta's mouth.

A drawing attempts to capture the elusive northern lights.

An early freeze caught five Nuiqsit hunters in the Beaufort Sea in September 1980, perhaps 40 miles (64 km) from the village. A helicopter dispatched from Prudhoe Bay later located the hunters gingerly crossing the sea ice on foot, their boat and most of their gear left behind on a barrier island, one of a broken ribbon of sand spits thrusting barely above sea level off the northern coast. The helicopter pilot carefully set his heavy machine on the soft new ice, cut the engine to idle, and exited the aircraft. The men of Nuiqsit politely asked the pilot if they could have a ride home, making no mention of their misfortune and offering no explanation for their dangerous trek over the uncertain ice. The pilot paused only long enough to ensure that these were the men he was hired to find, although it would have made little difference. The flier would have flown them to safety anyway.

Aboard the helicopter, the men consumed several gallons of hot soup and dozens of sandwiches; they had been without food for several days. In the village, only one hunter struggled to thank the pilot. The concept of expressing thanks is a white man's innovation; Eskimos traditionally return a favor or kindness with little or no comment.

On the Continent's Edge

Barrow, located to the west and just south of Point Barrow, the northernmost tip of North America, is the largest Eskimo settlement in Alaska. It is the headquarters of the North Slope Regional Corporation, a Native corporation formed to manage huge sums of money and vast tracts of land deeded to Alaska Native groups by the Alaska Native Claims Settlement Act of 1971. When that legislation was approved by the U.S. Congress, Barrow and other key Native villages in Alaska instantly became corporate centers, modern enclaves of big business in a traditional land. Barrow today stands as the ultimate contrast between tradition and technology.

The corporation, further enriched by money gained from oil leases, boasts large new buildings, buildings with entire walls of glass, even though built in this coldest and harshest of environments. When your land rests atop bil-

Snow-machining through the sun fog in the high arctic.

lions of barrels of petroleum, you can afford costly heating bills.

Yet in the shade of these glass monoliths perch clapboard shacks and drafty shanties of every description. Most of the owners haul water to their dwellings as blocks of ice cut from a nearby lake. One of the earliest goals of the North Slope Regional Corporation, headed during the 1970s by the late Eben Hopson, was to provide flush toilets in every home. It's still a dream, although coming closer to reality with every passing year.

Skin whaling boats still dot the coastline, but most are being replaced by modern aluminium craft as they wear out – few natives continue to make boats in the traditional way. Whaling captains teach their sons the secrets of harpooning and landing the bowhead whale, now more as a means of keeping the culture alive than as a necessary tool of survival.

Good teaching is a must; the International Whaling Commission allowed only 18 strikes on whales for 1985. A whale struck but not landed counts against the total, which is parceled out among the handful of villages along the north and west coasts of Alaska. Eighteen strikes, even landing a whale with each strike, could hardly feed the several thousand people residing near the whaling grounds.

The opportunity to see an ancient culture and its traditions, and a chance to stand momentarily on the continent's northern edge, lure visitors to Barrow – mostly as part of a package tour. Travel agencies offer overnight trips to Barrow from Anchorage and Fairbanks. A single fee covers a hotel room, a few local tours and the use of a parka.

Less timid souls venture into town on their own and perhaps discover **Pepe's North of the Border Restaurant,** which serves some of finest Mexican food in Alaska. Others may squeamishly try a bite of muktuk (whale blubber), or perhaps a piece of seal meat. These local delicacies are available sporadically, and visitors may have to search for them.

For all too many visitors, though, the most vivid memory of their Barrow trip is the brief moment they stood on the sand at the tip of the continent. It's only a windswept stretch of dark-sand beach, often shrouded in fog, and usually littered with ice. But it is the edge of a continent.

Eskimo Lore

It's unfortunate that most Barrow trips are so brief. Eskimo culture is varied and ancient, but for an outsider to gain a detailed knowledge of it is difficult and time consuming. And, although English is spoken by most Eskimos (except for the very old), traditional behavior sometimes interferes with communication. For example, Eskimos are not impolite when they fail to respond immediately to a question or statement. It is not their custom to do so. Outsiders who find this long pause uncomfortable often feel slighted, though there is no reason for such a feeling. Perhaps the best advice for tourists is to assume a slower-paced style of speaking and action, a pace more attuned to the traditional lifestyles of the region. Eskimos live not by the clock but by the change of seasons.

Prudhoe Bay's Oilfields

In addition to Barrow, tour companies also offer flights to the Prudhoe Bay oilfields. Travellers more attuned to 20th-Century civilization often find this a more comfortable experience; certainly, less chance for a clash of cultures exists. By and large, oil field workers come from an industrialized society, a society more familiar to most travellers.

Prudhoe Bay trips are managed just as the Barrow trips. A fixed fee provides a bed for the night, meals at a North Slope dining facility and round-trip airfare. Bus tours of the oilfields round out the arrangement. But you'll find few entertainment facilities, little local color and no planned activities – only a featureless landscape, broken here and there by modern metal buildings and an occasional oil derrick. The silver slash of the trans-Alaska oil pipeline originates here, then winds south toward the Brooks Range.

Prudhoe visitors meet men and women paid high wages to extract oil from the ground. They see a lot of sweat, a lot of grime and just enough luxury to maintain the morale of the workforce. Here beats the heart that pumps black gold, the life's blood of Alaska's economy.

Aerial view of the ice pack off Barrow.

198

DENALI
NATIONAL PARK

Alaskan Indians called it Denali, "The Great One." In later years, the mountain was officially designated **Mount McKinley** by the U.S. Government but Denali is the name still used by Natives and locals. Denali is the most spectacular mountain in North America. At 20,320 feet (6,195 meters), it is also the highest. In a sense, it could be called the highest in the world. The north face of Denali rises almost 18,000 feet (5,500 meters) above its base, an elevation gain which surpasses even Mount Everest.

The mountain is surrounded by one of the world's greatest wildlife sanctuaries—**Denali National Park**. A one day trip through the Park will almost certainly result in sightings of grizzly bears, caribou, Dall sheep, moose and perhaps even a wolf. A visit to Denali Park is a great adventure. It's like nothing you've ever seen before. When you arrive, be prepared for the ultimate Alaskan experience.

Geology and History

Denali is part of the **Alaska Range**, a 600-mile (960 km) arc of mountains stretching across the southeast quarter of the state. The oldest parts of what is now the Alaska Range consist of slate, shale, marble and other sedimentary deposits formed under an ancient ocean. Approximately 60 million years ago, the collision and subsequent overlapping of two tectonic plates produced such intense heat that portions of the earth's crust literally began to melt. A gigantic mass of molten rock was deposited beneath the current location of Denali. The molten material eventually solidified into granite.

Overlapping of the plates also caused the whole region to be uplifted. Granite and sedimentary rock were forced upward to form the ancestral Alaska Range. As this uplift gradually tapered off, the process of erosion slowly worked to wear down the Range. Since Denali is chiefly composed of erosion-resistant granite, it wore at a far slower rate than the surrounding sedimentary

rock. A more modern period of tectonic plate collision and uplift began 2 million years ago and continues to this day. This ongoing uplift is responsible for the towering height of Denali.

The first humans came into what is now Denali Park about 12,000 years ago, near the end of the last Ice Age. Use of the area appears to have been mainly limited to seasonal hunting trips. Ice Age hunters as well as the more recent Athabascans sought the region's big game species—but did not live here year round. Their permanent village sites were in lower, warmer and more sheltered locations. Almost all of the villages were built next to a lake or river which offered dependable fishing. The lack of significant numbers of fish in the Denali rivers probably limited Indian use of the region.

The Athabascans of the Yukon and Tanana rivers gave Denali its name. They said the mountain was created during a great battle between two magical warriors. The raven war chief, Totson, was pursuing his enemy Yako down a river. Totson threw a magic spear at his adversary but Yako turned a gigantic wave to stone and deflected the weapon. The solidified wave became the mountain called Denali.

In another Indian story, Denali is called "the home of the sun." (During the longest days of summer, the sun makes almost a complete circle in the local sky and drops below the horizon for only a few hours. From certain angles, it appears that the sun rises *and* sets from behind Denali.) An Athabascan hunting party once camped on the south side of the Alaska Range. That evening they saw the sun disappear behind Denali. A few hours later, it reappeared on the other side of the mountain. They told their chief, "Surely we found the home of the sun, as we saw with our own eyes the sun go into the mountain, and saw it leave its home in the morning."

The Highest Peak of the Continent

The first recorded sighting of Denali by a white man occurred in 1794. While sailing in the Cook Inlet, English Captain George Vancouver sighted "distant stupendous mountains covered with snow." He was undoubtedly seeing the Alaska Range. Other explorers, sur-

Preceding pages: Mount McKinley from Wonder Peak; fall tundra colors at Denali. Left, kiing the gorge at Ruth Glacier, Denali.

veyors and adventurers saw the mountain in later decades. Many of them commented on its great height. Some correctly guessed that it was the highest peak on the continent.

Denali became known as Mount McKinley through a strange set of circumstances in 1896. That year, a man named William Dickey went on a gold prospecting expedition in the area just south of Denali. While camped within sight of the mountain, he met other miners who argued at length with Dickey over whether gold or silver should back U.S. currency. (They were against the gold standard while Dickey was for it.) When Dickey later returned to the lower 48 states, he wrote an article about his Alaskan adventures. To spite the argumentative miners, he proposed that the highest mountain in the Alaskan range be named after Presidential Candidate William McKinley, the champion of the gold standard. McKinley won the 1896 election and the name stuck. At least it stuck in the lower 48.

The first white man to extensively explore the Denali region, Charles Sheldon, was also the first to suggest that it be set aside as a National Park.

Sheldon made a six-week trek through the area in 1906 and returned for a much longer trip from 1907 to 1908. To Sheldon, the opportunity to see and study wildlife was the most impressive feature of the region. After leaving Denali, he used his influence as a member of the powerful Boone and Crockett Club to gather support for his proposed Denali National Park. Largely due to Sheldon's efforts, the Park became a reality in 1917. To Sheldon's disappointment, Congress chose to call it Mount McKinley National Park.

While Sheldon was campaigning for the Park, others were endeavoring to make the first ascent of Denali. In late 1909, four miners, true Alaskan sourdoughs all, decided to climb the mountain. The four men (Billy Taylor, Pete Anderson, Charly McGonagall and Tom Lloyd) were quickly dubbed the Sourdough Expedition. They were not intimidated by the fact that they had never climbed a mountain before. They figured if they had survived the Alaskan winters they could do anyting. The Sourdough Expedition left Fairbanks with complete confidence to conquer the mountain.

Park shuttle bus is dwarfed by massive Mount McKinley.

On the morning of April 6, 1910, Taylor and Anderson set out for the summit from their camp at 12,000 feet (3,700 meters). By mid-afternoon they were standing on Denali's North Peak, the peak visible from Fairbanks and their mining claims. They had achieved their goal despite their total lack of experience. Unfortunately for them, the North Peak is 850 feet (260 meters) lower than the South Peak, Denali's true summit. Taylor and Anderson were never credited for being first on the top. For several years, no one even believed that these two miners had really climbed the North Peak. Taylor and Anderson insisted their story was true and claimed they had left a spruce pole in the snow on the top of the peak. A later climbing party was able to validate their claim when they saw the pole on the North Peak.

Hudson Stuck and a party of three climbers (Harry Karstens, Robert Tatum and Walter Harper) mounted the first successful Denali expedition in 1913. Using maps and route descriptions made by earlier parties, they ascended the Muldrow Glacier which flows down the east side of Denali.

After a long and difficult climb, they reached Denali Pass, the saddle between the North and South Peaks, only 2,100 vertical feet (640 meters) below the summit. The high elevation, low oxygen and extreme cold made those last few hundred feet the hardest part of their climb. Harper, a young Athabascan native employed by Stuck and the strongest member of the team was the first to stand on the summit of Denali.

Recent Changes

From 1917 to the early 1970s, visitation was relatively low in Mount McKinley National Park. The Park's remoteness and lack of direct access by vehicle combined to limit tourism. In the five years prior to 1972, the average annual visitation was only about 15,000. In 1972, the Anchorage-Fairbanks Highway was completed and it suddenly became much easier for both tourists and Alaskan residents to travel to the Park. In a short time, visitation jumped to over 140,000 per year, almost a tenfold increase over the previous figures.

This dramatic rise in use was foreseen by the National Park Service. Rangers were concerned about the effect it would have on the Park and the quality of visitors' experiences. One major problem was that the single dirt road which bisects the Park is too narrow to handle the increased traffic. Another concern was the Park's wildlife, which in the past had always been readily visible from the road. The extra traffic and noise created by a tenfold increase in visitation would likely drive the animals out of sight. In addition, huge influxes of people could result in more encounters with the Park's dangerous animals, the grizzly bears and moose.

The creative solution to these problems was the initiation of a free shuttle bus system for travel in the Park. Private vehicles are parked at the Park entrance and visitors board buses which run throughout the day. Because people are concentrated into the buses rather than a large number of private vehicles, wildlife experience little disturbance and still can be seen relatively close to the road.

In the late 1970s, Congress considered a number of proposals to establish new National Parks in Alaska. Most of the proposals also called for an ex-

Ranger shows young hiker Denali's sights.

dered a number of proposals to establish new National Parks in Alaska. Most of the proposals also called for an expansion of Mount McKinley National Park to include scenic areas and critical wildlife habitat which had been left out of the original boundaries. The Alaska National Interest Lands Conservation Act was finally passed in 1980. One section of the Act partially resolved an old controversy. Recognizing the long-standing Alaskan use of the name Denali, Congress renamed the area Denali National Park. (Although the Park is now called Denali, the mountain is still officially McKinley.)

Arriving in the Park

The entrance to Denali Park is on Alaska Highway 3, 240 miles (385 km) north of Anchorage and 120 miles (193 km) south of Fairbanks. Access to the Park is also provided by the Alaska Railroad which has daily service from both Anchorage and Fairbanks. The train depot, Information Center, Park Hotel, Riley Creek Campground, general store and Youth Hostel are all within easy walking distance of each other.

Denali National Park Hotel, McKinley Chalet Resort and **McKinely Village,** the only room accommodations in the park, offer an array of services. Visitors can book private wildlife bus tours, river rafting and flight-seeing. Complete packages are available including transportation to the park. For information, contact Denali National Park Hotel, 825 West 8th Ave., No. 240, Anchorage, AK 99501, (907) 276-7234. Accommodations are available from late May to mid or late September. The park is closed in the winter.

Campground and backcountry camping registration also takes place at the Information Center. Denali Park has six public campgrounds containing a total of 215 sites. No advance reservations are accepted for these campgrounds— everything is based on a first come, first served policy. During the peak summer season (late June to mid-August, all sites are often occupied by mid-morning. (Private campgrounds are located just outside the boundary and normally have space, even when the Park campgrounds are filled.)

The Poly-
chrome
Pass
overlook.

While in the Park entrance area be sure to visit the sled dog kennel, located behind the Park headquarters building at Mile 3 of the Park road. The kennel is the home of 30 of the hardest working government employees you'll ever meet. Since the 1920s, park rangers have used sled dog trips as a means of patroling the Park. Dogsledding is still the most practical means of getting around Denali in the winter months. The dogs have become so popular with visitors that rangers put on three dog sledding demonstrations every day during the summer season.

The Adventure Begins

The adventure of experiencing Denali National Park really begins when you step on a shuttle bus for an all day trip into the Park. The 40-passenger shuttle buses start their routes at Riley Creek Information Center. The rangers can give you a bus schedule, explain how the system works and get you a seat on the next available bus. Most shuttle buses turn around at Eielson Visitor Center, 65 miles (105 km) from the Park entrance. This round-trip usually takes 7 hours. Some buses make a 10 hour round-trip to Wonder Lake, 85 miles (136 km) from the entrance.

Your chances of seeing wildlife as well as Denali itself are increased by taking as early a bus as possible. The first few buses depart at 6 a.m. During the rest of the morning they leave every half hour. The early buses often are in high demand so it is worth it to arive at the Visitor's Center 30 to 60 minutes early. No food or drinks are available along the bus route so be sure to take with you what you'll need for the day. Always be prepared for cool temperatures and rain regardless of what the early morning weather might be.

The first leg of the bus route is the 14-mile (22-km) stretch between the entrances and the **Savage River**. The first views of Denali occur in this area. If Denali is visible, your driver will stop the bus, point it out and allow time for photographs. This section of the Park road goes through prime moose habitat. Anytime a moose or other animal is spotted the bus will stop to allow the passengers to watch and photograph it. Wildlife spotting on shuttle buses is a group effort. With 40 pairs of eyes

Park naturalist leads a nature walk.

looking for wildlife, your chances of seeing animals is far greater than if you were by yourself.

Moose are the biggest animals in the Park—mature bulls can weigh as much as 1500 pounds (680 kg). During the spring, watch for calves in this area. Cow moose usually have one or two calves each year. At birth, a calf weighs about 30 pounds (14 kg). Moose calves are one of the fastest growing animals in the world. By their first birthday, they often weigh over 600 pounds (270 kg).

Each September and October this portion of Denali Park becomes the rutting grounds for moose. The huge bulls challenge each other over harems of cows. The bulls are deadly serious when it comes to these fights. A bull can kill his opponent with his sharp antler points. Rutting bulls and cow moose with calves should always be considered extremely dangerous and avoided. If they are approached too closely, both cows and bulls will charge a human.

As your bus continues beyond the Savage River, you will pass a mountain to the north known as **Primrose Ridge**. Dall sheep are often seen on the higher slopes of Primrose. The sheep have

pure white fur, perfect winter camouflage, but in summer, they readily stand out against the green tundra or dark rock formations.

Like all wild sheep, the Dall sheep are almost always found on or near steep cliffs. The cliffs are their security. No predator can match their climbing speed or agility. Enemies such as wolves or grizzlies can only catch weak or injured sheep, or those that have wandered too far from the crags.

The Dall ewes utilize the steepest cliffs in this area as lambing grounds. With luck, you may be able to spot young lambs on the higher slopes. Within a few days of birth, the lambs can easily match their mother's climbing ability. The lambs spend hours each day playing games of tag, king of the mountain and head butting. All of this play helps them develop their strength, agility and coordination. When their lambs are young, the ewes are provided with free day care service. The mothers drop off their lambs with a designated babysitter. She will watch over up to a dozen lambs while the mothers go off to feed and rest. After a few hours the lambs get hungry and call out for their

Wonder Lake, Denali National Park.

mothers who then return to nurse their young.

Bands of rams may also be seen in the Primrose Ridge region. Rams are very concerned with the issue of dominance. A band will establish a pecking order going from the top ram down to the lowest. In almost all bands, the top ram will be the one with the largest set of horns. To a ram, horns are his most important status symbol. The older rams have horns of such large size that they can easily intimidate smaller rams.

Head butting contests which occur between big rams are fights to determine which animal will be dominant. The two rams back off and charge each other at speeds of 30 mph (48 kmph). They bash each other over and over until one gives up and backs off. The reward of dominance comes during the fall rutting season. The top rams are the ones who get to do most of the breeding.

By the time **Sable Pass** is reached at Mile 39 you are surrounded by tundra. Tundra is any area of plant growth above tree line. Sable Pass has an elevation of 3,900 feet (1,188 meters), well above the average local treeline of 2,400 feet (730 meters). The cool summertime temperatures and strong winds at these attitudes are too severe for trees. The low growing tundra vegetation survives by taking advantage of the slightly warmer and less windy microenvironment at the surface of the ground.

Sable Pass is grizzly country. So many bears use this area that the Park Service has prohibited all off-road hiking in Sable Pass. Denali Park's grizzly population is estimated at 200 to 300. Grizzlies are omnivores; like humans, they eat both meat and vegetation. They would prefer killing and eating large animals such as moose, caribou and Dall sheep but the bears are not often successful as hunters. For this reason, tundra plants make up at least 90 percent of the diet of most grizzlies. The tundra vegetation in such places as Sable Pass offers a dependable, easily obtainable source of nutrition.

Grizzly cubs are born in January or February in the mother's hibernation den. The sow gives birth to one to four cubs weighing about one pound each (.5 kg). By the time the family leaves the den in April, each cub has gained five to ten pounds (2 to 4.5 kg) from their

The Alaska Range, featuring Denali, from Wonder Lake.

mother's milk. Sable Pass is one of the best places in the world for viewing grizzly families. If a family is visible, you may see the cubs racing across the tundra, playfighting with each other or nursing from their mother. The sow usually drives her young off when they are two and a half years old. At that point they may weigh 100 to 150 pounds (45 to 67 kg). She then breeds again and gives birth to another set of cubs the following winter.

Without a doubt, the grizzly is the most dangerous animal in North America. Its behavior and reaction toward humans is very difficult to predict. Whenever you are in grizzly country, you have the responsibility of doing everything you can to avoid provoking a bear. Most of the local bears seem willing to avoid humans if given the opportunity. The few attacks by bears on people in Denali have almost always been provoked attacks—many made by mother bears on people who had deliberately approached their cubs. Park rangers can give you detailed information on ways to avoid problems with grizzlies.

Your shuttle bus will stop for a rest break at **Polychrome Pass** at Mile 45. The brightly colored Polychrome cliffs are volcanic rocks formed 50 million years ago. The spectacular view to the south includes part of the Alaska Range as well as a vast area of tundra.

Wolf Observation

Polychrome Pass is a good place to watch for wolves. A local pack uses these flats as its hunting grounds, especially in the spring when the caribou are in migration. Use binoculars to scan the tundra below Polychrome for wolves. The Denali wolves range in color from white to black but most are gray. They may be travelling singly or in small groups. If a pack is sighted, look for a wolf with its tail in the air. This will be the alpha wolf, the leader of the pack. He may not be the first wolf in line, in fact, he may bring up the rear. The alpha male often delegates the lead position to the beta wolf, his second in command.

In a wolf pack, the only members who breed are the alpha male and the alpha female. Their litter is born in the spring and all other members of the pack help to raise the young pups. The other wolves are almost always related to the alpha pair as brothers, sisters or previous offspring. The pack is really a large extended family. Feeding a litter of five to ten pups is a difficult job, even for the entire pack. If all of the pack members tried to breed, the park's territory could not support the resulting large number of offspring. The pack is better served by limiting breeding to the dominant pair, the wolves who have proven themselves to be the fittest animals.

Much of what is now known about wolves was discovered by Adolf Murie. Murie was a biologist who was assigned to the Park in the 1930's to study wolves and their relationship with their prey. He was the first scientist who extensively studied wolf behavior in the field. For years, Murie would drive out on the Park road and spend hours watching wolves. Much of his wolf observation took place in the Polychrome area. In 1944, Murie published the results of his studies in his book, *The Wolves of Mt. McKinley*, one of the great classics of animal behavior. Murie's book documented that wolves were primarily preying on the sick and weak Dall

Denali grizzly takes advantage of a sign for back-scratching.

sheep, caribou and moose. He concluded that wolves were a necessary part of the Denali ecosystem because they ultimately helped to keep their prey species in a healthy and strong state.

Caribou are commonly seen in the Highway Pass area at Mile 58. Caribou are the most social of the large Denali animals. In the spring, herds of several hundred caribou pass though this area as they head toward their calving grounds to the east. Later in the season, they migrate back through the area as they move toward their wintering grounds in the western and northern portions of the Park.

The herds are constantly on the move. Even as the caribou feed, they rarely browse for more than a few moments at any one stop. This style of light browsing is perfectly suited to the type of slow growing plants which live on the tundra. If the caribou herds spent too much time feeding in one area, they would likely kill off the fragile tundra vegetation.

Caribou, like moose, have antlers rather than horns. Antlers are formed of bone and are shed every year. Sheep horns consist of keratin, the same material as our fingernails, and are never shed. The caribou bulls' antlers are fully developed by September and are used to fight for harems. These matches usually occur between Highway Pass and Wonder Lake. After their rutting season is over, the antlers drop off. The weight of the massive antlers would be a major hindrance during the winter. Shedding the antlers enables the caribou to have a better chance of surviving the winter, the most stressful time of the year.

As your bus approaches **Stony Hill Overlook**, Mile 61, be prepared for a spectacular view of Denali. Stony Hill offers the first close up view of the mountain. From the Overlook, it is 37 miles (60 km) to the summit. On a cloudless day, the crystal clear Alaskan air makes the mountain appear far closer.

After a stop at Stony Hill, your bus will continue four miles (six km) to **Eielson Visitor Center**, where the view of Denali is equally as awesome. The park rangers at Eielson can answer any questions you might have and can suggest good hiking routes in the local

Moose are common sights along the Denali Park Road.

area. Restrooms, drinking water, maps and books are available at Eielson.

Some shuttle buses continue on to **Wonder Lake**, an additional 20 miles (32 km) beyond Eielson. The round-trip from Eielson to Wonder Lake adds about 2 hours to your day. If the weather is clear, the extra distance is definitely worth the time. Denali remains in full view along the entire route. On the way dozens of tundra ponds, home to many species of waterfowl, are passed. In the evening hours, beaver families can be seen swimming across these small ponds. At Wonder Lake you can use your break time for a walk or a rest on the shore of the lake.

Walks and Hikes

The shuttle system has been set up to encourage people to get off the buses and personally explore the Park. You may leave your bus, hike for a few hours and then return to the road to catch a later bus. Buses will stop to pick up passengers anywhere along the road. (Keep in mind that many buses may be full on busy days and that you might have to wait for one with empty seats.)

Denali National Park is a true wilderness. There are few official trails and these are mainly in the entrance area. In the rest of the Park, you are on your own. Despite the vast size of the Denali wilderness, route making is not difficult. Since most of the Park is open tundra, it is easy to visually choose a destination and hike straight to it. Most of the Park's rivers cross the Park road perpendicularly. Many hikers simply walk either up or down a river.

Good areas for day hikes include the Savage River, Primrose Ridge, Polychrome Pass, the Eielson area and Wonder Lake. Before you begin a day hike, talk to a ranger at Riley Creek or Eielson about tips on safety. Maps of the area you'll be exploring are available at both Centers. Permits are required for overnight hikes.

National Park Rangers offer a wide variety of interpretive programs to help you better understand and appreciate your Denali experience. Schedules of activities are posted throughout the Park. Slide shows and movies are presented in the auditorium behind the Park Hotel several times daily. Most campgrounds have nightly campfire

River rafting along the Nenana River.

talks.

A number of nature walks and half day hikes are given each day in different sections of the Park.

Denali Park is a paradise for watching and photographing wildlife. A pair of binoculars and a telephoto lens will greatly assist you in these activities. This equipment will allow you to observe and photograph the animals from a safe distance and in a way that won't disturb or drive them away.

Remember that some wild animals are dangerous and will attack if provoked. Never approach a grizzly—view them from the protection of a bus or Visitor Center. Always stay well away from a bull moose and a cow with calf. Dall sheep and caribou bulls are fairly tolerant of people if you abide by their rules. Allow the sheep or caribou to spot you when you are a still long way from them. (It is critical that they have a chance to identify you as a person, rather than a predator.) Making sure that you are always in their field of view, approach them at a very slow walk with frequent pauses. Before they exhibit any disturbance at your presence sit down and take out your binoculars and camera. This method of approaching wildlife will enable you to watch their behavior without causing them unnecessary stress.

The standard viewpoints for photographing Denali include Stony Hill, Eielson Visitor Center and Wonder Lake. Take shots from those angles but be sure to use your creativity to seek out less obvious photo points. A walk around some of the tundra ponds between Eielson and Wonder Lake will turn up many great Denali compositions. Lighting on the mountain is best in the early morning or late evening. Those are also the times Denali is most likely to be free of clouds.

A visit to Denali National Park is an ultimate Alaskan adventure. A stay of a few days or even a few weeks will show you only a small percentage of what the Park offers. Don't worry about seeing and doing everything during your first the mystique of the area; your perspectives will be different as a result of the experience.

And when you leave the Park, begin to make plans for your second visit. Denali is a hard place to forget.

Hikers survey the Alaska Range.

MYSTICAL MISTY FJORDS

There are only three ways to get to **Misty Fjords National Monument,** near Ketchikan: by water, by air, or by a cruise/fly combination tour. If your choice includes air travel you may receive, in addition to the flightseeing excursion you paid for, an unannounced, unexpected, guaranteed-to-thrill-you lesson in aerodynamics. What happens is this.

The cruise portion of your combination tour is completed, and Tim Goheen, your pilot, has picked you up in his float-equipped Cessna at a sheltered cove in the monument. After a noisy, full-throttle takeoff, some amazingly immediate wildlife viewing, and even a brief stop on a mountaintop lake, you are shortly at 3,000 feet (914 meters). The view is breathtaking.

Really breathtaking. It dawns on you suddenly that the pilot has cut back — *all the way back* — on power.

In the midst of some of the wildest, most isolated country in the north, your Cessna has become an instant glider.

As if that were not disconcerting enough, to the right of the aircraft — seemingly just inches from the wing — a sheer dark granite wall rises thousands of feet vertically from Punchbowl Lake. It all but fills the airplane's side window view.

"Not to worry," says calm Pilot Tim. "I always cut back on power on these tours ... to show people how safe an airplane really is. I can turn and bank, left or right," (and having said so, he does so) "and if we'd really lost our power I could easily land anywhere on the water I care to. We can glide a full mile in any direction for each 1,000 feet of altitude."

"Now, relax ..." he says, restarting the engine with a flick of the ignition switch, "... and enjoy one of Alaska's most magnificent and mind-boggling natural areas."

Thus, each summer, do hundreds of visitors to the Forty-Ninth State learn about the basics of sustained (and not so sustained) flight and about the beauty of an area that is, as pilot Goheen states, magnificent, mind-boggling and many an additional adjective as well.

Untouched Backcountry

The area, Misty Fjords, is a national wilderness as well as a National Monument, and within the 3,570 miles (9,246 sq km) of its largely untouched and untrammeled coast and backcountry lie three major rivers, hundreds of small streams and creeks, icefields, glaciers, snowcapped mountains and mountain-top lakes.

There are forest groves so thick you can barely see daylight through them, tiny coves and great bays. Misty Fjords wildlife includes brown bears, blackies, Sitka black-tailed deer, wolves, mountain goats, beavers, mink, marten, foxes and river otters.

As was noted earlier, no roads lead to Misty Fjords. Some cruiseships visit the monument as part of an Inside Passage experience. You can fly there with any of several Ketchikan air charter companies; you can cruise there by charter boat; or (probably most convenient) you can sign on with an outfit called Outdoor Alaska and take one of the yacht tours the company schedules each Sunday, Wednesday and Friday in the summertime. These latter excursions, aboard the 50-foot M/V *Misty Fjord*, can be round trip or one-way with either the coming or going portion by air.

Touring Misty Fjords

Here's what happens on a typical cruise/fly tour:

Departure from near downtown Ketchikan is at 9:15 a.m., but coffee is on the galley stove and donuts are on the serving table before then for passengers who arrive on the ship early. It's a wide, beamy, comfortable cruiser with plenty of walking-around room, big view windows, and tables and seating for 32. When the weather is nice about half that number can be seated, if they want to, on an open-air deck above the cabin.

The sightseeing begins as soon as the boat's lines are cast off and the vessel begins its southeasterly path toward the lower end of Revillagigedo (the locals say "Revilla") Island, on which Ketchikan is located. Passing dockside fish processors, supply houses and the town's main business district, the *Misty Fjord* soon cruises past the entrance to

Preceding pages, misty sea of the Alaska Panhandle. Below, the coast along Misty Fjords.

Ketchikan Creek. Late in the summer, many thousands of salmon will assemble here before ascending the creek — and formidable waterfalls — to spawn in the upstream shallows and then die.

Shortly after Creek Street (Ketchikan's former red light district) the *Misty Fjord* cruises past **Saxman,** an Indian village containing one of the largest collections of authentic Indian totems in the state.

By 10 a.m. or shortly after, the *Misty Fjord* passes **Bold Island** and passengers line the port (left) rails and windows of the vessel to glass a huge bald eagle perched in the spruce tree on the island. Shortly, the yacht will pass another of the proud birds, this one sitting on top of a navigational marker out in the middle of the channel. For southeast Alaskans, such sightings are commonplace, though never dull. For visitors, the frequent sight of America's national bird is a highlight of the trip.

At one point or another in the morning's cruise, almost every passenger will crowd into the yacht's little wheelhouse and talk to Dale Pihlman, sometimes skipper and all times owner of the *Misty Fjord* and the Outdoors Alaska excursion firm. Dale welcomes the intrusion. He's never reluctant to talk about the monument.

Glacial Scenery

Eons ago, he explains, great glaciers thousands of feet deep filled what are now Southeast Alaska bays and valleys. Slowly but relentlessly they ground their way seaward from mountaintop heights. In the process they carved and scoured great steepwalled cliffs that now plunge from mountain summits to considerable depths below sea level. The effect of this carving and scouring has never been more beautifully evident than it is in Misty Fjords.

"But Misty Fjords," he says, "is not only a place of scenery on a grand scale, though it certainly is that. It also has tremendous commercial value. Some of Alaska's most productive fish rearing streams are located there."

Dale Pihlman should know. He's been a commercial fisherman all his life and was, in fact, one of Alaska's fisherfolk who travelled back to Washington. D.C., a few years ago to lobby for the

Natives took advantage of the rich resources of the coastal fjords; below, a moose hunt by skin boat.

bill that created Misty Fjords National Monument in the first place.

Provisions of the bill, incidentally, do protect most of the monument today from destructive exploitation. Conservationists are fearful that if a giant molybdenum deposit being test-mined and developed in the monument by U.S. Borax is not very carefully controlled, the results for fish and wildlife values could be catastrophic.

Porpoise Companions

Shortly after 11 a.m., Jenifer Miller, the *Misty Fjord* guide, naturalist, cook and handyperson announces there are porpoises both fore and aft of the vessel. Everyone scrambles, half in each direction, for a view of the small whales. The porpoises swimming behind the yacht are too far away for a close look. They are visible only as leaping, playing creatures a hundred yards or more astern. But the ones in front are only a few feet away, clearly visible, and just as clearly having a wonderful time pacing the boat. For brief moments their dorsal fins break the surface

of the water; at other times they dive. It's obvious they could outdistance the 16-knot vessel easily. They prefer to stay and play, and they do so for a quarter hour or so.

By noon the vessel is in the monument and Dale guides the *Misty Fjord* through a narrow channel into an exquisite little tree-shrouded cove on **Rudyerd Island.** "Look at the steep granite rock formations on the shore," says Jenifer Miller. "See the occasional jet black vertical streaks, a few inches to a couple of feet or more wide, that appear among the brown granite walls?

Well, 60 million years ago there were earthquakes in this region that cracked the granite, and hot molten magma came up from below the earth's surface and filled those cracks. Those black streaks that you see is that magma."

Eddystone Rock

About 12:30 p.m. **New Eddystone Rock** comes into view. Spectacular sighting, this; depending upon the time of day you see it and the angle from which you approach it, it can resemble a man-made building, a ship under sail, or

Touring Misty Fjords waterfalls by floatplane.

it can look like what it is — a high-rising volcano "plug" from millennia past. It was named by the explorer Captain George Vancouver who thought it looked very much like Eddystone lighthouse off the shore of his native Plymouth, England.

About 1 p.m., if there are any overnight campers-kayakers aboard the *Misty Fjord,* this is the time they leave ship in their smaller craft to paddle the waters off Winstanley Island. There's a U.S. Forest Service cabin there, one of a relative few located on salt water sites in Southeast Alaska.

The comfortable, weathertight snug shelter is popular with campers who paddle around **Rudyerd Bay** during the day. The cabin can be rented for the outrageously reasonable rate of only $10 per night.

At 1:30 p.m. the cruiser enters Rudyerd Bay — and a welcoming committee of at least 20 seals lie basking on the rocks of an island to port. They pay us little mind.

Minutes later, within the bay, the *Misty Fjord* approaches the towering massive vertical walls of **Punchbowl Cove.** And it is here that the magical,

In the verdant coastal rain forest.

mystical effect of the place really comes upon you.

Mists and Mystique

It can be truly eerie hereabouts, especially when there are — as the monument's name suggests — mists or clouds or fog in the air. Steep, stark granite walls descend from heights hidden in clouds ... Waterfalls which range from torrents to trickles plunge from unseen sources just as high ... Trees both large and small hang tenaciously to many of the cliffsides, seemingly on surfaces that don't have enough ground cover to support a house plant ...

Waters around and beneath the boat are cold, slate gray, and they descend to depths of 750 feet (230 meters) or more. There had been no sea monster reported in these waters — but it's just the right kind of place for such.

Enough of musings and mystique. It is 2 p.m. and Jenifer Miller has set out luncheon of clam chowder, cold cuts and cheeses for make-your-own sandwiches. Then, best yet, fresh-caught, fresh-baked silver salmon. Superb.

Come 2:20 p.m. and the *Misty Fjord*

leaves Punchbowl Cove and cruises toward the head of Rudyerd Bay. Several of the passengers glass the shoreline that now replaces the steep cliffs, looking for brown bears, blackies, wolves or other wild creatures. Often visitors see them, more often they do not, but in any case it is exciting to know the critters are out there — hidden possibly, and looking directly at the vessel as it passes by.

Creeks and Waterfalls

At 3:15 p.m., another stop, this time at **Nooya Creek** where, in season, 1,000 or more pink salmon descend to saltwater each year from Nooya Lake in the high country. Here a trail leads to the uplands — much less steeply, says Dale, than one which also takes off, and up, from the Punchbowl Cove area visited earlier. The camping and trout fishing opportunities at the ends of the trails are, says Dale, outstanding.

About 3:30 p.m. and it's time for another memorable experience. Dale edges his boat right up to a large plummeting waterfall. Jenifer passes out paper cups and all on board have a great

laughing, splashing, shouting time getting half soaked while filling their cups and savoring the icy cold liquid. The drink, somehow to everyone's surprise, tastes just like what it is — water.

Promptly at 3:30, as well, it is time for those who will fly back to Ketchikan to leave the *Misty Fjord* and board the floatplane which landed during the water gathering excitement. It taxis gently to the rear of the ship.

From the Air

By 3:45 p.m. goodbyes are yelled to those remaining and Tim Goheen drifts his plane away from the vessel. He then gives the aircraft full throttle, and within a minute the aircraft is airborne. Within three or four minutes more you may well be spotting white, furry mountain goats, usually nannies and youngsters, negotiating impossible cliff faces to the right of the plane.

3:55 p.m. and yet another unexpected experience: the pilot brings the plane down for a landing on **Big Goat Lake** where another rental U.S. Forest Service cabin is located. The lake and the cabin are accessible only by air. Tim turns off the engine and lets the plane drift, allowing passengers to savor the sound of gentle winds, waters lapping on shore, and, at the end of the lake, a major waterfall that drops more than 1,500 feet (490 meters) straight down. For those who want to, there's even the opportunity to go ashore for a few minutes, to examine the high country flora.

Then it is time to be airborne again, and to experience that most unforgettable moment of all — when Tim Goheen cuts power and shows what happens to airplanes without engines.

Shortly thereafter the aircraft exits the monument, flying low over New Eddystone Rock and heading back to Ketchikan. The trip takes in hydro projects, logging shows, and no small quantity of land and water and mountain scenery in the process.

By 4:30 p.m. the trip is over. You pull in at the floatplane dock in downtown Ketchikan, walk up the ramp with a camera bag full of exposures and a mind full of one-of-a-kind memories, and it is hard not to reflect that visiting Misty Fjord is, indeed, one of Alaska's premiere experiences.

Left, a red fox investigates intruders. Right, a young hawk owl.

GATES OF THE ARCTIC NATIONAL PARK

Gates of the Arctic National Park and Preserve is located in the heart of northern Alaska, 200 miles (320 km) northwest of Fairbanks, and 200 miles south of Barrow, Alaska's largest Eskimo community. No maintained roads or trails exist within the park—no phones, TVs, radios, gas stations, restaurants, stores or hotels. No emergency services are available: no hospitals, first aid stations, ambulances, police or fire stations. Not even a park ranger is permanently based in the Gates.

Such wilderness offers a real opportunity to experience freedom from civilization and its attendant trappings. A person, liable to meet a bear, in 8 million acres (3.2 million hectares) of wilderness is on his or her own. Unless visitors arrange for someone to rescue them, no one will. People still freeze and starve to death in remote cabins in the Brooks Range wilderness; months may pass before their bodies are found. This unique experience is called self-reliance.

A Rewarding Risk

Yet inherent in the risks are opportunities for wilderness recreation on a grand scale. In the summer, the park provides opportunities for mountaineering, hiking and camping. The lakes, rivers and streams allow for motorboating, rafting, canoeing, kayaking and fishing. Photography is the most popular recreational activity. Also popular are birding, flight-seeing and wildlife viewing. The arctic summer provided 24-hour sunlight—no flashlight needed.

Fall activities include blueberry and cranberry picking, as well as hunting for bear, caribou, moose, ducks, geese, rabbits and ptarmigan. In winter, the park is quiet. The sun drops below the horizon in November and doesn't surface again until February. The temperature can drop to -70 degrees F (-57 degrees C).

As the sunlight comes alive between February and April, the park comes alive with cross-country skiing, dog-sledding and snowshoeing. The Coldfoot Classic, dogsled race which skirts the eastern edge of the park is held in April and is anticipated by local residents stuck indoors during the winter.

The Gates of the Arctic area is personalized by the Athabascan Indians and several Eskimo culture. The lifestyles of trappers, homesteaders and others who live in isolated cabins add color and character to the Gates. Visitors, flogging past an Indian fish camp, may see orange-red salmon strips drying on birch poles or an Indian fish net bobbing with the flow of the river. They may even encounter a trapper's secluded log home—with snowmachine outside, traps and a bearskin hanging from the cabin walls. But people are rare. The area population is less than one person per 5,000 acres (2,000 hectares).

Gates of the Arctic National Park and Preserve is remote, pristine wilderness. The meaning of "remote" becomes immediately evident when trying to reach the Gates. Visitors must fly there in their own plane or charter one. Those who

A CHILCAT MAN.
From a Drawing by Mrs. Willard.

The buckskin suit is trimmed with fur and quills. The narrow snow-shoe is used in hunting and running, and the broad one in packing.

Preceding pages, Brooks Range vista. Left, an old cabin sports a handy storage for snowshoes. Below, traditional transportation in the high mountains.

don't fly must have the time and physical stamina to backpack miles to the park, after driving the Dalton Highway.

The Dalton Highway winds through wilderness as wild and beautiful as the Gates and nears the Gates' vicinity at **Coldfoot**, approximately 250 miles (400 km) north of Fairbanks. In early September, when the birch leaves are golden in the hills and the weather is sunny and dry, the drive alone is worth the trip. Coldfoot was named when Klondike gold miners travelled that far north and got "cold feet." Coldfoot was then, and still is, history in the making. Here, the last frontier lives in truckers snaking up the haul road, in mountains and lakes with no names, and in people who tell bear stories from experience. The latter eye with disbelief visitors wanting to sleep in tents and travel unarmed through prime bear habitat.

A stop at Dick Mackey's **Coldfoot Services Truckstop** is a must for any visitor. A touch of the modern-day trucking frontier is evident in the racks of personalized coffee cups of the truck-

ers. In the lodge-style dining hall restaurant, meals are eaten on oilcloth-covered tables with wooden benches. mining camp-style. Motel rooms are also available. Dick and his wife add charm to the place with their openness and positive, yet practical, outlook–something so necessary to frontier life.

The most easily accessed trails into the park is in **Wiseman**, 15 miles (24 km) north of Coldfoot. Wiseman is a turn-of-the-century mining community. Its weathered buildings are still home to a small group of miners. The road from Dalton Highway to Wiseman extends on to several trails that enter the Park. The **Nolan-Wiseman Creek Trail** goes through the historic mining area of the park to the Glacier River. Another popular trail follows the Hammond River north from Wiseman.

Bettles: Gateway to the Gates

For those who fly into the National Park, the town of **Bettles** is the gateway to Gates. Another friendly outpost,

Canoeing in Gates of the Arctic Park.

Bettles provides visitors to the Gates with outfitters, guides, air taxi service and a lodge. From Bettles, any number of trips are possible into the park.

The most popular Gates of the Arctic trip is to the north fork of the Koyukuk River, where the peaks, **Frigid Craigs** and **Boreal Mountain**, stand guard. They are the climax of a backpacking trip that starts at **Summit Lake** and ends at **Chimney Lake**; a trip that averages 10 days. Another favored excursion involves flying down the river to the Eskimo village of **Noatak**, past exquisite mountain scenery. Moose and dall sheep are often spotted, and fishing for grayling, pike and char is excellent.

Float trips—and combination backpack/float trips—can be arranged throughout the Gates. Or seek fish-filled **Walker Lake**, a blue jewel nestled in the deep forested hills in the southern part of the park. **Walker Lake Lodge**, on the edge of the Lake, is the only place other than a few private cabins where a visitor can sleep indoors in the park. Winter cross-country ski trips, dogsled rides and ice fishing are also available at Walker Lake.

Anyone who wants to visit the Gates needs to do considerable research: terrain and customs can be likened to those of a third-world country. Topographical maps are a must, and problems must be anticipated and planned for. When you are hundreds of miles from the nearest tree it is *not* the time to inquire about how to start a fire without one!

For maps, information and supplies, Fairbanks is a recommended stop before going to the Gates. The National Park Service office in Fairbanks, which has jurisdiction over the Gates, has a complete list of air services, commercial services, information books, maps and pictures. Information is also available from the Alaska Department of Fish and Game, the Department of Transportation, the Alaska State Troopers, the State Department of Tourism and the Fairbanks offices of the Bureau of Land Management.

Fairbanks is generally the last stop to shop for supplies. Since all fuel must be

A beaver pulls an alder branch back to his dam.

flown in, many communities have erratic or nonexistent fuel supplies; camps stove fuel is not allowed on regularly scheduled airlines. Villages are often not equipped with facilities for visitors, so travellers should have adequate food supplies and arrange return air transportation well in advance.

Also check in at Fairbanks for road conditions on the Dalton Highway. (Call the Alaska Department of Transportation, road maintenance, 451-2294.) The road is rough gravel, very narrow and dominated by commercial trucks. Most local people refuse to take cars over the road, preferring vehicles with stronger suspension systems. Only two places sell gas (or anything else) on the road: the truckstop at the Yukon River Bridge and Dick Mackey's at Coldfoot. Beyond Disaster Creek, the Dalton Highway is closed to the public.

The world of air service opens the Gates to visitors. The average flight into the Gates lasts from ½ hour to 1½ hours and can cost from $150 to $300 per hour for flight time. The passenger pays for the pilot's return trip, plus fees for baggage in excess of 40 lbs (18 kg).

Those desiring to cut costs are encouraged to travel in a group. A trip for six from Bettles can cost $364 per person, less than half the cost of the same trip for two. An average two-week trip for two can add up to $2,000 per person. Compare services to prices and ask for references. Reputable guides will have names of people to contact who have taken their trips. The steep price of visiting Gates of the Arctic National Park can be an advantage. In 1984, only 470 groups visited the Gates. Just an elite few, endowed with finances, physique and time, vacation here.

Visitors whose goal is the solitude and isolation that this huge wilderness offers may be better off avoiding favored places, such as the north fork of the Koyukuk and the Gates of the Arctic peaks area, where they might meet other park visitors. Customized trips to unnamed valleys are available for those who want to vacation alone.

Hunting is only allowed in the pre-

A cache keeps animals and intruders away from backcountry supplies.

serve portion of Alaska and aliens must have a guide to hunt for certain big game animals. Given the remoteness and unique problems associated with hunting in the arctic wilderness, a guide who is familiar with local conditions is recommended even if not required. Some game can be taken only by permit or drawing. Contact the Alaska Department of Fish and Game for specifics.

Along with the bears–yes, guns are allowed for protection–the Gates is also home to hordes of mosquitoes. During certain times of the year, wilderness travellers survive the ever-present swarm of bugs by keeping their entire body, including their hands, completely covered. Carry a good mosquito repellent and a finely screened tent.

Another wilderness creature that inhabits the Gates is *giardia lamblia*, a microscopic water organism that causes "beaver fever," an unpleasant intestinal disorder. The best prevention is to boil all drinking water or use chemical disinfectants such as iodine or chlorine.

June and July are the wettest months in the Gates; thunderstorms are frequent occurrences. Rain has been known to start in mid-August and not quit until it turns to snow in September. Temperatures can range from -70 degrees F (-57 degrees C) to 92 degrees F (32 degrees C). Snow may fall in any month of the year. The average summer temperature ranges from freezing to 85 degrees F (29 degrees C), prime hypothermia (body-chilling) conditions. Wool clothing allows for both warmth and dryness, and hiking boots are needed to survive in wet, rocky and soggy conditions.

As a final word, avoid the tragic wilderness experiences. People have drowned sleeping on sandbars and others have suffered delays in their travel plans because a gentle stream became a raging white-water river in a matter of hours in a downpour. Three to 10 days leeway should be allowed for water level changes if any river or creek crossings are involved. The Gates is no place to live by the clock, and although offering a unique encounter with nature, requires some careful vacation planning.

Winter snows and a sled lend access to the cache.

GLACIER BAY NATIONAL PARK

Located in Alaska's southeastern panhandle, the park's center lies approximately 90 miles (145 km) northwest of Juneau and 600 miles (965 km) southeast of Anchorage. **Glacier Bay National Park and Preserve** encompasses 3.3 million acres (1.3 million hectares).

In a land comprised of three climatic zones—marine to arctic—seven different ecosystems support a wide variety of plant and animal life. From the endangered humpback whale and threatened arctic peregrin falcon to the common harbor seal, black and brown bears, mountain goat, marmot, eagle and ptarmigan, Glacier Bay provides a rich overview of Alaska's wildlife.

Whether navigating the narrow inlets by large cruiseship, small tour boat or kayak, or flying low over crevassed glaciers and rocky ledges in chartered aircraft, the emotions stimulated by the magic of Glacier Bay will remain for a lifetime. Gaze at towering walls of blue ice and laugh at the antics of lazy harbor seals sunbathing on floating bergs. Snap pictures of mountain goats perched precariously on steep slopes and take home tales of adventure and beauty.

Glacier Bay's physical environment is as diverse as any found in Alaska. Sixteen massive tidewater glaciers flowing from snow-capped mountain peaks of the **Fairweather Range** literally plunge into the icy waters of the fjords below. Besides the jagged icebergs, ice-scoured walls of rock lining the waterways, saltwater beaches and protected coves, numerous freshwater lakes and thick forests of western hemlock and Sitka spruce are also found within the park.

Prehistory and Exploration

Evidence of man's habitation in the Glacier Bay region dates back approximately 10,000 years. The absence of archeological remains over long time periods, however, prompts questions of early cultural success, as settlers struggled to survive postglacial eras. Researchers outline seasonal patterns of hunting, fishing and gathering from semipermanent winter villages. Native Tlingit folklore includes tales of village destruction periodically from shock waves and other natural forces.

European exploration of Glacier Bay began as early as July 1741, when Russian ships of the Bering Expedition sailed the region's outer coast. French explorer Jean Francois La Perouse arrived 45 years later. His detailed observations and map of Lituya Bay, published in 1797, with its five surrounding glaciers, provide scientists with valuable data, from which glacial changes over time are computed.

Other explorers such as Captain George Vancouver followed. But it was the widespread publicity soon after well-known naturalist John Muir's first reconnaissance of the area in 1879 that stimulated scientific investigations and early tourism.

Visitors to Glacier Bay today are treated to views much different from those observed in the 1880s. At that time, the network of fjords had not yet been established; a huge glacier extended into the area which is now open water.

Early steamship excursions into Glacier Bay during the 1880s carried up to 230 passengers. People came from around the world to ride the ships sailing close to the mighty icewalls. The flock of curious scientists and tourists halted abruptly, however, when on Sept. 10, 1899, a violent earthquake struck the area. The strong tremor caused tremendous amounts of ice from the Muir Glacier to calve, falling into the sea. An unbroken jam of floating ice choked the waterway and extended more than 10 miles (16.1 km) from the glacier's terminus.

When tour ships could no longer sail closer than five or seven miles (eight or 11 km) to the popular Muir Glacier, excursions to Glacier Bay ceased. Tourism slowly developed again after 1925, when Glacier Bay National Monument was established.

Glaciers and Icebergs

The glaciers of Glacier Bay National Park and Preserve have, over time, retreated and advanced due to severe climatic fluctuations. La Perouse and Vancouver both observed glacier ice at the mouth of the bay in 1786 and 1794. During Muir's trip to Glacier Bay in 1879, however, the ice had retreated 32 miles (51.5 km) to a point near what is now the mouth of Muir Inlet. Ninety years later, the Muir Glacier had receded another 24 miles (38.6 km).

Glaciers are rivers of ice, snow, rock, sediment, water and organic debris originating on land and moving downslope under the forces of weight and gravity. Alaska is one of the best places in the world to observe the impressive splendor of this natural phenomenon.

Visitors to Glacier Bay travelling either via water or air routes can often watch entire sections of glacier ice calve from 150-foot (46-meter) walls. From the water, the cracking ice produces a thundering roar. Huge bergs are set adrift. Waves sweep across sandbars outward from the glacier's tidewater base. Kayakers are warned to maintain a safe distance from the glacier faces.

Preceding pages: camp at Riggs Glacier, Glacier Bay National Park. Below, cruise-ship tours the Glacier Bay.

From the air, the sound emitted from the crashing ice cannot be heard over the drone of an aircraft engine, but the aerial perspective, the comprehensive view of shimmering ice flowing from mountaintop to sea will convince even the most ardent disbeliever that the forces of natures in Glacier Bay are alive and very active.

Those on the water, close to ice chunks slowly melting in the salty bay, may hear a crackling sound similar to Rice Krispies, seltzer water or champagne. Don't be alarmed! The sizzling actually comes from the release of thousands of air bubbles which became entrapped in the glacier ice from high pressure during its formation. The phenomenon, aptly named, is called a "Bergy Seltzer" or "Ice Sizzle."

Plant and Animal Life

Two hundred years ago, when a glacier entirely filled what is now a network of inlets in Glacier Bay, only a small number of plant and animal species inhabited the region. Since the rapid retreat of the ice, life in the water and on the surrounding land flourished. Today, the nutrient-rich waters of the fjords are important feeding grounds for large marine mammals. Even the wind-swept and insect-free upper slopes of the glaciers provide welcome refuge for mountain goats and other animals.

The four land and three marine ecosystems in Glacier Bay each supports lifeforms adapted to the environment. Near **Gustavus**, a wet tundra ecosystem is home to shrubby willow, lodgepole pine and Sitka alder. Sandhill

cranes rest in the open marshes here during migration, while river otter, wolf, bear, coyote and moose roam.

Bartlett Cove, the park's only area of major development, lies within a region dominated by coastal western hemlock and Sitka spruce. Watch for bald eagles flying overhead and perched in treetop nests.

Those who spend time in the magnificent backcountry of Glacier Bay National Park and Preserve may climb to elevations of 2,500 feet (762 meters). Here, in the alpine tundra ecosystem, the thick vegetation of lower elevations is replaced by shrubby plants—alpine grasses and dwarf blueberry. The terrain is rocky, and snow patches remain in early summer. Delicate flowering plants and lichens should be treated with respect, for regeneration in this environment is extremely slow.

Although few visitors venture onto the higher snowfields and glaciers, life in this seemingly barren, mountainous environment does indeed exist. The legendary "ice worm," the only earthworm known to live on snow and ice, feeds on a red-pigmented green algae and organic debris swept onto the frozen surface. Only three-quarters to an inch (two to 2.5 cm) long and as wide as a darning needle, these tiny black creatures hatch their eggs in subfreezing temperatures and remain extremely sensitive to heat. The Glacier flea—a vegetarian insect—also lives above treeline, as do many species of lichens—algae and fungus in a symbiotic relationship. Glacial history can actually be computed by studying lichen growth, a slow process which occurs at a steady rate.

Possibly the most controversial species found within Glacier National Park is the endangered humpback whale. A migratory marine mammal that winters near Hawaii or Mexico, humpbacks feed in the icy waters of southeastern Alaska and Glacier Bay in the summer. Killer and minke whales are sometimes spotted in the bay as well.

Besides small intertidal creatures, Glacier Bay is also home to many fish and shorebirds. Sea lion and otter, harbor seal and porpoise are frequently sighted.

There are no major roads leading to Glacier Bay National Park and Preserve, and the area is not serviced by Alaska Marine Highway ferries. Most visitors arrive by large cruiseship or package tour, but travellers on their own can reach the small community of Gustavus by either scheduled flights on Alaska Airlines or small air and boat charters from Juneau.

Overnight accommodations within the park are limited to **Glacier Bay Lodge**—55 rooms with baths, a dining room, cocktail lounge, lodge and gift shop. A 10-mile (16.1-km) road links the park headquarters in Barlett Cove to Gustavus, where lodges and cabins are open May through September.

Park Facilities and Attractions

A small walk-in campground located in Bartlett Cove usually fills to capacity only two or three times a season. **Sandy Cove**, approximately 20 miles (32.2 km) north, offers additional camping for those travelling by boat.

Although clear, warm days in the park are marvelous, providing unlimited views of the higher peaks and glacier walls, southeast Alaska is famous for its rain and fog. Summer temperatures in upper Glacier Bay can differ 20 degrees F (7°C) from those in Barlett Cove, where the average is 50 to 60 degrees F (10 to 16°C). Don't forget a warm sweater, hat and raincoat!

The main attraction in this beautiful national park is, of course, the spectacular scenery and abundant wildlife. The National Park Service provides interpretive programs and activities to make visits even more exciting. Guided nature and walking tours on two well-maintained trails start from Bartlett Cove, and slide-lecture shows are given in the lodge and on concessioner vessels—the *Thunder Bay* and *Glacier Bay Explorer*.

Backcountry travel in Glacier Bay is becoming increasingly popular. Kayakers often spend a week or more in the area, and July is usually the busiest month. (To protect the environment, the Park Services asks backcountry users to voluntarily disperse.) A floating ranger station in **Goose Bay** is open during the summer.

A trip to Alaska is not complete without a visit to Glacier Bay National Park and Preserve. In the sun, rain, fog—and magic—of southeast Alaska, Glacier Bay has it all.

The mystery of an ice cave.

KATMAI: VOLCANOES AND WILDERNESS

Nature is, simply put, "awesome" in **Katmai National Park and Preserve.** Here in this isolated location the scenery is breathtaking, the weather is unstable, the winds can be life-threatening, and the past is reckoned in terms of pre and post-volcanic eruption.

Located 290 air miles from Anchorage on the Alaska Peninsula, the Park is a haven for lovers of the unspoiled wilderness. No highway system touches this area; the usual access is by small plane. Within Katmai National Park and Preserve backcountry routes may be suggested to summer explorers, but the only trails they will find to follow are made by animals.

On **Naknek Lake** the Park Service maintains **Brooks Camp,** recipient of around 20,000 visitors, sightseers and flightseers, fishermen, hikers, climbers and canoeists each year. Northeast of Brooks Camp, lodges at **Kulik** and **Grosvenor Camps** are available for more serious fishing enthusiasts.

For those who prefer to enjoy the wilderness from a distance, air taxi services can be chartered for sightseeing and package tours are available, with guides, food and lodging provided. At Brooks Camp, tourists can enjoy several easy walks, bears can be viewed summer-long from a place of safety as they feed on spawning salmon, and a tour bus provides transportation to the scene of volcanic devastation in the **Valley of Ten Thousand Smokes.**

Three-quarters of a century after the eruption that justified this National Park, the Valley remains awe-inspiring. Ash, pumice and rocks from the 1912 eruption produced over 40 sq miles (100 sq km) of lunar landscape, desolate and forbidding, sculpted by wind and water. The once-verdant valley floor, covered with shifting pumice, still resists vegetation and quickly erases the imprint of a hiker's boot.

Historic Katmai

Before the great eruption, a portion of the historic Katmai Trail wound through this valley. Today the trail is no longer visible and its ancient route a path of obstacles. Blowing ash, rugged terrain, dense undergrowth, quicksand, narrow canyons and braided streams challenge the most seasoned hiker.

During severe weather travellers are warned against the old route at Katmai Pass at the head of the Valley of Ten Thousand Smokes. The interchange of air between the Gulf of Alaska and the Bering Sea streams through this pass and can cause winds over 100 miles per hour (160 kmph) — strong enough to blow a hiker off his feet and carry him along the ground.

Archeologists believe that two separate cultures once existed on either side of the Alaskan Peninsula. Some time after 1900 B.C., however. trade began across the Katmai Pass between the Pacific Ocean coast and Bristol Bay, and the dissimilar cultures began to merge.

As Russians infiltrated coastal regions in their quest for furs, the Katmai Trail was travelled by traders and missionaries. After Alaska's purchase by the Americans, traders still used this route, although less frequently.

The trail became popular again in 1898 when a flood of gold seekers found it a shortcut to Nome: prospectors used it to avoid a stormy sea passage around the Alaska Peninsula. Mail carriers also found this route convenient, but by 1912 the gold rush had subsided and the Katmai Trail was seldom travelled.

Earth Tremors and Eruptions

When the great eruption occurred in 1912, news was slow to reach the outside world because the area was so isolated. The closest account was furnished by a Native named American Pete, who was on the Katmai Trail only 18 miles (29 km) northeast of Mount Katmai when the violent explosions began.

Earth tremors that preceded the eruption were so severe that the residents of Katmai and Savonoski, small Native villages on the Alaska Peninsula, gathered their possessions and fled to Naknek, on Bristol Bay.

Later research gave credit for the devastation not to Mount Katmai, but to **Novarupta Volcano,** a volcano formed by the eruption itself. The explosion was heard 750 miles (1,200 km) away in Juneau, 650 miles (1,050 km) away in Dawson, and 500 miles (800 km) away in Fairbanks. Most heavily impacted were the Native villages of Katmai and

Savonoski, later abandoned because of heavy ashfall, and the town of Kodiak on Kodiak Island, across Shelikof Strait to the Southwest.

One hundred miles (160 km) from the eruption, Kodiak residents noticed a peculiar fan-shaped cloud in the sky. As the cloud grew steadily higher, darker and closer, they grew more and more uneasy. Especially alarming were flashes of lightning within the cloud, an oddity in an area where electric storms do not occur.

Terror increased as the sky became dark — in June in Kodiak there is almost continuous daylight — and earthquake shocks grew more frequent. As ash began to fall, accompanied by nauseating gases, people believed they would suffer the fate of Pompeii and be buried alive.

Kodiak's Ordeal

Mountain lake: a peaceful setting for fishing.

Ash sifted through cracks around windows and doors, clogged nostrils and scoured eyes, filling rooms with such an impenetrable haze that people could not see each other. A 20-room log building burned, yet residents who stood only a few hundred yards away saw no flame and felt no heat: falling ash was so heavy it insulated the air.

When the ash fall grew heavier the people of Kodiak tied dampened layers of cloth over their faces. Groping along fences and ditches they followed the sound of a foghorn to the harbor, where they boarded the revenue cutter *Manning* or the barge *St. James*. Five hundred people huddled on the decks of the *Manning,* so cramped they could not sit down. Lack of visibility made it difficult to leave the harbor, but eventually the vessel was anchored two miles away where an escape to sea would be possible if conditions worsened. But after two days and nights of terror, the cloud dispersed and the Kodiak people returned to their village. There they found ash 18 inches (45 cm) deep, landslides, collapsed roofs, choked water mains, pumice-laden rivers and streams overflowing their banks. Lakes normally five feet deep had been filled in, and wildlife was decimated. Fish died as the ash clogged their gills and the beaches were littered with dead sea life. Codfish, the native staple, disappeared; salmon destined for a new cannery never showed up.

Ash fall from the great eruption covered more than 3,000 sq miles (7,800 sq km). As far away as Vancouver, British Columbia, acid fumes weakened the threads in clothings hung out to dry. (Until the reason was known housewives accused merchants of selling inferior goods). In addition, particles from the ash cloud affected the upper atmosphere so much that the average annual temperature in the Northern Hemisphere was reduced by 1.8 degrees F (1°C).

Valley of 10,000 Smokes

In the following years several expeditions were sent to the eruption site by the National Geographic Society to satisfy worldwide interest and do scientific research. At first, prevented from reaching the source of the eruption, scientists encountered seas of mud, ash slides up to depths of 1,500 feet (450 meters), and evidence of one of the most powerful water surges in history.

In 1916 the crater of Mount Katmai was reached and a smoking valley discovered at Katmai Pass. The valley, named the Valley of Ten Thousand Smokes by explorer R.F. Griggs, covered up to 40 miles (100 sq km) and held thousands of steaming fumaroles. Some of these emitted periodic columns of steam that reached a thousand feet (300 meters) in the air. Here, explorers found that by moving their tents in relation to a fumarole, they could regulate floor temperature. Steam from the fumaroles, they found, could not only fry bacon, but would hold the fry pan aloft.

In 1918 the Valley of Ten Thousand Smokes was made a national monument in order to preserve an area important to the study of volcanism. Later additions for a wildlife sanctuary brought the Katmai National Park and Preserve to its present total of 4,268 acres (1,700 hectares).

When the Katmai monument was first created it was believed that the Valley of Ten Thousand Smokes would become a geyser-filled attraction to rival that of Yellowstone National Park in Wyoming. Scientists then believed that the geyser field at Yellowstone was dying. Since that time, however, the reverse has come about. The Yellowstone geysers are still active, but the fumaroles at the Valley of Ten Thousand Smokes have subsided, and now they number less than 10.

A Rugged Wilderness

Katmai National Park and Preserve makes available to visitors not only an area of amazing volcanic involvement but a representative and undisturbed portion of the Alaskan Peninsula. Great varieties of terrain in Katmai include the rugged coastal habitat of Shelikof Strait on one side of the Alaskan range and the rivers and lakes of the Naknek river watershed on the other. Mixed spruce-birch forests, dense willow-alder thickets and moist tundra are found at lower elevations, and alpine tundra on the higher slopes.

A series of small lakes and rivers provide opportunities for canoeing, kayaking and spectacular fishing. Rainbow trout, lake trout, char, pike and grayling are popular sport fish here, as well as sockeye, coho, king pink and chum salmon. Nearly 1 million salmon return each year to the Naknek river system.

Brown or grizzly bears are common in Katmai and can be safely viewed all summer at Brooks Camp as they feed on spawning salmon. Other wildlife that may be encountered are moose, caribou, land otter, wolverine, marten, weasel, mink, lynx, fox, wolf, muskrat, beaver and hare. Off coastal waters, seals, sea lions, sea otters and beluga and gray whales can be seen. Birdwatching is also a popular pastime at Katmai as waterfowl, shorebirds, raptors and song birds are numerous.

Weather in Katmai National Park is variable, and heavy rain is characteristic of most areas during the summer months. The most comfortable weather occurs on the northwestern slope of the Aleutian range, where at Brooks Camp average daytime temperature is 60 degrees F (15°C). Here, skies are only expected to be clear or partially cloudy 20 percent of the time. Warm clothing, rain gear and boots are recommended.

Katmai National Park and Preserve can be reached by an hour's jet flight from Anchorage to King Salmon, and a 20-minute trip by floatplane or amphibian chartered from King Salmon to Brooks Camp. More information about the park can be obtained from the National Park Service in King Salmon.

Bears frolick during the annual salmon run.

ALASKA'S WILDFLOWERS AND WILDLIFE

Some people think of Alaska as a wasteland, permanently covered with snow and ice. But the truth is, Alaska is a world teeming with life. From the humblest tundra flower to the mightiest grizzly bear, this land supports a vast array of wildflowers and wildlife. The most exciting part of an Alaskan adventure is discovering the flowers, birds and mammals of the state.

Fascinating Flora

All regions of Alaska, from the forests in the Southeast to the tundra on the North Slope, boast brilliant wildflower displays. Mid-June to mid-July is the peak season for flowers; in many areas, the blossoms are so thick you can't avoid stepping on them.

Fireweed is the most common Alaskan flower. The tall stalks, as high as a person, are topped with clusters of bright red blossoms. Fireweed lines the shoulders of almost all of the state's highways. Also common is the *forget-me-not*, Alaska's state flower. This 18-inch (46-cm) blue-flowered plant grows in tundra meadows and along streams. Around ponds and marshes, watch for *cotton grass*, a type of sedge capped with what appears to be balls of cotton.

The best place to find and photograph a wide variety of Alaskan flowers is on the tundra. Each spring, an explosion of white, yellow, pink, red, blue and violet flowers covers the tundra. A one-hour walk in Denali National Park will easily turn up thousands of flowers and scores of species. Many of these tundra plants are northern relatives of flowers found in the lower 48 states. Look for *arctic poppy, Alaska violet, alpine azalea, Siberian aster, wild geranium, Lapland rosebay* (rhododendron family), *arctic lupine, tundra rose, prickly wild rose, northern primrose, rock jasmine* and *whitish gentian*.

Preceding pages: naturalist Rick McIntyre captures the subtle beauty of wildflowers; from left to right, (1st row) Dwarf Dogwood, Northern Dwarf Larkspur, Cotton Grass, Lapland Rosebay; (2nd row) Shubby Cinquefoil, Scammon's Spring Beauty, Low-Bush Cranberry, Bearberry leaves; (3rd row) Northern Anemone, Diapensia, Bluebells, Pasque Flowers. Left, tundra flowers. Right, a hoary marmot, resident of Denali Park.

and *whitish gentian*.

Most of these species are dwarf versions of their southern cousins. To survive on the cold, windswept tundra, the plants must hug the surface of the ground, the warmest and least windy zone available to them. When winter comes, deep snow layers efficiently insulate the plants from the extreme cold temperatures. Some species, such as arctic poppy, have developed a flower shaped like a radar antenna. The poppy flower tracks the motion of the sun across the sky, its parabolic design reflecting the sun's heat on

the developing seeds. The inner temperature of the flower may be 18 degrees F (10 degrees C) warmer than the prevailing air temperature.

It is difficult to shoot a detailed photo of a field of tundra flowers. The beauty of these flowers is best shown in close-up shots, as near to the flower as your lens will allow. Winds are common on the tundra and swaying flowers may cause your shot to be blurred. Be patient when photographing tundra plants — if you wait a bit, you will probably experience a brief lull in the wind and can take a sharper photo.

If you enjoy learning about tundra flowers, consider purchasing one of the many excellent flower guide books available in local bookstores. The photographs, sketches and background information on the plants will enhance your appreciation of what you find.

Plants reproduce themselves through their flowering parts and picking a flower defeats this process. If these flowers have given you pleasure, repay them for this gift by not picking them.

Birds

At least 386 different species of birds have been officially documented in Alaska. With few exceptions, these species inhabit Alaska only during spring and summer and then migrate south. They come north to take

the *long-tailed jaeger* and the *arctic warbler*. Some plovers winter on the Hawaiian Islands while others migrate to Argentina. Tierra del Fuego, at the tip of South America, is the winter home of the surfbird. The jaeger spends its winters on the open ocean in the central Pacific or near Japan. The arctic warbler resides in southern Asia during winter months.

Alaska's state bird, the *willow ptarmigan,* was chosen not by politicians but by a vote of the state's school children. Along with its close relatives, the *rock* and *white tailed ptarmigan,* the willow ptarmigan lives in Alaska year round. A ptarmigan is brown in summer and white during winter, changing coloration to blend with the surroundings. During extremely cold winter weather, ptarmi-

advantage of the eruption of life which occurs on the tundra each spring. The tundra offers a nearly limitless banquet of food (plants, insects and small animals) to birds attempting to raise hungry young.

The *arctic tern* is the world's record holder for migration. These gull-like birds breed and nest on the shore of Alaskan tundra ponds. In late summer, the terns and their young start a migration which will eventually take them all the way to the Antarctic. Summer is just beginning in the Southern Hemisphere as the terns arrive. The round-trip flight from Alaska to the Antarctic and back is approximately 25,000 miles (40,000 km)!

Other long-distance commuters include the *American golden plover,* the *surfbird,*

gan keep warm by burrowing into snow drifts. The males fiercely defend nesting females: one male was actually seen attacking a grizzly bear who had stumbled on his mate's nest. Look for ptarmigan in willow thickets and on the open tundra.

Eagle Habitat

Alaska is the stronghold of the *bald eagle*. More bald eagles live in Alaska than in the other 49 states combined. Their white heads, white tails and eight-foot (2.4-meter) wingspan make them easily identifiable, even at a great distance. Look for them in places where fish are common, especially along coastal area, in Southeast Alaska. The best place to see bald eagles is near Haines in October and November. The Chilkat River, just north of town, attracts thousands of eagles to feed on dead or spent salmon. A single riverside tree may contain dozens of roosting eagles. Because fish are available throughout the winter in coastal area, these bald eagles do not migrate out of Alaska.

Golden eagles, the darker cousins of the bald eagle, are normally found in tundra and mountainous areas. They hunt rodents, such as the arctic ground squirrel, rather than fish. The Polychrome Pass area of Denali National Park is an excellent place to watch for golden eagles.

Alaska's birds can be seen and studied by anyone possessing time and a pair of binocu-

many communities have developed free bird checklists for their local area.

Mammals

Without question, the premiere wildlife area in Alaska is Denali National Park. *Grizzlies, moose, Dall sheep, caribou, red foxes, snowshoe hares, beavers, arctic ground squirrels* and *hoary marmots* are seen by almost everyone who visits Denali. With some luck, *wolves* may also be spotted. (See the section on Denali for information on grizzlies, moose, sheep, caribou and wolves.) Denali's shuttle bus system is designed to maximize wildlife sightings. Because the buses cause such little disturbance, many animals, including grizzlies, often can

lars. While near tundra ponds, look for *loons, grebes, geese, ducks, yellowlegs, phalaropes* and *sandpipers*. On tundra watch for *long-tailed jaegers, golden plovers, whimbrels, snow buntings, wheatears, sparrows* and *water pipits*. Owls, *goshawks, woodpeckers, gray jays* and *chickadees* are common in forested areas. *Gulls, terns, murrelets, auklets, shearwaters, cormorants* and *puffins* live along the coastlines.

Most National Parks, National Forests, National Wildlife Refuges, State Parks and

Left, stately caribou against a backdrop of fall tundra. Right, a standing grizzly in Denali Park.

be photographed within 100 yards (90 meters) of the road.

Denali and the other great Alaskan National Parks are textbook examples of what National Parks were meant to be. Each of these Parks protects an entire ecosystem in a condition nearly identical to its original state. The population levels of wildlife such as Dall sheep, moose and caribou are controlled not by humans, but by the area's natural predators, the grizzly bears and wolves. The vegetation, prey species and predators interact in the same manner that their ancestors did thousands of years ago. If you see a grizzly dig out a ground squirrel from its burrow or a wolf pack chase a caribou herd, you will be witnessing a scene which could have taken place during the last Ice Age.

Alaska's Bears

Katmai National Park is the place for *brown bears*, the coastal version of the Interior grizzly. At one time, the two bears were considered different species but most experts now feel they are the same animal. The brown bears in Katmai and other coastal areas live where large numbers of salmon are available. Partly because of the nearly unlimited salmon, these bears can grow to weights of more than 1,200 pounds (540 kg). The best time to see the Katmai bears is in July, the time of peak salmon spawning.

Polar bears live along the northern and

white settlers. In 1937, a law was passed which restricted reindeer ownership to Natives. Today, approximately 30,000 reindeer are in Alaska. The largest herd, 5,000 to 6,000 animals, lives near Kotzebue on the Seward Peninsula. Other herds of reindeer are located on Nunivak Island and Saint Lawrence Island. A small herd can be viewed at the Reindeer Research Station in Cantwell, 27 miles (43 km) south of the entrance to Denali National Park.

Alaska's wildlife live in one of the last great wilderness areas of the world. Regardless of how Alaska is developed in the future, the National Parks and National Wildlife Refuges will always be a safe haven for this great assemblage of animal species. The protection and preservation of this wildlife is

northwestern coast of the state. They are the largest land carnivore in the world. Some old males have weighed over 1,500 pounds (680 kg). Polar bears live on the ice flows of the Arctic Ocean and can readily swim long distances in the frigid ocean waters. A number have been seen 50 miles (80 km) from the nearest ice or land. Polar bears survive by hunting seals and other marine mammals. These nomads of the Arctic Ocean are seldom seen by travellers to Alaska.

Reindeer are the domesticated version of caribou, although both animals are considered the same species. The first reindeer were introduced into Alaska from the Old World in 1892 as a dependable source of food and clothing for native people and early

one of the greatest gifts America has made to the people of the world.

If you've never been to Alaska before, a whole world of wildlife and wildflowers awaits you. Your first sighting of a grizzly, your first bald eagle and your first walk over the profusely flowered tundra will likely be the high points of your entire trip. These are the experiences that make Alaska such an unique adventure.

Above: left, an arctic ground squirrel; right, a mature bald eagle. Right, Dall ewes on the slopes of Mount McKinley.

WORDS FOR THE WILDERNESS

In March 1981, a 35-year-old man was flown into the wilderness to an unnamed lake near the Coleen River, 150 miles (241 km) northeast of Fort Yukon. He planned to camp until August, spending his time photographing wildlife. All preparations had been made for his wilderness experience. He had ample provisions–shotgun, .30-30 rifle, .22 rifle, plenty of ammunition, reliable tent, wood stove, gas lamp and fuel, fishing equipment, plenty of matches and an ax.

On Feb. 2, 1982, Alaska State Troopers found the man's emaciated body in his tent. The camper, starving and suffering from frostbitten limbs, had apparently despaired and killed himself. The victim filled 100 pages of a diary that was found intact when his body was discovered. The diary is a poignant record of an idyllic outing that ended in tragedy.

The victim in this tale made two errors that eventually cost him his life. The first was made before he arrived at the remote lake–he failed to make firm arrangements to return to Fairbanks. The pilot told the man not to count on him for the planned August pickup, a fact confirmed in the diary.

The second error occurred in early fall when an Alaska State Trooper's airplane flew over his campsite. The starving man frantically waved both his arms over his head. When the plane flew over a second time, the victim again waved. The plane flew off. Days later, the man realized his mistake when he studied the back side of his hunting license. He had signaled, "everything ok, don't wait."

Travelling in Alaska need be no more hazardous than elsewhere in the world if proper precautions are observed. Due to the latitude and varying weather conditions around the state, the traveller must have the appropriate equipment and be physically prepared for the activities he wishes to pursue. Because there are so few roads and distances are so great, clear and precise communication while travelling is vital.

Preceding pages: climbers savor the vista over the Ruth Glacier, Denali Park. Left, an ice climber carefully negotiates a crevasse.

This section is not an exhausting discourse on any one topic; its purpose is to cite several common wilderness problems with remedies for Alaska travellers.

WEATHER

Coastal and Southcentral Alaska

The word to remember when selecting equipment for coastal Alaska is rain. If you are going to spend time in Southeast Alaska remember that portions of this area receive up to 200 inches (508 cm) of rainfall annually–a raincoat and an umbrella can be constant companions. Reliable raingear is a must. If you plan to be outside for long periods, a rainsuit (jacket, pants, and hat) will be used frequently. Rain is also the prime consideration when selecting a tent and sleeping bag. Tents must be able to withstand long wet spells. Sleeping bags filled with synthetic materials rather than down are a wiser choice as they retain more of their insulating qualities when wet.

The Interior

The Interior has dramatic seasonal contrasts. Summer temperatures are warm and winter temperatures can dip below -40 degrees F (-40°C).

Summer equipment and clothing may be lightweight although mountain travellers will face much colder temperatures. A light hat and at least one heavy long-sleeved shirt will be welcome additions to your wardrobe. A mosquito headnet takes little room and will be greatly appreciated if needed.

The extreme cold of winter makes only the best equipment suitable. A quality down jacket, a hat, mittens and warm boots are a must. Camping at this time of year is most rewarding (no crowds), but requires a sleeping bay comfortable at -40 degrees or colder.

The finest time, by far, to ski in the mountains is spring. Temperatures on the snow are so comfortable that people ski without shirts. However, snow-blindness is a very painful reality of spring for unprotected eyes. Mirrored sunglasses are best, but dark sunglasses will suffice.

The North Slope

If the password for coastal Alaska is rain, then the key word for the North Slope is wind. The area is technically an arctic desert with less than five inches (13 cm) of annual precipitation. This meager amount of precipitation should not be disregarded as it may fall as snow or freezing rain on any day of the year and be driven by gale force winds. Travellers to the North Slope need clothes that are windproof and warm. Camping equipment must also be able to withstand heavy winds.

and expected return date. *Make firm arrangements to be picked up.* Be certain that someone besides the pilot knows where you are. In one case, a fisherman was dropped off in a remote location and the pilot was the only person who knew of his whereabouts. The pilot has a fatal crash while returning to town, and several days of searching were required to locate the missing fisherman.

What happens if the plane crashes while you are in it? By Alaska law, all planes are to carry emergency equipment. The required list includes food for each person for two weeks, ax, first-aid kit, knife, matches, mosquito headnet for each person, gill net, fishing tackle and a pistol or rifle with

TRAVEL

Charter Flights

If your destination is a small village, confirm that there is regular service. Several commercial airlines service outlying Alaskan villages and communities. Again, check first to see it there is regular air service. This will save you a lot of money. If however, you are bound for the wilderness, a charter flight is necessary.

Before departure, be *sure* someone knows where you are going. If you must, inform the Alaska State Troopers of your destination

ammunition. A sleeping bag, snowshoes and one wool blanket are added to the list for winter travel. Although most flights carry some survival gear, sometimes the requirements are ignored. Check the survival gear before taking off. If you decide to bring your own, keep as much of it on your person as possible. In winter fill your pockets; in summer, use a small waist pack. You may have to evacuate the downed craft quickly.

Every plane in Alaska is also required to carry a downed aircraft transmitting device (Emergency Location Transmitter or ELT). Learn how to operate this device before you depart on your journey. If the pilot becomes incapacitated in a crash, you can activate the ELT and be rescued more quickly. Almost everyone arrives at his destination safely, despite all the gloom and doom. The above-mentioned precautions pertain to the less than 0.5 percent of flights during which an inflight problem does occur.

Automobile travel

This can be even more involved than air travel. There is no Alaska law which governs what survival equipment should be kept in a vehicle. Yet the average car is maintained less frequently than an airplane, which means that more cars break down while travelling. When travelling in sub-freezing weather, a breakdown can be life-threatening as well as inconvenient. The Alaska State Troopers recommend the following survival kit: down coat, boots, mittens, hat, snow-pants, sleeping bag, flare, candles, extra spark plugs, extra belts, shovel, chain, flashlight and high-energy food.

Automobile maintenance is vitally important. It is expensive and time-consuming to break down on the road, and towing charges are costly. Check the car carefully before leaving the city.

Be straightforward with the rental agency when hiring a car. Inform them of your proposed route and confirm that maintenance is available along your way. Most agencies have stringent rules about driving on gravel roads (e.g. the Dalton Highway). Solving problems before travel will avoid misunderstandings later.

Winter mandates snow tires or studded tires, an operating engine heater and ample electrical cord to reach a receptacle.

AVOIDABLE DILEMMAS

Mosquitoes

Whatever Alaska missed out on when it didn't get snakes or termites has been more than compensated for with the mosquito. Billed sarcastically as the "Alaskan State Bird," these insects are a wilderness force to be reckoned with. Use the most powerful repellents available, such as the "musk"

Left, crossing the Thorofare River. Right, always be prepared for rain in Alaska.

types or those with a high concentration of DEET. Even in the face of these strong measures (and probably in your face also), the mosquito thrives. Thick clothing will reduce the number of bites per square inch/cm, but sometimes relief is only a headnet away.

Bears

When bears and people cross paths in the wild, on one wins. Many Alaskans have stories about encountering bears at close quarters, but tragic accounts abound. Most bears turn tail and run upon encountering people, and vice versa. However, in some instances, the bear will stand its ground. At

this point, advice differs widely on what course of action to take next.

On school of thought preaches stay calm (right) and speak softly to the beast, encouraging it to leave. The second line of thinking contends that you should shout loudly to scare the animal away. Both schools agree that if the bear is a brown (coastal) or Grizzly (Interior), you should climb a tree if available. (Black bears may follow the climber). Should a bear attack, the *only* course of action is to "play dead." Protect your head and neck and try to lie on your stomach, but do not struggle. Bears have been know to walk away if they think the prey is dead.

Three important strategies should be used to minimize the number of chance meetings with bears. First, make plenty of noise while walking in the wilderness. Bears will hear your approach and leave. Secondly, be careful with food around camp. If possible, do not cook in camp and always store food away from your sleeping area. The final suggestion seems like common sense, but is easy to forget: If you see a well-worn path in the wilderness–it may even be grooved into the earth–remember the trail may belong to Mr. Bear. Be alert if you must walk along the path, make lots of noise, and do not pitch your tent on the trail, or you may have an unexpected tent mate.

Stay dry. Wet clothing loses most of its insulating value. Functional raingear is vitally important. Ponchos are nearly useless.

Avoid the wind. Wind carries body heat away much faster than still air. Wind also refrigerates wet clothing by evaporation.

Understand the cold. Remarkably, most people die of hypothermia between 30 and 50 degrees F (one and 10°C). Most hikers underestimate the severity of being wet at these temperatures. Sudden immersion in any Alaskan waters can be fatal and first aid measures must be taken immediately.

End the exposure. If a member of your party shows signs of hypothermia or if it becomes impossible to keep dry with exist-

Hypothermia

Beware of hypothermia, the sub-normal lowering of the body temperature. Hypothermia is caused by exposure to cold, but aggravated by exhaustion, wind and wet clothing. Left untreated, the hypothermic individual may become disoriented, incoherent, unconscious and may finally die. Never ignore shivering, it is the body's way of signaling for help.

The time to prevent hypothermia is during the period of exposure before complete exhaustion. The five following suggestions may help prevent an emergency:

ing clothing and conditions, make camp or end the trip.

Do not become overly tired. Make camp before you are exhausted, and bring high energy food to replenish your reserves.

Handle the hypothermic victim gently, replace wet clothing with dry, and warm the core area of the body. The procedure to warm the core is with a human sandwich: one person on each side of the victim, bare skin to bare skin, inside a warm sleeping bag. Do not give the victim any alcoholic drink as this could prove fatal. Also, do not rapidly warm the victim's extremities, as it takes much-needed blood away from the core and results in unconsciousness.

Avalanches

Avalanches pose a serious threat to winter mountain adventurers. Research has shown that most avalanches are triggered by people skiing through an avalanche zone.

An avalanche zone is a slope in which temperature range between 27 and 45 degrees F (-3 and 7°C). On shallower slopes, the snow usually does not accumulate. The two ways to avoid an avalanche are: a knowledgeable route selection and a careful trip planning. Avoid skiing through a likely avalanche zone–pass above or below it.

ation occurs in spring in Cook Inlet near Anchorage where high tide can be more than 38 feet (11.5 meters) above low tide. Tides of this size present two dangers for the sport fisherperson: swift incoming tides and strong currents.

Obtain a tide book from a fishing tackle shop, a hardware store, bar, or gasoline station if you plan to be on the water or along the shoreline. All too frequently, the fisherman standing on a rock working the incoming tide waits too long to retreat. This can develop into a life-threatening situation. People with vehicles travelling along the beaches must also be aware of the tides or risk losing their transportation–or–more. Large tides create

TOOT HORN ONLY IF BEAR IN CAMP

Spend as little time as possible near the zone. Choose the route carefully to avoid steep mountain faces, especially after a fresh snowfall. And remember, spring time is especially dangerous for avalanches.

Tides

Tidal variations are large in Southeastern Alaska. Prince William Sound, Cook Inlet and Bristol Bay. The extreme diurnal vari-

Left, hikers demonstrate mosquito headnets. Right, the battery of insect repellents available.

swift currents in constricted areas, such as the inlet to a bay. Travel by small craft is perilous during these times.

SAVOR THE MEMORY

This section was not intended to deter anyone from enjoying the wilderness. Great obstacles were overcome by early expeditions, which by today's standards had none of the proper equipment. Yet, parties with the best gear have experienced tragedies. Make the wilderness a part of your Alaskan vacation. Experience it, leave nothing but footprints, and always savor the memory.

BUSH PILOTS: A SPECIAL BREED OF FLYERS

In the 1920s Alaska and the airplane became partners in a relationship best described as complicated bliss. Despite an obvious need, early 20th Century Alaska wasn't equipped for airplanes. There were lots of places to go, but there was no place to land once you got there. This created a special breed of flyer: the bush pilot.

Referring to Alaska's boondocks as "the bush" was not an American idea. Credit belongs to Australian visitors at the turn of the century who viewed their own outback as the bush and figured the term was

Yukon River, then 100 miles (160 km) up the Tanana and Chena rivers to Fairbanks.

After the boxes arrived in Fairbanks, Martin reassembled the plane. It flew in exhibition for 11 minutes, was taken apart and carted out of the territory; that was Alaska's first taste of aviation.

After World War I, surplus "Curtiss Jennies" were available to anyone for about $600. Inevitably some of these found their way to Alaska. The first was *Polar Bear*, flown from New York by Clarence O. Prest in 1922. A year later Carl Ben Eielson lifted

appropriate in Alaska as well. The description stuck. Later, a pilot who flew anywhere away from the periphery of a town or village in Alaska became a bush pilot.

Being a bush pilot in the early years definitely lacked glamour. Consider Alaska's first performing flying machine. One James V. Martin contracted with three businessmen to fly an airplane over Fairbanks in honor of the 4th of July in 1913. He loaded his disassembled airplane on a steamship and sailed it to Skagway. There he transferred it to the Whitepass and Yukon Railroad for the 125-mile (200-km) trip to Whitehorse, Yukon Territory, Canada; finally he loaded it on a sternwheeler and steamed 800 miles (1,300 km) down the

this same plane from the ground in Fairbanks on July 3, 1923. This event was the initial appearance of Eielson, a man considered the foremost bush pilot of his era.

Where to Land?

For Alaska's early bush pilots, the size of their territory was summed up in the distances between cities, and only four really mattered in 1923: Juneau, Fairbanks, Nome and a small burg on Cook Inlet called Anchorage. From Juneau to Anchorage it's about 600 miles (965 km); Anchorage to Fairbanks, 275 miles (440 km); and Fairbanks to Nome, 450 miles (720 km). These were the business centers of Alaska, and a pilot wanting to fly for a living had to go between them regularly. This created a few problems.

The Old Jennies cruised at about 85 mph (135 kph) and carried only four hours worth of fuel. The only non-stop, city-to-city trip one could manage was between Anchorage and Fairbanks. This meant the baggage compartment on longer flights filled with fuel cans. Halfway between stops a pilot landed where he could, stopped, poured in fuel, and took off again.

It sounds easy, finding a place to land was

Alaska's winters, however, brought a host of other problems to pilots of open-cockpit biplanes. Noel Wien once took off when it was so cold he didn't know if his engine would stay warm enough to run. At 65 below zero he flew 350 miles with the cylinder head temperature steady at 100 degrees. Normally it's twice that.

Winter Weather

Winter stopovers were a real joy. As soon as the propellor stopped, a pilot drained the

the hard part. A pilot needed a long gravel bar on a river, or a stretch of level ground. Yet fields didn't exist in many places because Alaska had never been plowed. The land was natural, and Mother Nature rarely works in straight lines. In later years planes were equipped with floats for water landings. This eased the problem of selecting suitable landing sites.

Winter made landings easier. The rivers and lakes froze, snow filled the bumps on the ground, and pilots put skis on their craft.

Left, mail pick-up on Kodiak Island. Right, floatplanes land on an Interior river.

oil from his engine and carefully set it aside. He covered the engine with an insulated blanket, tied his plane down to withstand winds of up to 90 mph (145 kmph) and then looked to his own comforts.

In the wild, pilots had to fend for themselves. Most carried a wealth of gear for that kind of situation, including a tanned caribou hide. For sleeping in the cold there is no warmer ground cloth available.

Each of the early aviators would have the best sleeping bag he could find, two tents—one slightly smaller so it could be set up inside the other—and a stove of some sort for heating food, water and oil. The oil which had been drained from the plane on landing would be warmed almost to boiling and poured into the frozen engine prior to starting in the morning.

Alaska's menacing weather conditions are often caused by winds and clouds, both associated with mountains and sea coasts. Bush pilot Don Sheldon tells of the time he was flying at 120 mph (195 kmph) into the wind near Mount McKinley; when he looked over the side of his plane, he realized he was going backward relative to the ground. Figuring he wasn't getting anywhere, Don turned around and flew to an alternate, downwind destination.

Harrowing Moments

Weather conditions have often placed pilots in unusual roles. Steve Mills was

it had dropped through a hole in the fabric. As it happened, the poke had lodged under the cockpit deck. Had it fallen out of the plane in flight Wien would have had to make good the loss, which would have cost him everything he owned and then some. If that poke had disappeared, Wien Air Alaska may not have become one of the major air carriers in Alaska.

Everything a bush pilot owned or cared about depended on his airplane. This spawned humorous comments on occasion like, "a plane is only overloaded when it won't take off." Such antics didn't endear pilots to Department of Commerce officials. No matter how businesslike these bureaucrats tried to make their endless hearings, pilots made shambles of them. One flyer,

forced down by a blizzard while flying an appendicitis victim from Bethel to Anchorage on March 24, 1937. He nursed the woman all night in sub-zero cold until the weather cleared and he could complete the flight. And Katherine Clark was born in the back seat of Jim Dodson's *Stinson* in 1938. Jim's reward for one-handed flying and one-handed midwifery was to be named the baby's godfather.

Veteran bush pilot Noel Wien describes his worst flight as plagued not by weather but by problem cargo. He was carrying a nine-pound poke of gold to Fairbanks for a miner. Enroute, the leather sack slipped off the board under his feet where he had stowed it; Wien was not sure whether or not

when asked how much money his airline had, counted the bills in his wallet. Because he had some to count, his books were in the black, at least temporarily. It took a certain character and sense of duty to enforce aviation regulations in Alaska.

Eventually, regulations did start affecting Alaskan aviation. Pilots were licensed, and their cargoes were checked occasionally. They were required to keep records, which most of them despised.

Government rules were sometimes hard to live with, especially when imposed on a free-wheeling group like the early bush pilots. All recognized the requirements of safety, but the concern of Alaska's aviation pioneers was usually directed more to getting from here to there in one piece than to insuring that the proper federal form was filled out in duplicate or triplicate.

Rescues and Heroes

Cargo and passengers paid the bills, but the spectacular rescues—almost always volunteer—made the bush-pilot legends. In 1955 Don Sheldon, one of Alaska's last flying legends, made what was probably the most harrowing rescue ever attempted. An eight-man Army scout team from Fort Richardson, attempting to chart the Susitna River, was defeated by treacherous Devil's Canyon. Sheldon flew over the Army's proposed route after the team had been gone for two days. First he found pieces of

alongside the exhausted scouts required full throttle to hold the plane against the current. He eased over the the bank, and one man jumped aboard for the first trip. For steering control, and in order to slow down, he had to keep the plane pointed upstream—and drifting backwards down the canyon. Only after twisting out of the canyon could Sheldon turn around and make a safe, downriver takeoff.

The Pilot's Life

Sheldon made three more trips into the canyon, taking out two men each time. Later he found the eighth man 18 miles (30 km) downstream. For all his risk and the cost in time and gasoline, Don Sheldon received the

their wrecked boat floating in the river below the canyon. Then, in the middle of the canyon, he spotted seven men clinging to a tiny ledge just above the roaring water. Upstream was a fairly straight part of the canyon and Sheldon carefully guided his plane down through the tricky air currents.

Upon landing, he immediately found himself going backward at 30 mph (48 kmph) as the river swept the plane downstream. He kept the power on so as to slow his backward run and to allow him to steer. Pulling up

Left, wading from floatplane. Right, landing at Lake Hood near Anchorage.

going rate for rescues—a Certificate of Achievement.

But that was bush flying. The hazards were many, the pay uncertain, the hours absurd and the conditions unique. Yet from this beginning came the Alaska-based air carriers operating today.

Slowly but surely the planes have evolved, making it possible for passengers to fly in first-class comfort and luxury several miles above the earth. There is no need now of landing midway to your destination to pour in more gas. The plane is warm, it flies above most of the weather, and sophisticated electronics guide it almost effortlessly to its destination. It's a far cry from the good old days of the Alaskan bush pilot.

ALASKA AFTER THE OIL SPILL

When the tanker *Exxon Valdez* ran aground on March 24, 1989 in Alaska's Prince William Sound, 10.8 million gallons of black crude oil oozed out and eventually spread along 1,100 miles (1,770 km) of pristine shoreline. It was an ecological disaster of unprecedented proportions: the U.S. Fish and Wildlife service reported 90,000 to 270,000 sea birds, some 2,000 otters and countless other marine animals have died.

That summer, 12,000 workers descended on the soiled beaches and began one of the most exhaustive clean-up jobs. It was also one of the most expensive, with Exxon spending $2 billion the first year alone and expected to pay millions more, depending on the outcome of the more than 150 civil lawsuits filed against the giant oil company.

The first wave of workers, arriving by helicopter, military landing craft and an armada of fishing boats chartered by Exxon, fanned out in a broad perimeter along Alaska's southcentral coast to begin the messy task. All summer they bulldozed blackened beaches, sucked up gummy petroleum globules with vacuuming devices, blasted sand with hot water, polished rocks by hand, raked up oily seaweed, and sprayed fertilizer to aid the growth of oil-eating microbes—all this before bad weather forced them to suspend work for the winter.

For Alaska's tourism industry, the spill (the worst in American history) strained what already had been an uneasy relationship with the state's petroleum interests. Not only did it generate horrendous international publicity at a time when many would-be visitors were making their summer vacation plans, but the influx of clean-up workers over-extended the capacity of virtually every hotel, motel, campsite and restaurant in the Valdez area. "Clearly if they [tourists] had gone to see Prince William Sound it would have been impossible to find a room," said Bob Miller, executive director of the Alaska Tourism Marketing Council.

Prince William Sound, bound on the north by the Chugach Mountains, beyond which lies the city of Anchorage, is one of Alaska's most popular summer destinations, offering sailing, kayaking and cruises among picturesque islands, fjords and glaciers. Indeed, because of its easy accessibility to the sprawling Columbia Glacier—3.7 miles (6 km) wide and 200 feet (61 m) high at the face—it is for many as memorable a sight as Mt. McKinley which is only 31 miles (50 km) from the nearest road.

With so many factors against them, tourism officials braced themselves for a disastrous season and offset it with an aggressive advertising campaign paid for, in part, with $4 million provided by Exxon. The advertisements, which compared the spill to the beauty mark on Marilyn Monroe's face, seemed to pay off: the number of tourists rose by 4.3 percent, with 559,279 people visiting the state in the summer of 1989.

Still, authorities had hoped for a bigger increase and calculated that the clean-up would keep away 10,000 visitors and cost the tourism industry about $15 million. The commercial fishing industry was affected more severely, but most sport fishermen made out well financially by leasing their boats to Exxon to assist in the clean-up. "It was very lucrative to go into the oil clean-up business," said Gary Kranenburg, executive director of the Valdez Convention and Visitors Bureau. Of the 35 fishing boats in Valdez, all but two signed up with Exxon, he said. Ironically, sports fishermen who were scared off by the spill ended up missing the largest salmon catch in the state's history.

"Except for those visitors who attempted to book accommodations in the Valdez area, most probably never were aware of the spill," said Bob Miller. In fact, much of the damage was confined to remote areas and no oil came near the Columbia Glacier. Holland America line-Westours and Princess Tours, the two major cruise lines serving Alaska, didn't have to modify their itineraries when taking passengers north from Seattle, Washington since the oil was not visible along their popular, well-traveled routes.

While the wildlife loss was devastating, estimates said that only about 11.5 percent of the birds that died were killed in Prince William Sound, with the majority perishing in the remote Barren Islands region between the Kenai Peninsula and Kodiak Island.

Tourism officials, ever eager to portray the damage in the most favorable light, now are downplaying the effects of the accident and even point to some encouraging post-spill developments. "Basically, the average tourist isn't going to see any oil," said Kranenburg. Only those making difficult forays into Prince William Sound's remote islands will be able to observe oil-stained beaches and other evidence of the disaster, he said.

In fact, the clean-up efforts were more visible than the oil itself, with fluorescent paint and brightly colored ribbons marking affected areas, and discarded booms and absorbant material littering a number of beaches.

The onslaught of clean-up workers has

have long-term consequences, many scientists warn that the effects will be felt for years and possibly decades, The federal wildlife service predicts that certain devastated sea bird colonies may take up to 70 years to re-establish. In addition, though the oil may not be visible, it is far from gone. Alaskan environmental officials say that Exxon recovered less than 10 percent of the oil, and with less than 40 percent estimated to have evaporated, that leaves more than half of the 10.8 million gallons still soaking beach sand or ocean bottom. It will be extremely difficult, if not impossible, to recover much of this oil. The feared consequences range from warnings that there will be severe losses among

had a delayed beneficial effect for visitors, as there are many more rooms now in Valdez, Kranenburg reported. He said that the number of bed-and-breakfast inns more than doubled to house the workers. Perhaps the best news for those planning to visit the Prince William Sound area in the future is that the number of workers is expected to shrink from 12,000 to a crew of about 1,000.

Lest the idea be given that the spill will not

Above, hot water washing, La touche Island.

marine species to optimistic predictions that Mother Nature will be able to heal herself.

Meanwhile, the disaster has renewed calls for tighter controls over oil shipping, especially the requirement that all tankers be built with double hulls to prevent such catastrophic cargo losses. Oil from the North Slope region, pumped south to Valdez through Alaska's famed pipeline, provides 25 percent of America's energy needs, so no one is seriously considering cutting off the supply because of the spill. At the very least, though, the disaster should stand as a lesson that no place on earth is so remote that the careless hands of humanity can't mar it.

The Musher And The Entrepreneur — An Alaskan Friendship

One dresses for work in a suit, the other in a parka. One meets clients in an office; the other lives a self-sufficient lifestyle in Ruby, a Yukon River village. Both are 13-year Alaska residents and are headed for the top in their respective fields. And they're the best of friends.

Mark Freshwaters is a trapper and dog musher. Long-distance dogsled racing is his passion. He first entered the Iditarod, a 1,049-mile race from Anchorage to Nome, in 1981. In 1984 he placed 14th in the race, well in the money for this "last great race on

ka that first time, but only cost about $30 apiece. They made it to Fairbanks in June 1971, and spent their first summer at the Chena Campground.

John's great adventure that first summer was working as a meat packer on a hunting trip on Black Rapids Glacier. After becoming separated from his companions, he walked 35 miles and spent three days subsisting on two Snickers bars, some uncooked brown rice and a bit of Tang before a helicopter rescued him.

Mark also went hunting that first summer,

earth.

John Reeves is a career consultant, a candidate for a master's degree, and owner of a thriving Fairbanks business, University Resume Service and Alaska Life/Work Planning Center. He works with computers, a video recorder and a camera to prepare clients for job interviews.

Mark and John grew up together in Milwaukie, Wisconsin, becoming friends in their early teens. As a high school junior in 1970, Mark began planning a visit to Alaska after graduation. John agreed to go along. Both were 17 years old and intrigued by the state. Neither planned to settle in Alaska.

It took them 15 days to hitchhike to Alas-

with different results. He hitchhiked to Delta Junction and was picked up a man who took him in for the night. Mark stayed on to help build a cabin, and they trapped together that winter. While in Delta, Mark first saw people using dog teams for trapping. He started gathering dogs and vowed to have a good team someday.

For the next two years, Mark and John rarely met. They travelled a great deal, though not with each other. But they kept in touch. John attended the University of Alaska, Fairbanks, and worked on the trans-Alaska pipeline. Mark worked in Ketchikan as a logger.

In early fall 1974, Mark made plans to

spend the winter in the bush. He renovated a sunken riverboat he'd found, equipping it with two used outboard motors. He loaded it with $3,000 worth of gear, dogs, tools and supplies. By the time he finished loading, little of the boat showed above the water.

Pushing out from shore, Mark started the motor and turned into the current. The current pulled the bow under and Mark's attempts to raise it by adding power just made things worse. Mark ran the boat aground before it sank completely and waded ashore.

"I unloaded it, bailed it out, and was a little bit discouraged, to say the least. I thought about waiting till next summer to resume my journey down the river. But then the next day I got up and it was nice and sunny, and I thought, 'Well, what the heck, I'll give it another try.' I loaded the boat back up and shoved off, and never had any problems after that."

Several hundred miles downstream, Mark met a Native we'll call "Hank" working a fish camp on the river. After stopping to talk, Mark stayed to trap with his new friend that winter on the Nowitna River.

Their trapping camp was a wall tent insulated with spruce boughs — fairly primitive: the kind of place where one survived an entire winter on just a 55-gallon drum filled with food and a saw blade.

John flew out for a visit in February, and stayed for a month, helping Mark with the camp and the trapline. He enjoyed being back in the wilderness.

Becoming Established

By 1975 both had settled into stable lifestyles. Ruby became Mark's base camp. John built a house outside Fairbanks. Mark established a yearly rhythm with the land. John worked another year for the pipeline and then was hired as an adult education teacher.

In 1980, John risked starting his own business. The time felt right. Small, initial success.

Left, John Reeves at his computer. Right, Mark Freshwaters with his sled dog.

cesses lured him toward bigger projects and higher ambitions.

That same year Mark decided to run the Iditarod. He talked to mushers from earlier races and built up a dog team that could handle the rugged trail.

Mark searched for sponsors throughout 1980. (He figures his costs for a year's preparation were about $20,000.) He had little luck finding sponsors, but decided to run anyway.

Although he didn't even place in 1981, Mark learned from his experiences and per-

formed well under adverse circumstances. He applied the knowledge to other, shorter races and began winning. His 1984 bid for the Iditarod was well-thought out, as his high standing demonstrated.

John is gradually gaining recognition as an expert in his field. He has published his first book and finished his master's thesis.

John's worldliness is the flip side of Mark's functionalism, yet their friendship is unshakeable. Occasionally John comes home to find a dog team staked out in his yard. Mark listens with interest as John talks of computer programs and career development theories.

TIRED BUT CONTENT: TWO SISTERS IN THE ALASKAN BUSH

"All right, boys."

The soft command is all I need. As I pull the snow hook — the sled anchor — 12 rangy huskies bound forward in unison, slamming into their harnesses to send the loaded dog-sled and me flying down the steep hill below our isolated cabin.

"Gee, Loki!" At my order the lead dog swings hard right without breaking his stride, leading the loping dogs out the snowy trail going to our trapline and, 18 miles distant, our nearest line cabin.

The heavily loaded sled skids sharply around the corner, requiring all my weight to keep it from flipping as the dogs reach a top speed of 15 miles per hour. Already I've begun to perspire from the heavy work, and by the time the dogs settle into a 10-mile-an-hour trot I've shed my parka despite the 10-below weather.

A Good Beginning

It's been a typical start typical except for the remarkable lack of trouble. The sled did *not* clump a sapling in its careening descent; I did *not* have a dog fight, runaway dogs, a last-minute repair job, or a sloppily-loaded sled threatening to buck burlap sacks of frozen fish from the canvas tarp. The towline did *not* disconnect from the sled, sending the dogs flying in in formation away down that hill without me. I did *not* run into a one-ton bull moose challenging my right to use the trial.

Still, as the dogs glide effortlessly through two inches of fresh snow on the trail, I must remain constantly alert for unseen dangers: thin ice, deadly water hidden under deep snow, irritable moose, open creeks, or a fresh tree blown down across the trail.

These hazards usually crop up suddenly and without warning. Once I walked up to untangle the 60-foot towline and stepped backwards perhaps six inches off the trail only to have the ice collapse under me. A section of the slough caved in and I plunged into waist-deep water along with three of my dogs. Since I never let go of the towline, which had about 800 pounds of dogs attached to it, I had plenty of leverage for climbing out, but at 15 degrees below zero (F) the last 10 miles of that trip wasn't too pleasant.

While watching ahead I also have to con-trol the sled with its load of dog food, my own food, emergency gear, trapping gear, rifle and snowshoes — keeping the graceful wooden sled from skidding off the narrow trail into the deep snow. At the same time I must maintain a steady and constant control over the team of sled dogs, braking the sled as it plunges down banks, and running up hills to lighten the load. The dogs are guided verbally, with commands to tell a leader which trail to take, to order slack dogs to speed up, or to encourage the team as a whole when they begin to tire.

By watching form, ears, eye contacts and attitudes, I can determine whether the dogs scent a moose or an animal in a trap ahead, if they want to fight or balk, if they're happy, discouraged, tired or angry. Sensitive observation and interpretation of this subtle language enables me to keep the dogs at peak performance and alerts me to hazards I may not see myself.

After 10 years of driving dogs under conditions from 50 above to 50 below zero, I now possess a constant alertness for dangers,

Miki and dog team in a snowstorm.

which hit often and unexpectedly in the depths of the Alaskan bush where I live. Last fall we (twin sister Miki and I) returned from meeting the twice-weekly mail plane and found grizzly tracks on the beach in front of our house, tracks which had not been there in the morning. During the pitch black night the giant bear returned, plodding through knee-deep water up the bay past our house.

We were alerted by the 14 chained huskies as they roared with wild excitement. Miki, also my constant companion and trapping partner, challenged me to come with her into the darkness to protect drying fish and hanging moose meat from the great bear.

We crept softly toward the grizzly, listening to it splash by in the water. The bear passed uncomfortably close to us as we stood on the beach, but in the darkness he was just a great black blot against the deep gray water.

Miki fired a shot over the bear's head with our .308 rifle while I held a .264 ready in case he answered our challenge. Rather than speeding his departure, the explosion caused the grizzly to stop in mid-stride and raise his head to stare. A second shot had no effect at all, but at the third warning shot the bear moved off — not quickly, but fast enough.

An encounter like that tends to raise one's level of alertness far above normal. But then, so does stalking a bull moose or encountering a vicious, powerful wolverine caught in a feeble trap meant for a much smaller animal.

A Hard Rewarding Life

Life in the Alaskan bush is exhilarating but it is very hard and often tedious, too. Since very few jobs are available, many people like Miki and myself are self-employed, working as trappers, fishermen or handcrafters. Trapping is one of the hardest, least profitable professions I know, and the rewards are emotional and physical more than monetary. Still, we earn enough to support our dog team, and supplement this with small incomes from selling handcrafts and free-lance writing.

Gliding down the trail, the padding of paws and squeaking of sled runners muted by fresh snow, I feel tired but content. Yesterday I may have mushed the dogs 30 miles, tomorrow I may ski 15, but for now my goal is that tiny trapping cabin 18 (30 km) miles from home where my sister awaits with a warm fire in the wood stove and a hot meal.

If she were not there, if she were at home or farther out the line, I'd be looking forward to arriving long after the early darkness at a cabin as cold inside as the air outside. I'd have to unharness the dogs alone, light a fire, and chop a water hole through two or three feet of river ice, all in the darkness. After lighting a gas lantern I'd pack 40 gallons of water up the steep bank in five-gallon buckets, cook dog food, start my own meal, feed the dogs, and skin any fur I may have caught along the trail that day.

But today Miki will be there waiting for me, and this thought gladdens me, not only for the work she'll be helping me with, but for her companionship, for I have spent many days alone and know the true meaning of loneliness.

The dogs break into a run and I glance ahead to see their ears pricked tautly, every tugline tight as they strain forward. I see nothing here to spur them on but a set lies ahead, a trap laid in a small cubby baited with rotten moose hide.

"Straight on, Loki! Get up, straight on! Amber — Chevy!" My commands bark out in rapid staccato, first ordering the leader to force the excited dogs past whatever animal may be in the trap, and then guiding the whole team past, scolding the young dogs who have not yet learned to leave sets alone.

I find a marten in the trap, the first we have caught in 10 days. Although this rich, valuable fur animal is our prime catch, we trap them in cycles, sometimes doing well, and often doing very poorly.

After stopping at the set my dogs are eager to run and they lope on down the trail despite the fresh snow and heavy load. I have been pedaling with one foot on the runners behind the sled for an hour and won't stop until we reach the cabin. Pedaling is part of the routine, whether I am travelling five miles or 50. The work grows tedious and then tiring but I can't quit. With 50 to 80 miles of trapline to cover each week by dog team the huskies need that extra boost. Although the team is capable of doing 60 miles a day on a good trail, almost every week we have several inches of fresh snow or wind-blown snow covering the trails. Miki and I are constantly on the move trying to keep the lines open. Our pace is much slower, especially since we have to clean and bait traps after every snow.

Although we travel exclusively by dog team, most trappers use snow machines on their traplines, and during the summer we all travel by river boat or three-wheeler. Since few roads exist in the bush, any trip to the city is by airplane. Bush flying is a unique experience, and as a pilot I've had my share of adventures in bush planes.

Mistakes can be deadly when flying the Alaskan bush, for distances are great, villages few and far between, weather unpredictable and landing pots are rare or non-

run daily and the dogs fed with cooked whitefish and rice. Any extra fish are cut and dried for next winter.

In the slow summer months we build dog houses and dogsleds, sew sled bags, dog booties and harnesses. We also tan and sew furs from the winter's catch, making luxurious hats and mitts to sell for spare cash. This small business gives us a much-needed chance to sit quietly sewing for hours at a time — a relaxing break from our over-active lives. And once Miki and I brought a rich red-fox hat into a sporting goods store and traded it for a pair of snowshoes, two sleeping bags, a fish pole, some pots, gloves and several pairs of heavy winter socks.

During the fall we pick 15 or 20 gallons of

existent. I've been fortunate enough to survive the situations I've gotten myself into, although not always without damage. A plane crash some years ago left me with a stiff foot and a couple scars, and just last winter a broken valve in one cylinder crippled the engine of our Super Cub airplane. Although we finished the flight, we were forced to make an 80-mile detour around mountains because the engine couldn't develop enough power to gain altitude.

Our days are always full and productive. During the summer we grow a large garden to produce most of our vegetables for the year and spend long hours picking berries for fresh fruit and jam. The fish nets must be

cranberries. We shoot a moose, pack out the meat and hang it for the winter's food. Potatoes and root vegetables are harvested and stored and later in the fall, during the annual fish run, we net 500 to 1,000 whitefish, freezing them whole on a shelf outside in the brisk fall air for the winter's dog food.

As autumn spirals into winter, with graying skies, black ice snd white snow, a sense of urgency catches us. We *have* to catch a few more fish before the nets freeze in. We *must* finish that dogsled we've been working on. We *have* to repair our winter gear, a job we put off during the summer because the garden needed weeding or a fish net needed hanging.

Then the trapping season begins and we hit the trail with bouncing dogs and happy hearts, for the long, cold, dark season is our favorite. Now our union with our dogs is stronger, more intense, as we spend six to 12 hours nearly every day on the trail with them, scolding or praising them, loving and hating them, guiding, training and *living* dogs.

With winter comes the truly hard work: snowshoeing many miles through deep snow; skiing more miles to set trail; driving dogs 80 to 150 miles each week just to maintain the lines; clearing miles of new trails or brushing out overgrown old trails; and cutting cord after cord of firewood.

By late winter we are tired of the constant

So it goes. The yearly cycle, of putting food up in the summer and fall, of trapping and woodcutting in the winter and spring. The weekly cycle, measured by the mail plane and the trapline rounds, and the daily cycle of mushing dogs and feeding fires.

Home at Last

Now the dogs break into a lope again. We are near the cabin; dusk has fallen and we are tired but eager to be home. I smell the rich wood smoke of Miki's fire, see the cheery lantern light beaming through the window.

The dogs crowd by the door as she comes out and together Miki and I unhook

work in bitter weather. It's time for a vacation, the only vacation of the year. By early March the bitterest cold has drained away and we take our vacation: a cross-country dog team trip, a grueling journey which may take us 600 miles or more. We travel hard but without a care, the two of us alone with our dogs, following trails or breaking our own through the deep, powdery snow, stopping in villages to make friends but always eager to be off again.

Far left, bounty from Julie's summer garden; left, Miki sawing wood. Right, ready to embark on a canoe trip.

each dog and tie them up, unload the sled, and duck inside the warm, tiny cabin. A hot meal follows, of rich chili from ground moose and beans, or tender pot roast with potatoes and garden vegetables, or thick moose steaks with rice and steaming cornbread or raisin bread on the side.

I feed the dogs their meal too, fish and rice with a small piece of liver for each dog, with tallow, dried fish and commercial dog food to fill out their meal. Then, back inside, I pull off by fur mukluks and lie back on the bed, face flushed from the cold wind, muscles a little sore, a bruise on one knee from slamming into the sled when it hit a tree.

But most of all tired − tired but content.

INSIGHT GUIDES
Travel Tips

When it comes to planning an unforgettable vacation,

we wrote the book. *Amtrak's America.* A free, 82-page

IF YOU REALLY WANT TO SEE AMERICA, WE'LL SEND YOU A PERSONAL GUIDE.

travel planner that highlights the excitement of seeing

the country on Amtrak. With complete descriptions of

scenic routes. Our comfortable on-board accommoda-

tions. Even tour packages. And with over 500 destina-

tions, from cover to cover we'll take you coast to coast.

Amtrak's America. It's where great vacations begin.

For more information, or to order *Amtrak's America,*

call your travel agent or Amtrak at 1-800-USA-RAIL.

Please send my free copy of *Amtrak's America:*

Name _____
            Please Print

Address _____

City_____ State_____

Zip_____ Phone ( ) _____

Mail to: AMTRAK, Dept. 6000
P.O. Box 7717, Itasca, IL 60143

AMTRAK
THERE'S SOMETHING ABOUT A TRAIN THAT'S MAGIC.

TRAVEL TIPS

GETTING THERE

BY AIR

Not only is Anchorage the hub of Alaska's air route system, it is also the hub of a world-wide network of overseas airlines offering trans-polar service between continents. It's possible to fly nonstop to Anchorage from several European and Oriental cities as well as from the contiguous 48 states and Honolulu. Alaska is considered by some the air crossroads of the world. Anchorage is as close to Tokyo as it is to Houston in the lower 48 states. Eight U.S. domestic air carriers serve Alaska, mostly via Seattle, and 11 carriers offer international flights from locations as diverse as Brussels and Tokyo.

International air carriers using Anchorage as their international gateway are: Air France, British Airways, China Airlines, KLM Royal Dutch Airlines, Korean Airlines, Lufthansa German Airlines, Japan Airlines, Northwest Orient Airlines (to and from Japan), Sabena-Belgian World Airlines, SAS Scandinavian Airlines and Trans-Provincial Airlines.

U.S. domestic passenger carriers providing service from the lower 48 states are: Alaska Airlines, Delta Airlines, Hawaiian Air, MarkAir, Northwest Orient Airlines, United Airlines, Delta Airlines, and Reeve Aleutian Airways.

Besides Anchorage, connections from Seattle are available for Ketchikan, Sitka, Wrangell, Petersburg, Juneau, Cordova and Fairbanks.

BY SEA

Many visitors arrive in Alaska via a cruise ship. This is a luxurious and exciting way to visit. Cruise ships sail through the spectacular Inside Passage arriving at places like Skagway, Ketchikan, Sitka, Juneau, Misty Fjord, Whittier and infrequently Anchorage. Fifteen cruise lines served Alaska during the summer of 1988. Cruises normally start from Vancouver, B.C. and San Francisco with a few voyages leaving Seattle.

Cruise lines normally operate between May and September. They offer a variety of travel options including round trip or one-way cruises and cruises sold as part of a package tour. Tours may include air, rail and/or motorcoach transportation within Alaska.

For more information about cruise options and reservations, contact a travel agent or write to Alaska Northwest Travel Service, Inc., 130 2nd Ave. S., Edmonds, WA 98020, telephone (206) 775-4504.

Some popular lines which serve Alaska include: Admiral Cruises, Cunard/NAC Lines, Exploration Holidays & Cruises, Princess Cruises, Royal Viking Line, Sitmar Cruises, Travalaska, and Westours/ Holland American Line.

Another popular option for cruising the Inside Passage is to go via the **Alaska Marine Highway** system. This state ferry system carries vehicles in addition to passengers. It is in operation year round, however service in the summer is more frequent for the high tourist demand. Passengers and vehicles board in Bellingham, Washington. Southeastern ports of call include: Ketchikan, Wrangell, Petersburg, Sitka, Juneau, Haines and Skagway. The system also serves southcentral Alaska where ferries port in Kodiak, Homer, Seldovia, Seward, Valdez, Cordova and Whittier.

Vessels feature food service, a sightseeing solarium and staterooms. Passengers can also sleep in the public lounge or deck. During the summer months Forest Service naturalists offer interpretive programs on the larger ferries. Reservations should be made well in advance, at least six months. Bookings are accepted starting in January.

For current information and reservations contact: Alaska Marine Highway, P.O. Box R, Juneau, AK 99811, telephone (907) 465-3941 or toll free 800-642-0066.

BY RAIL

There is no rail service directly to Alaska, however the Alaska Railroad provides passenger service within the state. It connects Anchorage with Fairbanks to the north and with Whittier and Seward to the south.

For more information contact: Alaska Railroad, P.O. Box 1-07500, Anchorage, 99510-7500. By telephone: (907) 265-2623 or toll free 800-544-0552. Railroads offer a variety of packages to destinations like Denali National Park, Fairbanks and Seward with cruises on Prince William Sound. One day trips are also available to Talkeetna.

BY ROAD

Travelling the Alaska Highway is a great adventure and very safe. However because of the great distance, it can only be considered by visitors with an abundance of time.

BY BUS

Bus service and motorcoach tours are available to Alaska by way of the Alaska Highway. From Seattle, Greyhound connects with Canadian Greyhound Coachways, offering service to Whitehorse in the Yukon Territory, Canada. In Whitehorse, tours can

THE NOBLE TIME

JUVENIA

— 1860 —

Golden Age ®
COLLECTION

STEEL - STEEL/GOLD - 18KT GOLD AND WITH PRECIOUS STONES

Worldwide list of JUVENIA Agents available on request

JUVENIA MONTRES SA - 2304 LA CHAUX-DE-FONDS - SWITZERLAND
Tel. 41/39 26 04 65 Fax 41/39 26 68 00

For the fastest weekend refunds anywhere in the world.

Ensure your holiday is worry free even if
your travellers cheques are lost or stolen by buying
American Express Travellers Cheques from;

Lloyds Bank	Leeds Permanent Building Society*
Royal Bank of Scotland	Woolwich Building Society*
Abbey National*	National & Provincial Building Society
Bank of Ireland	Britannia Building Society*
Halifax Building Society*	American Express Travel Offices.

As well as many regional building societies and travel agents.

*Investors only.

Not all travellers cheques are the same.

AMERICAN EXPRESS **Travellers Cheques** ®

be arranged to Alaska and other Yukon destinations. Several companies offer motorcoach tours between the continental United States and Alaska. For more information contact a travel agent.

BY CAR

The newly improved Alaska Highway has made driving enjoyable and safe. However, distance may be the drawback, a non-leisurely drive (averaging eight hours a day) from the lower 48 to Anchorage would take two weeks one-way.

For more information about driving the Alaska highways refer to *The Milepost*, *(All-the-North Guide)*, published by Alaska Northwest Publishing Company, and *Alaska Yukon & British Columbia Travel Guide*, published by Alaska Travel Guide. Each gives a detailed description of the highway system and is updated annually. A free state-published brochure on the Alaska highways can be obtained through the Alaska Division of Tourism, P.O. Box E-301, Juneau, AK 99811.

TRAVEL ESSENTIALS

VISAS & PASSPORTS

Visitors entering Alaska from other than a U.S. port of embarkation will proceed through U.S. customs upon reaching the state. Canadian citizens entering from the Western Hemisphere do not need a visa or a passport. All other foreign visitors must be properly equipped with passports and the necessary documents.

MONEY MATTERS

American-dollar traveller's checks are advised to ease problems in dealing with the currency. National banks in Alaska's major cities–Anchorage, Fairbanks and Juneau – can convert foreign currency at the prevailing exchange rate. Outside of these metropolitan areas the opportunities to convert foreign money for use in Alaska are dramatically reduced.

There is no state sales tax in Alaska. However, different boroughs and municipalities in various parts of the state may impose a sales tax on all or some goods and services. If uncertain as to whether or not there is a local sales tax, ask any cashier or sales clerk.

WHAT TO WEAR

When packing your bags for Alaska, remember you are travelling north. While people who live in Alaska year-round may describe the climate as warm in the summer, those who visit from warmer climates find even the summer chilly. No matter what part of the state you are visiting, bring along a warm coat or jacket. A wool sweater, hat and mittens are also necessities.

Layering clothing is the best way to stay warm. While you may be able to run around in shirt sleeves for a few hours mid-day in the summer, the evenings always require a jacket or coat. Tour companies usually furnish speciality items such as parkas for overnight trips to Barrow, Kotzebue, Prudhoe Bay and other colder areas of the state.

The key for fashion in Alaska is casual and practical. Suits and evening dresses are rarely worn in the state unless for special occasions. Jeans, flannel shirts and tennis shoes are much more common. Pants are perfectly acceptable for women year-round and in any social situation. Dress for comfort. Alaska is not a place where you find residents wearing the latest *haute couture*. Since you will probably do a lot of walking, be sure to wear good walking shoes. And don't buy them right before your trip. Make sure they are broken in before you leave.

No matter where you visit in Alaska, you are likely to run into periods of rain. So suitable rain wear is recommended.

If your travel plans include flying to a remote area in a small plane, take and wear durable warm clothing; survival gear is required for cross-country flights in small planes. High-heeled shoes or neckties have little value if your pilot is forced to land on a riverbank to wait out the weather. Air services and charter flight operators normally carry sufficient survival gear as required by law; it's up to passengers to dress appropriately.

Getting Acquainted

State Song: Alaska's Flag
Nickname: The Last Frontier
State Flower: Forget-me-not
State Fish: King (chinook) salmon
State Bird: Willow Ptarmigan (pronounced tar-mi-gun)
State Tree: Sitka Spruce
State Sport: Dog mushing

POPULATION

Alaska is a sparsely populated state. The entire population is around 500,000 with half of the residents living in Anchorage. Alaska's population follows a boom or bust cycle, like its economy. Until the late 1980s the population was growing at an annual rate of 4 percent. In 1983 it peaked at an unprecedented rate of 10.8 percent. Today, the tide has changed and more people are leaving the state than moving in.

The general population of the state is young with the median age of 27½. Alaska has a higher percentage of males than any other state–53percent. This has resulted (among other things) in a new magazine called *Alaska Men*, which catalogs eligible males for female selection.

TIME ZONES

In 1983 the time zones in Alaska were reduced from four to two. Now 90 percent of Alaska residents live in the same time zone – Alaska Standard Time. The other zone is the Hawaii-Aleutian Standard Time zone which is in effect on the outlying islands of the Aleutian Chain and Saint Lawrence Island. Alaska Standard Time is one hour earlier than Pacific Standard Time, which affects the western portion of the contiguous United States.

CLIMATE

Alaska's vastness defies attempts to categorize its climate. For convenience, the state is divided into five regions about which some climatic generalizations can be made.

SOUTHEASTERN

This is Alaska's panhandle, a narrow ribbon of mountains and islands extending along the western edge of British Columbia. Wet and mild are the two best terms for describing its climate. Certain communities in the region receive more than 200 inches (5 meters) of rain annually. On rare, sunny days in summer, high temperatures might reach the mid-70°F (21°C) range. High 40s (4°C) to mid 60s (15°C) are the summer norms, under cloudy skies. Winter temperatures rarely fall much below freezing. Northernmost southeastern cities–Skagway and Haines – are usually drier and cooler in winter.

SOUTHCENTRAL

Anchorage and most of the gulf coast comprise this part of Alaska. Coastal communities are frequently as wet as southeastern cities, but the amount of rainfall lessens considerably just a short distance inland. Anchorage occasionally has summer highs in the 80s (26°C); 60s (15°C) and 70s (21°C) are normal.

INTERIOR

The broad expanse of inland Alaska, loosely centered on Fairbanks, gets perhaps 20 inches (50 cm) of moisture annually. Summer temperatures have reached 100°F (37°C) on occasions; 80°F (26°C) temperatures are the extreme opposite, occasionally falling as low as -75°F (-59°C) near Prospect.

ARCTIC COAST

This is a loosely described region encompassing most of Alaska's northern fringe and the west coast as far south as the Yukon River Delta. High winds are common, and average temperatures are too cool to permit trees to grow. Near Nome, summer temperatures can climb into the 60s (15°C) and sometimes the low 70s (21°C), but that's about as warm as it ever gets. Winter temperatures, though extreme, have never been recorded as low as some interior temperatures. This is also an extremely dry area receiving only minimal amounts of moisture every year.

SOUTHWESTERN & THE ALEUTIANS

The Aleutian Islands are justly famed for the most miserable weather on earth. High winds (williwaws) can rise without warning and smash through the islands at speeds of 100 mph (165 kph). Heavy fog is common, as are rain and cool temperatures. The southwestern mainland is the meeting point for Aleutian weather and interior weather, and often experiences unsettled conditions, frequently accompanied by high winds.

1993
spring-summer
COLLECTION

PART OF THE ART

swatch⊞
automatic

swatch⊞
SCUBA 200

POP
swatch

swatch⊞
C-H-R-O-N-O

swatch⊞

SWISS
made

THE WORLD IS FLAT

A.R. SMITH

Its configuration may not be to Columbus' liking but to every other traveller the MCI Card is an easier, more convenient, more cost-efficient route to circle the globe.

The MCI Card offers two international services—MCI World Reach and MCI CALL USA—which let you call from country-to-country as well as back to the States, all via an English-speaking operator.

There are no delays. No hassles with foreign languages and foreign currencies. No foreign exchange rates to figure out. And no outrageous hotel surcharges.

If you don't possess the MCI Card, please call **1-800-842-9144.**

The MCI Card. It makes a world of difference.

MCI

To reach around the world, use your MCI Card or call collect.° Just select the number next to the country you're calling from. An English-speaking operator will put your call through to anywhere in the 50 States as well as a growing list of participating World Reach countries.#

Australia	0014-881-100	Germany††	0130-0012	Mexico%	95-800-674-7000
Austria	022-903-012	Greece	00-800-1211	Netherlands	06*-022-91-22
Belgium	078-11-00-12	Hong Kong	800-1121	Norway	050-12912
Brazil	000-8012	Hungary	00*-800-01411	Portugal	05-017-1234
China**	108-12	Indonesia	00-801-11	Saudi Arabia	1-800-11
Colombia	980-16-0001	Ireland	1-800-551-001	Singapore	800-0012
Costa Rica	162	Israel	177-150-2727	Spain#	900-99-0014
Denmark	8001-0022	Italy	172-1022	Sweden	020-795-922
Egypt†	355-5770	Japan##	0039-121-(KDD)	Switzerland	155-0222
France	19*-00-19		0066-55-121 (IDC)	Turkey	99-8001-1177
				United Kingdom	0800-89-0222

#Country-to-country calling may not be available to & from all MCI CALL USA locations. Certain restrictions apply. *Wait for second dial tone. **Available from most major cities. †When dialing outside of Cairo, dial 02 first. +Limited availability. °Collect calls to U.S. only. In some countries, public phones may require deposit of coin or phone card for dial tone. %Service from public telephones may be limited. Rate depends on call origin in Mexico. ††Service available on a limited basis in eastern Germany © MCI International, Inc., 1993. MCI, its logo, and all other MCI products and services mentioned herein, are proprietary marks of MCI Communications Corporation. ##KDD & IDC are international telecommunications carriers in Japan.

Figures are Fahrenheit with Centigrade equivalent in parentheses.

City	January	July
Anchorage	13° (-10.5°)	58.1° (14.5°)
Barrow	-14.4° (-25.8°)	38.9° (3.8°)
Cold Bay	28.3° (-2.1°)	50.3° (10.1°)
Fairbanks	-12.8° (-24.8°)	61.5° (16.4°)
Juneau	21.8° (-5.6°)	55.7° (13.2°)
Kodiak	31.9° (0°)	53.7° (12.1°)
Nome	5.8° (-14.5°)	50.5° (10.2°)

ETIQUETTE

Tipping for services received is practical in Alaska just as it is in much of the world. Airport skycaps usually receive $1 for the first bag and 50 cents for each additional bag. (Don't expect skycap service outside of Anchorage.) Similar tips are appropriate for bellhops in the larger hotels.

Waiters and waitresses normally receive about 15 percent. Tipping as high as 20 percent for restaurants service shows you thought the attention excellent in all respects. Tips are inappropriate in most fast-food restaurants and cafeterias. Bartenders should get 10 to 15 percent depending on the quality of service.

If service is shoddy or the person performing the service is ill-mannered, no tip at all is appropriate.

BUSINESS HOURS

Government offices are normally open from 8 a.m. to 4.30 p.m. and frequently remain open until late at night; many are also open on Sunday, though hours may be limited. Banks are usually open between 10 a.m. and 3 p.m., Monday through Friday; some offer at least limited services until early evening.

Except for necessary public services (police and fire protection, for example), most government offices are closed on the following holidays. Banks and some retailers may also be closed on these dates.

HOLIDAYS & FESTIVALS

Alaska celebrates all traditional and official U.S. holidays. In addition there are many unique festivals occurring year round within the state. Some are created just for the amusement and pastime of local residents and others are part of the cultural heritage.

Dog mushing is state sport and sled dog races are held throughout the state in the winter. The most well known race which is becoming internationally acclaimed is the **Iditarod Trail Sled Dog Race**. It starts on the first Saturday in March from Anchorage. The trail covers 1,049 miles (1,752 km) to Nome, crossing vast tracts of wilderness and some of the most rugged country on the continent. Generally mushers arrive in Nome within two weeks, however the current champion Susan Butcher has set the record of 11 days. Other sled dog races are held in Fairbanks, Tok, Delta Junction and Nome.

Winter festivals are also popular in Alaska. The largest is **Fur Rendezvous**, held in Anchorage. It starts on the second Friday in February and lasts for 10 days with over 150 events occurring. A highlight of the event is the **World Championship Sprint Sled Dog Race**. Homer also celebrates a winter carnival in February and the North Pole Winter Carnival is held in March along with Valdez's.

For a rare opportunity to observe the rich Native culture, visitors can attend the **Savoonga Walrus Festival** held on St. Lawrence Island in May. This is not a tourist event, it is traditionally Eskimo. In June *Nalukataq* (**Whaling Feast**) is celebrated in Barrow by the Eskimo community.

In July the **World Eskimo-Indian Olympics** are held in Fairbanks. Here you can watch Eskimos compete in 25 different events which have been practised by the Natives for generations. They are games of strength, speed and endurance and serve to keep the Natives physically and mentally fit. Games include the one-foot high kick where the contestants hop in the air, kick a target and land again on the same foot. The event evolved from the ancient practice of signalling a whale kill to villagers in this manner. The Arm Pull is a display of strength using the same muscles that are needed to haul in seals or beaching whales. Contestants lock arms facing each other, then one tries to make the other straighten his arm.

Other festivals are held with tongue-in-cheek and for pure fun. Swimmers take to the icy waters of the Bering Sea in Nome for the annual **Polar Bear Swim** in May and locals join in the **Moose Dropping Festival** held in Talkeetna in July.

Festivals and holidays give visitors a chance to experience the local culture and join in the fun. Visitors are always welcome and should try to schedule at least one event into their trip.

Dates change annually and current schedules can be obtained from the Alaska Division of Tourism, P.O. Box E-301, Juneau, AK 99811, USA. (907-465-2010).

JANUARY

New Year's Day (1st)
Martin Luther King's Birthday (15th)
Russian New Year and Masquerade Ball,
  Kodiak
Alcan 200 Snowmachine Rally, Haines
Delta 8-Dog Classic Sled Dog Race, Delta
  Junction
Sled Dog Races, Tok

FEBRUARY

Abraham Lincoln's Birthday (12th)
George Washington's Birthday
(third Monday)
Cordova Iceworm Festival
Fur Rendezvous, Anchorage
Valdez Ice Climbing Festival
Nenana Tripod Raising Festival
Festival of Native Arts, Fairbanks
Gold Rush Classic Snowmachine Race,
Anchorage to Nome
Winter Carnival, Homer
Women's Champion Sled Dog Race, Tok

MARCH

Seward's Day (last Monday)
Spring Arts Festival, Homer
Beaver Roundup, Dillingham
Iditarod Trail Sled Dog Race, Anchorage to
Nome
North Pole Winter Carnival, North Pole
Fairbanks Ice Festival
Limited Class North American Sled Dog
Race, Fairbanks
Open North American Championship Sled
Dog Race, Fairbanks
Valdez Winter Carnival
Bering Sea Ice Classic Gold Tournament,
Nome
Nome Kennel Club's Dog Weight Pull
Skagway Windfest
Iditabike, Knik

APRIL

Spring Arts Festival, Homer
Alyeska Spring Carnival, Girdwood
Ski to Sea Race, Juneau
Copper Day Celebrations, Cordova
Alaska Folk Festival, Juneau
Biennial State Drama Festival, Haines
Nome-Kotzebue Sled Dog Race

MAY

Memorial Day (last Monday)
Jackport Halibut Derby, Homer
Savoonga Walrus Festival, St. Lawrence
Island
Wrangell Salmon Derby
Little Norway Festival, Petersburg
Ninth Annual Miner's Day Festival,
Talkeetna
Kodiak Crab Festival
Salt Water Fishing Derby, Kodiak
Haines King Salmon Derby
Petersburg Salmon Derby
Ketchikan King Salmon Derby
Sitka Salmon Derby

Valdez Halibut Derby
Tanana 100 Boat Race, Tok (Memorial Day
weekend)
Polar Bear Swim, Nome (ice permitting)

JUNE

Sitka Summer Music Festival
Nenana River Daze, Nenana
Alaska Renaissance Festival, Anchorage
Midnight Sun Festival, Nome
Mayor's Midnight Sun Marathon,
Anchorage
Nome River Raft Race
Colony Days Summerfest, Palmer
Great Tanana Raft Classic, Fairbanks
Nalukataq (Whaling Feast), Barrow
Yukon 800 Boat Race, Fairbanks

JULY

Independence Day (4th)
Rescue 21 Homer Halibut Tournament
Seward Jackport Halibut Tournament
Valdez Pink Salmon Derby
Valdez Gold Rush Days
Moose Dropping Festival, Talkeetna
$50,000 Big Lake Fishing Derby
Silver Salmon Derby, Ketchikan
World Eskimo-Indian Olympics, Fairbanks
Fairbanks Summer Arts Festival

AUGUST

Deltana Fair, Delta Junction
Cry of the Wild Ram, Kodiak
Valdez Silver Salmon Derby
Calico Salmon Derby, Talkeetna
Tanana Valley Fair, Fairbanks
Seward Silver Salmon Derby
Southeast Alaska State Fair, Haines
Alaska State Fair, Palmer
Alaska State Fair and Rodeo, Kodiak
Cordova Silver Salmon Derby
Wrangell Little League Halibut Derby

SEPTEMBER

Labor Day (first Monday)
Fall Fair, Dillingham
Tanana 500 Boat Races, Tok
Great Bathtub Race, Nome
Klondike Trail of '98 Road Road Relay,
Skagway to Whitehorse
Equinox Marathon, Fairbanks
Wrangell Silver Salmon Derby

OCTOBER

Alaska Day (18th)
October Arts Festival, Petersburg
Wrangell Winter Fishing Derby

NOVEMBER

Veterans' Day (11th)
Thanksgiving (fourth Thursday)
Great Alaska Shootout, Anchorage
Athabascan Old-Time Fiddling Festival,
    Fairbanks
Northern Invitational Curling Spiel,
    Fairbanks

DECEMBER

Christmas (25th)
Christmas Festival of Lights, Ketchikan
Midnight Madness and Christmas Tree Lighting,
Wrangell
Delta Winter Carnival, Delta Junction
North Country Faire, Cordova
Christmas Boat Parade, Sitka
Christmas Qitiks (Games), Barrow

COMMUNICATIONS

POSTAL SERVICES

Every community in Alaska, no matter how remote, has some sort of mail service. Cities and towns of sufficient size have one or more facilities with regular hours, usually Monday through Friday from 8:30 a.m. to 4:30 p.m. In large cities the main branch may have special sections open till midnight for such things as Express Mail service.

Small, remote communities probably open the post office window when the mail plane arrives. Meeting the mail plane is often a social occasion in these communities. Mail plane service can be daily, or it can be much more infrequent. Flights may also be subject to the whims of the weather.

First-class postage for letters mailed within the United States to other U.S. destinations, Canada and Mexico are 22 cents for the first ounce and 17 cents for each additional ounce. Rates are approximately double that for each half-ounce of airmail to other foreign countries.

Stamps can be purchased at all postal facilities,

from mail carriers and from vending machines, the latter mostly found in larger cities.

The Postal Service normally provides reasonably efficient service throughout the state. If travel plans include a stay in any particular community, mail can be addressed to you, care of general delivery, to that post office. You will have to call in person to collect your mail.

TELEGRAMS & TELEX

Western Union and International Telephone and Telegraph (ITT) will take telegram and telex messages by phone. Call 860-478-9500.

TELEPHONES

Public telephones can be found almost everywhere– hotel lobbies, stores, restaurants, bars, etc. Local calls cost from 15 to 25 cents.

Check the directory for local numbers or dial 411 for information. Information on telephone listings anywhere in the state can be obtained by dialing 555-1212. Information for other states and Canada can be obtained by dialing the appropriate three-digit area code and then 555-1212. The three-digit area code for all telephone exchanges within Alaska is "907," except for Hyder which uses "604".

MEDIA

Alaskans are kept informed by the good mix of local newspapers, ranging from the serious reporting to local gossip, television networks and radio stations.

NEWSPAPERS

The four major daily newspapers in Alaska are *The Juneau Empire*, *The Anchorage Times*, *The Anchorage Daily News* and the *Fairbanks Daily News-Miner*. *The Empire* deals with state political news.

Smaller communities put out newspapers which are a little more than local gossip to a few feisty ones more than willing to tackle local issues. For native issues, the *Tundra Times* and the *Tundra Drums* (*Bethel*) are good sources of information and editorials.

Bookstores and variety stores normally have one or more of the major dailies available for sale. In large cities, Seattle papers, *The New York Times* and *The Wall Street Journal* are normally available in bookstores. The New York papers are usually several days old. Foreign papers are rarely available in Alaska.

TELEVISION

Only Anchorage boasts enough stations to actively affiliate with the four major networks–CBS, Channel 11; ABC, Channel 13; NBC, Channel 2; and Fox Network, Channel 4. Other major cities will have one or more stations, loosely affiliated with one of the networks, but usually offering a spread of programs from all three of the major networks along with locally produced shows as well. Educational TV, public television, is thriving in most of the state.

Most of the programs are in English, although there may be some shows in southwestern Alaska which are broadcast in the Yup'ik Eskimo tongue. Most of these are on public television.

In the last few years, with the growing use of satellite communications equipment, even the most rural areas have gained access to television.

RADIO

Commercial radio stations in Alaska are still used daily to pass messages to remote-area residents living "in the Bush." Regularly scheduled times are set aside for transmitting anything from messages of endearment to appointments at a doctor's office.

The major radio networks have affiliates in major cities, and almost any town or village of any consequence has some sort of locally owned radio station. Quality varies from excellent to horrible on these local stations.

As with television, most programs are broadcast in English. There is some Yup'ik material broadcast in southwestern Alaska.

EMERGENCIES

SECURITY & CRIME

As in visiting any other place in the world, it is better to be safe than sorry. Alaska is not a crime-ridden state, but something about the "last frontier" image engenders a occasional outbursts of violence. Basic common sense precautions should be followed by all visitors.

Leave large amounts of money, traveller's checks, jewelry and other valuables in the hotel safe. Don't flaunt your money in public or display other valuables which could encourage a thief. Be careful where you leave packages, handbags and your luggage. Don't be paranoid.

Crimes rates for rape and murder are fairly high and burglaries are common. However, there are less muggings than in other parts of the United States. Stay away from areas of town that are known to be dangerous.

Two areas to avoid walking alone at night,

particularly if you are a woman, are Fourth Avenue in Anchorage and Second Avenue in Fairbanks. Problems in the latter have eased somewhat in recent years as Fairbanks has made a concerted effort of ridding Second Avenue of many of its problem bars, but things are still far from perfect.

The Alaska State Troopers have long been recognized as a thoroughly professional police force and in recent years they have been facing tough morale problems due in part to declining budgets, a huge influx of new residents and rising crime rates.

Dialing 911 on the phone will put you in touch with a dispatcher capable of providing almost any required emergency service. Be specific as to the nature of the problem and your location where you call.

MEDICAL SERVICES

Two major hospitals serve the general public in Anchorage, one in Fairbanks and another in Juneau. Additionally, there is a *Native* hospital in Anchorage run by the federal government. Treatment there is free for anyone who is one-quarter or more American Indian, Eskimo or Aleut.

Like hospital costs all over the United States, fees in the public hospitals are terribly high. Figure $300 a day for hospitalization, plus additional charges for almost every service provided. However, provisions can be made for indigent patients.

The major hospitals provide 24-hour emergency room service. Treatment is thorough and professional. Non-emergency medical care can be held in a doctor's office or in one of several medical clinics throughout Alaska.

Clinics are staffed by physicians, and occasionally dentists, who are ably assisted by nurses and a support staff. Most routine problems can be handled at a clinic. Appointments, scheduled in advance, are preferred, but walk-in patients can usually be accommodated if they are willing to wait.

Humana Hospital-Alaska, 2801 DeBarr Road, Anchorage, 276-1131.

Providence Hospital, 3200 Providence Drive, Anchorage, 562-2211.

Alaska Native Medical Center, 3rd and Gambell, Anchorage, 279-6661.

Fairbanks Memorial Hospital, 1650 Cowles, 452-8181.

Bartlett Memorial Hospital, 31/2 Mile Glacier Highway, Juneau, 586-2611.

PHARMACIES

Prescription drugs can normally be purchased at hospitals and medical clinics throughout Alaska, as well as in drugstores. If you require prescription medication after hours, most emergency rooms in hospitals and clinics can supply enough to meet requirements until the next business day.

GETTING AROUND

ORIENTATION

One of Alaska's major industries is tourism, so the visitor will find information easily accessible. To help in trip preparation, The Alaska State Division of Tourism annually publishes the *Alaska Vacation Planner*. It is a booklet crammed with fact about Alaska and a directory of where to stay, eat and tour. To obtain a free copy write to the Alaska State Division of Tourism, P.O. Box E-600, Juneau, Alaska 99811, U.S.A. Or call (907) 465-2010. By fax, (907) 586-8399 and telex 45331.

Most communities also have Visitor Information Centers and local Chambers of Commerce which provide specific details on their areas of location. Information can be received in advance by writing or in person when visiting the area.

CONVENTION & VISITORS BUREAUS

Anchorage Convention and Visitors Bureau, 201 East Third Ave., Anchorage, Alaska 99501, (907) 276-4118.

Centennial Hall Convention Center, 101 Egan Dr., Juneau, Alaska 99801, (907) 586-9442.

Fairbanks Convention and Visitors Bureau, 550 First Ave., Fairbanks, Alaska 99701, (907) 456-INFO or (907) 456-5774.

Juneau Convention and Visitors Bureau, 101 Egan Dr., Juneau, Alaska 99801, (907) 586-1737.

Kachemak Bay Visitors and Convention Association, Box 1001, Homer, Alaska 99603, (907) 235-6030.

Ketchikan Visitors Bureau, Box 7055, Ketchikan, Alaska 99901, (907) 225-6166.

Nome Convention and Visitors Bureau, Box 251, Nome, Alaska 99762, (907) 443-5349.

Sitka Convention and Visitors Bureau, Box 1226, Sitka, Alaska 99835, (90&0 747-5940.

Skagway Convention and Visitors Bureau, P.O. Box 415, Skagway, Alaska 99840, (907) 983-2854.

Southeast Alaska Tourism Council, Box 275, Juneau, Alaska 99802, (907) 586-8000.

Valdez Convention and Visitors Bureau, Box 1603, Valdez, Alaska 99686, (907) 835-2984.

Wrangell Visitors Bureau, Box 1078, Wrangell, Alaska 99929, (907) 874-3800.

CHAMBERS OF COMMERCE

Arctic Circle Chamber of Commerce, Box 284, Kotzebue, Alaska 99752, (907) 442-3401.

Cordova Chamber of Commerce, Box 99, Cordova, Alaska 99574, (907) 424-7260.

Delta Chamber of Commerce, Box 987, Delta Junction, Alaska 99737, (907) 895-5068.

Haines Chamber of Commerce, Box 518, Haines, Alaska 99827, (907) 766-2202.

Homer Chamber of Commerce, Box 541, Homer, Alaska 99603, (907) 235-7740.

Greater Juneau Chamber of Commerce, 311 Seward Street, Juneau, Alaska 99801, (907) 586-6420.

Greater Kenai Chamber of Commerce, Box 497, Kenai, Alaska 99611, (907) 283-7989.

Greater Ketchikan Chamber of Commerce, Box 5957, Ketchikan, Alaska 99901,(907) 225-3184.

Kodiak Area Chamber of Commerce, Box 1485, Kodiak, Alaska 99615, (907) 486-5557.

Nome Chamber of Commerce, Box 251, Nome, Alaska 99762, (907) 443-5535.

Greater Palmer Chamber of Commerce, Box 45, Palmer, Alaska 99645, (907) 745-2880.

Petersburg Chamber of Commerce, Box 649, Petersburg, Alaska 99833, (907) 772-3646.

Seldovia Chamber of Commerce, Drawer F, Seldovia, Alaska 99633, (907) 234-7816.

Seward Chamber of Commerce, Box 756, Seward, Alaska 99664, (907) 224-3094 (summer), (907) 224-3046 (winter).

Greater Sitka Chamber of Commerce, Box 638, Sitka, Alaska 99835, (907) 747-8604.

Skagway Chamber of Commerce, Box 194, Skagway, Alaska 99840, (907) 983-2297.

Greater Soldotna Chamber of Commerce, Box 236, Soldotna, Alaska 99669, (907) 262-9814 or 262-1337.

Tok Chamber of Commerce, Box 389, Tok, Alaska 99780, (907) 883-2381 or 883-5887.

Valdez Chamber of Commerce, Box 512, Valdez, Alaska 99686, (907) 835-2330.

Whittier Chamber of Commerce, Box 608, Whittier, Alaska 99693, (907) 472-2337.

Wrangell Chamber of Commerce, Inc., Box 49, Wrangell, Alaska 99929, (907) 874-3901.

DOMESTIC TRAVEL

The secret to conquering Alaska's vastness is air travel. Commuter airlines and charter aircraft services are everywhere. More often than not, even the most remote cabins in the wilderness have some sort of airstrip nearby, or a stretch of hard-packed sand on a river bar to serve as a landing strip.

Alaskans are rated the highest in having the capacity to fly an aircraft in the United States. On a per capita basis, six times as many Alaskans have a pilot's license as do residents of the rest of the country.

Virtually every community that merits mention on the map is served by a regularly scheduled air carrier. Most cities with a population that exceeds 1,000 people, serve as a base for one or more commuter airlines. If you know where you want to go, there's a pilot somewhere in Alaska who is prepared to take you there.

Charter aircrafts are available for those who don't wish to wait for regularly scheduled flights to remote destinations, or for those who wish to go into the middle of the wilderness.

Costs typically start at about $100 an hour (flight time) to charter a pilot and a plane capable of carrying one passenger and a small amount of baggage. Larger planes capable of carrying three or more people and considerable gear start at about $225 an hour and go up from there. If you're travelling with a large group, it's even possible to charter a vintage DC-3, a twin-engine plane capable of hauling large loads for long distances. Following are listed many of the carriers offering interstate scheduled air service. Interline service available to most rural Alaska points: check with carriers. Also check local air taxi operators for charter and commuter service to Alaskan communities.

FROM ANCHORAGE

Alaska Aeronautical Industries, Box 6067, Anchorage 99502 – To Homer, Kenai, Kodiak and Denali National Park (seasonal).

Alaska Airlines, 4750 International Airport Rd., Anchorage 990502 – To Fairbanks, Prudhoe Bay, Cordova, Yakutat, Juneau, Sitka, Wrangell, Petersburg, Ketchikan, Nome, Koetzebue and Gustavus/Glacier Bay (summer only).

MarkAir, 6441 S. Sir Park Pl., Box 6769. Anchorage 99502 – To Barrow, Bethel, Fairbanks, Dillingham, King Salmon, Nome, Koetzebue, Prudhoe Bay, Kenai and Kodiak.

Steve Aleutian Airways, 4700 W. International Airport Rd., Anchorage 99502 – To points on the Alaska Peninsula, on the Aleutian Islands and on the Pribilof Islands.

SEAIR, Box 6003, Anchorage 99502 – To Bethel, Dillingham, Aniak, Cordova, St. Marys, Galena, Unalakleet and King Salmon, with scheduled connections to over 60 bush communities from Akiachak to Ugashik.

Southcentral Air, 125 N. Willow St., Kenai 99611 – To Kenai, Homer, Seward and Soldotna.

Valdez Airlines, Box 6714, Anchorage 99502 – To Cordova, Homer, Iliamna, Kenai, Kodiak and Valdez.

FROM FAIRBANKS

Arctic Circle Air, P.O. Box 60049, Fairbanks 99706 – To Anaktuvuk Pass, Eagle, Fort Yukon, Bettles, Kaltag and other Interior Points.

Larry's Flying Service, Box 2348, Fairbanks 99707 – To Denali National Park.

FROM GUSTAVUS (GLACIER BAY)

Glacier Bay Airways, P.O. Box 1, Gustavus 99826 – To Juneau, Hoonah and Excursion Inlet.

FROM HAINES

LAB Flying Service, Box 272, Haines 99827 – To Juneau, Hoonah and Skagway.

FROM JUNEAU

Wings of Alaska, 1873 Shell Simmons Dr., Suite 119, Juneau 99801 – To Haines, Hoonah, Skagway and Gustavus/Glacier Bay.

FROM KETCHIKAN

Gateway Aviation, Inc., Box 8331, Ketchikan 99901 – To Craig, Hydaburg, Klawock, Metlakatla and other Southeast points.

Ketchikan Air Service, Box 6900, Ketchikan 99901 – To Hyder.

FROM KODIAK

Kodiak Western Airlines, Box 2457, Kodiak 99615 – To points on Kodiak and Afognak islands and to points in the Bristol Bay area.

FROM KOTZEBUE

MarkAir, Box 6769, Anchorage 99502 – To Nome. (See also From Anchorage.)

Ryan Air Service, P.O. Box 127, Unalakleet 99684 – To 11 villages.

FROM MCGRATH

Hub Air Service, Box 2, McGrath 99627 – To Nikolai, Telida, Lime Village, Takotna, Tatalina, Farewell and Flat.

FROM NOME

Bering Air, Box 1650, Nome 99762 – To Kotzebue and western Alaska points.

Ryan Air Service, Box 790, Nome 99762 – To 14 villages.

FROM PETERSBURG

Alaska Island Air, Box 508, Petersburg 99833 – To Kake.

FROM TANANA

Tanana Air Service, P.O. Box 36, Tanana 99777 – To Fairbanks, New Minto, Nenana, Rampart, Manley Hot Springs, Huslia, Hughes and Allakaket.

FROM TOK

40-Mile Air Ltd, Box 539, Tok 99780 – To Boundary, Chicken, Delta Junction, Eagle, Fairbanks and Tetlin.

FROM UNALAKLEET

Ryan Air Service, P.O. Box 127, Unalakleet 99684 – To Anchorage, Iliamna, McGrath, Galena and St. Marys.

WATER TRANSPORT

Besides sailing from Seattle for southeastern Alaska, the Alaska Marine Highway operates several vehicle and passenger ferries on the gulf coast. Seward, Homer, and Whittier on the Kenai Peninsular are connected to the Prince William Sound communities of Valdez and Cordova via the ferries. It's also possible to sail from Homer to Kodiak Island and thence to several Aleutian Island destinations. Check at the ferry office near the harbor if you're in any of the towns along the route, or call the Alaska Marine Highway in Seattle, (206) 623-1970 or Alaska Marine Highway, P.O. Box R, Juneau, AK 99811, (907) 465-3941 or toll free 800-642-0066.

PUBLIC TRANSPORT

Most communities with any road system at all will have some form of taxi service available. Taxis are nice for getting around town, but can be extremely expensive to ride for long distances.

RAILROADS

In addition to the Alaska Railroad, which offers travel by rail within the state, there is one other railroad in operation–the White Pass and Yukon Railroad out of Skagway. Service was discontinued for a few years, but the railroad is now back in full operation. The ride is a must for visitors to Skagway.

This historic railway was started in the days of the mad rush to the Klondike in 1898. The vintage 1890 parlor cars have been fully restored and are pulled along by Old Number 73 steam engine. The ride is breathtaking as the train climbs along the gray rocks cliffs and travels over a trestle which spans a gorge over the narrow box canyon.

Take the summit excursion to White Pass or scheduled through service to Fraser, B.C. where passengers connect with a motorcoach to Whitehorse, Yukon Territory. For more information and reservations contact a travel agent or White Pass & Yukon Route, P.O. Box 435, Skagway, AK 98840, telephone (907) 983-2214 or toll free 800-343-7373.

PRIVATE TRANSPORT

Most major U.S. car rental companies have offices in Alaska's larger cities. Generally, you have to be at least 21 years old, possess a valid driver's license and have a major credit card (VISA, Mastercharge, American Express or Diner's Club) to rent an automobile.

Shopping around with smaller companies such as Rent-A-Wreck or Rent-A-Dent can often save you money, although the car you get may not be anything to brag about.

There are usually extra restrictions imposed on drivers renting cars during the winter months. Although roads may be open, many companies do not allow their vehicles to be driven out of town or between cities. Check the rules carefully if renting during the winter months.

Package deals including transportation to Alaska, accommodations, and a car are available from most travel agencies. Check with a travel agent if you are interested in a combination price which is probably cheaper than arranging everything yourself.

MOTORING ADVISORIES

The maximum speed limit anywhere in Alaska is 55 mph (89 km). Speed limits are lower in residential areas, cities, and especially near schools. Obey posted speed limits and you should have few problems.

A right turn is permitted against a red light unless otherwise posted, but only after you stop long enough to confirm there is no traffic with which you will interfere. All drivers are required to stop for a school bus with its warning lights operating. Drivers may not proceed around or past a school bus until the lights have been turn off.

Drivers in Alaska will see a lot of hitchhikers; it's a popular form of travel for college students and others. Beware, you pick up hitchhikers at your own risk. Recent years have seen rising incidents of crimes involving hitchhikers in Alaska just as in most of the rest of the country. Prudence dictates you to slow your speed during the winter months. Highways in Alaska are far from the best in the world, and in combination with ice and snow, can be treacherous.

WHERE TO STAY

HOTELS & MOTELS

Accommodations in Alaska vary greatly. The larger cities offer plush top-quality hotels, which are of international standards. However, outside of the cities, facilities are mediocre and expensive. Visitors must keep in mind that Alaska is indeed the "last frontier" and hasn't risen to the standards of many other places.

There are a variety of accommodations available.

They range from well-known hotel chains to smaller local hotels and motels. There is also an extensive bed and breakfast program. For more information about bed and breakfast accommodation write **Alaska Private Lodgings**, P.O. Box 200047-TP, Anchorage, AK 99520-0047.

The Alaska Division of Tourism has an extensive listing of accommodations throughout the state in the Alaska Vacation Planner. For this free booklet write Alaska Division of Tourism, P.O. Box E-301, Juneau, AK 99811 U.S.A.

ANCHORAGE

Alaska Samovar Inn, downtown Anchorage, 68 rooms, moderate prices. Restaurant; lounge; coffee shop. 720 Gambell St., Anchorage, Alaska 99501, (907) 277-1511.

Anchorage Eagle Nest Hotel, 24 condo-style suites, five minutes from airport. 4110 Spenard Rd., Anchorage, Alaska 99503, (907) 243-3433.

Anchorage International Airport Inn, three minutes from airport. 333 International Airport Rd., Anchorage, Alaska 99502, (907) 243-2233, 1-800-544-0986.

Anchorage Hilton Hotel, downtown Anchorage, 410 rooms. Two restaurant/lounges; gift shops; travel office. Box 100520, West 3rd Ave., Anchorage, Alaska 99501, (907)272-7411 or (800)-HILTONS.

Arctic Inn Motel, near airport, 28 rooms, relatively low prices. Restaurants; cocktail lounge; laundromat. 842 West International Airport Rd., Anchorage, Alaska 99502, (907) 561-1328.

Best Western Barrat Inn, next to Spenard Lake, 150 rooms. Restaurant; lounge. 4616 Spenard Rd., Anchorage, Alaska 99503, (907) 243-3131.

Best Western Golden Lion Hotel, corner of New Seward Highway and 36th Avenue, 83 rooms. 100 East 36th Ave., Anchorage, Alaska 99504, 1-800-528-1234.

Big Timber Motel, waterbeds, some units with kitchenettes. 2224 East 5th Ave., Anchorage, Alaska 99501, (907) 272-2541.

Black Angus Inn, 1430 Gambell, Anchorage, Alaska,

Clarion Hotel, near airport and downtown. Located on scenic Lake Spenard with own float plane dock. Features 248 deluxe rooms. 4800 Spenard Road, Anchorage, AK 99517-3236, (907) 243-2300 or 800-544-0784.

Eklutna Lodge, 27 miles (44 km) east of Anchorage on Glenn Highway, 10 units. Restaurant; lounge. Star Route 2, Box 8165, Chugiak, Alaska 99567, (907) 688-3150.

Hillside Motel, two blocks from shopping mall. Several 24-hour restaurants. 2150 Gambell, Anchorage, Alaska 99503, (907) 258-6006.

Holiday Inn of Anchorage, center of downtown, 251 rooms. Pool; sauna; restaurant; lounge. 239 West 4th Ave., Anchorage, Alaska 99501. For reservations phone 1-800-HOLIDAY, telex 26647, or call any Holiday Inn worldwide.

Hotel Captain Cook, choice of mountain or bay view rooms in each of three towers. Restaurants; lounges; coffee shop; gift shops; athletic club with pool; travel agency. P.O. Box 102280, Anchorage, Alaska 99510-2280, (907) 276-6000, telex 25340.

Inlet Inn of Anchorage, condo-style rooms. Kitchen; saunas; beauty salon; laundromat. 1200 "H" St., Anchorage, Alaska 99501, (907) 277-0110.

Inlet Towers Hotel, condo-style rooms. Kitchen; saunas; beauty salon; laundromat. 1200 "L" St., Anchorage, Alaska 99501, (907) 276-0110.

John's Motel and RV Court, 16 units, 43 recreational vehicle hookups. Laundromat; showers. 3543 Mountain View Dr., Anchorage, Alaska 99508, (907) 277-4332.

Kobuk Hotel/Motel, Regular or waterbeds; Jacuzzi baths in some rooms. 1104 East Fifth Ave., Anchorage, Alaska 99501, (907) 274-1650.

Mush Inn Motel, 95 rooms. Some with Jacuzzi baths and waterbeds. 333 Concrete St., Anchorage, Alaska 99501, (907) 277-4554.

Northern Lights Inn, 136 rooms, restaurants, lounge, live entertainment, special low winter rates. 598 West Northern Lights Blvd., Anchorage, Alaska 99503, (907) 561-5200.

Sheraton Anchorage, downtown luxury hotel. Restaurant; lounge; cafe; nightly entertainment. 401 E. 6th Ave., Anchorage, Alaska 99501, (907) 276-8700, 1-800-325-3535, telex 25-325.

Super 8 Motel, 3501 Minnesota Dr., Anchorage, Alaska, (907) 276-8884,1-800-843-1991 for information.

Thunderbird Motel, 24 rooms with local phone service. 4404 Spenard Rd., Anchorage, Alaska 99503, (907) 243-4044/4004.

Tropic of the North Hotel, 120 rooms. Lounge. 3001 Spenard Rd., Anchorage, Alaska 99503, (907) 563-6640.

Voyage Hotel, downtown 38 large rooms. Walking distance to shops; restaurants; entertainment. 501 "K" St., Anchorage, Alaska 99501, (907) 277-9501 or 800-247-9070.

Westmark Anchorage, newly renovated, 200 rooms, formerly Sheffield hotel, heart of downtown (907) 264-0970 or 800-544-0970.

Barrow Airport Inn, near airport. Flush toilets; queen beds. P.O. Box 933, Barrow, Alaska 99723, (907) 852-2525.

Top of the World Hotel, 40 rooms. Phones; cable TV; adjoining restaurant. P.O. Box 189, Barrow, Alaska 99723, (907) 852-3900.

BETHEL

Kuskokwim Inn, 72 rooms, restaurants; flush toilets. Box 218, Bethel, Alaska 99559, (907) 543-2207.

BETTLES

Bettles Lodge, dormitory style rooms. Bunk beds; bathroom in hallway. Bettles Lodge, Bettles, Alaska 99726.

BIG LAKE

Klondike Inn, 10 rooms. Restaurant; bar. Reservations necessary. Box 17-320, Big Lake, Alaska 99687, (907) 892-6261.

CENTRAL

Arctic Cicle Hot Springs, Olympic-size hot springs pool; restaurant; beauty salon; service station. Box 69, Central, Alaska 99730, (907) 520-5113.

COPPER CENTER

Copper Center Lodge, meals available. Drawer J, Copper Center, Alaska 99573, (907) 822-3245.

CORDOVA

Prince William Motel, downtown in complex. Restaurant; bar; package liquor store. P.O. Box 848, Cordova, Alaska 99575, (907) 424-3201.

Reluctant Fisherman Hotel, overlooking boat harbor. Restaurant; lounge; gift shop; travel agency; beauty salon. Box 150, Cordova, Alaska 99574, (907) 424-3272.

DELTA JUNCTION

Alaska 6 Motel, eight rooms. Box 1115, Delta Junction, Alaska 99737, (907) 895-4848.

Bay Hotel, center of town near shopping center. Restaurant; bar. Box 160, Delta Junction, Alaska 99737, (907) 895-4646.

C's Motel, Singles and doubles; color TV; restaurant; lounge. Box 1121, Delta Junction, Alaska 99737, (907) 895-4437.

Evergreen Inn, Baths; restaurant; bar. Box 485, Delta Junction, Alaska 99737, (907) 895-4666.

Kelly's Motel, Lounge (featuring grill-your-own steaks and burgers). Box 827, Delta Junction, Alaska 99737, (907) 895-4667 or 895-4973.

DENALI HIGHWAY

Adventures Unlimited Lodge, 60 miles (97 km) from Denali Park. All manner of outdoor recreation available. Box 89, Cantwell, Alaska 99729.

Paxon Lodge, junction of Denali and Richardson highways, midway between Valdez and Fairbanks. Airstrip; restaurant; lounge; post office. Paxon Lodge, Paxson Alaska 99737, (907) 822-3330.

DENALI NATIONAL PARK

Camp Denali, Housekeeping cabins in the heart of the park. Box 67, Denali National Park, Alaska 99755, (907) 683-2302 (winter), (907) 683-2290 (summer).

Carlo Greek Lodge, Mile 224 of George Parks Highway, cabin resort on Carlo Greek. Box 185, Denali National Park, Alaska 99755, (907) 683-2512.

Denali National Park Hotel, 100 rooms with baths, 40 compartments in old railroad coaches. Restaurants; gift shop; tours. Denali National Park, Alaska 99755, (907) 683-2215 (summer); 825 West 8th Ave. #240, Anchorage, Alaska 99501, (907) 278-1122 (winter).

Healy Roadhouse, just north of park on George Parks Highway, 10 rooms. Dining room; lounge. Box 33, Healy, Alaska 99743 (907) 683-2273.

Kantishna Roadhouse, Cabin lodging; fine food; wilderness adventure. (907) 733-2535 or 683-2710. Box 130, Denali National Park, Alaska 99755.

McKinley Chalets, 216 two-room suites. Restaurant; lounge. Wilderness adventures. Denali National Park, Alaska 99755, (907) 683-2215 (sum-

mer); 825 West 8th Ave., #240, Anchorage, Alaska 99501, (907) 278-1122 (winter).

Mt. McKinley Village, on Nenana River near south entrance to park. Fifty rooms, two restaurants, lounge, gift shop, and gas station. 823 West 8th Ave. #240, Anchorage, AK 99501, (907) 276-7234.

North Face Lodge, near center of park. One and two-day all-inclusive packages including meals. Reservations. Box 67, Denali National Park, Alaska 99755, (907) 683-2290.

DILLINGHAM

Bristol Inn, 30 rooms. Restaurant; lounge. Box 71, Dillingham, Alaska 99576, (907) 842-2240.

Dillingham Hotel, downtown Dillingham. Box 194, Dillingham, Alaska 99576, (907) 842-5316.

ESTER

Cripple Creek Resort, seven miles (11 km) from Fairbanks, adjacent to famous Malemute Salon. Bunkhouse accommodations. Box 109, Ester, Alaska 99725. Phone (907) 455-2500 (winter); (907) 479-7274 (summer)

Fairbanks Alaska Motel, daily or weekly rates. Laundry facilities. 1545 Cushman St., Fairbanks, Alaska 99701, (907) 456-6393.

Captain Bartlett Inn, 200 rooms. Restaurant; lounge; jacuzzi; sauna. 1411 Airport Way, Fairbanks, Alaska 99701, (907) 478-7900, 1-800-544-7528.

Chena Hot Springs Resort, one hour's drive northeast of Fairbanks, rooms, suites and cabins. Hot spring pool; restaurant; bar. (907) 452-7867. 110 Antoinette, Fairbanks, AK 99701.

Fairbanks Hotel, downtown (relatively inexpensive) 455 3rd Ave., Fairbanks, Alaska 99701, (907) 456-6440.

Fairbanks Inn, 172 rooms, suites available. Dining room: lounge. 1521 South Cushman, Fairbanks, Alaska 99701, (907) 456-6602. I-800-544-0970, telex 35427.

Frontier Lodge, kitchens in all units. Motel; restaurant; bar. 440 Old Richardson Highway, Fairbanks, Alaska 99701, (907) 456-4733.

Golden North Motel, 62 rooms. Near shopping malls; restaurants. 4888 Old Richardson Highway, Fairbanks, Alaska 99701, (907) 479-6201.

Great Land Hotel, 90 rooms. Dining facilities; cocktail lounge. 723 1st Ave., Fairbanks, Alaska 99701, (907) 452-6661/1888, telex 35349.

Klondike Inn, 49 rooms. Restaurant; lounge; gift shop. 1316 Bedrock St., Fairbanks, Alaska 99701, (907) 479-6241.

Maranatha Inn, 100 rooms. Restaurant; health club. 1100 Cushman St., Fairbanks, Alaska 99701, (907) 452-4421.

Monson Motel, 50 rooms. 1321 Karen St., Fairbanks, Alaska 99701, (907) 479-6770.

Pioneer Hotel, downtown, 35 rooms. Restaurant; cocktail lounge; entertainment; kitchenettes. 401 1st Ave., Fairbanks, Alaska 99701, (907) 456-2600.

Polaris Hotel, 135 rooms. Two restaurants; bars. 427 1st Ave., Fairbanks, Alaska 99701, (907) 452-4451.

Ranch Motel, 31 rooms. Restaurant. 2223 Cushman St., Fairbanks, Alaska 99701 (907) 452-4783.

Tamarac Inn Motel, Kitchenettes; laundry facilities. 252 Minnie St., Fairbanks, Alaska 99701, (907) 456-6406.

Towne House Motel, 1010 Cushman St., Fairbanks, Alaska 99701, (907) 456-6687.

Traveler's Inn, 240 rooms. Two restaurants, two lounges. 813 Noble St., Fairbanks, Alaska 99701, (907) 456-7722, telex 36609.

Wedgewood Manner, Condo-style one-bedroom apartments. Fully furnished with dishes; linens cooking utensils; maid service; laundry service. 212 Wedgewood Dr., Fairbanks, Alaska 99701, (907) 452-1442.

Westmark Fairbanks, large downtown luxury hotel, 800 Noble Street, Fairbanks, AK 99701, (907) 274-6631 or 800-544-0970.

FORT YUKON

Gwitchyaa Zhee Lodge, four cabins ($40 per day per person.) Box 155, Fort Yukon, Alaska 99740, (907) 662-2468.

GLACIER BAY GUSTAVUS

Glacier Bay Lodge, 55 rooms, dining room, lounge and gift shop. Only hotel within the park. 1620 Metropolitan Park Building, Seattle, Wsahington 98101, 800-622-2042.

Gustavus Inn, accommodates up to 14. Family-style meals. Box 31, Gustavus, Alaska 99826, (907) 697-2254.

Salmon River Cabins, ($40 a day, bikes and sleeping bags extra.) Cooking/eating utensils; gas stove; wood heating. Box 13, Gustavus, Alaska 99825, (907) 697-2245.

GLENNALLEN/GAKONA

Caribou Lodge, 38 rooms. Food service. Box 329, Glennallen, Alaska 99588, (907) 822-3302.

Gakona Junction Village, located at the junction of Richardson and Glenn highways, 18 rooms. Restaurant; bakery; grocery store. Box 222, Gakona, Alaska 99586, (907) 822-3665.

HAINES

Cache Inn Lodge, rustic cottages. Cooking facilities; maid service. Box 441, Haines, Alaska 99827, (907) 766-2910.

Captain's Choice Motel, 20 rooms overlooking Portage Cove and Chilkoot Inlet. Box 392, Haines, Alaska 99827, (907) 766-3111.

Eagles Nest Motel, 10 rooms. Box 267, Haines, Alaska 99827, (907) 766-2352.

Fort Seward Condos, apartments overlooking Lynn Canal. Cregg Enterprises, Box 75, Haines, Alaska 99827, (907) 766-2425/2801.

Fort William H. Seward Lodge and Restaurant, Box 307, Totem Street, Haines, Alaska 99827, (907) 766-2009.

Hotel Halsingland, 60 rooms. Cocktail lounge; restaurant featuring locally caught seafood. Box 158, Haines, Alaska 99827, (907) 766-2000, 800-542-6363.

Mountain View Motel, within walking distance of downtown. Box 62, Haines, Alaska 99827, (907) 766-2900.

Thunderbird Motel, downtown. Box 159, Haines, Alaska 99827, (907) 766-2131, 800-327-2556.

HOMER

Baycrest Motel, 12 rooms, six with kitchens. Box 804, Homer, Alaska 99603, (907) 235-8716.

Best Western Bidarka Inn, Mile 172 Sterling Highway on Kachemak Bay, 64 rooms. Restaurant; lounge. Box 1408, Homer, Alaska 99603, (907) 235-8148 or 800-528-1234.

Driftwood Inn, one block from beach. (Bed and breakfast if desired.) 135 Bunnell, Homer, Alaska 99603, (907) 235-8019.

Heritage Hotel, downtown. Within walking distance of restaurants; shopping; entertainment. 135 W. Bunnell Ave., Homer, Alaska 99603, (907) 235-7787.

Land's End Resort, 56 rooms with full-service restaurant specializing in fresh seafood. P.O. Box 273, Homer, Alaska 99603, (907) 235-2500 or 235-2525.

Ocean Shores Motel, four blocks from down-town, all units apartment style. 3500 Crittenden Dr., Homer, Alaska 99603, (907)235-7775/6.

HOONAH

Huna Totem Lodge, north end of Chichagof Island, 30 miles (48 km) southeast of Glacier Bay, 28 rooms. Dining room; lounge; bar. (Reservations a must.) Box 320, Hoonah, Alaska 99829, (907) 945-3636.

JUNEAU

Alaskan Hotel, downtown, National Register of Historic Sites. Sauna; jacuzzi; laundromat; bar. 167 South Franklin St., Juneau, Alaska 99801, (907) 586-1000 or 800-327-9347.

The Baranof Hotel, newly restored, 226 rooms and suites. Coffee shop; lounge; restaurant; athletic club. 127 North Franklin St., Juneau, Alaska 99801, (907) 586-8315, 1-800-544-0970.

Best Western Country Lane Inn, indoor pool; jacuzzi. 9300 Glacier Highway, Juneau, Alaska 99801, (907) 789-5005, 1-800-528-1234.

The Breakwater, rooms with balconies overlooking harbor, some facing Mount Juneau. Restaurant; lounge; laundromat; gift shop. 1711 Glacier Ave., Juneau, Alaska 99801, (907) 586-6303, 1-800-544-2250.

Driftwood Lodge, 62 rooms. Laundry facilities; restaurant. 435 Willoughby, Juneau, Alaska 99801, (907) 586-2280 or 800-544-2239.

Prospector Hotel, downtown, 60 rooms. Restaurant; bar; music and dancing. 375 Whittier, Juneau, Alaska 99801, (907) 586-3737, 1-800-426-0670.

Super 8 Motel. (Low rates, free in-room continental breakfast.) (907) 789-4858, 1-800-843-1991.

Summit Hotel and Lounge, near ferry terminal. 455 South Franklin St., Juneau, Alaska 99801, (907) 586-2050.

Westmark Juneau, downtown on waterfront, 104 rooms and suites. Lounge; restaurant. 51 West Egan Dr., Juneau, Alaska 99801, (907) 274-6631, 1-800-544-0970, telex 25224.

KAKE

New Town Inn, ($64 a day, includes three meals.) Box 222, Kake, Alaska 99830, (907) 785-3472/3885.

KENAI PENINSULA

Gwin's Lodge, Mile 53 Sterling Highway, close to Russian River fisheries, 45 rooms. Manager, Mile 52 Sterling Highway, Copper Landing, Alaska 99572, (907) 595-1266/9295.

Kenai Merit Inn. 60 rooms. Restaurant; lounge. 260 South Willow, Kenai, Alaska 99611, (907) 283-7566 or 800-544-0970.

Sunrise Inn, on Kenai Lake, 10 units. Restaurant; lounge; gift shop. Mile 45 Sterling Highway, Copper Landing, Alaska 99572, (907) 595-1222.

KETCHIKAN

Gilmore Hotel, downtown near ferry terminal, 42 rooms. Restaurant; lounge. 326 Front St., Ketchikan. Alaska 99901, (907)225-9423.

Ingersoll Hotel, 60 rooms. Walking distance to government offices; shops; visitor attractions. 303 Mission St., Ketchikan, Alaska 99901, (907) 225-2124.

Super 8 Motel, on the waterfront between ferry terminal and downtown. Box 8818, Ketchikan, Alaska 99901, (907) 225-9088, 1-800-843-1991.

KLAWOCK

Fireweed Lodge, 20 rooms. Restaurant, lounge; fresh and saltwater fishing. Box 116, Klawock, Alaska 99925, (907) 755-2226.

KODIAK

Kalsin Inn Ranch, 30 miles (48 km) from downtown in heart of good fishing, 11 rooms. Coin-operated washers; driers. Box 1696, Kodiak, Alaska 99615.

Kodiak Star Motel, 26 rooms. Kitchenettes, laundry facilities. Box 553, Kodiak, Alaska 99615, (907) 486-5657.

Road's End, Rooms and camping area; dining room; bar. Box 5629, Kodiak, Alaska 99615.

Shelikof Lodge, 39 rooms overlooking city and harbor. Restaurant; lounge. Box 774, Kodiak, Alaska 99615, (907) 486-4141.

Westmark Kodiak, downtown on waterfront, 90 rooms and suites. Lounge; restaurant. 234 South Benson, Kodiak, Alaska 99615, (907) 486-5712, 1-800-544-0970, telex 25224.

KOTZEBUE

Nullagvik Hotel, 80 modern rooms overlooking Kotzebue Sound. Restaurants; beauty shop. Box 336, Kotzebue, Alaska 99752, (907) 442-3331.

MANLEY HOT SPRINGS

Manley Roadhouse, historic lodge built in 1906. Rooms; food; bar. 100 Landing Rd., Manley Hot Springs, Alaska 99756, (907) 672-3161.

NENANA

Tumwater Lake Lodge, cabins on five-acre (2 hectares) lake for swimming and boating. Groceries; liquor; gift; curio shop. Mile 290 Parks Highway, Nenana, Alaska 99760, (907) 683-2715.

NINILCHIK

Inlet View Cabins, Mile 135.5 Sterling Highway, close to two famed salmon streams, clam digging, and beachcombing. Restaurant; lounge; liquor store. Box 39050, Ninilchik, Alaska 99639, (907) 567-3330.

NOME

Nome Nugget Inn, 47 rooms. Lounge; retaurant. Box 430, Nome, Alaska 99762, (907) 443-2000.

NORTHWAY

1260 Inn, Mile 1260 Alaska Highway, five rooms. Baths; cafe; beauty salon; service station. Mile 1260 Alaska Highway, via Tok, Alaska 99780, (907) 778-2205.

PALMER

Eureka Lodge, Mile 128 Glenn Highway. Liquor store; gift shop. Star Route C, Box 8565, Palmer, Alaska 99645, (907) 822-3808.

Glacier Park Resort, Mile 102 on Glenn Highway. Rooms with baths; cabins; camping; laundromat; dining room; lounge. Box 4-2615, Anchorage, Alaska 99509, (907) 745-2534.

Hatcher Pass Bed and Breakfast, 60 miles (97 km) northeast of Anchorage. Cross-country skiing; loading; meals; bar; entertainment; sauna. Box 2655, Palmer, Alaska 99645, (907) 745-5897.

Pioneer Apartment Motel, eight rooms. Kitchenettes; showers. Box 2283, Palmer, Alaska 99645, (907) 745-3425.

Sheep Mountain Lodge, Mile 113 Glenn Highway, four cabins, three-bedroom trailer unit. Hot tub; sauna. Star Route C, Box 8490, Palmer, Alaska 99645, (907) 745-5121.

Valley Hotel, downtown Palmer, 35 rooms. Restaurant; cocktail lounge. Box 822, Palmer, Alaska 99645, (907) 745-3330.

PETERSBURG

Beachcomber Inn, seaside resort with king salmon and halibut fishing outside the door. Restaurant. Box 910, Petersburg, Alaska 99833, (907) 772-3888.

Scandia House, downtown, 30 rooms. Box 689, Petersburg, Alaska 99833, (907) 772-4281.

Tides Inn, downtown, modern rooms. Box 1048, Petersburg, Alaska 99833, (907) 772-4288.

SALCHA

Salchaket Homestead, 41 miles (66 km) southeast of Fairbanks on Richardson Highway. Restaurant; bar; post office. Box 140029, Salcha, Alaska 99714, (907) 488-2233.

SELDOVIA

Annie McKenzie's Boardwalk Hotel, 13 rooms on the waterfront with view of water or mountains. Several restaurants within three blocks. Box 72, Seldovia, Alaska 99663, (907) 234-7816.

SEAWARD

Breeze Inn Motel, 51 rooms. Restaurant; lounge. Box 935, Seward, Alaska 99664, (907) 224-5237.

Marina Hotel, Mile 1 Seward Highway overlooking bay and boat harbor. Box 1134, Seward, Alaska 99664, (907) 224-5518.

Murphy's Motel, downtown with dining area. Box 736, Seward, Alaska 99664, (907) 224-8090.

New Seward Hotel, downtown, 35 rooms. Snack bar. Box 675, Seward, Alaska 99664, (907) 224-8001.

Van Gilder Hotel, a National Historic Site, 26 rooms. Restaurant; bar. Box 775, Seward, Alaska 99664, (907) 224-3079 or 224-3525.

SITKA

Potlatch Motel, Eight blocks from downtown, 30 rooms. Restaurant; cocktail lounge. Box 58, Sitka, Alaska 99835, (907) 747-8611.

Sitka Hotel, downtown, 60 rooms. Box 679, Sitka, Alaska 99835, (907) 747-3288.

Westmark Sitka, 80 rooms downtown on waterfront. Restaurant; lounge. Box 318, Sitka, Alaska 99835, (907) 747-6616, 1-800-544-0970.

SKAGWAY

Gold Rush Lodge, modern rooms. Within walking distance of historical sites. Box 514, Skagway, Alaska 99840, (907) 983-2831.

Irene's Inn, Spacious rooms; restaurant. Box 538, Skagway, Alaska 99840, (907) 983-2520.

The Klondike, 220 rooms. Cafeteria; lounge; restaurant. Box 515, Skagway, Alaska 99840, (907) 983-2291, 1-800-544-0970.

Skagway Inn, 15 rooms with six hallway baths. Box 192, Skagway, Alaska 99840, (907) 983-2289.

Wind Valley Lodge, 12 rooms with private baths. Box 354, Skagway, Alaska 99840, (907) 983-2236.

SOLDOTNA

Bunk House Inn, 20 rooms with baths. Restaurant; lounge. Box 3100, Soldotna, Alaska 99669, (907) 262-4584.

Kenai River Lodge, rooms overlooking the famous Kenai River. Restaurant; lounge; Excellent sportfishing. 393 Riverside Dr., Soldotna, Alaska 99669, (907) 262-4292.

Soldotna Inn, 28 rooms. Restaurant; lounge. 35041 Kenai Spur Rd., Soldotna, Alaska 99669, (907) 262-4305.

SUTTON

King Mountain Lodge, Mile 76 Glenn Highway, five-room motel. Bar; restaurant; five cabins. Box 15, Sutton, Alaska 99674, (907) 745-4280.

TALKEETNA

Fairview Inn, National Historic Place in operation since 1923, seven rooms. (Reservations recommended.) P.O. Box 379, Talkeetna, Alaska 99676, (907) 733-2423.

TOK

Tok Lodge, Mile 124 Glenn Highway. Hotel; motel; restaurant; lounge, liquor store. Box 135, Tok, Alaska 99780, (907) 883-2851.

Westmark Inn-Tok, Alaskan lodge Atmosphere, luxury rooms, Mile 1315 Alaska Highway, Box 336, Tok, AK 99780 (summer) or 880 H Street, Suite 101, Anchorage, AK 99510 (winter). (907) 274-6631 or 800-554-0970.

FOREST SERVICE CABINS

For a totally unique Alaskan experience, visitors can stay in remote wilderness cabins maintained by the Forest Service and the Bureau of Land Management in Alaska. These rustic cabins are accessible by trails or by chartered air service (arranged by the renter). This is a real bargain at $15 per night. There are over 190 cabins scattered throughout the Tongass and Chugach National Forest in southeast and southcentral Alaska.

The cabins are located in beautiful areas and give visitors a chance to experience the great Alaska outdoors. However, they are very basic. They lack running water and electricity, averaging 12 by 14 feet (3.7 by 4.3 meters) in size. They come equipped with a table and oil or wood burning stove. Wooden bunks without mattresses are provided and outhouses are located a few steps away. Cabins located on a lake often have an aluminum boat or skiff available.

Renters are expected to bring their own food, cooking utensils and bedding. They are also expected to pack out their garbage and replace any fire wood they have burned.

Reservations are taken on a first come first serve basis up to 179 days in advance. For more information write for a copy of the *Recreation Facility* booklet. Send to Chugach National Forest, 201 East 9th Avenue, Suite 206, Anchorage, AK 99501.

CAMPING

Federal, state, municipal, and private campgrounds dot the landscape in Alaska. These can vary from barely organized tents sites to full-hookup recreational vehicle parking sites. As a general rule, there's usually one or more campgrounds nearby if you are anywhere along the road system.

Fees for overnight use vary from nothing for most state campgrounds to daily rate of up to $15 for full-

Put on the Cutter®
...because it's a
jungle out there.

Cutter® Insect Repellent. Effective, long-lasting protection.
So no matter how delicious you look, mosquitoes will know
it's look, but don't touch. Protect yourself with Cutter®
...because it's a jungle out there.

© 1993 Miles Inc.

Our history could fill this book, but we prefer to fill glasses.

When you make a great beer, you don't have to make a great fuss.

hookup sites in private campgrounds. In early 1985, state officials were beginning to look at instituting a fee system for state campgrounds.

Free state federal Bureau of Land Management campgrounds generally provide picnic tables, fire pits, outdoor toilets, a parking space, and space for tents or recreational vehicles. U.S Forest Service Campgrounds provide the same features but cost an average of $5 per day (noon to noon).

The two best sources for listings of public and private campgrounds are *The Milepost*, available from Alaska Northwest Publishing Co., and the *Alaksa Vacation Planner*, available from the Alaska State Division of Tourism, P.O. Box E-301, Juneau, Alaska 99811. Both of these publications are updated annually.

FOOD DIGEST

WHAT TO EAT

All Alaskan cities offer a variety of foods. Once out of the city, however, food ranges from great home cooking to poor fare. One thing that is consistent wherever you go is that prices are expensive. The rationale is that virtually all food products must be flown in and wages are high. Keep this factor in mind when planning your food budgets.

Alaskan restaurants do serve a variety of outstanding seafood. Both Alaska King and Dungeness crab are on the menu when in season. Other shellfish such as shrimp are plentiful. Fresh salmon is available year round and a wonderful treat. Don't miss the halibut offerings cooked in a variety of sauces. While travelling the backroads be on the lookout for a few rare treats such as moose burger, caribou steak and bear roasts.

Throughout Alaska you will find restaurants in all the major cities in addition to most fast food establishments. The best way to find a good restaurant is to ask for a recommendation from a local person.

DRINKING NOTES

The legal age for purchasing and consuming alcoholic beverages is 21; carry adequate identification. Alcoholic beverages are sold or served in specific liquor stores, lounges, and restaurants licensed by the state; licenses are allocated on the basis of one for every 1,500 residents of an area.

A number of small communities in rural Alaska have completely banned the importation, sale, and consumption of alcoholic beverages. You could be arrested, fined, jailed, or deported for violating these local ordinances. Before travelling to a remote destination, inquire as to local liquor laws.

THINGS TO DO

TOUR OPERATORS

One of the best ways to see Alaska is on an organized tour. Since the state is so massive, it is difficult for the individuals to maximize their time. You can arrange a tour for almost any activity-fishing, trekking, cruising, nature expeditions, photo tours, snow skiing, sled dog mushing, float trips, bird watching, glacier exploring, etc.

STATEWIDE

ABEC. Wilderness adventures on the rivers of Alaska. Rafting, kayak, canoe trips ranging from wildwater to relaxing floating basecamps in Brooks, Alaska, Aleutian and Wrangell-St. Ellias ranges. Backpacking trips in several areas. Write 1304 Westwick Drive, Fairbanks, AK 99712 (907) 457-8907.

Alaska Sightseeing Tours. Anchorage city and Portage Glacier tours. One or two-day Columbia Glacier circle tours by motorcoach, rail and boat (one day air). Golden Circle tour includes Anchorage, Valdez, Columbia Glacier, Fairbanks, Denali Park, Trailblazer tours to Haines or Skagway. Contact 349 Wrangell St. Anchorage, AK 99501. (907) 276-1305 or 800-421-5557.

Alaska Travel Adventures. Two, three and four day "tastes of adventure" in Alaska's backcountry, including Denali National Park, Prince William Sound, ant the Northern Inside Passage. All equipment, guiding, transportation and food provided. Contact 9085 Glacier Highway, Juneau, AK 99801. (907) 789-0052.

Alaska Wilderness Group. Scheduled custom guided float trips on various wilderness rivers. Flightseeing, camping, photography, hiking, fishing, wildlife viewing. 4341 MacAlister Drive, Anchorage, AK 99509. (907) 243-3068.

Camp Alaska Tours. Unique camping tours for persons age 19-40 through Alaska, British Columbia and the Yukon. Travel in small groups on five itineraries from 6-26 days with opportunites for scenic flights, cruises, hiking, rafting and nightlife. Tours depart from Anchorage and Seattle; May September. For brochure, write Box 872247, Wasilla, AK 99687, (907) 376-9438.

Hautanen Enterprises. Statewide fully guided big game hunting and/or photography trips with aircraft and/or boats. Specializing in brown bear and caribou. Licensed pilot and registered guide. Write N.E. "Butch" Hautanen, 3157 W. 64th Ave., Anchorage, AK 99502. (907) 243-5683.

Hugh Glass Backpacking Co. State quality guided wilderness adventures by registered guide/naturalists. Trekking, canoeing, river tours, ocean kayaking, fishing or photography. Also unguided trips, custom trips, logistical and advisory services. Write Chuck Ash, Box 110796, Anchorage, AK 99511. (907) 344-1340.

Kichatna Guide Service. Guided photographic safaris to Cathedral Spires in Alaska Range Mountains and on Kodiak Island. Also guided sporthunting in Alaska Range. Write Harold Schetzle, Box 670790, Chugiak, AK 99567. (907) 696-3256.

Midnight Sun Tours. Offers an exclusive array of Alaska tours and adventure programs. Executive and private charters, exclusive fishing packages, rafting and sailing programs, independent car/motorhome packages, mountaineering and hiking trips. Custom trip planning. Write Box 103355, Anchorage, AK 99510. (907) 278-3687. 800-544-2235.

Mountain Travel of Alaska Ltd. Expeditions and outings to wilderness areas of Alaska. Specialized guided tours feature travel by kayak, canoe, raft, or on foot to outstanding scenic, cultural and wildlife locations. Write 1398 Solano Ave., Albany, CA 99706. (415) 527-8100. Outside California 800-227-2384.

Mountain Trip. Year round mountain guiding service. Guided climbs on Mt. McKinley, Mt. Foraker, Mt. Hunter and more. Climbing seminars from two days to two weeks. Expeditions and seminars for women only. Write Gary Bocarde, Box 41161, Anchorage, AK 99509. (907) 345-6499.

Nature Expeditions International. Seventeen day expeditions to study the natural history of Alaska with emphasis on wildlife, culture and unique natural environments, including the Inside Passage, Glacier Bay, Katmai and Denali. Departures in June, July and August. Write Box 11496. Eugene, OR 97440. (503) 484-6529.

Northern Wilderness Adventures. Spectacular sportfishing on Wild and Scenic Rivers, from the Alaska Range to Bristol Bay. Guided power boat fishing, Alaskan guides and log cabin accommodations. Fishing float trips on class I to class IV rivers. P.O. Box 870834, Wasilla, AK 99687, (907) 376-0502.

Ouzel Expeditions. Guided river float trips in the Illiamna area, Brooks Range and close to Anchorage. Fishing trips, scenic float trips on whitewater and calm rivers. Superb fishing for salmon, pike, grayling and trout. Custom tailored to your wishes. Write 7540 E. 20th Ave., Anchorage, AK 99504. (907) 338-0620. (24-hour message service).

SOUTHEAST

Alaska Discovery. Wilderness tours by raft, kayak, canoe, backpack or skis. Completely outfitted expeditions into Glacier Bay, Admiralty Island, Hubbard Glacier and all S.E. Alaska. Custom trips designed. University credits. Charter floatplane available. Group size limited. Write 369 S. Franklin St., Juneau, AK 99801. (907) 697-586-1911.

Boat Rental. Kayaks, canoes and inflatable skiffs available in Juneau and Glacier Bay. Write Alaska Discovery, 418 S. Franklin St., Juneau, AK 99801. (907) 586-1911.

Alaska Frontier Yacht Excursions. 50' yacht charters, customized to your interests. One to 10-day excursions specializing in groups up to six. Fishing, glacier, fjord and Inside Passage cruising. Comfortable accommodations and home cooked meals. Airport transportation. Write or call, Box 32239, Juneau, AK 99801. (907) 789-0539.

Glacier Bay Yacht Tours. Eighteen years experience operating tours in Glacier Bay. Cruise close to glacier and wildlife including whales, puffins and seal rookeries. Fares all inclusive. Write 1620 Metropolitan Park Bldg., Seattle, WA 98101. 800-622-2042.

Sealaska Cruises, Inc. Customized vacation trips in SE Alaska aboard an 80' motoryacht, based in Sitka. Hunting, fishing, exploring, hiking, scuba diving, photography, or just relaxing and sightseeing. Accommodates four to six guests in three private two-berth staterooms. Write Box 1479, Sitka, AK 99835. (907) 747-6864 or 206-842-4666.

ANGOON

Admiralty Access. Travel booking service for boats and local guides, cabins, charter boats, and transportation scheduling either by charter aircraft, Alaska Marine Highway or Hydrofoil. Write P.O. Box 101, Angoon, AK 99820. (907) 788-3123.

Favorite Bay Inn. Canoe and boat rentals and moderately priced lodging. Write Favorite Bay Inn, P.O. Box 101, Angoon AK 99820. (907) 788-3123.

CRAIG

Karta Inn. Remote facility to Prince of Wales Island accepts small groups to provide personalized fishing, sightseeing. Floatplane access. No road access. 24-foot cruiser. We accept up to four guests. Non-smoker and family discounts. Write David Gusber, Box 114, Craig, AK 99921.

GLACIER BAY

Gustavus Inn Charters. If salmon or halibut fishing is part of your Alaska adventure you will enjoy fishing the Icy Strait Region. Two 30' cabin cruisers with long time residents guides take you fishing in Icy Strait and Glacier Bay. Write Box 31, Gustavus, AK 99826. Winter (907) 586-2006, Summer (907) 697-2255.

Gustavus Inn/Glacier Bay Tours. Offering sightseeing daily or overnight tours or customized private charters tours for small groups. We can help make your Glacier bay visit memorable, whether it is via a two person kayak or our chartered luxury yacht. Price all inclusive. Write or call, Box 31, Gustavus, AK 99826. Winter–(907) 586-2006, Summer–(907) 697-2255.

HAINES

Alaska Chilkat Bald Eagle Preserve. Approximately 20 miles (20 km) from Haines on Haines Highway. Largest concentration of eagles in the world. Best viewing November, December, January. Write Chamber of Commerce, Haines, AK 99827, (907) 766-2202.

Eclipse Alaska. Photograph thousands of American Bald Eagles as they gather on their winter feeding grounds to feed on spawning salmon. Located in the Chilkat Valley Eagle Preserve, Haines, AK. Tours October-February by a professional photographer/guide. Reservations and information call (907) 766-2670 or write to P.O. Box 698, Haines, AK 99827.

King Salmon Derby. Last weekend of May, first weekend of June. Write Box 677, Haines, AK 99827, (907) 766-2744 or (907) 766-2202.

Southeast Alaska State Fair. Combined with Horse Show held in mid-August every year. Write Manager, Southeast Alaska State Fair, Inc., Box 385, Haines, AK 99827. (907) 766-2476.

HOONAH

Hoonah Indian Association Culture Center. Hoonah AK, Small museum containing artifacts representing the Tlingit Indians. (907) 945-3600.

JUNEAU

Alaska Frontier Yacht Excursions. Personalized trips aboard your own private yacht, the 50' *Frontier Queen*. Fishing, sightseeing and whale watching while cruising the Inside Passage. Reserved for six guests maximum. Day or week. Fully outfitted. For reservations or brochure, call or write, 7850 Glacier Highway Juneau, AK 99801. (907) 789-0539.

"Alaska the Great Land." A movie filmed across the vastness of Alaska, the 180 degree wrap-around screen and six channels of sound transport you into the splendor of the last frontier. Showing on the hour daily, 10a.m.-10p.m., from May through September at Alaska Adventure Theater and Gift Shop. 245 Marine Way, Juneau, AK 99801. (907) 586-2419.

Alaska Up Close. See, touch, photograph and listen to Southeast Alaska's coastal rainforest as you explore with a natural history guide. Experience outdoor Alaska close up on gentle walking tour near city's edge, or meet Juneau artists and gallery owners. Small groups, van transportaton. Write Alaska Up Close, Box 2666, Juneau, AK 99803. (907) 789-9544.

Bike Rental. At Merchants Wharf in downtown Juneau. Three, five and 10-speed bikes at reasonable rates. Route maps. Create your own wheel adventure in Juneau. Eileen's Bike Rentals, P.O. Box 275, Juneau, AK 99802, (907) 586-8000.

Capital City Music Hall. Family entertainment starring J. Althea, Alaksa's hottest honky tonk piano player. Dancers perform the can-can, two step, charleston, waltz and foxtrot. Narrative on women's perspective on life in the dance halls and mining days. Prizes to audiences for off-key harmony and toe-tapping. Performances daily in summer. Group rates. 431 S. Franklin St., Juneau. AK 99801.

The Christmas Store. Visit Juneau's year round Christmas Store. Located in the historic Senate Building on South Franklin Street in downtown Juneau. Special gifts and Christmas ornaments from Juneau and all of Alaska. Take a little bit of Alaska back home for Christmas. Write the Christmas Store, Senate Building, 175 S. Franklin, Juneau, AK 99801 (907) 586-8000.

Eaglecrest Ski Area. 12 miles (19.3 km) from downtown Juneau, base lodge, food service, rental shop, ski school, mountain facilities, two chairlifts, one beginner's lift. Mountain top warming lodge and snack bar. Summer hiking, and sightseeing chairlifts ride. Winter offers 640 acres (259 hectares) of alpine/aordic skiing; 40 acres (16 hectares) of snowmaking. Bus service/package plans. Write Eaglecrest, 155 S. Seward, Juneau. AK 99801 (907) 586-5284.

Gold Creek Salmon Bake. Feast on Alaska's salmon barbequed over open fire served with salads, sourdough bread and all the trimmings. All you can eat for $15, kids half price. Explore abandoned gold mine, pan in Gold Creek. Free Bus leaves Baranof Hotel 6 p.m. Reservations only for groups over 15. Write 020993, Juneau, AK 99802. (907) 586-1424.

House of Wickersham. State Historic Site. Home once owned by Judge James Wickersham, early Alaska's outstanding statesman, historian and pioneering federal judge. Home contains impressive array of Alaskana. 213 Seventh Avenue, Juneau, AK 99801 (907) 586-9001 for information regarding tour availability.

Juneau Barbeque. Write Thane Ore House, 4400 Thane Rd., Juneau, AK 99801 (907) 586-3442.

Juneau Ferry Stop Tour. While the Alaska Ferry is berthed in Juneau or Auke Bay, experience the beauty and surroundings of nearby Mendenhall Glacier. Each tour is timed so ongoing passengers can disembark and reboard after an informative tour by bus to Mendenhall Glacier. Cost: $10.00 per person, Write Alaska Port of Call Tours, Box 2880, Juneau, AK 99803. (907) 586-8155.

Juneau Sportfishing. A complete fishing service representing an entire fleet of charter boats ranging in size from 26' to 50'. Includes bait, tackle, license, lunch and transportation. By day, week, or month for any type of fishing including lakes, rivers, ocean and fly-in. Call 800 544-2244 or write Box 20438, Juneau, AK 99802. In Alaska (907) 1887.

Masterson Charters. 46' diesel boat for three or more days of fishing, sightseeing or hunting trips. Sleeps eight. 22' boat for daily fishing for salmon and halibut. Write Donald Masterson, 8127 Popular Ave., Juneau, AK 99801, (907) 789-9061.

Mendenhall Glacier Float Trip. Half day guided float in large rubber rafts starting at Mendenhall Glacier, past the rain forests and high mountains of Mendenhall River Valley, with stop for snack of Alaskan treats. Mixture of rapids and calm water, for persons of all ages. Write 200N Franklin Street, Juneau, AK 99801, (907) 789-0052.

Mendenhall Glacier Hike. Professionally guided 10-hour hike on Juneau's famed Mendenhall Glacier offers exciting and awesome experience for anyone in good physical condition. No prior experience required. Equipment, lunch and transportation from downtown Juneau included. Write ATA, 200N Franklin Street, Juneau, AK 99801. (907) 586-6245 or toll free 800 227-8480, telex 090-45380.

Mendenhall Glacier Walk. One-day hikes on Juneau's Mendenhall Glacier. Write Alaska Discovery, 418.S. Franklin Street, Juneau, AK 99801 (907) 586-1911.

Millers Charters. Cruise beautiful S.E. Alaska aboard the M/V *Betty Jean*, 40' Bluewater Yacht. Sleeping accommodations for six features sightseeing, fishing, nature, photography, diving, hunting and floating base of operations. Custom tailored cruises to meet your desires. Write for brochure. Norman Miller, Box 2890, Juneau, AK 99803. (907) 780-6054 or 586-5887.

Puffin Charters. 37' modern, twin diesel powered cruiser. Fishing, sightseeing, cruising. Specializing in salmon and halibut fishing. Available for day charters for up to six passengers. For brochures and reservations write Puffin Charters, Inc., 4418 Mint Way, Juneau, AK 99801. (907) 789-0001.

Royal Highway Tours. Deluxe motorcoach city sightseeing tours to Mendenhall Glacier with experienced driver/guide. Write Royal Highway Tours, Second Avenue, Suite 400, Seattle, WA 98121. (206) 441-8428.

Windwalker. Enjoy a special evening of sailing and dining on the 36' sailing vessel *Windwalker*. Leave Auke Bay at 6 p.m., sail until 10 p.m. June-August. Write Capt. Bill Johnson, 800F Street, No L4, Juneau, AK 99801. (907) 586-6569.

KETCHIKAN

Alaska Fishing Adventure. Three-days, two-nights guided fishing charter and sightseeing of Misty Fjord. Excellent rates, delicious meals and excellent accommodations. Write 326 Front Street, Ketchikan, AK 99901. (907) 225-9423.

Alaska Salmon Charters/George Inlet Lodge. Complete salmon fishing charter packages guided or unguided. Also custom charters designed to your time and interests. Lodge accommodates 25 people in comfort with modern amenities including family-style meals, wet bar. Write Box 8215, Ketchikan, AK 99901. 247-2306.

Alaska Sightseeing Company. Ketchikan sightseeing tour includes Totem Bight, Totem Heritage Center, Creek Street and Dolly's House. Contact Alaska Sightseeing at Ingersoll Hotel, (907) 225-2740.

Graffin Marine Services. Charters for recreational cruises, Sportfishing and guided hunts. Each planned to suit your interests. Commercial charters for extended periods at attractive rates. Experienced and licensed for all of S.E. Alaska. Contact Frank Griffin, P.O. Box 6081, Ketchikan. AK 99901. (907) 225-3747.

Herring Bay Charters. Fishing day charters for two-four people for salmon, halibut, trout and crab. We will assist you in making local accommodations for lodging. Write 3225 Tongass Ave., Ketchikan, AK 99901. (907) 255-4869 evenings.

Ketchikan Marine Charters. Sportfishing and transportation charters, local and nearby area, day or overnight parties up to six. Association of Coast Guard certified boats and skippers. Write Box 7896, Ketchikan, AK 99901. (907) 225-2628.

Knudson Cove Marina. For skiff rental or skippered charters. Full bait and tackle shop. Fuel dock for regular, outboard premix or No.2 Diesel. Licenses, derby information and weigh-ins. Daily from 6 a.m. to 9 p.m. Snacks and sandwiches to go. Route 1, Box 965, Ketchikan, AK 99901. (907) 247-8500.

Royal Highway Tours. Ketchikan sightseeing to Totem Bight, a Tlingit totem site. Write Royal Highway Tours, 2815 Second Ave., Suite 400; Seattle, WA 98121. (206) 441-8428 or 800-647-7750.

Sea Charters. Guided fishing for salmon, halibut and crab in S.E. Alaska waters aboard 44' fully equipped yacht. Four guest maximum. Personal items, license available. Three-day two-night, to five-day, four-night charters. Also day charters. Write Box 677, Ketchikan, AK 99901. (907) 247-2490.

KLAWOCK

Klawock Wilderness Adventure. Log cabin camp grounds. R.V. hook-ups, rustic beach cabins, modern kitchen and bath. Outboards, skiffs, canoes. Fish in rivers, lakes, saltwater for salmon and halibut. Charters (licensed captain) canoe, hike, birdwatch, photography. Write Box 54, Klawock, AK 99925, (907) 755-2205.

West Coast Charters. Located on Prince of Wales Island, west of Ketchikan. Sightsee and fish for king or silver salmon and halibut is protected inside waters of SE Alaska. Bait and gear provided. Write Dick Echols, Box 133, Klawock, AK 99925. (907) 755-2205.

PETERSBURG

Moonlight Charters. Salmon, halibut and trout fishing for the serious or casual angler. Catch crab, shrimp and other marine delicacies or sightsee. Transportation for up to six persons to remote cabins. Specialize in evenings, weekends and early mornings. Contact Jim Schramek, Box 745, Petersburg, AK 99833. (907) 772-3337.

O'Neil Charters. Full and half-day excursions to spectacular LeConte, Glacier Bay and/or sportfishing charters on the 40' Cruise a Home *Without a Doubt*. Six guests mamimum. Write Skipper Bert O'Neil, Box 255, Petersburg, Alaska 99833. (907) 772-4700.

Tongass Marine Boat Rentals. Based in Petersburg, offers rental boats on two-day minimum basis for sportfishing, access to remote Forest Service cabins. Boats are suitable for inland light tackle fishing as well as deep water trolling. Write John Murgas, Tongass Marine, P.O. Box 1314, Petersburg, AK 99833. (907) 772-3905.

Viking Alaska Tours. Petersburg area fishing and hunting charters. 16' to 45' boats with equipment available for half-day, day and longer charter offerings. Local tour specialists. Box 787, Petersburg, AK 99833. (907) 772-4266.

SITKA

Alaska Day Festival. Historical commemoration of transfer of Alaska from Russia to the U.S. Original transfer took place in Sitka, capital of Russian America. Three-day festival features re-enactment of the transfer ceremony and other festivities culminating on October 18, an Alaska State holiday, with an annual costume ball. Write Vyola Belle, Box 102, Sitka, AK 99835. (907) 747-8814.

All Alaska Logging Championships. Seventeen events including world championships in the Hooktender's Race and Team Splicing. Over $10,000 in prize money. Write Vern Eliason, Box 1050, Sitka, AK 99835. Call (907) 747-225.

Allen Marine Tours. A two and one-half hour cruise from Sitka aboard the 63' *St. Aquilina*, featuring wildlife, scenic beauty and historical goldmining area. Depart daily June 1–August 31. Special runs for cruiseship passengers. Tickets available at Pursers Office. Write Box 1049, Sitka, AK 99835. (907) 747-8941 or 747-5111.

Connie Lyn Charters. Comfortable 36' tri-cabin boat available for salmon and bottom fishing, May through August. Six passengers maximum. Part day, all day, or weekend trips. Write 1101 Edgecumbe Drive, Sitka, AK 99835, or call (907) 747-8259 for further information.

Marine Wildlife Exploration. Travel by yacht and motorized raft through the islands and waterways that surround Sitka. Visit the seal rookery and bird refuge where you may see muir, puffin and cormorant colonies. Opportunities to sight sea lions, porpoises and whales. 9085 Glacier Highway, Juneau, AK 99801, telex 090-45380. (907) 789-0052.

Sea Comber Excursions. 60' yacht, sleeps eight in four staterooms. Gourmet food, fine wines, fishing, glacier flights, photography, duck/goose hunting and on-shore exploration. Experience past and present Native cultures and meet noted native artists (stress management seminar optional). Write 5443 California Ave., S.W. Seattle, WA 98136. 9206) 938-1846; telex 3247 Attn. SCE 313. 800-732-2662.

Sitka Ferry Stopover Tour. During ferry port arrival. Stops are made at Sitka National "Totem Park" and Sheldon Jackson Museum. Depending on the hour of arrival, the Russian Cathedral may be substituted for the museum. $8 Adult, $4 Child. Approximately 45 min. allowed for shopping. Call Prewitt Enterprises (907) 747-8443.

Sitka National Historical Park. This park is the site of the Battle of Sitka in 1804 between Tlingit Indians and the Russians. Located in a woodland setting with a magnificent collection of totem poles and an interpretive center for Russian and Indian history.

SKAGWAY

Alaska Sightseeing Tours. "Days of '98" tour to Gold Rush Cemetery, historic district, White Pass Railroad, Skagway lookout. Also tour to Dyea, historic jumping-off point for Chilkoot Trail. Contact Alaska Sightseeing at Golden North Hotel, (907) 983-2828. Also Trailblazer Tour to Anchorage via Valdez.

Days of '98 Show. Good family fun for all. Spend an evening gambling with our phoney money. See the gold rush history of Skagway unfold on the stage of our 250 seat theater. Shows mid-May through mid-Sept. nightly. Matinees for cruise ships. Tickets at the door, or write for reservations to: Soapy Smith, Box 1897, Skagway, AK 99840.

Gold Rush Cemetery and Reid Falls. Graves of many gold rush stampeders, including those of Soapy Smith, notorious gambler and gangster, and Frank Reid, town surveyor, who shot and killed each other, are located here. Nearby is Reid Falls. Cemetery is an easy two-mile (3.2 km) level walk from ferry terminal.

Relive the Klondike Goldrush! Explore trail head of the historic Chilkoot Trail. See gold rush artifacts, structures and cemetery. Includes sourdough pancake snack, gold panning, transportation from Skagway and guide. Contact 200 North Franklin St., Juneau, AK 99801. (907) 586-6245 or toll free 800-227-8480, telex 090-45380.

Royal Highway Tours. "Sourdough" tour by motorcoach. Sightseeing of historical Skagway highlighting "Days of '98." Write Royal Highway 2815 Second Ave., Suite 400, Seattle, WA 98121.441-8428. 800-647-7750.

Skagway Hack. Horsedrawn transportation in the Klondike National Park. Carriage rides and town tours available from 8 a.m. to 8 p.m. daily, June–September. Costumed guides tell tales of archvillian that ran 1898 Skagway on the Soapy Smith Excursion which departs 3rd and Broadway at 10 a.m. and 3 p.m. daily. (907) 983-2472.

TENAKEE SPRINGS

Snyder Mercantile Co. Cabins, cottages and boats for hire. Grocery store. Hot springs, fishing, hunting and hiking tours. Mr. Don Pegues, P.O. Box 505, Tenakee Springs, AK 99841. (907) 736-2205.

WRANGELL

4th of July Celebration and Logging Show. Annual salmon bake, crowning of queen, parade, logging show, fishing derby for king salmon, boat races and other festivities for all. Write Wrangell Chamber of Commerce. Box 49, Wrangell, AK 99929.

Garnet Ledge. Approximately five miles (8 km) north of Wrangell near mouth of Stikine River. Access by boat or plane. Rock hounds may search for garnets and, although most are fractured and not of gem quality, some can be faceted and can be hand polished. No charge for children, fee for adults and a permit is necessary. Contact Wrangell Museum, Box 1050-W, Wrangell, AK 99929. (907) 874-3770.

Tent City Winter Festival. Festival recalling early days when Wrangell was a city of tents erected by gold prospectors who wintered over there so they could get an early start for the gold fields in the spring. Long john contests, Shady Lady Ball, children's games, endurance race up Mt. Dewey. Write Wrangell Chamber of Commerce, Box 49, Wrangell, AK 99929.

Wrangell Charter Boat Association. Custom trips, sportfishing and one to two hours on the Stikine River, or a week of camping and exploring. Enjoy the Stikine River hot tubs with waters from natural hot springs. Trips also arranged for sightseeing and photography. Write Box 1078, Wrangell, AK 99929. (907) 874-3800.

SOUTHCENTRAL

Alaska Fishing and Wilderness Adventures. Offering trips into Katmai National Park. Lake Clark National Park and Kenai National Wildlife Refuge. Fish and explore some of the most incredible waters in Alaska. Contact Bill Wright, 938 P St., Anchorage, AK 99501. (907) 279-0919.

Alaska Float Trips. Experience the wildlife, fishing and sights of Alaska by canoe or raft. Led by Alaskans knowledgeable in your destinations. Scheduled custom exploratory and wilderness skill development experiences available. Half day to two weeks. May-Oct. Write Box 8264, Anchorage, AK 99508. (907) 333-4442.

Alaska Natural History Safari. Ten days includes Kenai National Wildlife Refuge, Chugach National Forest, Kenai Fjords National Park. Wide variety of outdoor wilderness adventures. First class safari equipment and guides. Contact Alaska Fishing and Wilderness Adventures, 938 P St., Anchorage, AK 99501. (907) 279-0919.

Alaska Pioneer Canoers Association. Guided or unguided trips, canoe rentals, sportfishing in the Kenai National Wildlife Refuge and Swan Lake Wilderness Canoe Trail. Write John Stephan, Box 931, Soldotna, AK 99669. (907) 262-4003.

Alaska Rivers. One to 14 days floats. Experience the untouched country and abundant wildlife of western Alaska, or chase the thrills of southcentral's whitewater. We float past wildlife, scenery, historical and cultural sites. Great photographic material. Write Alaska Rivers and Ski Tours. 1831 Kuskowim, Anchorage, AK 99508. (907) 276-3418.

Alaska Travel Adventures. Fly-drive adventure tours by camper or auto. Included on each of several routes are short, guided float trips, hikes, fishing, flightseeing and sightseeing. Camping and fishing gear are included. Write 200 North Franklin Street, Juneau, AK 99801. (907) 586-6245 or toll free 800-227-8480, telex 090-45380.

Alaska Wilderness Safaris, Inc. Located between Chugach and Talkeetna Mountains with transportation furnished from Anchorage. Complete room and board. Two, three or four-day horseback riding, hiking, backpacking trips. Dall sheep, grizzly/black bear, moose and caribou hunts. Seven-day fishing trips, extended outdoor adventure tour. Write SRC, Box 8512, Palmer, AK 99645. (907) 745-5118.

Alpine Llamas. Llama pack trips into beautiful Kachemak Bay State Park near Homer. Opportunities for exploring glaciers, birding, trout fishing, canoeing and non-technical mountain climbing. We offer personalized trips. Transportation, meals, gear and guide service all provided. Write Box 1557, Homer, AK 99603. (907) 296-2217.

Arctic Tramp. 48' motorsailor accommodates up to six passengers for two-five day cruises among islands, glaciers and fjords of Prince William Sound. Explore the ruins of Indians, miners and fox farms. Visit Columbia Glacier. Sportfishing and day trips also available. Write Alaska Charter Service, Box 827, Valdez, AK 99686. (907) 835-2378.

Columbia Glacier Cruises. Tours of Prince William Sound aboard the *Glacier Queen*, from Whittier to Valdez. Five hours one way, lunch served en route. Complete tour begins in Anchorage. For information, write Box 100479, Anchorage, AK 99510. (907) 276-8866, or toll free 800-544-2206.

Devil's Mountain Guiding and Outfitting Service. Mile 42 Nabesna Rd. Photography, backpacking, raft trips, sightseeing trips. SR Box 370, Gakona, AK 99586. (907) 822-3426.

Genet Expeditions. Guided climbing expeditions on Mt. Mckinley, throughout the Alaska Range and the Wrangell Mountains. Ruth Amphitheater ski trips, youth wilderness courses and custom trips anywhere in Alaska are also available. Write or call Genet Expeditions, Talkeetna, AK 99676. (907) 376-5120.

Kachemak Alpine Guides Service. Hiking, wildlife viewing, summer glacier skiing, rope climbs in the Kachemak Alps, river floats, ocean kayaking in Kenai Fjords, or any combination. All trips custom. Guide and all necessary equipment provided. Write SRA #31, Homer, AK 99603. (907) 235-6094.

Kenai Canyon Float Trips. Unique daily raft trips into the heart of Kenai National Wildlife Refuge in Cooper Landing. Great rapids, great lunches and great fun. Also overnights, fishing and rustic river cabins. Contact Alaska Fishing and Wilderness Adventures, Bill Wright, 938 P St., Anchorage, AK 99501. (907) 279-0919.

Kenai Fjords-Prince William Sound Seacoast Charters. Seacoast charters between Cordova, Alaska and Seward, Alaska including Columbia Glacier. Observe whales, rookies and marine mammals of all types. Can be geared to fishing or natural history. Contact Bill Wright, 938 P St., Anchorage, AK 99501. (907) 279-0919.

Keystone Canyon Tours. Daily trips through Keystone Canyon, one of Alaska's great river runs. Also expedition trips, special charters, raft support kayak trips. Trips vary from whitewater, wilderness expeditions, hunting charters to fishing float trips. Write Mike Buck, Box 1486, Valdez, AK 99686. (907) 835-5234.

Keystone Raft and Kayak Adventures. Wilderness whitewater adventures, fishing and camping. Raft trips from two hours to two weeks. Kayak support trips and class III, IV and V kayak excursions. Our guides will show you the real Alaska. Write P.O. Box 1486, Valdez, AK 99686. (907) 835-5234.

Matanuska River Day Trip and Lionshead Wildwater. Four hour raft trips on exciting rivers located about 76½ miles (123 km) N.E. of Anchorage. Cost includes transportation from Anchorage. Two-day helicopter and rafting trip on the Chickaloon River. NOVA Riverrunners of Alaska, P.O. Box 444, Eagle River, AK 99577. (907) 694-3750.

Mt. McKinley Alaska Glacier Tours. Independent travel arrangements throughout Alaska and Canada's Yukon and Northwest Territories with special one to five-day package economy tours and fly-drive packages from Anchorage. Write Box 102315, Anchorage, AK 99510. (907) 274-8539.

National Outdoor Leadership School. Comprehensive wilderness skills training. Mountaineering and backpacking in the Alaska, Chugach, Talkeetna and Brooks ranges; sea-kayaking in Prince William Sound and S.E.; kayaking in the Brooks Range; fishing in Wood-Tickchik Lakes. Write NOLS, Dept. K, Box 981, Palmer, AK 99645. (907) 745-332-6973.

Northsport. Guided raft trips through some of the most beautiful country in Alaska. Fishing, photography, sightseeing. Remote cabins available. One to seven-day trips. Air transportation via small plane available with advance notice. Write P.O. Box 40, Talkeetna, AK 99676.

Portage River Adventures. A scenic float trip beginning at beautiful Portage Glacier. Wildlife and glacier viewing en route. Safe and fun for all ages. Write Robert Crockett, P.O. Box 261, Girdwood, AK 99587.

River Adventure Frontier Trips. Write Skip Richards, Box 3401, Homer, AK 99603. (907) 235-7474.

Ski Adventure. One to ten-day cross country ski adventures. Fly into Ruth Glacier (Mt. McKinley) and stay in Don Sheldon's cabin at 6,000 feet (1829 m). Fly into a rustic wilderness lodge or ski cabin-to-cabin. Find the best snow of the moment from an Alaskan roadhouse. Write Alaska River and Ski

Tours, 1831 Kuskowin St., Anchorage, AK 99508. (907) 276-3418.

Stan Stephens Charters. Daily Columbia Glacier cruises aboard the 80' *Glacier Spirit*. For special overnight Columbia Glacier cruises the 52' *Vince Peede* departs at 1 p.m. Also available for overnight sportfishing, hunting and/or photography we have the 26' *Doreen* and 28' *Mary Helen*. Special interest charters are available. Write Box 1297, Valdez, AK 99686. (907) 835-4731.

St. Elias Alpine Guides. Specialists in the Wrangell/St. Elias National Park. Rafting, glacier exploring, backpacking, day hiking and sightseeing the old Kennicott mines. High altitude mountaineering expedition and International Mountain Camp. Guides and guides apprentice programs. Bob or Babbie Jacobs, Box 111241, Anchorage, AK 99511. (907) 277-6867.

Talkeetna River Service. Excellent trout and salmon fishing May through Sept. Guided and unguided trips, one or more days. Cabins and gear available. Transportation from Anchorage available via airplane with advance notice. Write Mac Stevens, Box 74, Talkeetna, AK 99676. (907) 733-2281.

Wild Country River Guides. Wilderness adventure for maximum six people. Float-fishing for five species: salmon, rainbow, dolly varden, arctic char and grayling from remote Iliamna watershed system. Wide variety wildlife, birds and wildflowers for viewing or photographing. Write Chip Marinella, SRA 180-F 12020 Timberlane Dr., Anchorage, AK 99515. (907) 349-9173.

Wilder Tours. Scenic historical tours to the Cook Inlet region. Wilderness river tours. Fly-in and jetboat tours for the photographer. Daily historical tours. Cook Inlet tours, wildlife, Mt. McKinley and wilderness river tours. Fishing in Bristol Bay or river float fishing trips. Write 2502 W. 43rd Court, Anchorage, AK 99503. (907) 243-6813.

Wrangell-St. Elias Mountaineering. Scheduled mountaineering, skiing, trekking and float expeditions in Wrangell-St. Elias National Park. Climbing trips to Mt. Sanford, Mt. Drum, Granite Range. Float trips on the Copper River. Trekking in the Chitna Valley. Write for a brochure. David Staeheli, Box 11-1816, Anchorage, AK 99511. (907) 688-9958.

Zephyr North River Expeditions. Eagle River and Matanuska River guided trips daily with paddle rafts or oar boats. One-half and one day trips include lunch. Discounts available for groups and families. Two to six days trips on the Gulkana, Talkeetna and Copper Rivers. Charters and white-water school. Write/call 2915, Glacier Street, Anchorage, AK 99508. (907) 338-2688.

ANCHORAGE

Alaska Show and Sourdough Buffet. Watch a show and eat with Alaska's Ambassador Larry Beck doing Robert Service and his own poems, songs, stories and other Alaskana. Dinner and show or show only. Write Larry Beck,945 West 12th Ave., Anchorage, Alaska 99501 or call (907) 278-3831 for reservations and information.

Alaksa Sled Dog Racing Association. During winter months sled dog races held every Saturday and Sunday at 11 a.m. and 1 p.m. at Tudor Road sled dog race track. Teams from all over Alaska and the rest of the world gather for these events. Spectators are welcome. Write Box 10-569, Anchorage, AK 99501. (907) 243-0608 evenings.

Alaska Women's Run. Held in early June. Write Larry Ross, 3605 Arctic No. AA, Anchorage, AK 99503.

Alyeska Portage. Two days/one night. Coach down Turnagain Arm to Portage Glacier and Alyeska Resort. Ride chairlift for a panoramic view and lunch at the Skyline Restaurant. Pan for gold at historic Crow Creek Gold Mine. Next day, time for shopping and a river rafting tour down the Portage River. Write Discovery Tours, Box 8800, Ketchikan, AK 99901. (907) 279-7033.

Alyeska Resort. Year round resort 40 miles (64 km) S.E. of Anchorage on Seward Hwy. Five double chairlifts, nightskiing, hotel and condominium accommodations, daylodge, convention facilities, Sitzmark Bar and Skyride Restaurant, ski school, alpine and telemark skiing, ski rental and repair, ski shops, dog sledding and sleigh rides. Summer sightseeing chairlift ride. Write Box 249, Girdwood, AK 99587. (907) 783-2222.

Crow Creek Gold Mine. Eight-hour tour begins with scenic drive down Turnagain Arm to Portage Glacier, then to resort area of Mt. Alyeska for chairlift ride to the Skyline Restaurant for lunch. Try your luck panning for gold at Crow Creek Mine and return to Anchorage late afternoon. Write Discovery Tours, Box 8800, Ketchikan, AK 99901, or call (907) 279-7033.

Crow Creek Mine. 1898 historic gold mining building with artifacts, now on National Register of Historic Places. Open to tourists to pan, play, purchase gold in our shop. All equipment furnished, gold guaranteed for panners. Overnight camping. Accommodate groups up to 200. Write Cynthia Toohey, Box 113, Girdwood, AK 99587.

Ft. Richardson Fish and Wildlife Center. Open summer Mon-Fri., 9 a.m.-5 p.m., Sat. 10 a.m.-4 p.m.; Sun. 12 noon-4 p.m.. After Sept. 1 Mon-Fri., 9 a.m.-5 p.m. Building 600, Rm 114, Ft. Richardson, AK 99505. (907) 863-8113 or 8288.

Goose Lake Dog Sled Rides. Take to the wooded trails of downtown Anchorage in a dog sled and get the feel of Alaska bush travel. One-half and one hour tours operating Nov. 15-Apr. 15. Bob Crockett, Box 757, Girdwood, AK 99587. (907) 272-3883 or 783-2266.

Grayline of Anchorage. Motorcoach city sightseeing tours including tours of Portage Glacier and Alyeska Resort, Matanuska Valley and the Columbia Glacier. Package tours to Mt. Mckinley, Fairbanks, Valdez, Whitehorse and Skagway. Write P.O. Box 100479, Anchorage, AK 99510. (907) 276-8866, or toll free 800-544-2206.

Mayor's Midnight Sun Marathon. Write Jim Mayo, Municipality of Anchorage Parks and Recreation Dept., Pouch 6-650, Anchorage, AK 99502.

Old Anchorage Salmon Bake. June 1-Sept. 15, seven days a week, 11 a.m. to 9 p.m. Near the site of the Original 1916 Tent City, North of Bluff at 3rd and "K" Streets. Salmon, halibut, reindeer sausage, special salad bar. Free transportation from Anchorage area. (907) 276-4325.

Quest Charters. Motorcoach pick-up and return from downtown Anchorage hotels for daily sightseeing of Seward and tours of Resurrection Bay. Overnight cruises, sportfishing aboard 70' motor yacht *Pacific Star*. Homer halibut fishing and sightseeing daily aboard 53' sportfishing vessel *Resolution*. May-Sept. Write 2240 East Tudor Rd., Suite 116. Anchorage, AK 99507. (907) 337-6532.

Royal Highway Tours. Deluxe motorcoach tours of Anchorage area including Portage Glacier, Whittier and the Matanuska Valley. Write Royal Highway Tours, 2815 Second Ave, Suite 400, Seattle, WA 98121. (206) 441-8428 or 800 647-7755.

University of Alaska, Anchorage. Special events include: First Interstate Hockey Classic, Great Alaska Shoot-out and the Northern Lights Invitational. For information on any of the above write to Tim McDiffett, 3211 Providence Dr., Anchorage Dr., Anchorage, AK 99508.

CORDOVA

Cordova, "Alaska's Best Kept Secret". Guided tours available to see this picturesque fishing town on Prince William Sound. Visit Million Dollar Bridge, Sheridan Glacier, ride chairlift to the top of Eyak Mountain, see Alaska birds and wildlife, tour a salmon cannery. Call or write: Irene Gunnerson, Box 1210, Cordova, AK 99574. (907) 424-6200.

Cordova Iceworm Festival. Feb 1-3, 1985. Annual celebration of the emergence of the legendary iceworm of Robert Service fame. Cordova battles mid-winter cabin fever with a parade, blessing of the fishing fleet, talent show, arts and crafts display, photo show and culinary delights. Write Box 819, Cordova, AK 99574. (907) 424-5168.

HOMER

Alaska's Last Frontier Show. P.O. Box 3124, Homer, AK 99603. (907) 235-8713.

Alaska Wild Berry Products. Manufacturers of Alaskan Wild Berry Jams and Jellies. Our taster's stand is open May-Sept. to sample free Wild Berry jams and jellies begin made. Gift shop, Alaskan artifacts on display. Write Alaska Wild Berry Products, 528 E. Pioneer Ave., Homer, AK 99603. (907) 235-8858.

Homer Tours. Visit beautiful Homer Alaska, where the land ends and the sea begins. Kachemak Bay four-hour tour includes local artists, fish processing plant, bird and wildflower identification, Pratt Museum, Berry Kitchens and much more. Contact Gert Seekins, Box 1264, Homer, AK 99603. (907) 235-8996.

Homer Tours Charters. Booking charters for halibut and salmon fishing on beautiful Kachemak Bay. Also sightseeing and glacier tours of the Bay. Contact Floyd and Gert Seekins, Homer, AK (907) 235-8996.

Inlet Charters. Sportfishing for halibut in Kachemak Bay. Three six-passenger boats with enclosed cabins; equipment and bait furnished. Located on the Boardwalk on Homer Spit. Write Maxine Barr, Box 2083, Homer, AK 99603. (907) 235-6126 or 235-5544.

Kachemak Bay Horse Trips. A unique wilderness beach experience for two to eight people 12 years old or older. One to four-day trips include overnight lodging in a rustic, cozy homestead cabin, all meals, your own horse and gear, experienced, bilingual (English/German) wrangler. Vacation cabins available. Write Mairiis Davidson, Box 2004, Homer, AK 99603. (907) 235-7850.

Pratt Museum. Natural and cultural history of Kenai Peninsular. Over 4,000 Alaskan objects, including marine aquarium, botanical garden, Alaskan mammals, marine birds, Eskimo, Indian and Aleut tools and clothing, model marine vessels and whale skeleton. Film program Thursday nights June-August. Open 10 a.m.-5 p.m. daily. Brochure available. Write 3779 Barlett St., Homer, AK 99603.

Rainbow Tours. On the boardwalk at Homer Spit. One and one-half to six hour tours; Natural History tour to Peterson Bay, five hours; Gull Island Bird Rookery, one and one-half hours. Water taxi for camping, hiking etc. also available. Hotel accommodations in Seldovia can be arranged. Group rates. P.O. Box 1526, Homer, AK 99603. (907) 235-7272.

Silver Fox Charters. Sportfishing for halibut in Cook Inlet. Six radio-equipped fiberform boats, maximum six per boat. Gear and bait furnished. Write Donna Hinkle, Box 402, Homer, AK 99603. Reservations required. (907) 235-8792.

KENAI

Kenai Guide Service. Guided and unguided hunts, fishing trips, wilderness backpacking. Write George R. Pollard, Master Guide, Kasilof, AK 99610. (907) 262-5496.

Kenai River Driftboat Fishing. Offering a special way to fish the Upper Kenai River. Work the pools and eddies to catch king and silver salmon, rainbows and dollies. Available daily. Located south of Anchorage in Cooper Landing. Rustic river cabins are also available. Box 26, Cooper Landing, AK 99572. Free 800-334-8730 or (907) 595-1279.

Kenai River Fishing. Fish for world's largest king salmon in May, June, and July. Silver salmon fishing August, September and October. All gear furnished. We handle all arrangements, including hotel reservations. Write Harry Gaines, Box 624, Kenai, AK 99611. For reservations, call (907) 283-4618.

Pacific Coast Charters. Fishing from March through September, specializing in steelhead, trophy king salmon and fall silvers, on the Kenai Peninsular and southeast Alaska. Box 3807, Soldotna, AK 99669, (907) 262-4493.

PALMER

Alaska State Fair, Inc. Located Mile 40 on the Glenn Highway. Showcases of agriculture for Alaska during the 11-day event ending annually on Labor Day. More than 5,000 prime exhibits depicting all phases of agriculture and homemaking. Write Marsha M. Melton, Box 1128, Palmer, AK 99645. (907) 745-4827.

Matanuska Guest Ranch and Riding Stables. Horseback trail riding daily 9 a.m. to 5 p.m. Also summer horse camp for girls and boys 8 thru 14. Matanuska Lake on Trunk Road near junction of Glenn and Parks Highway, 34 miles (55 km) north of Anchorage. Write SRA 6157, Palmer, AK 99645. (907) 745-3693.

PRINCE WILLIAM SOUND

Choice Marine Charters. Experience the beauty of Prince William Sound. Plan a recreational outing at a location of your choice. Cruise Alaska waters on the motoryacht *Waterbed*, 38' twin diesel, luxurious accommodations. CG licensed captain, documented vessel. One-night and custom excursions. Write Jack Gilman, Box 3592, Anchorage, AK 99501. (907) 243-0069.

Columbia Glacier Cruise. 65' yacht cruises daily May 24-Sept. 15 from Valdez to Whittier, featuring Alaska Pipeline terminal facilities, then to Columbia Glacier. Harbor seals, sea lions, otters, whales and birdlife may be seen. One-two day packages offered. Write Alaska Sightseeing Co., 349 Wrangell Ave., Anchorage, AK 99501. (907) 276-1305. 800-637-3334.

Sea Hunter Charters. Sportfishing, hunting, sightseeing in Prince William Sound. Overnight or extended trips available. Food and tackle provided. Licensed ocean operators. Write Don, Box 621, Eagle River, AK 99501, (907) 694-2229.

Water Wilderness Guides and Outfitters. Explore the deep bays and fjords of Prince William Sound. Accept the challenge of safely venturing along a bird-filled shoreline. 2-7 days, 4-8 persons. Customs trips available for all budgets and interests. Statewide recognized guides. University credit available. Write Helen Woodings, Box 1386, Palmer, AK 99645. (907) 745-3487.

SEAWARD

Fantasea Charters. Fishing and sightseeing on beautiful Resurrection Bay at Seward. Mid-April through Sept. Fish for halibut, salmon, bottom fish. Sightsee Kenai Fjords and Resurrection Bay. Small parties welcome. For reservations call (907) 248-0302 or write 9221 Kirkwall Circle, Anchorage, AK 99515.

Mt. Marathon Races. Annual Independence Day event in Seward. Tough, grueling race attracts runners from all over the world. Junior race held at 11 a.m. and Seniors at 2 p.m. with entry limited to 200 per race. Write Director, Mt. Marathon Races, Box 756, Seward, AK 99664. (907) 224-3046.

SLANA

Hard D Ranch. Located at Slana, the community Post Office. At the ranch you will find the Fine Art Gallery, studio of bronze sculptor, Mary Frances DeHart, featuring extensive wildlife trophy display. Hard D sled dogs may be photographed in their own "Husky Village." Write Mary Frances Dehart, Slana, AK 99586. (907) 822-3973.

SOLDOTNA

Alaska Outdoor Services. We can help you with your fishing, hunting, photography, hiking, transportation or accommodations. Our services are aimed at your needs and budget. Guided, unguided and outfitted trip available. Group and family rates. Write Box 1066, Soldotna, AK 99669. (907) 262-4589.

Johnson Bros. Salmon Charters. Fish for the largest strain of king salmon in the world on the Kenai River. 20' river boats. King salmon run during June and July, average 40 pounds (18 kg). Pinks and silvers run during August and September. Write Box 3774, Soldotna, AK 99669. (907) 262-5357.

Rex's Kenai River Fishing Charters. Fish the Kenai River for king and silver salmon. 18' Alumuweld river boats. Experienced, licensed guides. Two 5-hour charters per day. Fishing gear provided. May 15- Oct. 1. Call or write 4120 Dorothy Dr., Anchorage, AK 99504. (907) 333-0092, or P.O. Box 4525, Soldotna, AK 99669. (907) 262-7499.

STERLING

Wrangell R Ranch. Outfitting point for trail rides and family trips which include photography, sportfishing, rockhunting and wilderness sightseeing. Write Box 10, Sterling, AK 99672. (907) 262-4678.

TALKEETNA

Mahay's Riverboat Service. Sportfishing for rainbow, dolly varden, grayling, salmon. Camping and gear rentals. Write Stephen T. Mahay, Box 133, Talkeetna, AK 99676. (907) 733-2353 or 733-2223.

Miners Day Celebration. Local festival held the 3rd weekend in May of each year. Write to Talkeetna Chamber of Commerce-VP, c/o Ms. Pam Rannals, President, Talkeetna, AK 99676.

Moose Dropping Festival. First weekend in July. Write: Talkeetna Historical Society, Talkeetna, AK 99676.

Race for Gold. 10-K footrace held the third weekend in May as part of the Miners Day Celebration. Write: Fairview Inn, P.O. Box 379, Talkeetna, AK 99676.

Talkeetna Bachelor's Society. Bachelor Ball held the first weekend in December. Activities include dog sled rides, music, dancing and the Bachelor Auction. Write: President, Talkeetna Bachelor Society, c/o Fairview Inn, P.O. Box 379, Talkeetna, AK 99676.

VALDEZ

Coho Charters. Fishing, hunting, sightseeing, marine taxi. Full day, half day or hourly charters. Reasonable rates. U.S. Coast Guard licensed and insured operators. Charters restricted to six or less passengers. All bait and gear furnished. Write Box 1103, Valdez, AK 99686. Or call (907) 835-4435.

WILLOW

Capital Speedway. Racetrack open one week before Memorial Day until one week after Labor Day. Superstocks, B-stocks, mini-stocks and bomberstocks. Gates open every Sunday at 5 p.m. Also restaurant and liquor store. Mile 75.5 Parks Highway, north of Willow. (907) 495-6420.

INTERIOR & FAR NORTH

Alaska Fish and Trail Unlimited. Backpacking, fishing, river rafting, wildlife photography in Alaska's Brooks Range. Write 1177 Shypoke Dr, Fairbanks, AK 99709. (907) 479-7630.

Arctic Treks. Wilderness backpacking and rafting in Brooks Range. Two-week combination trips and 7-10 day base camp day hiking trips in Gates of the Arctic and remote Arctic National Wildlife Refuge. Recognized Outfitters and Guides – Alaska Wilderness Guides Assoc. Write Box 73452, Fairbanks, AK 99707. (907) 455-6502.

Brooks Range Expeditions. Guided river, hiking trips in Brooks Range. Canoe, raft, hike with Alaska Wilderness Guide Association certified guides. Unguided trips, canoe rentals. Brochure available. Write Box 7, Bettles, AK 99726. (907) 692-5333 or 692-5444..

Sourdough Outfitters. Guided and unguided wilderness trips in the central and western Brooks Range. The oldest outfitting business in the Arctic offers canoe, raft, kayak trips and backpacking throughout the Brooks Range; dogsled, cross-country ski trips, raft, canoe, cabin rentals. For brochure write Box 90, Bettles, AK 99726, or call (907) 692-5252.

Wilderness Alaska. Fifteen years experience guiding Brooks Range backpacking, river and cross country ski trips. Custom and scheduled trips throughout the Brooks Range. Special focus on wilderness skills and field biology unique to the high arctic. Write to 6710 Potter Heights Drive, Anchorage, AK, (907) 345-3366 for brochure.

DELTA JUNCTION

Deltana Fair. Held first full weekend in August in Delta Junction. Highlights are the Chamber of Commerce barbeque, University of Alaska Coopera-

tive Extension Agricultural Tour, Lions Club Pancake Breakfast. Write Box 408, Delta Junction, AK 99737. (907) 895-4627.

DENALI PARK

Alaska-Denali Guiding. Join us for one day to one week at our remote, lakeside log cabin or for a three-week Alaska Wonder Tour. We also offer Denali Expeditions and other climbs within Denali National Park. Hiking, rafting and cross-country skiing. For information, write Alaska-Denali Guiding, Box 566, Talkeetna, AK 99676. (907) 733-2649.

Denali Raft Adventures. Float fishing trips of various lengths. A total river-fishing experience at reasonable prices. Comfortable tent camps with everything furnished. Write Drawer 190, Denali Park, AK 99755. (907) 683-2234 or 337-9604.

Camp Denali. In the geographical heart of Denali National Park. Wilderness vacation retreat featuring "bush" country living. All-expense "Sourdough" vacations, housekeeping, cabin rentals, hiking, canoeing, goldpanning, photo workshops. Naturalist guides and interpretive programs. For brochure write Mile 156 Parks Highway, Box 13229, Trapper Creek, AK 99683.

Denali National Park Central Reservations and Travel, Inc. Central booking service for Denali National Park area. Lodging, tours and activities. Full service travel agency for all of Alaska. P.O. Box 597, Denali National Park, AK 99775. (907) 274-5366. Denali office open May/Sept. Anchorage office open year round.

McKinley Raft Tours. Float the western boundary of Denali National Park on the Nenana River. Great whitewater, beautiful scenery and a wildlife viewing. Raingear provided. Open from mid May through mid September. Reservations recommended. Write for free brochure. P.O. Box 138, Denali National Park, AK 99755. (907) 683-2392 or 683-2581.

Tundra Wildlife Tour. Six to seven-hour tour through the Alaska Range in Denali National Park. Buses depart from McKinley Chalets and Denali National Park Hotel daily at 6 a.m. and 3 p.m. Write 825 W. Eight Avenue, #240, Anchorage, AK 99501. (907) 276-7234.

FAIRBANKS

Alaskaland. Features historical exhibits and artifacts from all over Alaska. Gold Rush Town historical log cabins house gift shops, Native Village and Pioneer Museum. Mining Valley, Big Stampede Show, Bear Art Gallery, 30-gauge railroad rides. Commuter tram from downtown area. Write Park

Office, 410 Cushman, Fairbanks, AK 99701. (907) 452-4529.

Alaska River Charters. Tours of the Chena and Tanana Rivers from Fairbanks. Phone (907) 455-6825.

Alaska Salmon Bake. Open seven days a week, 5 a.m.-9 p.m. from June 1 to mid-Sept. Free transportation from hotels. Located in Alaskaland Pioneer Park. (907) 452-7274 or 452-3049.

Alaska Sightseeing Company. City and riverboat "Discovery." Trailblazer tours to Haines. Golden Circle tour to Anchorage, Valdez, Denali Park. Contact Alaska Sightseeing at golden Nugget Motel, 900 Noble, Fairbanks, AK 99701.(907) 452-8518 or toll free in "Lower 48 states" 1-800-426-7702.

Gold Rush Tours. See the many attractions Fairbanks has to offer. Take a ride on our Historical City tour, Sternwheel Riverboat cruise. Gold Dredge tour, or the Ragtime-Evening tour and enjoy the Old Golden days atmosphere. Write c/o 1170 Propwash, Fairbanks, AK 99709 (907) 455-6208.

Golden Days Celebration. Citywide pageant held each July commemorating the discovery of gold near Fairbanks in 1902. For information contact the Fairbanks Chamber of Commerce, 550 First Ave., Fairbanks, AK 99701. (907) 452-1105.

Grayline of Fairbanks. Motorcoach city sightseeing tours including Malemute Saloon. Four hour cruises on stern-wheeler "Discovery" on the Chena and Tanana Rivers. Package tours to surrounding areas including Mt. McKinley, Anchorage, Whitehorse and Skagway. 820 Noble Street, Fairbanks, AK 99701. (907) 452-2843 or 800-544-2206.

Lambert's Guide Service. Fishing trips available. Write Bill Lambert,1419 Second Ave., Fairbanks, AK 99701. (907) 456-6472.

Little El Dorado Gold Camp. Three expeditions daily, including a sourdough buffet in a rustic log cabin reminiscent of a miners' dining hall. Gold pan for nuggets. Reservation. Write Andy Wescott, 1132 Lakeview Terrace, Fairbanks, AK 99701. (907) 456-4598.

North America Sled Dog Race. Held annually in March. Contact Alaska Dog Sled Mushers Association, Box 662, Fairbanks, AK 99707. (907) 452-MUSH.

Old F.E. Company Camp. Located 27.5 Mile Steese Highway. Built in 1921, now a Registered National Historical Site, provided room and board for miners for over 30 years. Hotel rooms, hall baths, gift shop, dining room, bar, swimming pool. Open year round.

Royal Highway Tours. Fairbanks city sightseeing on deluxe motorcoaches and four hour cruises on sternwheeler, "Discovery" on the Chena and Tanana rivers. Also tours to the Malemute Saloon. Write 2815 Second Avenue, Suite 400, Seattle, WA, (206) 441-8428 or 800 647-77500.

Skiland. Downhill skiing. About œ mile (805 m) east of 20.5 Mile Steese Highway. Two rope tows: lower 1,700 feet (518 m), upper 1,300 feet (396 m). Vertical drop 700 feet (213 m). Cross country skiers welcome. Open Saturday and Sunday 10 a.m.-5 p.m. Nov. to May. Write Box 1191, Fairbanks, AK 99707. (907) 456-4518. Bill Whitcher.

Summer Solstice '85. Annual festival celebrating longest day of the year with a weekend of music, dance, crafts and Alaskan arts. Held in pastureland near Fairbanks. City bus service available. Limited camping facilities. Children's programs. Write Box 90908, Fairbanks, AK 99708. (907) 456-5055.

University of Alaska Animal Research Station. Formerly the Muskox Farm. A biological research station with colonies of muskox, caribou and reindeer. Write Muskox Resarch, Institute of Arctic Biology., University of Alaska, Fairbanks, AK 99701. (907) 474-7207.

NOME

Camp Bendeleben. Located at Council, 73 miles (117 km) N.E. of Nome. Fishing for arctic char, four species of salmon, trophy size grayling. Unguided American plan available. Write John Elmore, Outfitter, Box 1045, Nome, AK 99762. (907) 443-5535.

TOK

Burnt Paw. Mile 1314 Alaska Highway, the Sled Dog Capital of Alaska. Featuring sled dogs and dogs mushing equipment. See and photograph the various dogs and sleds used for freighting, trapping and racing. Dog team hook-up demonstration, wildlife exhibit, native crafts. Husky pups usually available. Box 7, Tok, AK 99708. (907)883-4121.

SOUTHWEST

Alaska Fishing Adventures. Nine-day wilderness float trips in Wood-Tikchik State Park in Bristol Bay. Designed for the fisherman, photographer and wilderness enthusiast. Five species of salmon, trout, grayling, pike. 1334 Bannister Drive, Anchorage, AK 99508. (907) 272-1137.

St. George Pribilof Island Tours. Features a unique naturalist experience for bird watching, seal observation, wildlife photography and beautiful scenery. Write for brochure to 400 Old Seward Highway, Suite 302, Anchorage, AK 99503. (907) 562-3100.

DILLINGHAM

Beaver Roundup. Annual event held in March celebrates the end of the winter trapping season. This winter festival consists of dog sled races, games and other community activities.

KODIAK

Island Terrific Tours. Full one-day guided motor tour of scenic historic Kodiak and nearby attractions. Write Box 3001, Kodiak, AK 99615. (907) 486-4777.

Kodiak Sea Charters. Boat tours for fishing, sightseeing, photography, harbor touring. Insured, certified and licensed. Write Box 2156, Kodiak, AK 99615. (907) 487-2683.

MEKORYUK

Nunivak Island Guide Service. Wilderness trips include beachcombing, sportfishing and sightseeing of wildlife here on the Nunivak National Wildlife Range. For information, write Ed J. Shavings, Sr., Box 31, Mekoryuk, AK 99630 or call (907) 827-8213.

PUBLIC PARKS & LANDS

With eight national parks (many with attached preserves), four national monuments, three separate national preserves, 16 wildlife refuges, 25 wild and scenic rivers, and 12 designated federal wilderness, Alaska holds more land in the public trust than any other state. There's more federally protected land in Alaska than there is land within the boundaries of California.

National park rangers, U.S. Fish and Wildlife Service personnel and U.S. Forest Service rangers patrol these vast acreages on foot; from airplanes; in canoes, jetboats, outboard motor boats and ocean cruisers; and by vehicle. The best sources for general information about parks and other wilderness areas are:

National Park Service, 2525 Gambell Street, Anchorage, Alaska 99503, (907) 271-2643.

U.S. Fish and Wildlife Service Alaska Regional Office, 1011 East Tudor Road, Anchorage, Alaska 99503, (907) 786-3487.

Admiralty Island National Monument – Southeastern Alaska island located 15 miles (25 km) west of Juneau across Stephens Passage. Primary access is by boat or floatplane from Juneau; wheeled planes allowed to land on beaches. Mountainous terrain in coastal rain forest. Monument totals approximately 900,000 acres (364,500 hectares). Contact: Forest Service Info. Center, 101 Egan Dr., Juneau, AK 99801.

Alaska Maritime National Wildlife Refuge – Scattered coastal units from southeastern Alaska all the way around to the west coast, including the Aleutian Islands. Marine mammals and marine birds. Approximately 4,500,000 acres (1,822,500 hectares). 202 W. Pioneer Ave, Homer, AK 99603.

Alaska Peninsula National Wildlife Refuge – Alaska Peninsular of southwestern Alaska. Salmon, brown/grizzly bears, moose, caribou, wolves and wolverines. 3.5 million acres (1,417,500 hectares).

Aniakchak National Monument and Preserve – Difficult but not impossible hiking access from Port Heiden, about 10 miles (16 km) overland, no trail. Port Heiden reached by charter aircraft from King Salmon. Located on eastern side of Alaska Peninsular. Monument and preserve total 514,000 acres (208,170 hectares). Contact: Box 7, King Salmon, AK 99613.

Arctic National Wildlife Refuge – Extreme northeastern Alaska bordering Canada. Porcupine, caribou herd (120,000-plus animals), Dall sheep, polar bears on coast, grizzly bears, wolves, wolverines and black bears. 8,894,624 acres (3,602,323 hectares).

Becharof National Wildlife Refuge – Alaska Peninsular between Katmai National Park and Alaska Peninsular National Wildlife Refuge. Primary attractions are brown/grizzly bears most evident along local streams during salmon spawning runs. 1.2 million acres (486,000 hectares). Box 277, King Salmon, AK 99613.

Bering Land Bridge National Preserve – Northern edge of Seward Peninsular, accessible by charter aircraft fron Nome or Kotzebue. Preserve totals 2,457,000 acres (995,085 hectares). Contact Superintendent, Bering Land Bridge National Preserve, National Park Service, Nome Alaska 99762.

Cape Krusenstern National Monument – This monument was designed primarily to protect evidence of early man in western Alaska. Monument totals approximately 560,000 acres (226,800 hectares). Contact: Superintendent, Cape Krusenstern National Monument, NAtional Park Service, Box 1029, Kotzebue, Alaska 99752.

Coronation Island Wilderness, Maurelle Islands Wilderness and Warren Island Wilderness – Small grouping of islands off the west coast of Prince of Wales Islands in southeastern Alaska. Wilderness total 34,899 acres (14,134 hectares). Boat or floatplane access only. Contact: U.S. Forest Service, Ketchikan Area, Tongass National Forest, Federal Building, Ketchikan, Alaska 99801.

Denali National Park and Preserve – Home of Mount McKinley, highest peak in North America, and called by some a zoo without fences. Attractions include mountain climbing, wildlife tours (Dall sheep, grizzlies, moose and caribou to name some species seen frequently). One of Alaska's most popular lures for visitors. Park and preserve total 5,696,000 acres (2,306,880 hectares). Located 140 (225 km) miles south of Fairbanks, 220 miles (354 km) north of Anchorage, on Parks Highway. Contact: Superintendent, Denali National Park and Preserve, National Park Service, Box 9, McKinley Park, Alaska 99755.

Endicott River Wilderness – Western edge bounds eastern border of Glacier Bay National Park. Located west side of Lynn Canal about 45 miles (72 km) northwest of Juneau. Wilderness totals about 94,000 acres (38,070 hectares). Contact: U.S. Forest Service, Chatham Area, Tongass National Forest, Sitka, Alaska 99835.

Gates of the Arctic National Park and Preserve – The peaks and valleys of the central Brooks Range, north and south of the continental divide, lie within the 7,952,000 acres (3,220,560 hectares) of the park and preserve, 200 miles (322 km) northwest of Fairbanks. The most convenient access is by air. Scheduled service from Fairbanks to Bettles, 40 miles (64 km) south of the park. Charter aircraft available in Bettles for flightseeing or drop off in the park. True wilderness hiking and raft trips available. Contact: Superintendent, Gates of the Arctic National Park and Preserve, National Park Service, Box 74680, Fairbanks, Alaska 99701.

Glacier Bay National Park and Preserve – Located 50 miles (80 km) northwest Juneau at the northern end of Alaska's panhandle, Glacier Bay is an ever-changing wilderness of tidewater glaciers, marine mammals and northern birds. Park and Preserve total 3,328,000 acres (1,347,840 hectares). Contact: Superintendent, Glacier Bay National Park and Preserve, Juneau, Alaska 99802.

Innoko National Wildlife Refuge – Central Yukon River Valley, two sections totaling 3,850,000 acres (1,559,200 hectares), 80 percent of which is wetlands. Primarily for water fowl.

Izembak National Wildlife Refuge – Tip of Alaska Peninsular in southwestern Alaska, on Bearing Sea side. Migratory birds (mostly waterfowl) and caribou. 320,893 acres (129,962 hectares).

Kanuti National Wildlife Refuge – Mostly wetlands south of Bettles. Waterfowl. 1,430,000 acres (579,150 hectares).

Katmai National Park and Preserve – Initially set aside 1918 as a National Monument to protect the Valley of 10,000 Smokes created by a massive volcanic eruption in 1912. Park and preserve total 4,268,000 acres (1,728,540 hectares) on the Alaska Peninsular, approximately 250 miles (402 km) southwest of Anchorage. Contact: Superintendent, Katmai National Park and Preserve, National Park Service, P.O. Box 7, King Salmon, Alaska 99613.

Kenai Fjords National Park – Boat or floatplane charters from Seward, on the Kenai Peninsular 130 road miles (209 km) south of Anchorage, are the usual means of access. Park totals 567,000 acres (229,635 hectares). Contact: Box 1727, Seward, AK 99664.

Kenai National Wildlife Refuge – Kenai Peninsula across Turnagain Arm south of Anchorage. Major attraction is moose. About 2 million acres (810,000 hectares).

Kobuk Valley National Park – This western Brooks Range Park is 350 miles (563 km) northwest of Fairbanks, and 75 miles (121 km) west of Kotzebue. Canoe, kayak, and raft trips are primary recreational opportunities. Park totals 1,710,000 acres (692,550 hectares). Contact: Superintendent, Kobuk Valley National Park. National Park Service, 1029, Kotzebue, AK 99752.

Kodiak National Wildlife Refuge – Kodiak and Afognak islands southwest of Anchorage. Kodiak brown bear, salmon and wterfowl. 1,865,000 acres (754,325 hectares).

Koyukuk National Wildlife Refuge – Heavily forested with extensive wetlands on Koyukuk River floodplain. Waterfowl, including trumpeter swans. 3.55 million acres (1,437,750 hectares).

Lake Clark National Park and Preserve – Across Cook Inlet from Anchorage, the Lake Clark area has long been favored by outdoorsmen. Fishing and hiking are major recreational opprtunities. Park and preserve total 3,656,000 acres (1,480,680 hectares). Contact: Superintendent, Lake Clark National Park and Preserve, Box 61, Anchorage, Alaska 99513.

Misty Fjords National Monument – About 22 air miles (35 km) from Ketchikan near the southern tip of Alaska's panhandle. Misty Fjords is a wet, scenic region of steep mountains descending into deep fjords. Floatplane or boat access only. Monument totals 2,285,000 acres (925,425 hectares). Contact: Misty Fjords National Monument, U.S. Forest Service, 3031 Tongass Ave., Federal Building, Ketchikan, Alaska 99901.

National Wildlife Refuges – For information on any or all, contact: U.S. Fish and Wildlife Service, Regional Office, 1011 East Tudor Road, Anchorage, Alaska 99503.

Noatak National Preserve – Just a few miles north of Kotzebue, this northwestern Alaska preserve has no road access. Charter flights from Kotzebue are the normal means of getting to the area. Preserve totals 6,460,000 acres (2,616,300 hectares). Contact: Superintendent, Noatak National Preserve, Box 1029, Kotzebue, AK 99752.

Nowitna National Wildlife Refuge – Lowland basin bordering Nowitna and Yukon rivers in westcentral Alaska. Wetlands for waterfowl. 1.56 million acres (631,800 hectares).

Petersburg Creek-Duncan Salt Chuck Wilderness – Kupreanof Island across Wrangell Narrows from Petersburg in southeastern Alaska. Wilderness totals 50,000 acres (20,250 hectares). Contact: U.S. Forest Service, Stikine Area, Tongass National Forest, P.O. Box 309, Petersburg, Alaska 99833.

Russel Fjord Wilderness – Heavily glaciated fjord about 25 miles (40 km) northeast of Yakutat. Wilderness totals about 307,000 acres (124,355 hectares). Contact: U.S. Forest Service, P.O. Box 1980, Sitka, Alaska 99835.

Selawik National Wildlife Refuge – Northwestern Alaska about 360 miles (579 km) northwest of Fairbanks. Caribou and waterfowl. 2 million acres (810,000 hectares).

South Baranof Wilderness – Southern portion of Baranof Island in southeastern Alaska. Floatplane or boat access from Sitka or Port Alexander. Area can receive 200 inches (5 meters) or more of rain annually. Wilderness totals 314,000 acres (127,170 hectares). Contact: U.S. Forest Service, Chatham Area, Tongass National Forest, P.O. Box 1980, Sitka, Alaska 99835.

South Prince of Wales Wilderness – Approximately 40 air miles (64 km) southwest of Ketchikan on Prince of Wales Island. Wilderness totals 97,000 acres (39,285 hectares). Contact: U.S. Forest Service, Ketchikan Area, Tongass National Forest, Federal Building, Ketchikan, Alaska 99901.

Stikine-LeConte Wilderness – Southeastern Alaska mainland a short distance north of Wrangell. Boats capable of navigating the Stikine River are most common means of access. Wilderness totals 443,000 acres (179,415 hectares). Contact: U.S. Forest Service, Stikine Area, Tongass National Forest, P.O. Box 309, Petersburg, Alaska 99833.

Tebenkof Bay Wilderness – About 50 miles (80 km) west of Petersburg on Kuiu Island. Usual access is by boat or floatplane. Wilderness totals 65,000 acres (26,325 hectares). Contact: U.S. Forest Service, Tongass National Forest, P.O. Box 309, Petersburg, Alaska 99833.

Tetlin National Wildlife Refuge – South side of Alaska highway at Canadian border. Waterfowl, moose, some caribou, black bears, wolves and wolverines. 700,000 acres (283,500 hectares).

Togiak National Wildlife Refuge – Southwestern Alaska on coast between Kuskokwim Bay and Bristol Bay. Marine mammals, sea ducks, brant and other waterfowl. 4 million acres (1,620,000 hectares).

Tracy Arm-Fords Terror Wilderness – Southeastern Alaska between Tracy Arm and Endicott Arm, bordered on the east by Canada. Access is by boat. 656,000 acres (265,680 hectares). Contact: U.S. Forest Service, Chatham Area, Tongass National Forest, P.O. Box 1980, Sitka, Alaska 99835.

West Chichagof-Yakobi Wilderness – Western portions of Chichagof and Yakobi islands in southeastern Alaska. Pelican is the nearest community. Access by boat or floatplane. Wilderness totals 265,000 acres (107,325 hectares). Contact: U.S. Forest Service, Chatham Area, Tongass National Forest, P.O. Box 1980, Sitka, Alaska 99835.

Wrangell-St. Elias National Park and Preserve – Wrangell-St, Elias occupies the southeast corner of the mainland, tucked against the Canadian border. This huge park/preserve is the largest in Alaska, and totals 12,318,000 acres (4,988,790 hectares). Portions of the road system either enter the park/preserve or pass close to it. Usual access is by air from Glennallen. Contact: Superintendent, Wrangell-St. Elias National Park and Preserve, National Park Service, Nome, Alaska 99588.

Yukon-Charley Rivers National Preserve – Preserve includes a portion of the Yukon River near Eagle, approximately 325 road miles (523 km) northeast of Fairbanks by road. Also accessible by road is Circle, outside the western boundary, about 140 road miles (225 km) from Fairbanks. Preserve totals 1,713,000 acres (693,765 hectares). Contact: Superintendent, Yukon-Charley Rivers National Preserve, National Park Service, Box 64, Eagle, Alaska 99738.

Yukon Delta National Wildlife Refuge – Deltas of the Yukon and Kuskokwim rivers in southwestern Alaska. Waterfowl and sea birds–170 species seen in the area; 136 species known to breed here. 19,624,458 acres (7,947,905 hectares). Box 346, Bethel, AK 99559

Yukon Flats National Wildlife Refuge – Eastcentral Alaska about 100 miles (161 km) north of Fairbanks. Highest density of nesting waterfowl in Alaska. 8.63 million acres (3,495,150 hectares). Box 20, Fairbanks, AK 99701.

CULTURE PLUS

MUSEUMS

Alaska is not known as a hub of culture, in the international sense. However, the visitor should not overlook the many wonderful museums and cultural attractions that are available. While not numerous, they are worth a visit.

Shedon Museum and Cultural Center. Historical Tlingit and pioneer exhibits, slide and cassette programs and movies on request. Adults $2, under 18 free if with parent. Box 236, Haines, AK 99827. (907) 766-2366.

Juneau History, Cultural and Mendenhall Glacier Tour. Capital City tours for small, personalized groups feature photo stops at various attractions including the Juneau Historic District, Governor's Mansion, Russian Church, Auke Bay Harbor, Mendenhall Glacier, Mendenhall Wetlands Refuge, and Alaska State Museum. Write Box 2880, Juneau. AK 99803. (907) 586-8155.

Tongass Historical Society Museum. Collections emphasize Tlingit, Haida and Tsimshian cultures and Ketchikan's past as a mining and salmon fishing center. Ketchikan, AK 99901. (907) 225-5600.

Totem Bight State Historical Park. Historic park dedicated to Southeast Alaska's native cultures. Trail winds through rainforest to group of replicas of Tlingit-Haida totem poles. For information contact Divsion of Parks, Pouch M-D, Juneau, AK 99811. (907) 465-4563.

Duncan Cottage Museum. A National Historic Site restored by State of Alaska in 1972. Built in 1894 by Tsimpshean pioneers, it was the home of William Duncan, missionary and teacher to the Tsimpshean Indians. Open 9.30 a.m.–4 p.m. Mon.-Fri., on weekends by request, year round. Write LaVerne Welcome, Curator, Box 282, Metlakatla, AK 99926. (907) 886-6926.

Clausen Memorial Museum. Collections depict life of early pioneer Petersburg families. Good collection of historic fishing gear and displays relating to fishing industry and fur farming. Corner of 2nd and F Sts. May 1-Sept. 30, 1 p.m.–4 p.m. daily. Oct. 1-

April 30, 1 p.m.–4 p.m. Wed. and Sun. Box 708, Petersburg, AK 99833. (907) 772-3598.

Historical Society and Museum. Located in Sitka Centennial Building. Exhibits on local history and includes a model of Sitka as it was in 1867 based on sealskin maps from that era. For information write Sitka, AK 99835 or call (907) 747-6455.

Sheldon Jackson Museum. Located on the campus Sheldon Jackson College. Includes valuable Russian artifacts and one of the finest collections of Indian and Eskimo art in Alaska. Many of the artifacts were collected by the early missionary for whom the college was named. Write to Sheldon Jackson Museum, Sitka, AK 99835. (907) 747-5228.

Sitka Historical Tour. Approximately three-hour tour including Sitka National "Totem Park," Sheldon Jackson Museum, St. Michaels Cathedral, Old Sitka National Historical Park and Indian Cultural Center. When cruiseships are included. Cost $16/Adult, $8/Child. Call Prewitt Enterprises (907) 747-8443.

Trail of '98 Museum. Extensive collection of Gold Rush memorabilia. Open daily 8 a.m.–8 p.m. May 1-Sept. 30, Box 415-D, Skagway, AK 99840.

Wrangell Museum. Located two blocks from ferry terminal, features local Tlingit history, totem poles, basketry, local wildlife exhibit. Write Ms. Pat Watson, Director, Wrangell Museum, Box 1050, Wrangell, AK 99929, (907) 874-3770.

Alaska Wildlife and Natural History Museum. Alaska's rare, fascinating mammal and bird species exhibited in natural panoramic settings, gift shop, exhibit room, theatre and coffee shop. Easily accessible from major hotels and main highways. Open daily thru Sept., Wed-Sun, Oct-May, Corner 4th and Ingra. Box 101820, Anchorage, AK 99510. (907) 272-3510 or 272-3519.

Anchorage Museum of History and Arts. Exhibits the history of man in Alaska from prehistory to present. Temporary exhibitions from national and international sources. Admission free. 121 West 7th Ave, Anchorage, AK 99501. (907) 264-4326.

Elmendorf Wildlife Museum. Displays of varied Alaska wildlife. Open to the public. Elmendorf Air Force Base-VP, Anchorage, AK 99506.

Cordova Museum. 622 First Street, downtown Cordova. Exhibits of history and industry of area, including former Copper River and Northwestern Railroad. Write Curator, Box 391, Cordova, AK 99574. (907) 424-7443.

Fort Kenai Museum. Log building which houses the museum is a replica of barracks at one of the state's first U.S. Army posts set up in Kenai in 1869. Heritage collections of Indian artifacts, early Russian mementos, antiques of pioneers on Kenai Peninsula. Write Pat Porter, 361 Senior Court Kenai, AK 99611. (907) 283-4156 or 7294.

Knik Museum and Dog Mushing Hall of Fame. Displays memorabilia of famed dog mushers of Alaska. Located at Mile 14, Knik Goose Bay Road, Knik, AK (907) 376-7755.

Alaska Historical and Transportation Museum, Inc. Located near Palmer next to the Alaska State Fair Grounds, Mile 40.2 on the Glenn Highway. The museum exhibits and interprets artifacts concerning Alaska's industrial and transportation history. Open seven days a week, 8 a.m. to 4 p.m., no admission charged. Write Star Route B, Box 920, Palmer, AK 99645. (907) 745-4493.

Resurrection Bay Historical Society Museum. Located at Fifth and Adams. Collection of Alaskan historical artifacts and photographs of Seward and the Kenai Peninsula. Write Resurrection Bay Historical Society, Box 871, Seward, AK 99664.

Talkeetna Historical Society Museum. Located in old school house. Includes display on history of mountain climbing, local art exhibits and historical library. Talkeetna, AK 99676. (907) 733-2487.

Valdez Heritage Center. Historical museum in Centennial Building. Artifacts include Hinchinbrook lighthouse lens, early firefighting equipment, '64 earthquake photos, display of terminal of Alaska Pipeline illustrated with color panels and button activated tanker and schematic drawing of terminal. Open year round. Write Director, Box 307, Valdez, AK 99686. (907) 835-2764

Wasilla-Knik-Willow Creek Historical Society and Museum. Historical park includes first school house in Wasilla, old gold miner cabin, home of pioneer family and a blacksmith shop. Slide collection. Wasilla, AK 99687, (907) 376-2005.

Circle District Historical Society Museum. Serving Central, Circle and Circle Hot Springs. Local history museum with exhibits of gold rush days, trapping and early agriculture relics of the region. Located in Central, AK 99730.

Eagle Historical Society Museum. Contains Judge Wickersham's (Alaska's pioneer federal judge) original court house and many exhibits representing transportation, trapping, hunting, mining, houses and school room of the early 1900's. Eagle, AK 99755. (907) 683-2215.

Goldstream Dredge Number 8. Mile 9 Old Steese Highway, 200 yards (183 m) from Alaska Pipeline pulloff. Built 1928, now on National Register of Hisorical Objects. Guided tour, gold panning, Dredge-O-Drama, 12-bedroom bunkhouse. Open May 15-Oct. 15. Write John Reeves, Box 81941, Fairbanks, AK 99708. (907) 456-6058.

University of Alaska Museum. Northernmost professional museum in the United States. Natural history, animal life, Native art, art history and culture of Alaska. Write 907 Yukon Drive, Fairbanks, AK 99701. (907) 474-7505.

Dinjii Zhuu Enjit Museum. Translated from the Athabaskan, this means "Museum for the People of Yukon Flats". Contains exhibits ranging from Prehistoric era to the Hudson Bay era (when the white man first arrived). Extensive beadwork display. Contact Museum, Fort Yukon, AK 99740. (907) 662-2487.

Kotzebue Museum. An excellent city museum, Ootukahkuktuvik, "Place Having Old Things," contains among other things, a raincoat made from walrus intestine and a coat fashioned from bird feathers. Kotzebue, AK 99752.

NANA Museum of the Arctic. Provides two hour program including diorama show. Enables visitor to know land and Native culture. Kotzebue, AK 99752.

Carrie McClain Memorial Museum. Exhibits on the Bering Land Bridge, natural history of the region, Eskimo cultures and the gold rush. Box 53, Nome, AK 99762. (907) 443-2427.

Adak Community Museum. A small museum containing World War II memorabilia, wildlife displays and Eskimo artifacts. Since this is on a U.S. Naval Base, military clearance is required for admittance. Adak, AK.

Yugtarvik Regional Museum. One of the finest collections of Yup'ik Eskimo art and artifacts is displayed here. Also a marketplace for Native-made art objects and craft items. Bethel, AK 99559.

Dillingham Heritage Museum. Collection consisits of varied native arts and crafts. Also features traveling exhibits from other regions of Alaska. For further information, contact the Museum at (907) 842-5610.

Baranof Museum. The Baranof Museum exhibits a collection of Aleut, Koniag, Russian and American artifacts on display in the Erskine House, a National Historic Landmark, open daily in summer and six days a week in winter, closed Thursday. Write Box 61, Kodiak, AK 99615. (907) 486-5920.

MUSIC/DANCE/DRAMA

Chilkat Center. 350 seat auditorium featuring authentic Indian dances, melodrama and Alaska film series. Shows daily during summer months. Located at historic Fort Wm. H. Seward. Write Chamber of Commerce, Box 518, Haines, AK 99827. (907) 766-2202.

New Archangel Dancers. Folk dances from various of Russia. Performances timed to docking of cruiseship or by special arrangements. Tickets available at door of Centennial Building, admission $2 per person. Write New Archangel Dancers, Box 1687, Sitka, AK 99835.

Pioneer Repertory Players. Second season for show with buffet with Pioneer Repertory Players doing melodramas, comedies and musicals. Dinner and show or show only. Write Box 2882, Sitka, AK 99835. Phone 747-6616 for reservations.

Sitka Summer Music Festival. Acclaimed by critics of *New York Times* and *Washington Post*, select classical soloists perform in the beautiful glass walled Centennial Building. First three weeks in June each year with concerts Tuesdays–Fridays and some Saturdays. Open rehearsals. Reservations encouraged. Box 201988, Anchorage, AK 99520.

Southeast Alaska Fine Arts Camp. Annual Fine Arts Camp and Summer Arts Institute conducted during the month of July and the first week of August. Guest artists instruct Jr. and Sr. high school and adult students in music, mime, dance, painting, ceramics, writing, computer graphics and more. Make the Arts part of your summer. Box 2133, Sitka, AK 99835. (907) 747-8177.

Fairbanks Summer Arts Festival. Starting in late July, on University of Alaska campus. Thirty-one nationally known guest artists and teachers including Philadelphia String Quartet, Westwood Wind Quintet, Boston Pops musicians. Workshops and concerts. UAF credit and housing available. For brochure, send self-addressed stamped envelope to Jo Ryman Scott, P.O. Box 80845, Fairbanks, AK 99708.

Annual Festival of Native Arts. A week long Alaska Native culture celebration held on University of Alaska, Fairbanks campus. Traditional singers, dancers and storytellers, arts and crafts demonstrations, blanket toss and craft sales. Write Festival of Native Arts, UAF, Fairbanks, AK 99701. (907) 474-7181.

Cry of the Wild Ram. Historical outdoor drama presented in the Frank Brink Amphitheatre at Monashka Bay on Kodiak Island. Play depicts history of Russian America. Write Kodiak-Baranof Productions, Box 1792, Kodiak, AK 99615. (907) 486-5291.

CULTURAL TOURS

The Northwest Native Fair. Invites you to our Eskimo games, traditional fashion show, Eskimo dance competition and many other activities. July. Take part with "Inupiats sharing their Celebration of life from the Land". Write Clara Taylor, Box 49, Kotzebue, AK 99752. Or call (907) 442-3301.

Alaska Indian Culture Study Tour. One and two-day study on Alaska Indian villages, totem poles, petroglyphs and tribal cultures. Tours fit cruise and ferry schedules. Metlakatla Indian village tour includes flying with an Alaska bush pilot, salmon cannery tour and fresh salmon dinner. Write Alaska Bound, Box 2880, Juneau, AK 99803. (907) 442-3301.

Totem Heritage Center. Original, unrestored totem poles and house posts are preserved here along with an impressive collection of primitive art. Workshops in design, wood carving and silver engraving are conducted by recognized artists in native arts. Ketchikan, AK 99901. (907) 225-5900.

Bear Tribal House. Tlingit Tribal House of the Bear on Chief Shakes Island. Nine totems and community house open for cruise ships during summer and by appointment year-round. Admission. Write Box 868, Wrangell, AK 99929. (907)874-3503.

Alaska Experience Theatre and Gift Shop. Thrill to the wonders of the 49th State as the huge domed screen surrounds you with the scenic grandeur, history, culture and wildlife of this great land. Open daily all year round. 705 West 6th Avenue, Anchorage, AK 99501. (907) 276-3730.

ARTS & CRAFTS

Alaska Native and Crafts Association. Native owned and directed non-profit craftspeople's marketing association representing work of Eskimo. Tlingit, Athabascan, Tsimshian and Aleut artists of Alaska. Monday through Friday 10a.m. to 6p.m., Saturday 10 a.m. to 5 p.m. 425 D St., Anchorage, AK 99501. (907) 274-2932.

Oomingmak Musk Ox Producers' Co-op. Exquisite garments handknit in traditional patterns by Eskimo villagers from the rare wool, Qiviut, combed from the Arctic musk ox as he sheds on our farm each spring. A unique northern gift. For information and brochures, contact Oomingmak Musk Ox Producers' Co-op, 604 H Street, Anchorage, AK 99501. (907) 272-9225.

Whittier Historical Society and Fine Arts. Fine art displays by local and native artists. St. Lawrence Island artifacts and relics from area's old fishing villages and canneries. Whittier, AK 99693.

SHOPPING

Many unique crafts and products are available throughout the state. Popular items include gold nugget and jade jewelry. Don't expect a bargain, but do expect quality made goods. Gold nugget jewelry is a speciality and makes a wonderful Alaskan souvenir or gift. Jade is found locally in Alaska and in addition to jewelry, it is carved. Jade stones occur in various shapes of green, brown, black, yellow, white and red.

Alaska also is home to many wonderful artists, whose works can be purchased at local galleries and shops. Their works are generally inspired by the beauty of the land. In addition to works of art and jewelry look for seal oil candles, carved wooden totem poles, canned food products and clothing.

Native crafts are abundant and feature items carved from walrus ivory, soapstone and jade. Scrimshawed ivory is an authentic Native handicraft. Scenes or objects are etched on the ivory. Visitors who wish to take ivory to a country other than the United States must obtain an export permit from the U.S. Fish and Wildlife Service. Be sure to ask about restrictions when your purchase is made.

Alaska Native women make some of the most intricately woven baskets in the world. Materials used for the baskets include beachgrass, birch bark and whale baleen. These items have become very popular over the years and command a high price, some selling for several hundred dollars. They also make beaded slippers from seal skin and wolf hair. Unique porcupine quill earrings are affordable and attractive.

Alaska crafts are identified by three different types of labels. If an item was manufactured in Alaska the tag features a polar bear and the words, "Made in Alaska." Authentic Alaska handicrafts are identified by a tag featuring an "Alaskan Flag" and Native made products feature a hand with the designation "Native Handicraft." Both tags state "Authentic Handicraft from Alaska."

SHOPPING AREAS

The suburban shopping mall has come to Alaska's larger cities to stay, to the joy of some, and the disgust of most old-timers. Malls abound throughout Anchorage, and three major ones sort of surrounding Fairbanks. Smaller communities are beginning to establish mini-malls of their own.

IN THE CITY

Diamond Center, located at the corner of Diamond Boulevard and the Old Seward Highway in Anchorage, is the largest mall in Alaska. Besides major department and chain stores there are a variety of smaller shops. An ice rink is located at the southern end, in addition to several fast food restaurants.

Northway Mall, on the Glenn Highway just northeast of Anchorage, ranks as probably the second-largest mall in the state. Nearly 100 stores and small shops comprise this facility, easily spotted as you drive into town from the north.

Bentley Mall, corner of College Road and the Old Steese Highway, is Fairbanks' largest mall. That and other local malls were a direct outgrowth of the building of the mid-1970s. Although big by Fairbanks' standards, it cannot compare in size or variety to the larger Anchorage malls.

Alaska is still "folksy" enough that many of the best places to shop are *Mom and Pop* operations scattered almost everywhere. It would take a book almost this size to list all shopping places in Alaska that might be interesting. Your best bet is just to wander slowly through whatever town you're in and take the time to check even the most rundown looking stores. Ivory, Native crafts, novelties, and just anything is available.

Major hotels in Anchorage have gift shops featuring Alaskan products, ivory carvings, and the like. If your trip includes visits to rural areas, don't buy until you've had a chance to investigate local offerings. Although opportunities to pick up bargains from the actual producers have declined markedly in recent years, it's occasionally possible to strike a good deal in the villages. If you find nothing in the villages that appeals to you, the stores in Anchorage will still be glad to see you when you return there from other excursions.

ON THE FARM

You may be able to buy something unusual from the handful of residents trying to eke a living from the soil in Alaska's harsh climate, but don't count on it. The best bet is to visit the state fair in Palmer at the end of August. There, at least, you can photograph an 80-pound (37 kg) cabbage, even if you can't take it back with you.

There are, however, locally produced edibles which should be investigated. Canned, smoked fish as well as jams and jellies made from wild berries and rose hips are available in many locations on the Kenai Peninsula, south of Anchorage. Berry products are also available in other areas. Brave souls in places like Barrow or Nome might find an opportunity to sample *muktuk* (whale blubber), seal meat, or reindeer.

DUTY FREE

Duty free goods are available in the International Terminal of the Anchorage Airport for purchase by passengers embarking on flights to foreign destinations.

SPORTS

PARTICIPANT

No professional or college football is played in Alaska. There are only limited facilities for tennis—mostly in Anchorage—and there is no formal competitive play. Golfers can find a rough course in Anchorage, but little other in the way of playing areas. In 1985, however, more golfing facilities were under development.

Several "golf" tournaments are played, mostly as a joke. A nine-hole course is laid out on frozen Norton Sound near Nome in March for a few hardy souls. Since the course is different every year, there is no established par.

CYCLING

Hundreds of cyclists make long-distance trips by pedal power along Alaska's road system every year. These trips are often as much a test of the ruggedness of the bikes and riders as they are a pleasurable journey. But, for the hardy, a bicycle makes a wonderful vehicle for exploring the state's road system. It does take time, though. It's a long way between cities, even on the road system.

Anchorage and Fairbanks have elaborate networks of bike paths/jogging trails. Where available, these are splendid, safe paths set well off the road.

CANOEING/KAYAKING

Surely there is no better way to explore the Alaskan outdoors than in a lightweight craft you paddle yourself. Most rivers are navigable, to some extent at any rate by a canoe, and there are enough white-water thrills available for kayakers to last a lifetime.

Anyone setting out on an extensive canoe/kayak trip in Alaska, should leave a detailed itinerary with the nearest Alaska State Trooper office. People who don't come out of the woods when expected are certainly a lot easier to find if the rescue agencies have some idea of where to start looking.

A particularly good canoeing experience is the Swanson River system of canoe trails near Soldotna on the Kenai Peninsula. Weekend adventures or two-week expeditions are possible in this region, just a three-hour drive from Anchorage. For more details, write to: Refuge Manager, Kenai National Wildlife Refuge, Box 2139, Soldotna, Alaska 99669.

DIVING

Recreational diving in Alaska is not for the faint-hearted. The water is cold. Local divers prefer dry suits to the older, more-common wet suits. Currents in salt water are treacherous. Inquire locally before undertaking any dives.

Once underwater, however, the cold northern seas can offer much. The water is clear, except near the mouths of major, slit-laden rivers. Abalone can be plucked off the bottom in southeastern Alaska waters for an unforgettable meal. Several shipwrecks have also attracted divers in recent years.

Those diving in freshwater will be swiming in a much sterile enviroment in most cases. Alaska's short summer season limits the growth of aquatic plants. Major rivers, usually heavily laden with silt from headwater glaciers, should be avoided by divers.

FISHING

The number of people who have long dreamt of fishing Alaska's pristine waters for massive king salmon, leaping trout, and wily northern pike must surely number in the millions. All those fish are there, and more. But they're not inclined to just leap in your boat. Prime fishing takes a little bit of planning and a few logistics.

Most roadside streams and lakes experience more fishing pressure that they can naturally stand. Thus any fish you catch from these waters are likely to be small. However, you don't always have to mount a major expedition to find good fishing.

Streams that cross the various roads in the state will be heavily fished near the highway. A short walk upstream or down should put a person in all-but-unfished territory. The easiest way to calculate the necessary walking distance is to walk until there are no more footprints visible at stream side. There are exceptions to this rule, particularly in streams with heavy runs of salmon, but if trout or grayling are your quarry, hiking up or down a clear stream rarely fails.

Those wishing to catch a monstrous salmon would do well to enlist the services of a fishing guide. Guide services are located near most of the major fisheries.

About $100 a day or less per person should provide more adventure than most anglers ever can imagine. Best bet for salmon fishing with guides is on the Kenai River near Soldotna. The king salmon and red salmon fisheries in the area are famed throughout the world.

Fishing licenses are available at almost all sporting goods stores and most variety stores. All persons 16 years old or older must have a fishing license in their possession when angling on Alaskan waters.

Halibut fishermen flock to Homer every year for the opportunity to latch onto a bottom fish that can weigh 400 pounds (182 kg) or more. Several fish of 250 to 300 pounds (114 -136 kg) are caught every year by charter boats operating from the Homer Spit. Again, about $100 buys a day's fishing per person. The recent oil spill in the Prince William Sound area, however, has altered some fishing practices. The three principal ports affected by the spill are Kodiak, Prince William Sound and Cook Inlet. State health authorities advise against eating shellfish from these polluted areas. In 1990 there was a record salmon catch in Prince William Sound but poor catches in Lower Cook Inlet and Kodiak Island. (See chapters on Prince William Sound and Kodiak for more information, pp. 101-128). Write to Public Communications, Alaska Department of Fish & Game, Box 3-2000, Juneau, AK 99802 (907-271-5960) for the latest "catch" information. In recent years, a rash of first-class fishing resorts have developed in many areas of the state. These are usually in remote areas, and involve flying in via float plane. For those who have the $2,000 or more per person for a week's fishing, these offer an unforgettable experience. Contact the Alaska Sportfishing Lodge Association, 500 Wall Street, Suite 401, Seattle, Washington 98121, for a listing of more than 20 lodges and brochures.

BACKPACKING

Extensive hiking trips into Alaska's back country differ significantly from backpacking trips in most of the rest of the country. With the exception of the Resurrection Pass trail system on the Kenai Peninsular, there are few trails. Hiking in Alaska is an overland-navigation experience, but one that can be rewarding in the extreme.

Hikers should take precautions to avoid unfriendly encounters with bears, particularly the Alaska brown/grizzly bear which thrives throughout most of the state. Make noise as you walk, keep campsites clean, keep food away from sleeping areas, and always travel with one or more companions. Statistically, the larger the group, the lower the chances of encountering a hostile bear.

If attacked by a bear, experts agree that the victim should roll over on his/her stomach and play dead. Trying to run from a bear may incite a charging reflex. The best bet is to give bears as wide a berth as possible. Alaska is their domain.

Those going on extensive hikes in the Alaskan wilderness should leave an itinerary with the Alaska State Troopers or, when appropriate, at the headquarters of a national park.

HUNTING

A significant portion of Alaska's visitors are interested in the state for its big game hunting opportunities. There's good reason for this; Alaska provides some of the finest opportunities for wilderness hunting in the Western Hemisphere.

Citizens of the countries other than the United States must enlist the services of a licensed hunting guide for hunting any big game animal in the state. Guided hunts typically cost from $2,000 for a single-species hunt to $10,000 or more for particular high-quality or multi-species hunts. A typical $2,000 hunt buys a few days of hunting for a caribou. The $10,000 might buy 20 days or more of hunting from several lodges or camps. A complete list of registered and master guides is available from: Department of Commerce, Guide Licensing and Control Board, Pouch D, Juneau, Alaska 99811. Only the men and women licensed by the department can contact to provide guided hunts within Alaska.

U.S. residents of other states besides Alaska can hunt big game animals without a guide, except for brown/grizzly bear and Dall sheep. For these animals, non-Alaska-residents and U.S. citizens must engage a guide or be accompanied by a family member who is a resident of Alaska and within the second degree of kindred—father, mother, sister, brother, son or daughter—by blood or marriage.

Regulations affecting hunting areas, bag limits, and methods and means are extremely complex and vary from region to region around Alaska. Copies of the hunting regulations and game unit maps can be obtained by writing to: Alaska Department of Fish and Game, Box 3-2000, Juneau, Alaska 99802. Study the regulations and the game unit map carefully before hunting. If in doubt about any regulation, inquire locally with the Alaska Department of Fish and Game.

LICENSE & TAG FEES

A non-resident hunting license costs $60. Tags allowing the taking of big game animals must be purchased before hunting. Hunting licenses and appropriate game tags must be carried while in the field. Non-resident tag fees: brown/grizzly bear, $250; black bear, $200; bison, $300; caribou and/or moose, $300; Dall sheep, $400; elk or goat, $250; deer, $135; wolf, $150; wolverine, $150; musk ox, $1,100.

SPECTATOR

Alaska boasts one of the most impressive semi-pro baseball leagues in the country. The Fairbanks Gold Panners, the Anchorage Glacier Pilots, the Anchorage Bucs, and the Kenai Peninsula Oilers are just some of the teams with intense fan loyalty.

BASEBALL

Baseball games are played on ball diamonds built in the cities. Double headers and extra-innings games go until late at night without lights.

Prices are cheap. A few dollars get you into the bleachers. Be sure to carry plenty of insect repellant, especially to Fairbanks-area games.

A good bet is the Midnight Sun Game in Fairbanks, which starts late at night on June 21, without lights. Play usually continues until well after midnight.

BASKETBALL

Basketball is probably the most-watched spectator sport in Alaska is high-school basketball. Every community with seven or more students has its own school and probably enough players to field a team. Regional tournaments abound in late winter, with the state championship played out in Anchorage in March. The Great Alaska Shootout held the weekend after Thanksgiving in Anchorage attracts top rate college teams from across the United States.

ART/PHOTO CREDITS

Photography by

97, 99, 107, 106/107, 155, 163, 202/203, 260	Roy Bailet
36, 37, 41, 48, 54L&R, 59, 87, 112, 146, 157, 169, 171, 180, 196, 219, 227, 231	Bruce Bernstein Collection
endpaper, 77, 94, 226	Maxine Cass
271	Florence Collins
197, 268, 270R	Julie Collins
270L	Miki Collins
90R, 96, 98, 159, 230	Lee Foster
8/9, 80, 84, 90L, 100	Hara
66/67, 72/73, 213, 218, 237	Kim Heacox
235	Holland America Westours, Inc.
266	Carol Kaynor
44, 108/109, 117L, 120/121, 127, 140, 216/217, 228, 261	Kyle Lochalsh
265	Gary Lok
30/31, 32, 52, 56, 144/145, 149, 150, 154, 156R, 166, 212, 248R, 255	James McCann
6/7, 51, 75, 89, 91, 186/187, 206, 207, 209, 211, 215, 222, 229, 242/243, 245, 246, 248L, 249, 254, 256	Rick McIntyre
267	Pat Pearlman
27, 35, 82, 86, 111, 113, 115, 116, 117R, 130/131, 156L, 188, 199, 210, 221, 258	Allan Seiden
19, 20, 21, 22, 34, 45, 47, 60, 62, 64/65, 68, 78, 81, 83, 102, 103, 110, 135, 139, 158, 164, 170, 173, 174/175, 181, 182, 184, 193, 204, 220, 223, 232/233, 241, 244, 247, 250/251, 252, 257, 259, 263	Jeff Shultz
14/15, 16/17, 43, 124, 125, 162, 262	Mark Skok
cover, 10/11, 18, 55, 58, 119, 224/225, 239	Tony Stone Worldwide
5, 12, 28, 38, 39, 49, 57, 114, 122, 129, 147L&R, 153, 160, 161, 167, 168, 172, 177, 178, 183, 185, 190, 191, 194	Vautier-de-Nanxe
24, 25, 26, 29, 53, 63, 76, 79, 88, 95, 104, 134, 136, 151, 189, 192, 200/201, 208, 214	Harry M. Walker
40, 92/93	Angela White
Maps	Berndtson & Berndtson
Illustrations	Klaus Geisler
Visual Consulting	V. Barl

INDEX

A

INSIGHT GUIDES

COLORSET NUMBERS

You'll find the colorset number on the spine of each Insight Guide.

INSIGHT *Pocket* GUIDES

EXISTING & FORTHCOMING TITLES:

• •

United States: **Houghton Mifflin Company, Boston MA 02108**
Tel: (800) 2253362 Fax: (800) 4589501

Canada: **Thomas Allen & Son, 390 Steelcase Road East**
Markham, Ontario L3R 1G2
Tel: (416) 4759126 Fax: (416) 4756747

Great Britain: **GeoCenter UK, Hampshire RG22 4BJ**
Tel: (256) 817987 Fax: (256) 817988

Worldwide: **Höfer Communications Singapore 2262**
Tel: (65) 8612755 Fax: (65) 8616438

❝ I was first drawn to the Insight Guides by the excellent "Nepal" volume.
I can think of no book which so effectively captures the essence of a
country. Out of these pages leaped the Nepal I know – the captivating
charm of a people and their culture. I've since discovered and enjoyed
the entire Insight Guide Series. Each volume deals with
a country or city in the same sensitive depth, which is
nowhere more evident than in the superb photography. ❞

Sir Edmund Hillary